ROUTLEDGE LIBRARY EDITIONS:
HOUSING POLICY AND HOME OWNERSHIP

Volume 7

CITIES, HOUSING AND PROFITS

CITIES, HOUSING AND PROFITS

Flat Break-Up and the Decline of Private Renting

CHRIS HAMNETT AND BILL RANDOLPH

Routledge
Taylor & Francis Group
LONDON AND NEW YORK

First published in 1988 by Hutchinson Education

This edition first published in 2021
by Routledge
2 Park Square, Milton Park, Abingdon, Oxon OX14 4RN

and by Routledge
52 Vanderbilt Avenue, New York, NY 10017

Routledge is an imprint of the Taylor & Francis Group, an informa business

British Library Cataloguing in Publication Data
A catalogue record for this book is available from the British Library

ISBN: 978-0-367-64519-9 (Set)
ISBN: 978-1-00-313856-3 (Set) (ebk)
ISBN: 978-0-367-68211-8 (Volume 7) (hbk)
ISBN: 978-1-00-313473-2 (Volume 7) (ebk)

Cities, Housing and Profits:

flat break-up and the decline of private renting

Chris Hamnett

Bill Randolph

Hutchinson

London Melbourne Auckland Johannesburg

Hutchinson Education

An imprint of Century Hutchinson Ltd
62 – 65 Chandos Place, London WC2N 4NW

Century Hutchinson Australia Pty Ltd
PO Box 496, 16 – 22 Church Street, Hawthorn,
Victoria 3122, Australia

Century Hutchinson New Zealand Ltd
PO Box 40-086, Glenfield, Auckland 10, New Zealand

Century Hutchinson South Africa (Pty) Ltd
PO Box 337, Bergvlei, 2012 South Africa

First published 1988

Typeset in 10/12pt Times by Saxon Printing Ltd., Derby
Printed and bound in Great Britain by
Anchor Brendon Ltd, Tiptree, Essex

British Library Cataloguing in Publication Data
Hamnett, Chris
Cities, housing and profits : Flat break-up and the decline of private renting. —— (The Built environment series).
1. Housing —— England —— London
I. Title II. Randolph, B III. Series
363.5'09421 HD7334.L6

ISBN 0-09-173235-2

Contents

Preface

This book attempts to address several issues simultaneously. It is most obviously concerned to document and explain the emergence of flat 'break-ups'—the sale for individual owner occupation of blocks of flats which were previously privately rented. These have played a major role in the transformation of the private housing market in London since the late 1960s. The effects of flat break-up have been most marked in central and inner London, because it is here that the majority of England's privately rented blocks of flats were built during the late nineteenth century and again during the 1930s.

But, as we attempt to show, the flat break-up market in London is not a unique phenomenon. It is but one of the latest and most geographically concentrated manifestations of the trend for sales from private renting to owner occupation which has been established in Britain since the 1920s. What is new is that the sale of privately rented property was confined to the sale of houses until the late 1960s. In order to explain why the sale of flats took off when it did, it is necessary first to explain the features which are specific to the purpose-built flat sector and the causes of the decline of the privately rented sector in general. This interrelationship between the causes of the decline of the privately rented sector in Britain and the features specific to the flat market comprises the second theme of the book.

One of the features which is most specific to central London's purpose built blocks of flats is its ownership structure. Unlike the privately rented housing in the rest of Britain, which is largely dominated by small landlords who own a few houses each, the flat market in central London has been dominated by large, professionally run, residential property companies—some owning thousands of flats. Unlike smaller landlords for whom residential property ownership often represents something other than just a financial asset, central London's corporate landlords view their assets purely in profit maximizing terms.

These companies are very sensitive to changes in financial and economic conditions, and the analysis of the flat break-up market in London highlights one way in which the housing market and the social structure of urban residential areas can be transformed by private capital in search of greater profitability. The sale of rented flats in to owner occupation represented their most profitable use in the period after 1960, and the importance of profitability in reshaping cities is the third theme of the book. Most of the capital raised from selling flats has been reinvested in other, more profitable areas. The Church Commissioners, to take just one example, are currently investing the proceeds from the sale of their Maida Vale flats in North American real estate in Silicon Valley and North Carolina. We believe it is only by attempting to understand such investment decisions that is it possible to explain what has happened to the central London flat sector since 1965. We are unashamedly espousing a 'supply-side' explanation of urban residential change. Individuals' choices and decisions about where and in what they would like and can afford to live are made in the context of a structure of supply shaped by profitability.

But there is no single response to changes in financial and economic conditions. Changes in the financial environment affect different companies differently, and the fourth theme of the book is the variability of response among different companies. Some sold early, some sold late and some failed to sell quickly enough and were taken over by their more dynamic and aggressive competitors.

One of our discoveries during the course of our research was that flat break-ups were not unique to London. Similar processes have taken place in many large European and North American cities—where it is termed condo conversion—and the fifth theme of the book is the comparative analysis of these processes and their effects. We have examined the variations in the consequences of the process and the policy response to break-ups in Holland and the USA and it is clear that in England security of tenure legislation and the peculiar nature of English real property law-in particular, the existence of leasehold ownership—played a key role in influencing both the social consequences of the process and the policy response.

The research on which this book is based had a quite unexpected spin-off, in that it led to us both becoming involved in the Nugee Committee of Inquiry into the management problems of privately owned blocks of flats which reported to the Minister of Housing late in 1985. Despite the limited nature of some of the reforms proposed, we have been heartened by the fact that the government accepted most of the major recommendations of the Committee and introduced the Landlord and Tenant (No 2) Bill in 1987. It received all party support in Parliament and became law in the week before Parliament was dissolved for the 1987 General Election. The only pity is that the Act was not passed 15 years earlier. It would have saved the residents of blocks of flats a great deal of pain.

Finally, it is perhaps appropriate to say a word about how the the research on which this book is based came to be done. Although we know that the search for profitability and profit maximization on the part of the owners and developers of land and buildings is one of the principal motive forces of urban change, the specific form and nature of these processes of change vary widely depending on current circumstances and opportunities. They can rarely be deduced from some a priori theory. In fact, most urban research has its genesis in the simple act of observation: in noticing the first signs of social or physical change and then pursuing explanations by inquiry and theorization.

Anyone walking round parts of Camden, Islington or Hammersmith in inner London in the early 1970s could not have failed to notice the large number of rubble filled builders' skips standing in the streets outside partly renovated terraced houses with estate agents' 'sold' signs outside. It was clear that something unusual was happening. After decades of neglect and decay, houses were being rapidly renovated and the long established population of working class private renters was being slowly replaced – or displaced—by a new population of middle-class home owners.

These changes aroused our intellectual curiosity. We wanted to find out what was happening to inner London and why. The answer, of course, was 'gentrification', and since the early 1970s it has transformed the housing market and social structure of large parts of inner London. In the late 1970s our curiosity was again aroused—not by builders' skips but by the appearance of a large number of 'flat for sale' boards outside blocks of flats and some articles in the financial press on the large profits being made from flat 'break-up' in London. We believe that the observation of such changes in the form and structure of cities comprises a fruitful source of new urban research. It is, of course,necessary to develop and apply theories in order to explain these changes and this is not an easy task. The world does not neatly present itself ready made for us to understand. The point we wish to make, however, is that it is rarely possible to deduce what is happening by application of a priori theories. We believe that the builders'skip and sale board theory of knowledge has something to offer.

We would like to thank the Social Science Research Council—now the Economic and Social Research Council—for funding the research on which this book is based and hope that the government appreciates the potential policy relevance of much social science research. It is an an amusing reflection on the popular press in Britain that our initial survey of the problems faced by residents of blocks of flats was the subject of a 'social science snoopers' story by a well-known Sunday newspaper. We wish that their coverage of the problems faced by the residents of the blocks of flats in London had been as assiduous as their attempt to discredit research on the problems. This book spans the eras of handwritten manuscripts and word processors. We apologize to Eve Hussey and Carol Oddy for inflicting our handwritten early drafts on them. We would also like to express our thanks to the Rent Officer Service in Camden, Westminister, and Kensington and Chelsea for allowing us access to rent registration data and to the *Estates Gazette* for allowing us access to their library, the information from which formed the basis of much of the analysis in Chapters 5, 6, 7 and 8. The analysis, however, is our own and any mistakes and errors in interpretation are our own responsibility.

Acknowledgements

The authors and publishers would like to thank the following for their kind permission to reproduce copyright material:

Allsop and Co for figure 9.3;
David Lewis and Partners for figure 6.4;
Druce and Company for figure 6.7;
The Estates Gazette Ltd;
The Economist for figure 8.2;
Folkard and Hayward for figure 6.1;
Freshwater Property Management for figure 8.3;
Gross Fine for figure 6.3;
The Investors Chronicle for table 6.1;
Keith Cardale Groves for figures 7.1 and 6.9;
The Knight Frank and Rutley Group for figure 8.1;
Peachey Property Corporation plc for figures 2.1, 2.2 and 2.3;
Windsor Life Assurance Company Ltd for figures 8.4 and 8.5;

1 The production and transformation of urban residential space

Introduction

Central London is rightly renowned for its many squares and terraces of fine period houses. It is much less well known for its numerous blocks of late-nineteenth and early-twentieth century private flats. Discreet and anonymous, frequently built above a row of shops, and bearing more than a passing similarity to the late-nineteenth century and interwar office blocks, central London's purpose-built blocks of flats for long remained largely unknown and their crucial role in central London's private rented housing market went largely unappreciated to all but those who either lived in them or owned them.

During the course of the last 15 to 20 years, this picture has changed dramatically. Since the late 1960s London's privately rented blocks of flats and the problems which surround them have become a focus of increasing resident unrest, media attention and political concern as a result of the 'break-up' and sale of the blocks. The term 'break-up' refers not to the physical demolition of the blocks, but to a more subtle but none the less important form of change: the tenurial transformation of the blocks from private renting to individual owner occupation as a result of landlords' decisions to sell. The 'break-up' is therefore one of ownership and control and the effects have been traumatic. What had, for years, been a rather sleepy backwater of up-market residential landlordism was transformed in just a few years into an area of intense speculation in search of quick capital gains.

Although break-up and sale has transformed the tenurial and social structure of London's privately owned purpose-built flat market over the last 15 to 20 years (see Chapter 2), it has had few visible external manifestations apart from the growth of a forest of 'flat for sale' boards throughout central London and the almost complete disappearance of 'flat for rent' advertisements in London papers. It has had a number of major—if less directly visible – social consequences. Not only has the functioning, unfurnished, purpose-built flat sector in London been almost totally destroyed, but the traditional residential investment companies which had owned the blocks for many years have been replaced by a new, aggressive breed of speculative break-up companies whose principal interest is not long-term rental income but the short-term capital gains to be derived from flat sales. This, indeed, is the sole reason they have acquired the flats. The term 'landlord' is a misnomer for what are, in effect, no more than residential asset strippers.

The break-up process is not unique to London, however. Nor is it unique to blocks of flats or to Britain alone. On the contrary, flat break-up is merely one expression of a wider process of tenurial transformation from renting to owning which has been common to many Western capitalist societies over the last 30 years. To this extent, flat break-ups serve as a particularly interesting and illuminating vehicle for the consideration of a series of wider questions concerning the decline of the privately rented sector in Britain and the production and transformation of urban residential space in general. We therefore see this book not just as a specific study of the causes and consequences of the transformation of the residential structure of London, but as a contribution to a series of much wider questions and debates concerning the production and transformation of urban space.

Understanding the production and transformation of urban residential space

How and why does urban residential segregation arise and persist? This question has intrigued and fascinated social observers and social scientists ever since the advent of capitalist industrial urbanization in late-eighteenth and early-nineteenth century Britain led to the creation of both a large urban proletariat and the rise of residential class segregation. Unfortunately, the answers have often been far from satisfactory. Although a wide variety of nineteenth century commentators, from Cooke Taylor to Engels, Booth and Masterman, clearly recognized the class character of much residential segregation, this perspective was never systematically developed. Although Engels identified and described the concentric class zoning of Manchester and other large cities as early as 1844, he made no attempt to analyse the causes of this 'hypocritical plan' apart from recognizing the role of land values and voicing his suspicions that: 'the liberal manufacturers, the Big Whigs of Manchester, are not so innocent after all, in the matter of this sensitive method of construction' (Engels, 1969).

This lack of attention to the actual processes by which urban class segregation was produced and maintained was continued when attention shifted in the early decades of the twentieth century to the burgeoning cities of the New World. In his classic essay 'The growth of a city', Burgess (1925) outlined his famous concentric model of residential differentiation based on

Chicago. But, although he attempted to describe the way in which different areas were differentiated in the process of urban expansion, the discussion of the *process* of segregation was confined to passing references to 'invasion and succession' and the 'sifting and sorting of individuals and groups by residence and occupation'. As Firey commented as early as 1945: 'nowhere in this theory is there a definite statement of the *modus operandi* by which people are propelled to their appointed niches in space'. By focusing on the geographical pattern of residential differentiation, Burgess fostered a concern 'with the isolation of models *per se*, rather than with the isolation of those forces which operate within the urban area to produce residential patterns' (Robson, 1969, p132).

As Harvey (1973, p.133) has observed:

> The line of approach adopted by Engels in 1844 was and still is far more consistent with hard economic and social realities than was the essentially cultural approach adopted by Park and Burgess. It seems a pity that contemporary geographers have looked to Park and Burgess rather than Engels for their inspiration.

Given that urban social areas are composed of 'people, living in houses distributed in space' (Robson,1975,p.13),it follows that an analysis of the structure and operation of the housing market is crucial to an understanding of the processes of residential differentiation in cities. Unfortunately, the absence of such an analysis is now seen to have constituted a glaring lacuna at the heart of Burgess's model. As Bassett and Short (1980, p.24) commented:

> by considering the nature of housing supply and allocation in early twentieth century North America as a constant, given and often 'natural' variable,(it)is unable to say anything meaningful about the structure of the housing market and consequently has little explanation to offer for the patterns of residential differentiation which it describes.

This concern with the identification and analysis of geographical patterns of differentiation at the expense of process persisted for decades as successive generations of urban geographers and sociologists continued their attempt to 'hunt the Chicago model'. Where attempts were made at explanation, the focus was almost exclusively on demand-oriented, behavioural explanations which stressed the role of choice and preference in residential decision making and intra-urban migration. It is now generally accepted that such explanations are of only limited value, not least because they fail to locate individual choices within the context of the different structures of opportunity and constraint within which such choices are made. As Short (1978) put it: 'The decisions of individual households are more adequately explained as a form of adaptive behaviour in relation to the nature of the housing system..than by...consumer preference argument"(pp.545-6). The first major break with this behavioual form of analysis was pioneered by Rex and Moore's (1967) study of housing allocation, race and segregation in Birmingham, but it was not until the early 1970s that the focus of attention finally moved from the identification and description of static residential patterns to the analysis of housing market processes.

Initially, most studies dealt with the consumption and allocation of housing rather than with its production. The realization that housing in capitalist economies was a commodity produced and exchanged for profit was slow to dawn. Although the central role of landownership and investment in the production of residential space had long been recognized by urban historians (Cannadine, 1980; Chalklin, 1968; Dyos, 1961, 1968; Kellett, 1961; Parry Lewis, 1965; Reeder, 1965; Thompson, 1974), it was not generally appreciated by contemporary urban geographers until the mid 1970s. (Lamarche, 1976; Massey and Catalano, 1978; Boddy, 1981; Badcock, 1984). So vast was the intellectual gulf separating the contemporary focus on abstract general models of urban residential land use from the historical analysis of specific development processes that it could easily have been concluded that the role of capital investment in the production and transformation of the environment ceased around 1945. The intellectual hegemony of ecological and neo-classical demand-oriented economic approaches to residential structure was so great and all-pervasive that, with few exceptions (e.g. Form, 1954), the built environment was treated as though it had sprung, fully formed, out of nothing. The social relations of ownership and production were almost entirely ignored and one of the principal goals of this book is to reassert their importance.

It is only relatively recently that the realities of investment and profitability have been brought into the forefront of concern from the historical backwater in which they had languished. Not until 1974, when Harvey and Chatterjee's work on the structuring of residential space by government and financial institutions in Baltimore was published, was the role of investment and disinvestment pushed back into the centre of the contemporary urban residential stage. Their analysis of the geographical impact of mortgage finance and mortgage guarantee policies is too well known to merit repetition here, but it can be argued that the most important aspect of their work lay in their attempt to relate residential differentiation, housing choice and the structure and operation of the housing market. Having established the geographical structure of the housing finance and mortgage market, they suggested that this structure forms a 'decision environment' in which individual households make housing choices which largely conform to and reinforce the existing structure. They concluded:

> This geographic structure is continuously being transformed by the ebb and flow of market forces, the operations of speculators and realtors, the changing potential for home-ownership, the changing profitability of landlordism, the pressures emanating from community action, the interventions and disruptions brought about by changing governmental and institutional policies, and the like. *It is this process of transformation of and within a structure that must be the focus for understanding residential differentiation.* (p.25)

We believe this statement to be of considerable importance for a number of reasons. First, it sets the analysis of socio-spatial structure firmly within the wider social context as a basis for understanding and explanation. Second, it embodies a historical perspective which stresses the essentially dynamic nature of socio-spatial structure and accords priority to the processes of change. Third, it does not exclude the role of housing choice. Instead, it places 'choice' within the framework of a spatially and socially structured housing market produced and shaped in its broad lineaments by financial, economic and political forces. The statement also avoids the crude and functionalist supply-side determinism which has characterized some of the recent literature on housing markets.

Although the actual decision to move or not to move house is taken by the individual household unit, this 'direct' decision cannot be examined independently from the 'decision environment' within which the decision is taken. One of the most important aspects of this decision environment is the interaction between the structure of housing demand, particularly the distribution of income and wealth between households, and the structure and characteristics of the available dwelling stock, particularly tenure, price and location. As anybody who has ever tried to buy or rent somewhere to live knows very well, the final 'decision' is generally as much or more determined by the constraints on what is available, where and at what price, than it is by household choice and preference.

Choices and preferences, for those fortunate enough to possess them, are invariably exercised within the constraints of what is available and affordable. *Tenure* plays a crucial role in this and, to the extent that the tenure structure of central London – or, indeed, of any other residential area – is significantly changed by supply-side decisions such as the decision to sell blocks of flats for owner occupation, this will have profound implications for the nature of residential choices. Whilst some increasingly affluent people will be able to afford to move in and buy, many potential residents will find themselves effectively debarred by the change in tenure and its associated price structure. They become priced out of the market and, over time, such changes in the tenure and price structure of housing supply can and do effect radical changes in the social composition of residential areas of cities independently of any changes in the structure of household demand or choice or preference.

The tenurial transformation of the city

The residential structure of most Western capitalist cities has undergone a variety of transformations during the course of the last 40 years but it is no exaggeration to say that, with the exception of suburbanization, none has been more fundamental and far reaching than the transformation from renting to owning and, in Britain, from private renting to public housing

(Bourne, 1981; Kemeny, 1981; Harloe, 1985). Nowhere has the scale of this tenure transformation been greater than in Britain. On the eve of the First World War approximately 90 per cent of households in Britain rented their accommodation from a private landlord. Britain may have been 'two nations' in terms of class and living standards, but private renting in some form was the major housing tenure across all social classes from the Gorbals of Glasgow to London's Mayfair. Council housing scarcely existed and no more than 10 per cent of households owned their own homes. Today, the picture is radically different. Over 60 per cent of households either own their own home outright or are buying it on a mortgage, and another 30 per cent rent from a local authority. Outside the older inner areas of the larger towns and cities, private renting has been reduced to a small and relatively insignificant residual tenure and, even in the inner areas, it rarely accounts for more than a third of all households. In the space of just 70 years the tenure structure of housing provision in Britain has undergone a radical and dramatic transformation.

This transformation has had two components. First, virtually all housing in Britain built subsequent to 1945 has been for owner occupation or council renting. New building for private renting has been very limited since 1945 and, with the exception of a short period during the 1930s, there was little new building for private renting after the turn of the century. But not all the growth of owner occupation and council renting has arisen from new building. The growth of owner occupation also involved a massive shift from the existing rental stock and it is *the explanation of this shift* which forms a major theme of this book. The privately rented sector in Britain fell from 7.1 million units in 1914 to 2.9 million in 1975. Of the loss of 4.2 million dwellings, no less than 3.7 million, or 88 per cent, were sold for owner occupation and these sales accounted for 41 per cent of the growth of owner occupation between 1914 (0.8 million) and 1975 (9.9 million dwellings). The sale of rented property for individual ownership has also been widespread in the United States (Bourne, 1981; Grebler and Mittelbach, 1979) but, there, rented property has declined far less rapidly than in Britain—from 53 per cent in 1900 to 35 per cent in 1976. This transformation has been of major importance for several reasons, not least because it has altered the structure of tenure opportunities within which housing choices and preferences can be expressed. For most people, private renting is no longer a real option: the dwellings simply do not exist. They are therefore forced either to buy or, if they cannot afford owner occupation, to move into the council sector. Given the marked geographical variations in the distribution of housing tenure between inner cities and suburbs, there is a broad reciprocal relationship between housing tenure and residential location and a change in one frequently implies a change in the other (see Bonnar, 1979).

Towards an explanation of tenure transformation:demand or supply

The crucial question, of course, is why did this shift from private renting to owner occupation take place and what were its causes? The explanations which are put forward by the property lobby and their sympathizers exhibit a rather paradoxical duality. On the one hand, the classic explanation put forward by landlords lays all the blame at the door of rent control which was first introduced in Britain in 1915 under Lloyd George's Government and has remained, in various forms, ever since. As the *Financial Weekly* put it in 1980: 'David Lloyd George first signed the death warrant of the private landlord. That has been sealed by decades of rent control.' On the other hand,the growth of owner occupation has also been interpreted by the building societies and others in terms of the idea of 'natural preference'. The government White Paper *A Fair Deal for Housing*, published in 1971, asserted that: 'Home ownership is the most rewarding form of housing tenure. It satisfies a deep and natural desire on the part of the householder to have independent control of the home that that shelters him (sic) and his family.'(Department of the Environment, 1971).

While we do not dispute that home ownership may confer some degree of ontological security (Saunders, 1984), any attempt to explain the fundamental tenurial transformation in terms of natural preference is both simplistic and erroneous. We argue in Chapters 3 and 4 that the causes of the decline of private landlordism and the rise of owner occupation this century owe more to the structure of taxation, interest rates and financial opportunities for investors than they do to rent control *per se* or the idea of natural preference on the part of home owners. In capitalist economies housing is a commodity which is produced and exchanged for profit like any other commodity. Whether the commodity is produced at all and the form in which it is produced depend almost entirely upon one thing: profitability. If one form of production is unprofitable or less profitable than others it will be scaled down or stopped. The converse is also true. If alternative opportunities for more profitable forms of production or exchange open up, potential producers or speculative entrepreneurs will quickly emerge to take advantage of them. Such a process is not, of course, unique to housing. On the contrary, the search for profitability, new markets, and success and growth at the expense of competitors is the basic motor of all kinds of commodity production and exchange in capitalist economies and housing is no exception. But if a commodity is not profitable it will not be produced. This point is a crucial one which has a major bearing on the relative importance of producer and consumer in the process of housing production. It is frequently asserted that in market economies the consumer is sovereign. Producers may spot a potentially profitable gap in the market, but, if the product is not what the consumer wants or if the price is too high, it will not be bought and the producer will rapidly have to adapt or go out of business. This is true only to a certain extent. Potential demand may exist for many products but, and this is crucial, such demand is only met to the extent that it is profitable to do so.

In general, demand is expressed within the constraints set by the economics of supply. If potential suppliers cannot or will not to supply at a given price or level of profitability, there is very little that consumers can do about it other than attempt to provide the commodity for themselves. The same applies to the form of production. To the extent that the structure of finance, taxation, interest rates and relative profitability point towards certain forms of production rather than others, consumer demand will necessarily be expressed within the framework of supply. As Henry Ford declared of his first Model T cars, the customers could have any colour they wanted as long as it was black. The levels of profitability in different sectors of the market determine what, if anything, is produced. The level and nature of supply is determined by suppliers in the light of their objective to make the best return possible on their capital consistent with continuing capital accumulation. This may seem glaringly obvious but it is crucially important given the stress on demand in traditional economic accounts. As Bourne (1976) has observed: 'the supply of housing in most micro-economic models is not considered to be much of a problem. Supply...follows automatically from the structure of demand' (p.124).

This may seem an esoteric argument, but it has an important bearing on the explanation of the tenure transfer process that we advance in this book. As we shall seek to show, the decline of the privately rented sector is a direct consequence of the decisions made by landlords to disinvest in the light of prevailing financial conditions and relative levels of profitability. New housing production was also switched into owner occupation for essentially the same reasons. While some housing consumers may have preferred to buy, the decline of private landlordism has meant that many households today have little other option. The structure of housing production and opportunities is such that most of those who can buy must buy. While a substantial number of small resident landlords continue to let a room or two in their houses, renting from commercial landlords has ceased to be a feasible option for most people outside the high rent luxury part of the market, and the ever diminishing number of regulated tenants who continue to hang on. The structure of tenure opportunities in the private sector is essentially a product of the profitability of different forms of supply—not consumer choice and preference.

As we show in Chapters 5 and 6, the flat break-up market is very much a supply-led rather than a demand-led process. Although effective demand has played a key role in underpinning the break- up market, the decision to break up and sell in the late 1960s and the 1970s was made by the owners of the blocks - not the residents. It was the owners who set about creating a market, and there are close parallels between the flat break-up market today and the break-up and sale of estates of rented houses from the 1920s onwards. Both needed the active mediation of property owners to create the conditions in which profits could be made.In both cases it proved crucially important to convince tenants of the financial attractions of purchase over rental and to provide mortgage finance for the initial buyers in order to 'prime the pump'. The role played by landlords and others in the shaping and creation of markets forms another major theme of this book. As we argue in Chapter 6, landlords did not passively respond to the pressure of external forces: they actively helped to mediate them.

Varieties of response

The decline of private landlordism has not proceeded evenly across time and space. Although large scale new building for rent effectively ceased in 1939, the extent and rapidity of the decline of existing privately rented property has varied considerably from one part of the country to another and, crucially, from one sector of the privately rented market to another. While the explanation for flat break-ups can be related to the explanation for the decline of the privately rented sector in general, the timing of break-ups is very much a product of unique physical, social and ownership characteristics of the sector. There has been no one mechanical response to the changing conditions of profitability across the private rented sector as a whole.Indeed, profitability has varied considerably within the purpose-built flat sector itself, as we show in Chapters 7 and 8.

Flat break-ups have transformed the tenure structure of central London, but it should not be merely assumed that they have proceeded uniformly across all sections of the market. On the contrary, although the 'conditions of profitability' for the traditional large corporate residential landlords changed radically, neither the timing nor the form of the landlord response to the changes in their 'decision environment' has been uniform. Not only did different landlords find themselves in different positions by virtue of differences in their company structure, their level of borrowings, the size, location and quality of their stock, and their business orientations, etc., they also perceived and reacted to the underlying trends in a variety of different ways. While some companies perceived the profitable opportunities for disinvestment to be derived from break-ups at a relatively early stage, other companies were much slower to react and some only began breaking in a desperate attempt to fend off a takeover bid or because of other internal problems.

The description and explanation of this 'variability of response' on the part of landlords which is developed in Chapters 7 and 8 is a key element of the book. Although all entrepreneurs have to respond in the long term to changing conditions of profitability and the dull compulsion of the market or go out of business, there is no uniform, mechanistic response by landlords to either the changing conditions of profitability or changing investment opportunities. Instead, responses vary widely according to the position and perception of individual companies. Although, in the final analysis, all landlords have to remain profitable to stay in business, different companies face different constraints and have different opportunities and goals. Some companies are also more ruthlessly profit-orientated than others. This is especially true at the more speculative end of the market where entrepreneurs and speculators are constantly searching for new opportunities to make a quick financial killing. We therefore strongly reject the deterministic and functionalist interpretations which have characterized some approaches to the production and transformation of the built environment in the late 1970s. Instead, we would stress the 'competitive anarchy' of the market. As Gough (1979) has pointed out:'The secret of capitalism is that *nobody* plans it.' Although resident choice and preference have played little part in the *causes* of flat break-ups in London and elsewhere, the break-up process has had major social consequences for the social composition of the affected areas and for the residents themselves. The sale of privately rented property for high priced owner occupation has led to the replacement of older, lower income renters by younger, higher income buyers. It has also inflicted major social costs on the existing residents and, in Britain, on the new buyers, as many of the new speculative owners of the blocks have increased rents and service charges and reduced the level of service provision and maintaince. As Chapter 9 shows, their capital gains have been made at the residents' expense.

The comparative analysis of cross-national variations

The scale and incidence of flat 'break-ups' are particularly marked in London, but neither the process nor the problems are confined solely to London or even to Britain. On the contrary, the tenurial and social transformation of rental apartment blocks to owner occupation has been a common phenomenon in Canada, the United States and Australia throughout the 1970s under the name condominium conversion. Condo conversions have generated a great deal of controversy in North America as a result of the large volume of associated tenant displacement and they have been the subject of major governmental and congressional inquiries. In the Dutch cities of Rotterdam and Amsterdam,the equivalent phenomenon of 'appartementen-splitsing' has also proceeded rapidly. The widespread occurrence of the phenomenon of tenurial transformation across a number of Western capitalist societies raises a series of important questions concerning comparative explanation. How far is it possible to assimilate a variety of different national processes to a common explanation and how do essentially similar underlying processes take on different forms in different national contexts?

These questions are the subject of two specific chapter at the end of the book which examine the condo conversion phenomenon in the Britain, the United States and Holland. Although the causes are broadly similar, the actual form of the process and its social and political consequences have differed considerably from one country to another as a result of the considerable differences in landlord-tenant law and the forms of real property ownership. Finally, both flat break-ups and condo conversions raise questions about the extent, nature and timing of state intervention designed to control, halt or otherwise modify the process. As we shall show, state intervention has often been far more marked in 'free enterprise' California than it has been in Britain. In Britain, the belated attempt at state intervention owes a great deal to the embarrassing political pressures generated by the concentration of break-ups in a small number of predominantly Conservative London constituencies, strongly opposing 'the unacceptable face of capitalism' operating, literally, on their own doorstep.

Not suprisingly, the new breed of owners have tended to manage their blocks very differently from their traditional and rather conservative predecessors. They view their blocks of flats not as long-term sources of rental which require regular maintenance and attention if they are to preserve their asset value, but as a commodity to be bought and sold as profitably and as quickly as possible. Whereas the traditional landlords had a vested interest in the maintenance of good landlord tenant relations, the new generation of breakers tend to view tenants not as a valued source of rental income, but as an unfortunate impediment to the realization of capital gains. As a consequence of these changes in the structure, goals and operation of landlords from the late 1960s onwards, tenants have been faced with substantial rent increases, declining maintenance and physical deterioration of their blocks, landlord harassment and a variety of other problems. Nor have the growing number of long-leasehold owner occupiers had an easy ride. They have faced problems over repairs, rapidly escalating service charges,decling services, unexpected bills, lack of consultation and the like.

As break-ups affected an ever larger proportion of the purpose-built, privately rented flat market in London, the protests from tenants and owners grew in volume to the point where they could no longer be ignored. In November 1983 the then Conservative Minister of Housing and Construction stated in the House of Commons that 'Concern has been expressed on both sides of the House about the problems of management in privately owned blocks of flats, especially in London'. He then went on to announce that he was setting up a Committee of Inquiry into the nature, scale and incidence of problems for both landlords and tenants arising from the management of such blocks. The Committee reported in late 1985, and in March 1987 the government put legislation before Parliament based on the committee's recommendations. This won all-party support, and the Landlord and Tenant Act, 1987, was rushed through on the last day before

Parliament was dissolved for the 1987 General Election. Once again, government has had to clear up the mess left by capital in its search for continued profitability, and the break-up market provides a valuable insight into the ways in which the the tenurial and social structure of contemporary cities has been transformed in the course of this search.

2 London's many mansions: the tenurial transformation of London's purpose-built flat sector.

Introduction

Paris, Vienna, Berlin are all cities of flats. But London,[1] the 'Unique City' as Rassmussen (1982) termed it, is distinguished by virtue of the fact that it developed primarily as a city of houses rather than flats. Throughout the eighteenth and nineteenth centuries the principal building type was the terraced house (Summerson, 1978; Methesius, 1982), and the 1920s and 1930s were characterised by the growth of what Jackson (1974) has termed 'semi-detached London'. Although much of the great boom in council building in inner London since the last war has been in the form of blocks of flats, the introduction into London from the 1850s onwards of both artisans' tenements and the middle-class block of privately rented flats constituted a radical innovation in building design. The history and development of 'model dwellings' for the working classes in London has been well documented by Tarn (1969, 1974) and others (Stedman Jones, 1971; Dennis, 1985). But, although the construction of large numbers of middle class blocks of privately rented flats from the 1870s through to the end of the 1930s transformed the residential structure of central London and left a substantial and enduring imprint across much of the rest of London, relatively little is known about either the growth of the sector, its size, distribution and importance or its subsequent transformation from the late 1960s onwards into one of the most speculative and rapidly growing owner occupied markets in London. In subsequent chapters we focus on the causes and consequences of this transformation. The purpose of this chapter is to set the scene by providing an overview of the historical and geographical development of London's purpose built privately rented flat sector, its size and importance, and the quantitative scale of the transformation which has taken place since the mid 1960s.

Origins and development

The origins of the middle class block of flats in London can be traced back to 1853 when Victoria Street in Westminster was being cut through one of Victorian London's many 'rookeries'. According to the *Builder* (1857), the first block of mansion flats in London was built by a Mr Mackenzie as 'his own speculation, and the idea, we believe, originated with him'. The middle class block of flats has been the basis of many speculative fortunes since Mr Mackenzie first realized their potential, but 'French flats', as they were termed, were slow to take off in London. Not only does there appear to have been a strong cultural antipathy to flat living amongst the British middle classes (Tarn, 1974), but Olsen (1976) suggests that they were also associated in the middle-class mind with the equally novel development of model dwellings for the working class. He quotes the *Building News* of 1868 as saying:

> The fact of its being a philanthropic movement . . . created such a prejudice against it in the minds of the classes just above them . . . We are aware of only one building in London divided into flats and let to tolerably well-to-do occupants of the middle classes.

But while this association may have put off the middle classes, it apparently did not deter the upper classes, and Tarn (1974, p.24) suggests that:

> The idea of living in a flat in the middle of London attracted the rich, perhaps because they could usually regard it as a second home . . . Only later did they attract the middle-classes who were one-house families.

Despite this slow start, Escott could observe in 1879 that

> The 'flat' system, borrowed from France, has now existed on a considerable scale in London some fifteen years, and at the present time is in great and growing favour. In the course of five years the rents of flats have doubled. Victoria Street, Westminster, is about equally divided into the offices of parliamentary lawyers, colonial agents, engineers, and into domestic dwellings. These last consist in every case of flats.

The 1880s appear to have marked a turning point in the fortunes of the mansion flat, and during the course of the next 25 years a large number of such blocks were built throughout central and inner London. Opinions differ as to the causes of this boom. Tarn suggests that the rapid increase in the population of London and the city's considerable outward growth placed an increasing pressure on the central, high status residential areas from the 1870s onwards. This pressure may have been instrumental in weakening the traditional English antipathy to flat dwelling. 'The journey to work and the problems of transport in a city where it was no longer possible for many to walk to work altered the popular view of life in the central area' (Tarn, 1974, p.30). The convenience of centrally located flats may have outweighed any residual dislike of flat living, and Escott (1879, p.38) refers to their 'great advantage to busy men or women who are anxious to purchase the seclusion of domestic life at the cost of as little inconvenience as possible'.

Certainly a demand seems to have existed for such flats. Writing of Henry Hankey's Queen Anne's Mansions, a large 14-storey block on the edge of St James's park started in 1873 and finished in 1888, Escott noted that 'The rents paid are fixed at figures which might seem prohibitory, yet few sets of rooms ever remain long vacant'. But why was demand so buoyant? The most likely explanation is that the growth of specialized office employment in the City and elsewhere, and the resultant growth in white-collar professional and clerical occupations referred to by Escott in his description of the Victoria area, created a growing demand for scarce central area accommodation.

What is certain is that such development would not have been undertaken were it not profitable. As the *Builder* noted in 1877: 'when a floor containing six rooms, without any grounds, commands £300 per annum, and two rooms £60 per annum, there is a strong encouragement to continue the erection of such a class of structure'. Indeed, there is a good case for arguing that just as 'The size and shape of the London house have been conditioned from the first by the economic need to get as many houses as possible onto one street' (Summerson, 1978), so too the redevelopment of sites for blocks of flats permitted an intensification in land use. In both cases, however, the motivation was essentially similar: the maximization of dwelling numbers on scarce, high value central sites. The block of flats merely represents a more extreme version of the same process. As we show in later chapters, the maximisation of profitability has continued to shape the more recent development of the flat market and it remains the dominant force in determining the nature and timing of events in the sector.

The last two decades of the nineteenth century and the first 5 years of the twentieth century saw the building of a considerable number of blocks in

Table 2.1 *The number and distribution of privately owned blocks of flats in Greater London by age*

	Pre 1919		*1919–39*		*Post-1939*		*Total*	
	Blocks	*Flats*	*Blocks*	*Flats*	*Blocks*	*Flats*	*Blocks*	*Flats*
INNER LONDON								
No.	1,065	38,320	818	39,429	994	29,340	2,877	107,089
% of blocks by age	37.0	—	28.4	—	34.6	—	100	—
of which, central London:								
No.	*571*	*21,875*	*402*	*22,324*	*418*	*14,595*	*1,391*	*58,794*
%	*41.0*	—	*28.9*	*—30.1*	—	*100*	—	
OUTER LONDON								
No.	87	2,355	509	16,913	1,974	45,243	2,570	64,511
%	3.4	—	19.8	—	76.8	—	100	—
GREATER LONDON								
No.	1,152	40,675	1,327	56,342	2,968	74,583	5,447	171,600
%	21.1	—	24.4	—	54.5	—	100	—

Source: Unpublished Valuation Office survey, 1978

both central and inner London. By 1919 there were over a thousand blocks of 10 flats or more accounting for 40,000 flats (Table 2.1). These were particularly concentrated in the three central London boroughs of Camden, Kensington and Westminster which collectively contained some 22,000 flats in 570 blocks. Westminster alone contained just over half the total and when the substantial number of blocks containing less than 10 flats are taken into account, the total number of blocks in London could be up to 40 per cent greater.

Unfortunately, little is known of the type of capital involved in the development of blocks of flats during this period although it is likely that the sheer size of many of the blocks would limit them to the large speculative investors. There is, however, some limited evidence to suggest that flat development in this period was associated with the early growth of the property investment companies such as the Middle Class Dwellings Company, founded in 1888 and later to be incorporated into the London County Freehold and Leasehold Company (owners of the famous Key Flats empire) which was to become a dominant force in the 1930s (see Chapter 7), the Artisans' and General Property Company, now Artagen Ltd, the London Housing Society and the aptly named New Century Estates. All that can be said with certainty is that building petered out rapidly between 1906 and 1910 in line with the general swing away from housing investment (Greve, 1965). The market was not to revive for 25 years.

The 1930s flat boom

The physical evidence of the 1930s boom is everywhere apparent in London. In central and inner London, large new blocks were erected on cleared sites; in the older, nineteenth-century suburbs large Victorian villas were demolished and the sites redeveloped, and in the outer suburbs new blocks were built on green field sites.

> Blocks of self-contained flats, frequently with the name '————— Court', were erected in completely new areas such as Edgware and Cockfosters (adjacent to newly built tube lines) as well as on the sites of large Victorian villas in the older suburbs. In return for rents ranging from £70 to £150 a year, the tenants enjoyed central heating, the services of a resident porter and the maintenance of communal gardens, in addition to the accommodation which usually comprised one reception room, two bedrooms, a kitchen and a bathroom. (Jackson, 1974, p.136)

The 1930s witnessed the construction of many of the largest blocks in central and inner London. When it was finished in 1934,the 360 flat Latymer Court in Hammersmith was said to be the largest single block of flats in Europe, but it was soon overtaken by the 800 flat White House in Albany Street, just off Regent's Park. Other large blocks rapidly followed, including the 500 flat Russell Court just off Russell Square, the 550 flat Park West just up the Edgware Road from Marble Arch and the 780 flat Du Cane Court in Balham south London. The largest development by far was the massive Dolphin Square complex in Chelsea. Built on a 7 acre site, its 1,250 two to five roomed flats were let at rents of between £75 and £275 per annum. There were two quite distinct markets for blocks of flats at this time. The White House was largely comprised of one room 'flatlets' or 'service flats' like those at Russell Court and, like many suburban blocks of the period, it was specifically designed to accommodate the growing army of middle-class white collar office workers. In central London, however, many blocks were built for the 'persons of position' referred to by the *Builder* in 1877, the larger four to seven roomed flats being let at rents of up to £300 per annum.

Evidence regarding the pace of building in the mid to late 1930s is found in the general summaries of trends in the London property market published each year by the *Estates Gazette*. They present a picture of a booming market throughout the period. The survey for 1934, for example, observed that

> The demand for the smaller type of utility flat at a modest rent continues unabated and the ever increasing additions to the number and variety of the new blocks of flats that are appearing with such rapidity has resulted in considerable competition not only with regard to the rentals asked but also to the amenities offered. Numerous large blocks have been erected in London and the suburbs and suitable sites have been eagerly sought after. A noticeable feature has been the large increase in the number of flats in the outer suburbs. (Estates Gazette, 5 January 1935, p.13).

The survey of 1935 noted that 'In the centre of London the rate at which new blocks of mansion flats have been constructed has hardly diminished' and the 1936 survey commented that 'With regard to flats, the best answer to those who toy with hackneyed catchwords like "saturation point" is to point to the promptitude with which new accommodation is being taken' (Estates Gazette, 10 December, 1936, p.1079).

References to specific major new developments tail off rapidly in 1938, but indirect evidence of the very real demand for good quality prestige central London developments is provided by a number of passing references to pre-lettings in the *Estates Gazette*. In 1935 there was a reference to the fact that 22 of the 49 flats in Crompton Court in Fulham had been let even though the building was not completed. Similar reports in 1936 noted that 75 per cent of the flats in Kings Court, Chelsea, had been let on completion and in nearby Chesil Court half the flats had been let prior to completion. In 1936 the *Evening News* carried a full page of advertisements every Wednesday for luxury flats.

A large number of new units were added to the existing stock of flats during the 1930s boom, and by the outbreak of war in 1939, a further 56,000 flats in 1,300 blocks of over 10 flats had been built in Greater London. Some 39,000 flats in 800 blocks were built in inner London and 17,000 flats in 500 blocks in outer London (Table 2.1). Of the inner London total no fewer than 22,000 or 57 per cent were built in the three central London boroughs. Although the majority of both flats and blocks were built in central and inner

London, the number built in outer London increased dramatically compared to before the First World War. This is, of course, partly a reflection of the massive physical growth of outer London between the wars.

The modern flat: a machine for living in

The evidence for pre-lettings notwithstanding, the central London flat market in the 1930s was clearly a very competitive one in which developers vied with one another to offer the most comprehensive and up-to-date facilities in their blocks. In 1936 the *Estates Gazette* commented that Carrington House in Mayfair was 'the first block to be equipped with television facilities for reception by tenants sets'. Eaton House, another Mayfair block, was described as 'the first block of luxury flats in England, and probably in Europe, to be air-conditioned', and Kings Court, Chelsea, was recorded as having all modern conveniences, lifts, central heating and constant hot water, refrigerators, roof gardens and decorations to tenants' requirements. In 1938, an advertisement in the London *Evening News* for Park West stated that 'Every possible convenience to modern luxury is evident in the flats, even to a rent-free telephone and a refrigerator'.

The selling value of the comfort and facilities of the new blocks is a recurrent theme the importance of which cannot be overstressed. Modern blocks in the 1930s were definitely regarded as a new form of living, as 'a machine for living in' to quote Le Corbusier's telling phrase, and flat developments attracted the attention of many leading contemporary architects. The efficiency and convenience of modern blocks were frequently stressed and one 1936 feature in the *Estates Gazette* (11 April 1936) suggested that

> When discussing the increasing popularity of the modern flat among the middle and upper classes people usually try to explain it by contrasting the simplicity of the flat with the difficulties caused by the shortage and cost of domestic labour in the large or old-fashioned house. This, of course, does play a great part in influencing people's minds; but equally important factors are the very high standard of comfort and efficiency offered by the up-to-date blocks of flats, their astonishingly complete equipment, and the comprehensive 'all-in' services that are available to every tenant.
>
> The term 'block of flats' is an inadequate one nowadays. Flats are designed today not to be a mere collection of apartments, but to function as smooth-running organisations which not only accommodate the tenant under the most private, comfortable and sanitary conditions, but provide him with more and more amenities, from siesta and sunbathing gardens on the roof to underground garages and household store-rooms in the basement. Once regarded as a temporary home in which one might 'make shift' for a year or so, the flat as it is being erected today is to many discriminating people an 'ideal home'.

The prize for panegyrics however, must go to an article on Grove Hall Court, St John's Wood, entitled 'New Services for Flat Dwellers'. As a hymn of praise to modernity and an example of the hard-sell technique it is scarcely equalled.

> One of the outstanding achievements of the twentieth century is that smooth running organism, the block of 'luxury flats' - a vast machine dedicated to efficiency in living, where, under one roof, all important needs can be satisfied, and life achieves a simplicity and material perfection beyond the dreams of our fore-fathers. One of the most striking examples of such an achievement is Grove Hall Court . . .
>
> The building includes a lido; gymnasium; garage accommodation; a roof garden; restaurant; pets' parlour; coiffeur; valet service; library service; domestic service; hoover service; cold storage; refrigeration; free telephone service; electric current at 1/2d per unit; central heating; constant hot water; wall safes; coal fires to principal bedrooms; trunk storage; pram lift; pram cleaning service; medical service; and free telephone communication to Messers Selfridges', Whiteleys', and Barnes'. (Estates Gazette, 27 June 1936, p.151)

The 1930s flat boom was closely associated with the establishment of the property investment company as a major force in property development. While the involvement of larger corporate developers partially reflected the size of many of the developments and the necessity for ready access to secure and plentiful finance, it also reflected the profitable and trouble- free nature of the block of flats as a safe investment commodity. The type of tenant for whom the flat market was oriented—the salaried, non-manual households—the level of rents obtainable, and the compact and orderly nature of the developments which allowed for efficiency in management, all contributed to the appeal of flat development for corporate investors.

While some of the companies involved in the 1930s boom were already long established, this period also saw the rise of some newly established property companies run by astute speculative entrepreneurs who had little or no direct experience of the property world. Bell Property, jointly founded in 1931 by Anthony Somers, a businessman engaged in hire purchase, and Reginald Toms, who made his fortune on war surplus dealing and pirate bus operations (i.e. running private services illegally to compete with licensed services) in the 1920s, was responsible for a number of the most prestigious and imposing block developments. Park West, Marble Arch (550 flats), Highlands Heath, Putney (144 flats), Chiswick Village (280 flats), Greenhill, Hampstead (135 flats), and the High, Streatham (174 flats), are all examples of Bell Property schemes which in the 6 years between 1933 and 1939—the heyday of the flat developer—constructed at least 2,700 'up market' flats in and around London (see Figures 2.1, 2.2 and 2.3).

The parallels with the 1970s are striking. While the 1930s saw the rise of speculative builders and developers, the 1970s saw the rise of the speculative flat breakers. In both periods, the people involved often had little expertise in property. But they had a nose for money and speculative profits and flats—for rent in the 1930s, or for sale in the 1970s—offered

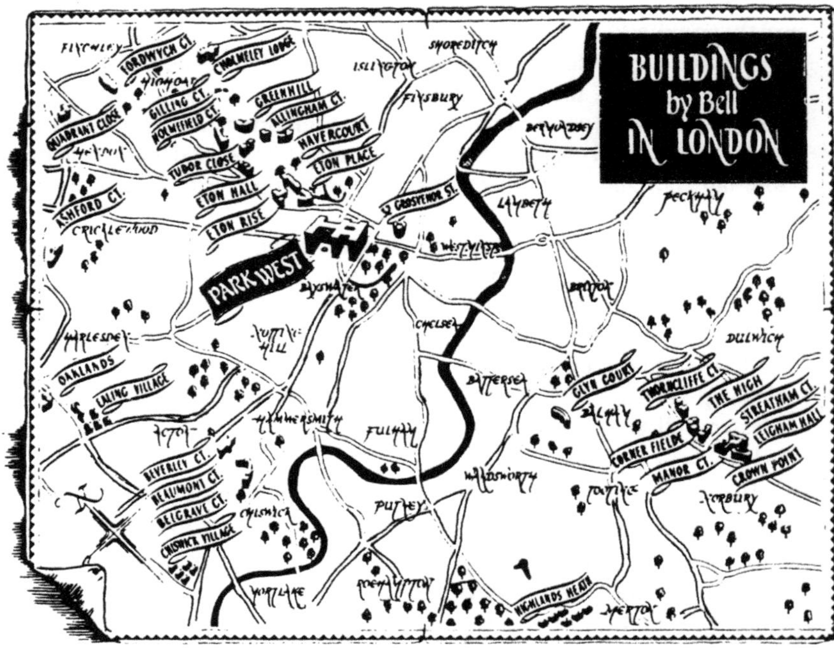

***Figure 2.1** Blocks of Flats built by the Bell Group in London in the 1930s*

***Figure 2.2** A typical 1930s block of flats in Central London*

***Figure 2.3** Park West: a block of 550 flats in Central London*

opportunities for rich pickings for the shrewd entrepreneur. In the 1930s as in the 1970s, adequate finance on the right terms was crucial for success. The Bell developments were financed on loans from the joint stock banks and by mortgages from the Royal Liver and Eagle Star Insurance Companies. In general,

> the promoter had to put up about one quarter of the cost himself, borrow the rest at around 5 percent and hope to get 8 percent on the cost. Once the flats...were let, the developer would attempt to borrow long-term finance from an insurance company or some established lender. (Marriott, 1967, p.35)

The banks would put up the initial short-term finance at several points over base rate and, once the building was completed and rents were coming in, the now secure investment could be refinanced on a longer term basis at lower interest rates from more cautious institutional sources. While this is the classic financing method utilized throughout the property development sector, it illustrates the need fo. · ¬th substantial initial capital backing and good institutional links - both a remote possibility for smaller landlords and developers. As we shall see, successful break-up operations in the 1970s were also dependent on institutional financial backing.

Crucial though the structure and organization of development is, the demand side of the equation cannot be ignored. As in the late nineteenth century, the source of demand derived once again from the growing army of middle class white-collar workers, and Jackson (1974) has argued that flats were increasingly built for the growing number of small households as 'the house market reached saturation in the middle thirties'. Developers had a shrewd eye on the changing structure of demand at this time and marketing was the key to success. The marketing strategy of the Bell Group was 'to decide on the type of resident for whom the property is to cater...plan the flat...that will best suit their needs...then decide on the fittings and equipment which will help them live with the minimum of labour and expense' ('Homes by Bell', 1947). The development of the flat market was clearly not left to chance. Flats were carefully marketed to elicit a demand from the potential clientele. As we shall see, similar techniques were to underpin the marketing of flats for sale some 40 years later.

Alien elements: the opposition to suburban blocks of flats

Despite their apparent appeal to both developers and tenants, the development of purpose built blocks was not without conflicts. These were particularly marked in established residential areas where developers commonly sought to demolish large old houses and redevelop the sites for blocks of flats. These sites frequently had restrictive covenants on them which prohibited higher density or cheaper developments. But the 1925 Law of Property Act enabled developers and others to apply to have any restrictive covenants on land and property lifted. There was often strong opposition by existing residents. The most common grounds for objection were that such developments would have a detrimental effect on the immediate properties by virtue of light, view, shadow, etc., and that they would generate excessive traffic and depress property prices. But perhaps the most important objection was that the cheaper blocks would lower the tone of such areas by introducing lower class or 'alien elements'.

The *Estates Gazette* carried regular reports on hearings under the 1925 Act and the application to redevelop Richmond House, Aldenham Road, Bushey, in 1939 provides a typical example of the importance of social class in these hearings. The *Estates Gazette* (10 April 1939, p.628) reported one opponent as arguing that

> the neighbourhood in question was a high-class residential one which had been developed with properties of a better type...the erection of the proposed flats must seriously depreciate the houses in their immediate vicinity. Not only would they dominate the surrounding properties by reason of their height and bulk, but they would also be occupied by a different class of tenant from those living in the neighbourhood.
>
> The same objection was made time and time again. A witness opposing an application to redevelop two semi-detached houses in Croydon in 1937 argued that the district was 'a good class residential one, occupied predominantly by owner occupiers....An *alien element* would be brought into the neighbourhood if flats were erected' (*Estates Gazette*, 17 April 1937, p.744)

The chief targets were smaller cheaper flats for the growing number of lower-middle class, white-collar workers. In the 1934 application to develop a site on Richmond Hill as 68 flats next to the existing Richmond Hill Court, the opposition argued:

> There were 'flats' and 'flats'. In this case the flats one visualised were not attractive. Furthermore, the class of tenants might be the most undesirable...In the proposed flats all the cooking would have to be done in the one living room and they would possess only one bedroom. The type of person attracted would not be willing to pay more than £70 per annum. They would certainly not be the kind of tenants one expected to find in the premier position of Richmond Hill. I will go further and say that these flats would attract undesirables. (*Estates Gazette*, 10 March 1934, p.398)

While these conflicts were not always resolved in favour of the developers, it is clear that the reason for squeezing as many flats as possible onto a site, indeed the very rationale for redeveloping sites as blocks of flats, was the increased yield they brought. Increasing land values and rents and the growing demand for and acceptance of flats as a way of living raised the possibility of profitable land use intensification. As we shall see, it was the search for enhanced profitability that led to the break-up and sale of such blocks during the 1970s. As Chapter 9 shows, this more recent activity has also created considerable conflicts—both between owners and residents and between tenants and long leaseholders. As ever, the drive to maximize private profitability tends to generate social costs.

London's many mansions

The development of the purpose built privately rented block of flats in London from the mid-nineteenth century onwards has left an enduring stamp on London's housing stock. In 1966, the high-water mark of the sector immediately prior to the advent of break-up and sale for owner occupation, the 10 per cent sample census enumerated some 173,550 such flats in Greater London. They accounted for 7.4 per cent of the total housing stock and 28 per cent of the stock of privately rented *dwellings*, and accommodated

188,200 households. In central and inner London they played a far more important role. As Table 2.2 shows, such flats comprised 13 per cent of the total housing stock and 33 per cent of the total privately rented dwelling stock in inner London. In central London the figures were even higher at 27 and 48 per cent respectively, and they accounted for no less than 53 percent of the total stock of unfurnished privately rented dwellings. Central London accounted for no less than 27 per cent of the total number of purpose-built privately rented flats in London, and Westminster alone accounted for half of these. The geographical concentration of such flats in central and inner London is shown in Figures 2.4 and 2.5. The significance of this sector in the central London housing market in 1966, immediately prior to the onset of break- up is clear-cut.

Table 2.2. *Privately rented, purpose-built multi-dwellings in Greater London, 1966*

	Central London	Inner London	Greater London
PURPOSE-BUILT RENTED MULTI-DWELLINGS			
Unfurnished	43,430	110,470	164,800
Furnished	4,350	6,480	8,760
Total	47,780	116,940	173,550
ALL RENTED DWELLINGS			
Unfurnished	81,560	325,380	557,100
Furnished	17,440	33,880	55,350
Total	99,900	359,260	612,450
% PURPOSE-BUILT MULTI-DWELLINGS			
Unfurnished	53.2	40.0	29.6
Furnished	24.9	19.1	15.8
Total	48.3	32.6	28.3
Total number of dwellings	175,390	880,076	2,237,630
Purpose-built multi-dwellings as a % of all dwellings	27.2	13.3	7.7

Source: Sample Census of Population, 1966; all figures have been multiplied by 10

The size distribution of blocks

The size distribution of blocks can be assessed from two sources. The unpublished valuation office statistics for all non-council blocks of 10 flats or more in London in 1978 (see table 2.1) (Department of the Environment, 1985) give a total of 171,000 flats in 5,447 blocks in Greater London -an average of 31 flats per block. When the figures are disaggregated, they show that the average block size of 42 flats in central London is greater than the inner London average of 37 and significantly greater than the outer London average of 25. These differences reflect the fact that blocks built before the Second World War tend to be larger than postwar blocks and that the

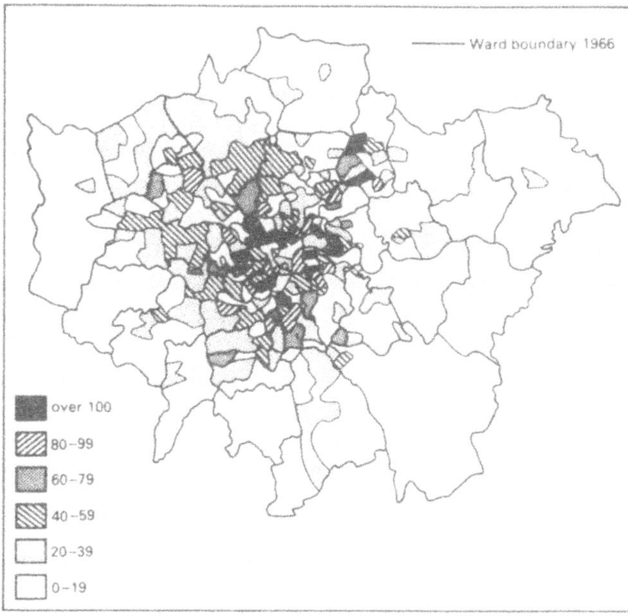

Figure 2.4 *The geographical distribution of purpose-built blocks of flats by ward in London, 1966. (Source: 10% sample census)*

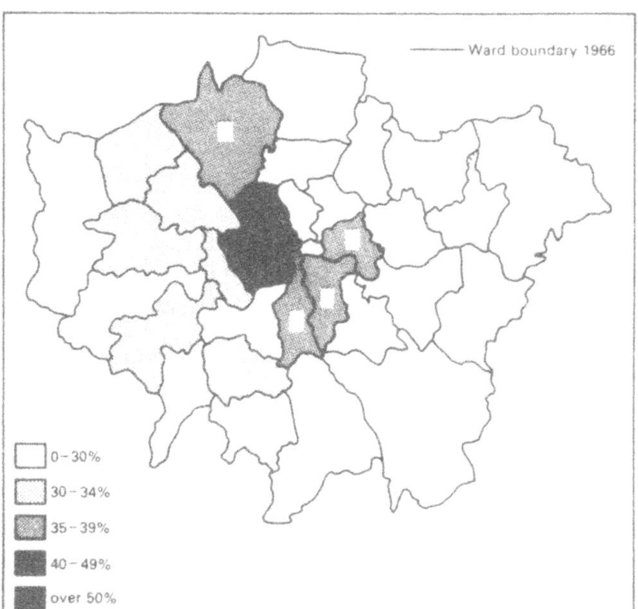

Figure 2.5 *Privately rented flats as a percentage of all privately rented unfurnished dwellings, by borough, 1966. (Source: 1966 sample census)*

proportion of new blocks inncreases as distance from the centre of London increases. Thus, the average size of pre-1919 blocks in greater London is 35 flats, compared to 42 and 25 for interwar and postwar blocks. And while in 1978 inner London contained no less than 92 per cent of all the pre-1919 blocks in Greater London, it contained only 62 per cent of inter-war blocks and 50 per cent of postwar blocks. These figures are distorted, however, by the fact that they include all non-council blocks, including new blocks purpose-built for owner occupation and blocks owned by housing associations but excluding all blocks of fewer than 10 flats (see table 2.1).

Analysis of the data on purpose-built privately rented blocks contained in the rent registers of the Rent Officer Service for the three central London boroughs of Camden, Kensington and Chelsea, and Westminster reveal that of a total of almost 43,000 flats in 1,239 blocks—an average of 35 flats per block. There are a large number of small blocks and a small number of large blocks. The size distribution of blocks by the number of flats they contain is therefore negatively skewed. Table 2.3 shows that just over a third of the blocks had fewer than 10 flats and half of all blocks had 14 flats or less while only 10 per cent of all blocks had more than 80 flats. This 10 per cent, comprising the largest blocks, accounted for no less than 50 per cent of all flats. Conversely, the 50 per cent of blocks with 14 flats or fewer accounted for only 10 per cent of all flats. It is apparent that a small number of large blocks account for a disproportionately large number of flats.

Regarding the size of accommodation offered in the sector in terms of rooms per flat, Table 2.4 compares the distribution of flats by number of rooms both in Greater London in 1966 and in a sample of 102 large blocks in central London in 1971. The figures show a considerable contrast between the two. In Greater London as a whole, there is a preponderance of units in the medium size range of four to five rooms, whereas the central London blocks possess a large (44 per cent) proportion of one or two roomed studio units. It therefore appears that the central London flat sector is strongly oriented towards a very specific market – that of small (one and two-person) households. At the other end of the scale, the central London figures also reveal a higher proportion of units in the seven plus rooms range. This reflects the concentration of the large luxury flat market in areas like Kensington and Mayfair.

Flat break-up in London: the scale of the transformation

In order to assess the scale of the break-ups and their contribution to the decline of London's privately rented sector two major sources of data were used. The first was the rent registration data from the rent offices of each of the three central London boroughs. The second,and principal data source was the 1981 census which, fortunately, included a published table giving details on building type by tenure down to the borough level. This enabled a comparison to be made with the 1966 census data.

Table 2.3 *Frequency and cumulative percentage distribution of blocks by size in Camden, Kensington and Westminster*

Size band (no. of flats per block)	*Flats* *No.*	*Flats* *Cumulative %*	*Blocks* *No.*	*Blocks* *Cumulative %*
0–4	518	1.2	170	13.7
5–9	1,726	1.5	257	34.5
10–14	2,133	10.0	186	49.5
15–19	1,736	13.9	104	57.9
20–9	3,281	21.4	137	68.9
30–9	2,124	26.2	62	73.9
40–9	2,622	32.2	60	78.8
50–9	2,337	37.5	43	82.8
60–9	2,200	42.6	35	85.0
70–9	1,487	45.9	20	86.7
80–9	2,027	50.6	24	88.6
90–9	2,238	55.7	24	90.6
100–19	3,700	64.1	34	93.3
120–39	3,323	71.7	26	95.4
140–59	1,936	76.1	13	96.4
160–79	2,010	80.7	12	97.4
180–99	1,500	84.0	8	98.1
200+	6,987	100.0	24	100.0
Total	43,887		1,239	

Source: Borough rent offices' registration data

Table 2.4 *Percentage distribution of privately rented purpose built flats by size. Greater London, 1966, and central London, 1971*

	Number of rooms 1/2	3	4	5	6	7	Total
Greater London, 1966	11.1	20.0	37.3	20.6	7.2	3.7	188,200 (100%)
Central London, 1971	43.8	20.3	13.8	8.6	6.6	6.9	12,216 (100%)

Sources: 1966: 10% Sample Census, Greater London
1971: Census, unpublished Small Area Statistics, Sample of 1J2 Central London Enumeration Districts

Before looking at the rent registration data it is important to describe briefly the nature and limitations of the data source. In addition to introducing security of tenure for all unfurnished privately rented tenancies, one of the the provisions of the Labour Government's 1965 Rent Act was the establishment of a procedure for registering 'fair' rents with the newly established Rent Officer Service. Either landlords or tenants could apply to have a 'fair' rent determined and registered by the rent officer. The registered rent was then entered along with details of the tenant, the landlord and the property itself in rent registers available to the public for inspection. Once registered, a new application for a change of rent, almost invariably an increase where landlords were concerned, could not be made for a further 3 years (reduced to 2 years under the 1980 Housing Act).

While rent registration was designed to introduce a measure of certainty and security into the privately rented market, it was a voluntary procedure and there is therefore no guarantee that rent registration data provide a comprehensive or even a representative source of information. We found, however, in the course of an examination of *all* rent registration records for blocks of flats in the three central London boroughs, that not only were some 90 per cent of applications made by landlords, but that they appeared to be remarkably comprehensive. Although the number of registrations increased only slowly in the first few years, it seems that the great majority of landlords progressively registered the majority of their purpose built flats. Our evidence for this is derived not only from the rent registers themselves but from a comparison of the total number of flats in blocks listed in the rent registers with the evidence of the 1966 census.

The 1,240 blocks identified from the rent registers in central London contained an estimated total of some 43,887 flats (by no means all of which were registered). The figure recorded in the 1966 census was 47,780 and this included some 3,600 flats owned by the charitable trusts such as Guinness and Peabody which were excluded from our analysis of rent registrations. When these are deducted from the 1966 census figures, the census total is almost identical to the figure derived from the rent registers.

Given that break-ups did not get underway until after 1965 and that very little in the way of new building for rental took place after the end of the 1950s, the 1966 census and the rent register estimate provide an accurate picture of the size of the privately rented purpose built flat sector in central London immediately prior to break-up. Although we cannot directly infer from the rent registration data that all flats in the blocks identified were privately rented, the 1966 census revealed that out of a total of 51,090 private sector flats in central London only 4,350 or 8.5 percent were owner occupied. The remaining 91.5 percent were privately rented.

The number of purpose built flats in central London which had currently registered rents in mid 1980 was only 12,757. Although it is possible that this figure excluded a substantial, if unknown, number of non-registered rented flats, this figure comprises only 30 per cent of the total number of privately rented flats contained in the blocks in 1966. It thus appears that up to 70 percent of central London's privately rented, purpose-built flat sector had disappeared from the rent registers by mid 1980. Useful though the rent registers are in indicating the degree of tenure transformation which may have taken place, it would be dangerous to base an analysis of change solely on this basis alone. This data source also tells us nothing about what happened to the missing flats or what happened outside central London during the years since 1966. In order to answer these questions and to check the changes indicated by rent registration data for central London, it is necessary to compare the results of the 1966 and the 1981 censuses.

Intercensal change 1966–81

Table 2.5 *The changing tenurial composition of privately owned blocks of flats in Greater London 1966–81*

	Inner London	*of which central London*	*Outer London*	*Greater London (Inner) & outer)*
1966[1]				
Owner occupied	11,240	*3,290*	36,910	48,160
Rented unfurnished[2]	110,470	*43,450*	54,330	164,800
Rented furnished	6,480	*4,350*	2,280	8,760
Total	128,190	*51,090*	93,530	221,720
1981[3]				
Owner occupied	35,645	*14,947*	77,794	113,439
Rented unfurnished[4]	54,166	*21,877*	37,853	92,019
Rented furnished	8,184	*4,586*	5,544	13,728
Total	97,995	*41,410*	121,191	219,186
Change 1966–81				
Owner occupied	+24,405	*+11,657*	+40,874	+65,279
%	+217.1	*+354.3*	+110.7	+135.5
Rented unfurnished	−56,304	*−21,573*	−16,477	−72,781
%	−50.9	*−49.7*	−30.3	−44.2
Rented furnished	+1,704	*+236*	+3,264	+4,968
%	+22.8	*+5.4*	+143.2	+56.7
Total change	−30,195	*−9,680*	+27,661	−2,534
%	−30.8	*−18.9*	+24.6	−1.1

1 Purpose built multi-dwellings; restricted to households present on Census night.
2 Includes dwellings rented from private person or company, but excludes other tenures and not stated category.
3 Household spaces in purpose-built falts; residents' household spaces.
4 Includes falts rented unfurnished or from housing associations *but excludes* rented with business by virtue of employment.

Table 2.5 shows the number of households living in private (i.e. non local authority) purpose-built flats disaggregated by tenure in central, inner, outer and Greater London for 1966 and 1981. The tenurial changes all reveal a sharp decline in the number of households renting unfurnished accommodation and a large increase in owner occupation. In Greater London as a whole the unfurnished sector declined by almost 73,000, or 44 per cent, while owner occupation increased by over 65,000, or 135 per cent, and the furnished sector increased by 5,000, or 57 percent. While these aggregate change figures seem to balance very closely, they conceal a number of factors which complicate the analysis and it cannot simply be assumedd that there has been a direct transfer from unfurnished renting to owner occupation as a result of flat break-up and sale across London as a whole. First, the figures for the unfurnished sector include a large housing association component, the size of which has increased enormously since 1966. In fact, of the 92,000 unfurnished households remaining in the sector in Greater London in 1981, no fewer than 42,369, or 46 per cent, were accounted for by housing associations. As a result, the decline of the non housing association, private, unfurnished sector is very considerably understated.

The second complication is revealed when the individual figures for central, inner and outer London are examined. In outer London, the absolute decline of 16,477, or 30 per cent, in the unfurnished sector is far outweighed by the gain of almost 41,000, or 111 per cent, in the owner occupied sector, and the figure for the private sector as a whole shows a net increase of almost 28,000 households. The net increase in this sector is primarily a result of the high level of new flat building for owner occupation in outer London during the 1960s and 1970s.

In central and inner London, where there has been very little new building for owner occupation, the change figures reveal large net losses from the rented sector.In inner London the owner occupied sector increased by over 217 per cent, or 24,000 households, while the unfurnished sector declined by more than 56,000 households. There was thus a net loss of 30,000, or 31 per cent, in the number of usually resident households. In central London, owner occupation increased by almost 12,000, or 354 per cent, while the unfurnished sector declined by nearly 22,000. The result was a net loss of 10,000, or 19 per cent, of usually resident households from the purpose-built sector as a whole. While the large increases in the numbers of owner occupied households in both central and inner London are almost entirely a product of the sale of previously privately rented flats, a large part of the rented sector appears to have disappeared without trace between the censuses into a quantitative 'black hole'.

How can we account for these seeming losses? First, there has been a small, though not precisely quantifiable, reduction in the size of the sector in inner London as a result of municipalization in the early 1970s and the compulsory acquisition and demolition of some of the poorest blocks. Camden, for example, is known to have municipalized at least 1,500 flats during this period, and a number of working-class artisan blocks have been cleared in the boroughs of Southwark, Lambeth, Tower Hamlets and

Islington where the net losses from the private purpose built sector have been greatest. But, while local authority acquisitions and clearances clearly account for a considerable though unspecified proportion of the losses in a number of inner London boroughs,an examination of the rent registers for the three central London boroughs from 1966 to 1980 revealed that very few blocks had been either demolished or municipalized. The explanation must lie elsewhere.

The primary cause of the decline in the number of households enumerated as living in flats in central and inner London is, we suggest, the very considerable increase in the number of flats which are either vacant or not occupied on a permanent basis. The 'unit of count' employed in the 1981 census was that of 'usually resident' households. By definition this excludes vacant flats and flats where the household was either absent or not usually resident. It is, of course, impossible for the census to disaggregate such household spaces by tenure, but by using the 1981 data on vacancies and tenure characteristics of some 101 of the largest central London blocks each of which formed comparable enumeration districts in the 1971 and 1981 censuses, it is possible to show the magnitude of the increase which has occurred in the number of vacant and not usually resident household spaces during the intercensal decade. Table 2.6 shows the tenure distribution of the 12,900 flats in these blocks for the two dates. The figures have been expressed as a proportion of the total household spaces, including vacant spaces, in order to illustrate the impact of the large increase in vacant and non-resident occupied household spaces (i.e. flats) in these blocks. While the changes from 1971 to 1981 are not directly comparable with those derived from the 1966 to 1981 analysis, the 12,900 household spaces in these large blocks account for a quarter of the 1966 central London total. They thus provide a significant indication of change.

Table 2.6 *Tenure and vacancy changes for household spaces in 101 blocks in central London 1971–81*

	1971	%	*1981*	%	*1971–81*	%
Owner occupied	814	6.3	2,969	23.0	+2,155	+264.7
Local authority	320	2.5	436	3.4	+116	+36.3
Rented unfurnished	9,241	71.4	4,266	33.0	−4,975	+53.8
Rented furnished	1,425	11.0	948	7.3	−477	−33.4
Vacant	1,137	8.8	4,302	33.2	+3,165	+278.4

Sources: Census of Population, 1971 and 1981

The trends shown in Table 2.6 broadly reflect those previously discussed for central London as a whole between 1966 and 1981. Owner occupation increased by 265 per cent, growing from just 6.3 to 23 per cent of all household spaces, while unfurnished private renting declined by 55 per cent, from 71 to 33 per cent of all household spaces. The key figure is the 278 per cent increase in the number of vacant and not usually resident household spaces from 9 per cent in 1971 to no less than 33 per cent in 1981. Further confirmation was obtained from an analysis of electoral registration data for a sample of 13 of these large blocks of flats in Westminster which collectively contained some 1,486 flats. The proportion of these flats for which there was no entry in the electoral registers rose from 12 per cent in 1968 to 32 percent in 1981. These figures are very close to those obtained from the analysis of intercensal voids and, although registration for British nationals eligible to vote is not compulsory, they point to the existence of a significant increase in the number of flats which are either vacant or not permanently occupied or occupied by foreign nationals who are ineligible to vote.

While it is not possible merely to extrapolate from either the vacancy or the electoral register figures to the sector as a whole, they none the less provide a clear pointer to the cause of the otherwise inexplicable 'disappearance' of a large proportion of central and inner London's purpose-built private flat stock between 1966 and 1981. They also provide further confirmation of the scale of the transformation of London's privately rented purpose built flat sector between 1966 and 1981. Not only have a large proportion of flats been sold for 'usually resident' owner occupation, but a large proportion of flats have been either sold to non-resident foreign nationals or held vacant pending sale.

The decline of the privately rented sector in central London

Central and inner London have long occupied a unique position within the British housing market. Although 90 per cent of all households rented privately in Britain in 1914, this figure had fallen to just 21 per cent by 1961. In inner London however, some 64 per cent of households still rented privately in 1961 and in central London the figure was no less than 80 per cent. Central and inner London constituted an island of private renting in a sea of owner occupation. Central and inner London are also unique by virtue of the composition of the privately rented dwelling stock. The privately rented stock in England and Wales is characterized by small purpose-built terraced houses or larger houses which have been converted to multi-occupancy and split into flats and rooms (Paley, 1978; Office of Population, Censuses and Surveys, 1981). In central and inner London, however, purpose-built flats have long comprised a large part of the housing stock.

The consequences of flat break-up for the tenurial structure of central London have been profound. The proportion of households renting privately in central London declined from 80 per cent in 1961 to 70 per cent in 1971 and 47 per cent in 1981. The absolute changes have been even greater. The number of households renting privately in central London fell by 22 per cent during the 1960s and 46 per cent during the 1970s. The proportion of owner occupiers rose correspondingly from just 9 per cent of all households in 1961 to 27 per cent in 1981. In absolute terms the number of owner occupiers in central London increased by 31 per cent between 1961 and 1971 and by 49 per cent between 1971 and 1981. Over the 20 years as a whole, owner occupation in central London grew three times as fast as it did in inner London with the result that whereas the level of owner occupation in central London was little more than half the level of that in inner London in 1961, the 1981 figures were almost identical. Given the number of flats now being held vacant pending sale and the financial incentive for landlords to sell rented flats as soon as they gain vacant possession, we would expect the 1991 census to reveal a substantial further decrease in the privately rented sector and a considerably larger owner occupied sector. The tenure structure of central London is in the throes of a long-term transformation from renting to owning.

The Ownership Structure of Central London's Purpose Built Flat Sector

We have established that the housing market in central and inner London in 1966 was distinguished by the large proportion of purpose-built blocks of privately rented flats in the dwelling stock. We have also shown that by 1981 this sector of the housing market had experienced a major tenure transformation from renting to owning. In subsequent chapters we show how this transformation came about as a result of the landlords' decision to break-up and sell their blocks for individual owner occupation and we explain the changes in the relative profitability of sales versus renting which underpinned both this transformation and the decline of investor landlordism in general in Britain. First, however, it is necessary to set these changes in context by briefly examining the highly unusual ownership structure of central London's blocks of flats. As we show in later chapters, the ownership structure of central London's purpose built flat sector is crucial to an understanding of the transformation because it cannot merely be assumed that the changing external structure of financial and economic market conditions impinge equally on all sectors of the market. Not only do changing market conditions affect different sectors of the market differently at different times, but they may also be perceived and acted upon in very different ways depending upon the particular characteristics and position of different types of landlord.

Given the secrecy surrounding private property ownership in Britain, and the fact that, outside Scotland, there is no publicly accessible register of property ownership, information on the ownership structure of the privately rented sector in Britain has tended to be derived almost exclusively from sample surveys. They have produced a consistent picture of a sector in which the majority of landlords are very small scale, owning one, two or at most a handful of properties, but where the majority of properties are owned by a small minority of large landlords.

Paley's (1978) survey of private lettings in England and Wales in 1976 showed that the 77 per cent of landlords who owned between 1 and 4 lettings collectively owned only 27 per cent of lettings, whilst the 1 per cent of landlords who owned 50 or more lettings collectively owned 38 per cent of all lettings. These findings echo those of the 1965 Report of the Milner Holland Committee on Housing in Greater London which found that 60 per cent of landlords in London owned only 1 letting and a further 25 per cent owned between 2 and 4 lettings. These two groups of landlords owned only 14 and 16 per cent of all lettings respectively, so 85 per cent of all landlords owned just 30 per cent of all lettings. At the other end of the scale, only 1.7 per cent of all landlords owned more than 25 lettings and only 0.3 per cent owned more than 100. Significantly, however, this latter category owned 32 per cent of all lettings, and 15 per cent of all lettings were owned by only 40 to 50 landlords who each owned 1,000 properties or more.

Paley and Milner Holland also found that the marked divergence in the size of holdings was paralleled by a marked divergence between individual and corporate ownership. Whereas the great majority of small landlords were individuals, the great majority of large landlords were companies, charitable or other trusts, insurance companies or other bodies. Milner Holland also found that landlord type tended to be related to the type of dwelling, company landlords dominating the purpose built flat sector. As the report put it: 'Companies were responsible for more than two-thirds of the lettings in purpose built flats...In the other groups taken together, over half the lettings were by individuals' (Milner Holland, 1965, p.316).

This picture is confirmed by our own detailed study of the ownership details of all blocks of flats listed in the rent registers of the three central London boroughs. Looking at the period 1966-9, just prior to the start of large-scale break-ups, ownership details were identified for some 700 blocks containing 30,000 flats—an average of 43 flats per block (see Table 2.7).

These blocks were owned by just 368 landlords, giving an *average* holding of 82 flats in 2 blocks per landlord. Of the total number of landlords, no fewer than 272, or 74 percent, were property companies, with the remainder being more or less equally divided between insurance and pension funds, miscellaneous companies, institutional landlords such as the Church Commissioners, private trusts and executors and individual landlords. Such a classification is, of course, an essentially superficial one which tells us little or nothing about the form of the different 'property relations' involved (Allen, 1983), and this area is explored in subsequent chapters which examine the transition from investment to trading landlordism. None the less, this classification reveals both the dominance of property companies in the central London purpose-built flat market and the marked differences in the size of holding from one broad category of landlord to another.

Table 2.7 *The ownership structure of privately rented blocks of flats in central London, 1966–69*

Property companies	Misc. companies	Insurance Cos, pension funds	Institutional landlords	Trusts and executors	Individual landlords	All landlords
272	20	23	6	23	24	368
74.1	5.5	6.3	1.6	6.3	6.5	100
538	21	65	14	32	26	696
77.2	3.0	9.3	2.0	4.6	3.7	100
24,492	256	3,049	1,084	790	318	29,989
81.7	0.8	10.2	3.6	2.6	1.1	100
45.5	12.2	46.9	77.4	24.7	12.2	43
1.98	1.05	2.8	2.3	1.4	1.8	1.9
90	12.8	133	181	34.3	13.2	81.5

Table 2.8 *The ownership structure of privately rented of flats in central London, 1977–80*

Property companies	Misc. companies	Insurance Cos, pension funds	Institutional landlords	Trusts and executors	Individual landlords	All landlords
333	32	21	19	30	69	504
66.1	6.3	4.2	3.8	5.9	13.7	100
663	44	58	50	44	73	932
71.3	4.7	6.2	5.4	4.7	7.8	100
26,854	1,071	2,069	2,798	841	717	4,350
78.2	3.1	6.0	8.1	2.5	2.1	100
40.4	26.9	35	55.7	19.1	13	36.8
2.0	1.4	2.8	2.6	1.5	1.1	1.8
80.6	33.5	98.5	147.3	28	10.4	68.1

Whereas the 6 per cent of individual landlords owned just under 4 per cent of all blocks and 1 per cent of all flats, the 74 per cent of property company landlords owned 77 per cent of all blocks and no less than 82 per cent of all flats—an average of 2 blocks and 90 flats per landlord compared to just 1 block and 13 flats for individual landlords. The insurance companies and pension funds had even larger holdings—averaging 3 blocks and 132 flats per landlord. Not only did individual landlords collectively own a very small proportion of blocks and flats in central London, they also tended to own much smaller blocks—an average of 13 flats per block against the 45 flats per block for property companies, the 47 flats per block for insurance companies and pension funds and the 77 flats per block for institutional landlords who owned an average of 180 flats each. It is significant that whereas individual landlords, private trusts and miscellaneous companies together accounted for almost 20 per cent of landlords, they owned under 5 per cent of all flats. Property and insurance companies, by contrast, owned between them no less than 87 per cent of all blocks and 92 per cent of all flats identified in central London.

Data for 1977-80 (Table 2.8) reveal a similar, though slightly less marked concentration of ownership. Ownership details were identified for some 932 blocks containing some 34,350 flats—an average of 37 flats per block. These blocks were owned by just 504 landlords. Of these landlords, no fewer than 333, or 66 per cent, were property companies. Individual landlords were next with 13.7 per cent, followed by miscellaneous companies (6.3 per cent), private trusts and executors (6 per cent), insurance companies and pension funds (4 per cent), and other institutional landlords, principally the Church. Whereas the 13.7 per cent of individual landlords owned just 6 per cent of all blocks and just 2 per cent of all flats, the 66 per cent of property company landlords owned 70 per cent of all blocks and 77 per cent of all flats-an average of 2 blocks and 81 flats per landlord compared to just 1.1 blocks and 10 flats for individual landlords. Not only do individual landlords collectively own a minute proportion of both blocks and flats, they also tended to own much smaller blocks—an average of 13 flats per block as against 40 flats per block for property companies, 35 for insurance companies and pension funds and 56 for other institutional landlords. The 6 per cent of landlords who were private trusts and executors also owned only 2.4 per cent of flats. Although these two categories of landlord accounted for almost 20 per cent of landlords they only owned 4.5 per cent of flats compared to the 94 per cent of flats owned by property and miscellaneous companies, insurance companies and pension funds and other institutional landlords.

We can conclude from this analysis that the central London purpose-built private flat market has been dominated by large corporate and institutional owners. In fact, the concentration of ownership in the hands of a relatively small number of companies is even greater than these overall figures suggest. Out of a total of 24,492 company owned flats for which ownership details were available during the period 1966-9, some 20,859, or 85 per cent, were owned by the 25 largest owners and out of a total of 26,854 company owned flats for which ownership details were available in the period 1977-80, some 19,680, or 73 per cent, were owned by the 25 largest owners. The reduction in the degree of ownership concentration between the two periods is, as we shall show, a product of large-scale disinvestment by some large, traditional investment landlords and the purchase of blocks by smaller break-up operators for the sale of individual flats. The implications of this are examined in detail in Chapters 7, 8 and 9. The central point to be established here is the extent to which ownership and control of the central London purpose built private flat market has been dominated by a small number of very large property and insurance companies. As we shall show in subsequent chapters, the transformation of this market from one dominated by private renting to one dominated by owner occupation and vacant units is esentially a product of the investment and disinvestment decisions of these large corporate owners.They viewed their blocks as investments whose profitability they sought to maximize. The central London flat sector contains very few of the traditional small landlords who often lack wider investment opportunities and expertise and take a more personal, proprietorial view of their property holdings. The central London flat sector is therefore a particularly good vehicle for the examination of the impact and importance of changes in profitability and investment opportunity in the transformation of the urban housing market and residential space. But, before we look at the transformation of the central London flat market from renting to owning from the mid 1960s, it is first necessary to examine the causes of the decline of the privately rented sector in Britain as a whole. This is done in the next two chapters. Chapter 3 analyses the rise and fall of investor landlordism and Chapter 4 focuses on the tenure transfer process which first got underway in the 1920s.

Note

1 Central London contains the boroughs of

Camden
Kensington and Chelsea
Westminster

These three boroughs, together with the following eleven, form inner London:

City
Hackney
Hammersmith
Haringey
Islington
Lambeth
Lewisham
Newham
Southwark
Tower Hamlets

Wandsworth

Outer London comprises the boroughs of

Barking
Barnet
Bexley
Brent
Bromley
Croydon
Ealing
Enfield
Greenwich
Harrow
Havering
Hillingdon
Hounslow
Kingston on Thames
Merton
Redbridge
Richmond on Thames
Sutton
Waltham Forest

Greater London is the area within the boundaries of the erstwhile Greater London Council.

3 The rise and fall of investor landlordism in Britain

Introduction

While the specific empirical focus of this book is the flat break-up market which emerged in the 1960s, it represents only one facet of a much more far reaching transformation of the British housing market over the past century. In order to fully understand flat break-ups, we first need to consider the wider historical transformation within which this particular process has developed. This chapter aims to develop this historic context by charting the rise and fall of the system of housing provision which created the flat market, namely domestic investor landlordism.

The decline of investor landlordism contrasts to the emergence of owner occupation as the dominant tenure form in the provision of housing during the first half of the twentieth century. The fundamental shift in the tenure structure of private housing provision at this time represented the outcome of a competitive struggle for the hearts, the minds and, most important of all, the pockets of the private housing investor who, with the landlord and the tenant, formed the key components of investor landlordism. The principal protagonist in this struggle has been the building society movement.

This is an important point, for the demise of investor landlord cannot be understood in isolation from the wider conditions in which housing is provided and, most crucially, financed. The failure to recognize the central role of finance in structuring housing provision has been a consistent feature of the arguments of those commentators who have for many years placed the blame for the decline of the private investor landlord solely on rent controls and direct political intervention in the rental market. But before we develop these arguments, it is necessary, first, to consider the structure of housing provision more formally in order to establish the framework within which the discussion can be placed.

Housing tenure and the commodification of housing provision

Housing, despite its many forms, is a commodity. Like all other commodities, housing is produced and consumed for its use value, in this case as the location for domestic life. But in common with other commodities produced under capitalist social relations, housing is also produced to accumulate capital - in other words, for profit (Boddy, 1976; Ball, 1978). Wherever capitalist production prevails, the imperative of accumulation pervades the operation of the housing market and exerts the underlying influence on the direction and outcome of decisions taken by house producers, house owners and house consumers. This basic condition—profitability—is the starting point for any analysis of the housing market.

However, housing is not a simple commodity. It is very expensive in relation to average incomes and is used and re-used over a very long period. These two characteristics have important consequences for the way in which housing is provided and utilized. Because of its expense, there are few households who can afford to purchase housing outright from earnings or even savings. This poses a major problem for housing producers – builders – for if they wish to maintain a steady output they need to be able to sell houses more or less as soon as they are completed in order to recoup their costs, make their profit and invest in new production. Clearly, this would prove impossible if households were left to buy housing from cash in hand.

For mass housing production to be viable, some mechanism has to be interposed between builder and household to ensure both a sufficiently rapid turnover of output for the realization and reinvestment of profit for the former and a reduction in the immediate cost of accommodation to an affordable level for the latter. At the risk of sounding excessively functionalist, the mechanisms which provide a solution to these 'realization' and 'affordability' problems are the various housing tenure systems which have evolved to bridge the builder-household gap. In essence, modern housing tenure systems provide the means by which mass housing consumption is made possible. It is in this sense that Ball (1983) has referred to tenures as 'structures of housing provision'.

But even when a house is sold, the problems of housing consumption continue. The same difficulties exist for households who want to move into existing houses as for those who wish to occupy new ones. Given that the housing market is dominated by existing housing and the vast majority of households are therefore involved in the consumption of second-hand housing, then tenure systems also function to allow households to move between existing houses without the 'affordability' problem causing insurmountable obstacles.

In the mass housing market which developed in the nineteenth century, which was characterized by the absence of a large scale domestic consumer credit system, the realization problem was initially 'solved' by the evolution of a particular tenure system which we can term 'domestic investor landlordism'. Investor landlordism brought capital, in the form of private mortgages, into the housing consumption process to buy the finished housing from the builder and 'sell' it on to the householder. But the fact that credit formed such a central component of the system meant that housing took on a use other than that of a mere commodity for consumption. The principal attraction of this form of landlordism lay in the value of housing as a capitalized investment commodity which provided long-term investment income from the flow of rents and the maintenance or enhancement of the value of invested capital by periodic increases in rents.

In these conditions, housing assumed the characteristics of a financial asset which returned an interest payment in the form of rental income. In other words, the form of housing provision which emerged at this time transformed domestic property into a fully fledged investment commodity. Consequently, landlords are not 'housing merchants', buying housing wholesale and selling on to households retail, but *investment capitalists* using rents and capital gains as a form of investment income. The commodification of housing in this way reflects the domination of capitalism in the provision of housing and the integration of housing into the developing system of credit and capital markets (Ball, 1981; Nevitt, 1966).

But the role of housing as an investment good also has an important bearing on the way in which it is capitalized or valued, for it follows that the value a house takes on is a function of its interest-yielding qualities. In the final analysis, of course, these qualities are limited by the effective potential of households to purchase housing for its use value, through either rents or mortgage payments. But while houses do not have a value independent of this potential, the way in which this potential is expressed in house values reflects its ability to provide a return on the capital invested in it. The level of this return will in turn depend on the interplay of a variety of influences—general level of interest rates, the availability of competitive alternatives for investment, the volume of money available for investment, the level and direction of subsidies, and so on—and not just on the basic income potential of the consumer households.

This has the impact of greatly increasing the complexity of the mechanism by which housing derives its value. Not only do the vagaries of housing production play their part, but once housing is completed, a further level of complexity is added by the investment market into which housing is injected. It is only by recognizing that housing is primarily an investment good and not a simple, if expensive, consumer good (although, of course, its investment good status is a direct consequence of its cost and longevity as a consumer good) that an understanding of the importance of capital and credit within the housing market can be developed.

Moreover, as each tenure is characterized by a particular fiscal and financial structure, then differences in these structures between tenure systems will result in a different value accruing to a house depending on which tenure it is in. The reasons for this are straightforward enough. They stem from the differential effects of the various real rates of interest which are paid to capital in the different tenure systems, the varying levels of subsidy and taxation, the differences in the structure of loan repayments, the varying costs and expenses which the participants include in their financial calculations, their different perceptions of the returns or benefits which the tenures impart, and so on. To put this simply, a unit of credit applied to the purchase of a privately rented property will be expressed as a different unit of house value from if it were applied to the same property in, say, owner occupation.

The conditions in which structures of housing provision are formed and maintained are constantly changing and, in consequence, so too are the values of housing which result from these structures. We only have to look at the impact that changes in such things as interest rate levels, mortgage availability, subsidy arrangements or household incomes have on house prices to appreciate the way in which changes in these structures are expressed in concrete terms. But these are not the passive components of a theoretical economic model. They reflect the outcome of real relationships between institutions and agents which exist in an environment of economic and political tension and competition. It is here that the motives for the changes in the structure of housing provision are to be found.

Particular tenure systems are the product of particular historic circumstances and once in place they are relatively enduring. But eventually they are subjected to pressures—both political and economic—to which, in their existing form, they are unable to adapt fully. The result is a crisis in the provision of housing during which the existing tenure form is displaced by other tenure forms which reflect these changed circumstances. In the private sector (i.e. where provision depends ostensibly on 'market forces'), the mechanisms underlying this displacement process are changes in the structure of profitability of housing as both a commodity and an investment. These relate not only to the production of new housing, but also to the utilization of existing housing. Consequently, shifts between structures of housing provision will be reflected in a wave of revaluation, or indeed devaluation, throughout the housing market as all housing values readjust to the new relations of exchange which accompany the new structure of provision.

Herein lies the basis of the tenure transfer process with which we are concerned. When the structure of private housing provision switched from private renting to owner occupation in the early part of the twentieth century, the repercussions were felt not only in the form in which new housing was produced, but also in the structure of the existing housing stock, particularly in relation to property values. In effect, the emergence of owner occupation as the dominant structure of private housing provision after the First World War recapitalized the existing private rented sector, thus providing a source of profit from housing – capital gains through the sale of rented housing into owner occupation – hitherto denied to housing investors. It was the appropriation of these capital gains which provided the economic rationale for the tenure transfer process.

The decline of domestic investor landlordism from its dominant position in the nineteenth century has therefore been accompanied by a reversal in the perceived value of housing as an investment good, away from a primary concern with investment income (rents) and towards the capital value component. But the role of housing as an interest-yielding investment good has not disappeared. It is merely the form in which this investment value is appropriated through the housing system which has changed. The private investment which funded landlordism in return for an interest payment now funds the building societies.

The origins of this shift in the structure of housing provision are to be found in the changing fiscal and financial conditions in which investor landlordism found itself by the early decades of the twentieth century. Although both economic and political influences were behind these changes, what were important were the tensions which these changes set up within the structure of investor landlordism which cumulatively impaired the relative profitability of the sector and led to active disinvestment. It is to a discussion of the development of this situation in the British housing system and the basis of the re-capitalization process that we now turn.

Investor landlordism in the nineteenth century

Domestic investor landlordism was an integral component of the generalized market for the speculatively built housing which accompanied industrial urbanization. It can be seen not only as the expression of capitalist social relations which came to dominate the provision of housing by the beginning of the nineteenth century, but to have also been part of that 'solution' to the problem of housing the growing urban populations best suited to the economic and social conditions of the period (Kemp, 1982; Harloe, 1985). Throughout the nineteenth century, incomes were generally low and, in the absence of an organized labour market, wages were subject to considerable fluctuation over the lifetime of a household. At the same time, sources of generally available consumer credit were also extemely limited in the absence of an organized capital market. In these circumstances large-scale domestic debt encumbrance in the form of house mortgages proved impossible, as the limited impact of building societies in stimulating and maintaining demand for home ownership during the nineteenth century testifies (Pawley, 1978). These social conditions were reflected in a flexible housing system which could provide a wide variety of housing opportunities at varying cost for a population whose economic resources were limited and uncertain.

From the supply side, housing provided an eminently suitable outlet for small to medium investment capital throughout the nineteenth century (Dyos, 1967; Nevitt, 1966). Investor landlordism formed the crucial nexus through which much of the savings of the growing ranks of the middle classes—the 'petty bourgeoisie' – were channelled into profitable investment (Daunton, 1983). Investment in housing, either directly by landlords or through the provision of mortgage funds for both builders and landlords, formed a relatively safe source of income, especially as few other forms of investment were available which offered the flexibility and guaranteed returns that housing could.

With interest rates at 4–5 per cent for most of the latter half of the nineteenth century, a landlord could expect a return of about 8 per cent gross on residential property to provide an adequate return after costs on whatever capital was invested (Parry Lewis, 1965). Although the maintenance of the value of any capital invested was an important consideration, capital gains were of secondary consideration compared to the requirement of a steady income yield (Elliot and McCrone, 1975; Gauldie, 1974). For the mortgagors who put up the bulk of the capital which landlords used to fund their businesses, housing provided a relatively trouble free and flexible outlet for savings, often forming the basis of a retirement income. Moreover, a considerable proportion of the investment which flowed into housing represented the capital of family trusts and settlements which sought the safety and security provided by the housing market.

The integration of the housing landlord into the wider system of credit and capital investment is clearly summed up by Kemp (1982, p.1440):

> Thus, in the late nineteenth century the existence of the housing landlord was a critical facet of the housing production process. The particularly precarious nature of speculative house building and its long period of rotation of capital, the very high cost of housing, the relatively limited development of the credit system and the relative attraction of house letting in the absence of suitable alternative investment outlets all operated to make private renting from independent housing landlords the dominant means of realisation of the commodity housing.

Rented housing therefore served as the major investment medium for the owners of small to medium capital during this period.

The origins of the landlords' long decline

By the end of the nineteenth century, however, the conditions which had led to the emergence of investor landlordism as the dominant form of housing provision after the industrial revolution had begun to break down. Four interrelated reasons – two mainly political and two mainly economic—can be identified for this: (1) the role of increased state intervention; (2) the declining political importance of the landlord lobby; (3) the changing relative taxation position of the investor landlord; and (4) the impact of the growth of competing investment alternatives on the structure and availability of housing capital.

1 The growth of state regulation in housing

The increasing level of state intervention in the regulation and control of housing provision, especially in the public health sphere, was beginning to have a significant impact on the quality of housing production, and hence on its profitability. Until the middle of the nineteenth century, housing could be profitably provided for low income households by the simple expedient of overcrowding (Dyos, 1967; Wohl, 1971; Stedman Jones, 1971). In other words, slums were not only created in existing buildings, but could be built as such (Merrett, 1979). But this 'solution' to the provision of working-class housing became increasingly recognized by the middle classes as a threat to social order, welfare and industrial efficiency (Dyos, 1967). At the same time, the working class had itself brought increasing political pressure to bear as its organized strength began to grow (Clark and Ginsberg, 1975). From the pioneering Liverpool Building Act of 1842, a whole series of legally enforceable orders and Acts of Parliament regulating housing provision began to impose imcreasing costs which eroded the profitability of landlordism. The impact of this growth of legislation aimed at improving the standard of housing provision was straightforward: 'The supply of housing at rents which working people could afford became increasingly difficult and much less attractive as a speculative venture' (Murie *et al.*, 1974, p. 180). Thus throughout the latter half of the nineteenth century, increased state intervention into the regulation and provision of housing imposed increasing constraints on the profitability of the housing landlord. At the same time, the expansion of the system of local taxation through the rates can also be attributed to the increasing scale of government activity at the local level (Offer, 1981). This added a further cost to the housing landlord which increased the upward pressure on rents and constrained profit margins.

2 The decline in the landlord's political influence

The growth of state intervention reflected the steady erosion of the political position of the private landlord as the various Reform Acts gradually extended enfranchisement to an ever widening spectrum of the population. By the end of the nineteenth century property no longer constituted the main determinant of adult suffrage. In consequence, the political influence of landlordism, in all its forms, had declined substantially. This loss of power is reflected in the growing inability of the landlord lobby to resist the political challenges to its legal, fiscal and economic position, particularly from the encroachment into private property rights by the state. The culmination of this process was the imposition of rent control and security of tenure in 1915. It was also reflected in the increasing public criticism of the landlord as the appropriator of 'Mammon's Rents' and the source of many social ills. There were, of course, other structural reasons for this decreasing political power. For example, Hennock (1973) describes how the petit bourgeoisie in Birmingham declined in political influence after the mid 1800s in contrast to the growing power of the larger business and professional classes. This decline was also related to the longer term erosion of the influence of landed capital and the importance of land and property ownership as a dominant social relation since the end of the feudal period (Nevitt, 1966; Massey and Catalano, 1978). This cumulative and steady loss of political clout made landlords increasingly susceptible to the economic pressures they were facing.

3 The impact of direct taxation

The third factor in the deterioration of the position of the investor landlords was the increasingly unfavourable taxation position they faced in relation to other commercial investments. With the exception of the local rating system, the major taxation disadvantage which applied to landlords has been the assumption, which dates from the beginnings of modern taxation in Britain in 1802, that buildings last for ever and therefore no depreciation allowances need be given. This is based on a second assumption that the value of land and buildings can be expected to rise over time. The lack of depreciation allowances could therefore be viewed as a form of built-in capital gains tax.

This became a significant problem after 1878 when depreciation allowances for plant and machinery were introduced for manufacturers. Residential landlords were excluded from these provisions (Nevitt, 1966). Although some allowances were introduced in 1894 to enable landlords to deduct the costs of repairs from their Schedule A assessments, the deduction allowed was fixed at one sixth of the total assessment, which not only provided little incentive to undertake extensive repairs, but provided little opportunity to allow for reasonable sinking-fund payments. If anything, this fixed allowance, which was introduced because it was feared that a more flexible system would be open to abuse, gave more incentive to neglect repairs and maintenance, given that the landlord would receive the allowance regardless of whether or not improvements were carried out. As Nevitt concludes: 'the taxation policy of government since at least 1878 has been so designed that capital has flowed from renting dwellings into other forms of investment which rank for more favourable tax treatment' (1966, p.47). She goes on to note that while returns on rented property were at times sufficiently large to minimize this tax disadvantage, as taxation levels generally increased, the disadvantage became more serious.

4 The increasing competition for capital

This increasingly disadvantaged taxation position was reflected in the fourth, and perhaps most important, difficulty facing investor landlordism by the turn of the century, namely the development of an integrated and nationally organized capital market which offered increasingly attractive investment alternatives for housing capital. This had the dual repercussions of not only reducing the amount of credit flowing into landlordism but also of increasing the costs of that capital which remained available for investment in rented housing.

The supply of credit has a major influence on the rate of investment in housing, either by builder or landlord. This supply will fluctuate depending on the availability of and level of yields on alternative investments. Until the middle of the nineteenth century, housing represented one of the few secure outlets for private investment other than government stock, and the flow of capital into housing was generally closely related to the fluctuations in the yield on consols. If the yield rose, the supply of loans into housing would dry up as investors switched to the more secure government stock (Parry Lewis, 1965; Burnett, 1978).

But by the end of the century a wide range of investment opportunities were effectively competing for capital, drawing it away from investment into housing regardless of the relative attraction of government stock. The introduction of limited liability in 1844 led to the gradual expansion of investment in an organized and regulated stock market and investment outlets in the industrial and commercial sectors. The ownership of private stock remained relatively limited, however, even up to the First World War, and it could be argued that the development of the stock market and the flow of capital into international speculation was more relevant to large capital than to the sort of small to medium capital which characterized the domestic property investment sector at this time (Dyos, 1967; Kemp, 1982). Nevertheless, despite the local and segmented nature of housing capital, it was becoming increasingly sensitive to changes in the wider capital market (Daunton, 1983).

The growth of an institutionalized financial and banking sector was also becoming influential. Restrictions on joint stock banking were removed by 1833 and by 1855 banks had achieved corporate status greatly freeing their activities. As a result the late nineteenth century saw the emergence of an increasingly organized and sophisticated finance and banking system in which the Bank of England assumed the major stabilizing role. The growth of the National Debt (e.g. the Boer War loans of 1900 and 1901) also extended the institutional financial market and offered greater security than domestic property. Other channels for small capital investment were developing. Bowley notes there was an expansion of investment trusts by the early 1900s:

> These offered small and rather timid investors opportunities of investment in industrials combined with professional advice and dispersed risks over a wide field. Moreover it was a form of investment free from commitments, the investors had no responsibility for mortgage interest and repayment and no liability for repairs. (Bowley, 1945, p.88)

But the real challenge to the private landlord lay elsewhere, however, in the form of the increasing control that the building societies were exerting on the direction of investment into the housing market (Pawley, 1978; Nevitt, 1966). As the building society movement gradually shifted from the small-scale terminating friendly societies typical of the early nineteenth century to a more permanent and integrated system of savings and loans institutions with a greater interest in attracting investment than in providing housing *per se*, a crucial new investment medium opened up for the small investor. The strength of the building societies as financial institutions was based on the stability of domestic property values to maintain the capital invested in them. Their principal role as investment institutions rather than the promoters of home ownership can be seen in the insignificant growth of owner occupation during the nineteenth century despite a century of activity (Pawley, 1978). Pawley notes that by the 1850s building societies 'were already financial institutions rather than instruments of thrift' for would-be house purchasers (1978, p.40).

After the 1874 Building Societies Act granted the societies corporate status along the lines of banks, the expansion of the movement accelerated. By maintaining their interest rates in a period of generally falling interest rates and prices (the Bank rate fell as low as 2 per cent in the early 1890s), the societies attracted an increasing volume of funds (Boddy 1980). Much of this came from the small investors who were the financial backbone of private landlordism. But the effect of the growth of building societies on the landlord at this time was rather more complex than this might suggest. While landlords (and house builders) derived much of their loan capital from private mortgages and loans, often from private trust funds channelled through solicitors (Dyos, 1968), the other major source of funding came from the building societies themselves. In fact, the major proportion of building society business was directed towards funding the building of new housing for rental. Nevitt (1966) notes, however, that there were distinct advantages in obtaining private as opposed to society mortgages due to the repayment structure. Annual repayments on a private loan only entailed the payment of the interest due on the principal, while the principal was repaid in full on the expiration of the loan, typically after 10 years. Thus the current costs of such loans were relatively low and at the end of the loan period a new mortgage could be raised to repay the original principal if necessary. This was relatively easy at most periods in the mid to late nineteenth century (Dyos, 1968). In this way it was possible to defer the payment of loans virtually indefinitely provided the property remained an acceptable investment risk for the mortgagor.

For the mortgagor, the advantage of this form of investment was that the loan could be called in at short notice, making it highly liquid. The corollary of this was that mortgagors were willing to lend on lower rates of interest than were generally available. Thus private loans offered landlords a cheap and flexible form of capital. The viability of private loans as the source of finance for landlordism depended, however, on an adequate supply of fresh mortgagees to take the place of those withdrawing their capital. This was no particular problem while private loans were plentiful, but as alternative investment opportunities opened up for private investors, credit became less freely available and more expensive. One of the principal alternatives was the building societies who, as a result of their favourable tax treatment, could offer almost as high a rate of return on a depositor's capital as he or she would have obtained by lending it out directly to a mortgagor and the capital was easily accessible if needed.

As private credit began to get scarcer, landlords were forced to seek other sources. The major alternatives were the very building societies who were helping to siphon off their existing credit. But this only compounded their difficulties. Building society mortgages take the form of amortized loans. These involve the concurrent repayment of both interest and principal throughout the life of the loan. This has the effect of significantly increasing the costs of borrowing compared to the private loan, and therefore reducing the net yield on any given rent. In other words, building society loans were much less profitable to landlords than were private loans.

In effect the societies were squeezing landlords from two sides simultaneously. On the one hand they were depriving landlords of their traditional sources of private capital and on the other they were lending landlords the money which now accrued to them in a form which greatly increased the costs of borrowing to the landlord. Nevitt leaves no doubt as to the importance of the amortized loan in the decline of landlordism: 'This invention is of such importance in housing economics that it should rank with the invention of the steam engine in changing the face of Britain' (1966, p.8).

The shifts in the organization of the capital market in the 50 years or so preceding the First World War therefore had an important impact on the structure of loan capital available to the housing investor. The private loan market, which until the middle of the nineteenth century had been largely localized and variable in character, became increasingly stabilized and integrated into a national system of institutionalized investment opportunities. These institutions competed for the local capital that supplied investor landlords who remained essentially local in character.

The funding of investor landlordism, therefore, became increasingly problematic and yields were being squeezed. As a result, not only did the small investor who supported the housing landlord move away from direct involvement in the housing market, but landlords themselves were also being drawn away from housing investment. Moreover, this restructuring of the housing capital market, and the increasingly dominant role played by the building societies in it, was to have a crucial impact on landlordism in the period immediately following the First World War. Not only did the building societies deprive landlords of a vital and cheap source of capital, they were also to undercut them in the competition for their customers—the private householder.

Taken together, then, the difficulties which housing landlords were facing as a consequence of the changing political, fiscal and financial conditions of the latter half of the nineteenth century led to increasing pressure on the profitability of their investments. The pressure on yields was reflected in the steady inflation in rents over this period. By 1910 rents were 85 per cent higher than in 1845, but both wholesale prices and building costs were not significantly higher than they were in the 1840s (Parry Lewis, 1965). In the decade leading up to 1914 there was a marked swing away from investment in housing. Costs were rising, finance was becoming increasingly scarce and expensive, household incomes were depressed and the introduction of land taxation in the Liberal's 1909 Budget all contributed to the depressed state of the housing market (Greve, 1965; Daunton, 1983). The late Victorian housing boom petered out in 1905 leaving a glut of middle-class housing but increasing overcrowding for the working class, and by the time war broke out a growing crisis in housing provision was evident. Investor landlordism was simply failing to deliver adequate housing at an acceptable price. The war, while significantly changing the political framework in which landlordism had to function, merely served to bring the crisis of investor landlordism to a head. As Parry Lewis has stated: 'war speeded the revolution in housing' (1965, p.225). The point, of course, is that this revolution was under way long before the war started.

The First World War: the end of the private housing investor

Perhaps the most immediate consequence for the housing market of the outbreak of war in 1914, apart from the virtual cessation of new building, was the 1915 Increase in Rents and Mortgage Interest (Restrictions) Act. This retrospectively controlled rents on working class housing to their level on 3 August 1914 and gave tenants of controlled housing protection from unreasonable eviction. It also restricted the interest rate which landlords had to pay on their mortgages to a maximum of 6 per cent and prevented the calling in of existing mortgages.

Much has been written about this Act, which is generally attributed to the political necessity on the part of the state to defuse a potentially revolutionary situation in a period when nothing could be allowed to interfere with the war effort (Swennarton, 1981). As is well known, the 1915 Act was introduced as a consequence of the unrest following the rapid escalation in rents as landlords sought to exploit the influx of workers into urban areas for war work—most notably the munitions workers in Clydeside. As a consequence, the Act has been viewed both as an example of a working-class victory over the private landlord as the result of direct political action

(Community Development Project, 1976), and as the deliberate 'sacrifice' of the private landlord in the interests of industrial capital acting through the state during a period of crisis (Dickens, 1977; Byrne and Damer, 1980; Saunders, 1981; Daunton, 1983). Intriguing though this question is, our concern here is with the impact that this legislation had on the financial structure of landlordism.

The repercussions of the 1915 Act on landlords' profitability were straightforward and, in the event, not too severe. Not only were the levels of rents controlled, so too were the costs of finance. The controls on mortgages had been introduced to ensure that landlords were not unfairly penalized as a result of the immediate political necessity to control rents. As such, their interests had been safeguarded as far as was possible in the circumstances. Seen in this light, the 1915 Act was far from the defeat of the landlord it is popularly portrayed as being. By controlling both rents *and* costs, the financial position of the landlord was not greatly impaired, at least in the short term. Returns were effectively maintained at their pre-war level, although maintenance was increasingly affected as time went on. We therefore have to look elsewhere for the real impact of this legislation.

In fact, the greatest burden of the 1915 Act fell squarely on the shoulders of the 'hidden' half of housing landlordism, namely the housing mortgagor. But even here, its effects were selective. The clearing banks, no doubt due to their considerable influence and power, were excluded from the provisions of the Bill from the outset. The building societies also managed to get mortgages which were repaid monthly over a period exceeding 10 years excluded from the Act by the time it was passed (Dickens, 1977), effectively freeing the typical owner occupier mortgage from interest restriction. This was achieved in order to protect the small but growing market in owner occupied housing which had emerged in the decade or so before the war, a move which had been prompted by the building societies in order to maintain investment levels in a period when landlords' investment had slumped (Jackson, 1974). This exemption from the Act reflected the growing influence of an increasingly organized and nationally integrated building society movement.

The same could not be said for the private mortgagor, for the main type of mortgage caught by the Act was the 10 year loan typically made by private investors to landlords. The restriction on interest levels was, of course, a major blow to the profitability of the private loan market in a period of rising interest rates. But, more importantly, by freezing existing mortgagees into their investment, the whole functioning of the loan market, which was founded on the principle that the invested capital was easily realizable at short notice, was fatally undermined. This began to cause considerable difficulties, especially on the death of landlords and mortgagees by delaying the winding up of estates indefinitely.

Thus the 1915 Act threw the whole system of housing finance into confusion. It is difficult not to conclude, then, that the main 'victim' of the 1915 Rent Act was not the landlord or the profitability of renting *per se*, but the localized and fragmented private mortgage market on whose capital landlordism had developed over the previous century. When the effects of the Rent Act on this component of landlordism were combined with the rapidly increasing demand for investment capital from the government to service the wartime National Debt, the rationale for the withdrawal of capital from the private housing market at this time becomes clear. The controls on mortgagors remained in force after the war and, although the permitted interest rate ceiling was raised to 6.5 per cent in 1922, they continued to be a major deterrent on the flow of capital into the rented sector and increased the incentives for existing investors to disinvest if at all possible. From this time on, private landlords and, in particular, the private mortgagor, formed a decreasing component of the total housing system. The rate of decline in the role of private mortgages invested in housing can be gauged from the fact that between 1897 and 1914 the proportion of private property held in the form of mortgages averaged 6.5 per cent. This had fallen to 4.5 per cent by 1920-1 and further to 2.7 per cent by 1937-8 (Nevitt, 1966). Although private landlordism remained for a considerable time as a major source of housing provision, and even made a limited comeback in the 1930s, the close links between the private investor and the private landlord forged in the urbanization which followed the industrial revolution were broken for ever.

The role of direct political intervention in the post war housing market

1 The advent of rent control

Before considering how the housing market responded to this situation after the First World War, it is worth assessing the effects that rent control, introduced by the 1915 Act, and direct state subsidies for housing provision, introduced in 1919, had on the private rented sector. As it has been common to credit almost the whole blame for the decline of the landlord to these measures, particularly the former, this question is of more than passing interest.

When the war ended the housing system was in crisis. Bowley (1945) estimated that there was a shortage of 600,000 houses in the immediate post war period as a combined result of the slump in housing production in the years preceding 1914, the virtual cessation of new construction during the war, and the collapse of the property investment market. But there was no return to pre-war conditions. Political expediency dictated the maintenance and indeed extension of the 1915 legislation. In 1919 and each of the two following years rent control was progressively applied to cover some 98 per cent of the housing stock (Parry Lewis, 1965). At the same time, in recognition of rising costs, controlled rents had been increased by 40 per cent over their 1914 level. But from 1923 onwards, successive Rent Acts freed increasing proportions of existing housing from controls, especially in the middle to high value sectors.[1] Nevitt concludes that 'During the period 1923 to 1933 landlords who held property in the expectation of future decontrol were in general able to get a competitive return on their capital' as 'rents were probably controlled at about their market value' (1966, pp.114-15).

While rents may well have started to fall behind their market level for the remaining controlled properties at the bottom end of the market from the mid 1930s onwards, there was no impediment on profitability at the top end of the market and there were increasing opportunities for rents to reach open market levels for the middle range of properties. In other words, the profitability of renting out existing property increasingly improved in the years after 1920, and in any case yields had not been greatly affected due to the control of finance costs. New properties were, of course, never controlled. Perhaps the most important effect of rent control during this period was the uncertainty it created amongst investors and landlords. For although it was widely accepted that the measures would eventually be repealed, there was no certainty as to *when* this would happen. The effect of this was summed up by Barnes, who, speaking of the impact of the legislation in 1923, stated:

> The factors which have operated to drive away investment money from new house-property are both financial and psychological. In the first category comes the high price of building ... there is still a gap between the commercial rent of a new house and the rent which may legally be charged for a similar house erected before April 1919 ... but the demand for houses at a rent rather than for purchase is so great that this alone would probably not deter investors from purchasing new houses from speculative builders were it not for the psychological factor. This factor is, of course, the aversion to statutory control of any kind, aversion which is the result of experience of control since 1915. The primary investor, the property owner, dislikes the prospect of increasing interference by the State in the relations between himself and his tenant; and both he and the secondary investor, the mortgagee, desire securities that can be realised at short notice, especially if, as was the case to a considerable degree with investors in mortgages, they are trustees. (Barnes, 1923, p.204)

In other words, apart from the disruption to the organization of the housing finance system discussed above, rent controls had their greatest impact on the perceptions rather than the pockets of housing landlords. While this may well have had the effect of pushing up the yields required from the rental market to tempt investors, we can conclude that, on their own, rent controls were not, and indeed have never been, the principal cause of the loss of private rented accommodation.

2. The emergence of housing subsidies

If the first major political response to the post war housing situation was the continuation of rent control, the second was the 1919 Housing and Town Planning Act. This placed a statutory responsibility for the provision of new low-rent housing onto local authorities. Public housing was not a novel idea and statutory provision for direct state intervention in housing production dated from the Lodging Houses Act of 1851.[2] What was new was the commitment by the state to the direct subsidy of working-class housing which the 1919 Act introduced. The Act guaranteed government funds to meet any deficit incurred by local authorities on the cost of housing provision not covered by the product of a penny rate. A substantial commitment to some form of direct housing subsidy had been established during the war due to the realization that, after the war, a return to pre-war conditions in which the 'free market' could be expected adequately to meet housing needs after the war was unlikely, particularly given the problems landlordism had been facing in the decade or so preceding 1914. The 1919 Act was the product of the recognition that private landlordism could no longer be relied on to produce decent working-class housing at affordable rents, if indeed it ever had.

Although the direct impact of the Act was limited to the 170,000 houses built between 1920 and 1928 when its subsidy arrangements finally ended, it had set the precedent for direct state intervention, although on an increasingly restricted basis, in the subsequent Housing Acts of 1923 and 1924 and the various slum clearance and overcrowding Acts of the 1930s. But while the subsidized public sector produced over 1.1 million houses by 1939, the households it accommodated were not generally those on the lowest incomes simply because despite the subsidy, rents were set at levels higher than lowest income tenants could afford. As Kemp states, 'the more 'marginal' families were left to sink or swim in the private sector' (1980, p.24). In other words, public housing effectively deprived private landlordism of the better-paid and most profitable section of working-class demand.

While the main emphasis of direct state intervention in the immediate post war period was placed on local authority provision, the Coalition Government did not ignore the private sector. The Housing (Additional Powers) Act of 1919 introduced a subsidy arrangement for private sector house building regardless of whether the houses were for sale or rent.[3] These provisions were extended in a modified form by the Housing Acts of 1923 and 1924. But the objective of these subsidies was to encourage private house construction, not private landlordism, the subsidy being paid to the builder. Landlordism appears to have been more or less deliberately excluded from the housing subsidy structure that emerged during this period and has remained excluded ever since. While some 430,000 subsidized private sector houses were eventually built between 1920 and 1939 when the provisions ended, largely under the 1923 Act's provisions, the majority of these were produced for sale for owner occupation (Bowley, 1945; Jackson, 1974).

The extent to which the exclusion of landlords from this legislation represented deliberate policy decisions on the part of governments to support alternative tenures at this time is not at all clear. Although the Labour Party, which came briefly to power in 1924, was clearly committed to the replacement of the private landlord by council housing, the Conservatives' attitude as to which tenure to support was less clear. However, they appear to have become increasingly predisposed towards owner occupation as a favoured tenure by the early 1920s.[4] Home ownership offered the Conservatives a vital ideological weapon to counter the collectivist ideals implicit in the growing support that general needs council housing was attracting. At the same time there was little political mileage to be gained from a major effort to resuscitate the private landlord. But as the political representative of both landlordism and the building society movement, the Tory Party could hardly be seen to be favouring one at the expense of the other. Nevertheless, the Tories' ambivalence towards the question of their preferred tenure may partly rest in their failure to recognise fully the changes in the conditions of housing production which had taken place. The vast majority of housing was still firmly privately rented and the changes were felt mainly at the margin of new production (which at most represented no more than 2 per cent of the housing stock per year), while the sale of existing rented housing to owner occupiers had yet to have any real impact.

The net effect of this conflict of interest for the Conservatives was that the issue was simply left to the 'market' to sort out. And, eventually, the market did. But despite the tremendous shortage of housing and even with generous subsidies to reduce the costs of housing production, private landlordism was patently unwilling or unable to respond. The point, of course, is that the supply of private rented housing was not a function of the needs or incomes of households *per se*, but of the opportunity for profitable investment by landlords and mortgagees. Why, then, was landlordism unable to reassert itself at this time? The answer is largely to be found in the economic conditions prevailing in the housing market after 1918 and their consequences for the housing investment market.

The post war housing market: economics and expediency

As Bowley (1945, p.8) has argued:

> Investment in housing to let will only appear to be profitable if there is reason to believe that prospective rents will be sufficient to provide some margin of profit as well as covering the interest charges on the capital cost of the houses and cost of repairs and management. If building costs and interest rates are abnormally high, this condition is not likely to be satisfied. Further, if building costs and interest rates are likely to fall, or are actually falling, prospects of

> profits are still more gloomy and actual losses are probable. For if either costs or interest rates fall it is impossible to let profitably any new houses built after the fall in costs, or in interest, at lower rates than houses built at higher levels of cost. Competition from the new cheaper houses will tend to drag down the rents of the older houses with consequent loss to their owners.

This was exactly the situation facing landlords after the First World War. By the early 1920s, building materials and labour costs were at an all time high[5], as were interest rates, which had reached 7 per cent in April 1920. The effects of this cost inflation on investment were clear, and as Barnes stated at the time: 'This rising tide has submerged private enterprise in house building, and it now lies like the lost city of Atlantis in the region of legend and myth' (1923, p.170). As a result, house prices were up to four times their pre-war levels. For example, local authority tender prices for three bedroom houses in England and Wales rose from £235 in 1914 to £708 in 1919 and reached £881 by 1920. Thereafter the decline in prices was just as rapid, falling to £643 in 1921 and to £380 in 1923 (Merrett, 1979). Similarly, the cost of a standard non-parlour, three bedroom speculatively built house reached £930 in mid 1920, but had fallen to £436 by early 1923 (Jackson, 1974). Clearly, no landlord would have entered the market in these circumstances.

But why was there no significant return to construction for private renting once conditions began to stabilize after 1923? The reasons are complex, but the restructuring of the housing finance market which had accompanied the war and was consolidated in the decade or so after it was of central importance.

During the war the building societies had been major beneficiaries of the redirection of private capital but had been unable to expand business due to the absence of new construction. When the war ended they were under increasing pressure to find new outlets for lending in order to maintain their investment position. But there were few landlords willing to use building society funds for new investment. The societies had, however, managed to circumvent controls on their lending to owner occupiers. There had been a small but significant move towards increased funding of sales to owner occupiers in the decade or so before the war (Jackson, 1974), mainly in response to a decline in demand for funds from landlords during this period. This market now offered itself as a opening into which the war time build-up of funds could be directed, either for the purchase of new housing, or, just as importantly, for the sale of existing rented houses. At the same time, builders were facing a major problem as demand for their product had slumped. While local authorities filled the gap in demand for housing at the lower end of the market to some extent, the rest of the housing market was effectively devoid of investment. The sale of houses for owner occupation offered the greatest scope for sustaining output in the absence of demand from investors.

Thus the post war conditions in the housing market literally forced both builders and, more importantly, building societies to develop alternative means of maintaining their viability. This meant turning their joint attention towards the expansion of the previously limited market for owner occupation Consequently, the established system in which landlords played a key role in the 'realization problem' and which had prevailed for the previous century was effectively broken. Viewed in this light, the switch to owner occupation was a direct outcome of the situation prevailing in the private housing market after the First World War. It was, however, contingent on the political and economic developments which had been accumulating for some time and which the war brought to a head, as well as the added impetus generated by the wartime conditions themselves.

Owner occupation was certainly not a new tenure form but at a critical period it provided the opportunity for an alternative system of housing production to fill the vacuum left by the departure of the private housing investor. As Bowley states: 'The modern owner occupier, aided and abetted by the building societies, stepped neatly into the place deserted by investing owners' (1945, p.88). Exactly how the building societies created the market for owner occupation in the 20 years between the two world wars and in doing so created the conditions in which the tenure transfer process thrived will now be considered.

The 1930s housing boom: an unequal contest

Despite the fall in building costs throughout the late 1920s and early 1930s, the low level of investment and high interest rates restrained the level of new house building for private consumption, which hovered around the 120,000-140,000 level until 1932. Although there are no figures to indicate the proportions that were sold as opposed to rented, the general consensus is that few were purchased for investment by landlords (Marshall, 1968). The supply of new rented housing to working-class households was almost entirely confined to local authority provision. New housing provision for the private sector was more or less exclusively directed to meet the demand of the growing sector of middle-income, skilled manual and, particularly, white collar and middle-class workforce, continuing the pattern established since the 1890s (Burnett, 1978). This sector of the market undoubtedly provided the greatest opportunity for private landlordism to make a comeback when conditions once more became favourable for investment during the early 1930s, and new housing had never been subject to rent control. Yet it was precisely in the provision of new housing for middle and high income households that landlordism failed so conclusively compared with its major competitor in the latter half of the interwar period.

The housing boom which followed the return to power of the Conservative-led National Government in 1932 was spectacular given the prevailing economic conditions. The most important change which stimulated the surge in building was perhaps the abrupt switch to a cheap money policy following the sterling crisis of 1931, the abandonment of the gold standard and the expenditure cuts initiated by the new coalition government. The fall in interest rates which followed coincided with the falling trend in building costs which had continued since the early 1920s and into the depression.

But the conditions which were now favourable to building were also favourable to new investment in rented property and there was a significant return to building for private rental from 1933 onwards. By 1935, as Bowley has argued, 'Interest rates were low and might be expected to remain so. It seemed improbable that building costs would fall any further. They were more likely to rise than fall. The situation was favourable for investment in houses to let for the first time since the Great War' (1945, pp.81-2). This point was also made forcibly by the Housing Policy Review, which noted (Department of the Environment, 1977, vol. III, p.64) that:

> With interest rates back to where they were in 1907-10 (lower than in 1913), and building costs considerably lower relative to income than before 1914.... A return of about 4 or 5 per cent on the original cost was possible, which compared reasonably well with returns elsewhere.

The considerable shortage of housing relative to households added to the possibility of achieving a profitable return, and economic rents were within the reach of the better paid wage earner.

In all some 350,000 dwellings, or 28 per cent of all private sector housing with rateable values below £26 produced between 1933 and 1939, were built for rental. As 57 per cent of these were dwellings with rateable values below £13, it is usually assumed that this represented low-value housing for the working class (Marshall, 1968). At an average of roughly 60,000 per annum, this represented a return to the level of rented output not seen since before 1910 (Kemp, 1980). The general explanation for this return to renting was that it represented a response to over- supply for the owner occupier market which more or less forced builders either to rent the houses out or to sell to investors in the absence of demand from home owners. But to the extent that the over-supply thesis is correct, it was the higher-value sectors where demand failed to keep pace with production, spurred on by speculative competition (Merrett, 1982).

In fact, as Jackson notes, demand from middle-income home owners had been 'more or less met by the middle thirties and, from then on until the outbreak of war, the builders increasingly turned their attention to the minimum cost house, to maisonettes and to self-contained flats in large blocks' (Jackson, 1974, p.192). Thus the provision of lower-rated rental housing was not simply the result of over-supply for owner occupation. It also reflected a deliberate shift back into investment landlordism. Moreover, far from representing a disproportionate amount of construction for 'working class' rental, much of the lower-rated property which entered the rented sector at this time represented purpose-built flats aimed principally at middle income, white-collar demand. An estimated 100,000 to 200,000 purpose-built flats were constructed between 1933 and 1939 - perhaps 50 per cent of all rented dwellings produced at this time (Department of the Environment, 1977). In a period of low costs, access to cheap and stable banking and insurance credit in quantity, and high demand, especially in the major urban areas, rented flats were a profitable investment alternative.

Despite the return to new rental construction, especially for flats, the housing boom of the 1930s and the suburbs that it generated saw the overwhelming triumph of owner occupation and its mentor, the building society. The conditions which favoured the investment landlord were also conducive to the building societies' desire to foster owner occupation. But in a straight fight for the provision of housing for the middle income household, the chronic disadvantages of landlordism in the twentieth century were plainly exposed. Landlordism simply lost the battle for the average housing consumer.

The battle lines, such as they were, were being drawn up throughout the 1920s. Not surprisingly, the decisive factor which was to determine the outcome was the lines of supply to sources of credit. The situation was summed up by Walter Harvey, sometime chairman of the Building Society Association, who maintained that the societies 'were drawn off financing the building of houses to let by the ... much more profitable business of financing house purchase at scarcity prices, mainly for the benefit of the builder-seller' (quoted in Boddy, 1980, p.15). Boddy concludes: 'the societies, which had previously been providing loans on a significant scale to private landlords, came by the end of the thirties to concentrate more on financing owner-occupation' (Boddy, 1980, p.15).

The basic explanation of this is once again to be found in the changes within the system of housing finance itself as well as in the relationship of the system to the wider economic and political situation. As the 1920s drew to a close amidst the severest depression industrial Britain had faced, and a world wide economic crisis, the building societies found themselves embarrassingly overburdened with investment funds. Their combined assets rose from £68 million in 1919 to £300 million in 1929.

The shift in investment patterns was the product of a number of related factors. The lack of investment opportunities in the privately rented sector after 1918 was itself closely related to the growth of the societies' funds. According to Pawley (1978, p.65), 'money which a generation before might have been invested in building houses to rent, found its way instead into building society shares'. This reciprocal shift in investment patterns therefore reinforced the shift in tenure patterns that were emerging. The depression and associated financial collapse after 1929 also led to alternative investments, particularly in the stock market, declining in competitiveness with the societies' terms. This was compounded by the uncertainty of the capital market in general at this time. And despite high unemployment, real incomes grew steadily for those with jobs, especially among the salaried white collar sectors. Personal disposable income per head rose from £305 in

1920 to £391 by 1938 at 1970 prices (Merret, 1982). With a depressed consumer market, much of this income went into savings, particularly via the societies' accounts. In short the building societies became one of the few reliable outlets for investment capital and they deliberately maintained their attraction by keeping interest rates to depositors consistently higher than the normal market rate.

But this shift of private funds into the building societies was not simply a response to interest rate differentials or the ease and security of investment. The societies possessed a vital advantage over all other forms of investments, namely the composite tax rate charged on their investors' interest payments. This composite rate had been established in 1894 in a compromise arranged between the Inland Revenue and the societies. Under this voluntary agreement, interest on society amounts was taxed at source, but at only 50 per cent of the normal rate of tax. This was to allow for the fact that few investors earned high enough incomes to justify the payment of the full tax rate. In a period of low taxation (4d in the pound during much of the nineteenth century) this had only limited impact. But with the substantial increase in taxation leading up to the First World War standard income tax rates had risen to 5s in the pound by 1916. The advantage of this system began to be increasingly appreciated by higher-income investors. In 1921 a further agreement was reached between the Inland Revenue and the societies in which the effective tax rate on their investment interest was set at 25 per cent of the new higher standard rate, again in order not to penalize excessively the lower-income investor (Nevitt, 1966). The attraction of this tax rate to standard rate taxpayers was only too evident. By 1926 a limit of £5,000 per investor had to be imposed in order to stem the flow of funds seeking this preferential treatment (a measure quite easily circumvented in practice). Building societies had become a most effective tax haven by the late 1920s.

At no time before or since has the composite tax arrangement been so favourable to investment in building societies. Although the composite rate had risen by a series of adjustments to 36 per cent of the standard rate of 5s 6p by 1938-9, this concession represented a major attraction for investors in the middle wealth ranges throughout this period. The tax-compositing arrangement therefore represented a substantial and little appreciated subsidy to the societies at this time and gave the societies a considerable advantage over landlordism. It is hardly surprising then that by the mid 1930s few small investors bothered to take advantage of the more profitable conditions for investment in rented housing that existed and it also helps to explain why the limited return to investment landlordism was principally made by large scale corporate investors for whom the attractions of the building societies were largely incidental.

The build up of funds as a result of these developments placed a considerable pressure on the societies in the generally depressed housing market of the 1920s and early 1930s. Some mortgage business had been generated through the funding of sales of existing rented property (see Chapter 5) but even this failed to soak up the continued flow of investment. Consequently, the societies made further moves to stem the influx of money. By 1932, faced with an increasing mismatch between the growing accumulation of funds and low demand for mortgages, the major societies decided not only to reduce interest rates to new investors from 5 per cent to 3.5 per cent (following the fall in government stock yields by a similar amount), but to restrict increases in existing investment amounts and to limit new accounts to a maximum of £50. Nevertheless demand for mortgages was still insufficient and these measures were supplemented by a major drive to boost mortgage take-up, and with it, owner occupation. As Pawley concludes:

> in the end it appeared that the only answer for the societies was to promote the building of new homes for sale as fast as possible. Only unprecedented rates of new building could absorb the funds at the societies' disposal, and from this need sprang the great speculative housing boom of the 1930s. (Pawley, 1978, p.66)

As a consequence, a whole series of measures were introduced by which the societies restructured their mortgage lending practice in an attempt to reduce the effective cost of owner occupation, notably by lowering the entry costs to ownership and the subsequent repayments. First, mortgage rates were pushed down to their limits. Following the general fall in interest rates in 1932, the mortgage rate fell to 5 per cent by 1933 (it had reached 6.5 per cent in the 1920s). But pressure from builders to push sales up further forced the societies into reducing their rates to 4.5 per cent by 1935. As builders moved into the business of providing mortgages themselves in order to boost their sales, the intense competition for suitable mortgage business kept the mortgage rate at this level for the remainder of the 1930s despite the general rise in the yields on government securities after 1936. Second, effective demand for mortgages was stimulated by the general extension of repayment periods from the established 15-16 years to 25 or even 30 years. This reduced weekly repayment levels considerably, thus increasing competitiveness with rent levels, to which end it was deliberately aimed.

Demand was also fuelled by the increase in maximum advance on property valuations from the 75-80 per cent traditionally given to 90 per cent. This was initially effected by an insurance payment to meet any loss over the 75 per cent valuation which might result from defaults and foreclosure. In practice, life assurance policies, securities and other forms of personal security were often accepted as collateral in the general scramble for custom. The mortgage guarantee system reached its peak in the 'builders' pool' which became widespread by the mid 1930s. In its simplest form, the house builder supplied a collateral payment to the lending society to enable the house purchaser to receive a 95 or 100 per cent mortgage. This deposit was repaid once the purchaser had completed an agreed number of repayments and the risks of default had presumably passed. The system benefited both builders and building societies by boosting sales and mortgage lending. As a result houses could be purchased with as little as a £5 deposit by 1934 and Jackson (1974) quotes John Laing, the head of one of the major building contractors involved in speculative house building, as estimating that the builders' pool had enabled about three times as many people to consider home ownership as would have been the case under the traditional deposit system.

Though not without its risks, the builders' pool cemented the link between builders and building societies in a mutually beneficial and reinforcing association. 'By this ingenious means societies and builders became bound together according to an infinite variety of secret arrangements, with each endeavouring to pressure the other into accepting less advantageous terms' (Pawley, 1978, p.68). This association, formed out of necessity in the investment vacuum after the First World War, had by the mid 1930s developed into an efficient and effective system of housing production and consumption. The private landlord played no part in this system, however. It was simply more profitable for builders to use the close relationship they now enjoyed with the building societies and backed by the stable funds from the banking sector to fund building to sell direct to the household consumer. The growing purchasing power of the owner occupier could be simply appropriated by the builder without the necessity of any mediating agent.

The increasing economic power of the building societies was also reflected in their increasing political influence. The 1933 Housing Act, which helped shape housing policy for the remainder of the decade, was 'placed in the Statute Book simply because the building societies were absolutely bursting with money ... in order that people might be driven into the hands of the building societies and called upon to purchase houses for themselves' (Boddy, 1980, p.14). By cutting the subsidy system of the Wheatley Act and pushing local authority building into slum clearance and away from general needs provision, the 1933 Act forced local authorities out of housing provision for those households that the societies were desperate to attract into home ownership – the skilled working-class and lower-income, white-collar workers. The removal of the general subsidy arrangements freed the private market to respond to the changed conditions (and opportunities) of the 1930s without hindrance. But although the Act contained no obvious bias towards either owning or renting, 'The winding down of the great government housing programme ... made apparent the true extent of the switch from rental to ownership which was now taking place' (Pawley, 1978, p.64).

How far did this shift in tenure relations reflect change in demand preferences or were these changes largely constrained by predetermined shifts in the nature of housing supply? Boddy quotes Walter Harvey as stating, 'The new owner occupiers were so by necessity rather than choice.... The main source of the increased demand for building society mortgages came from people forced to become owner occupiers because there were no houses to let' (Boddy, 1980, p.15). Jackson, talking of the new breed of non-manual owner occupiers, notes:

> 'Still close to their working-class origins, white-collar families practised frugality and financial prudence almost instinctively, but their large-scale conversion to owner occupation did not come about by deliberate choice. If they wanted a new house, they had virtually no alternative but to buy'. (Jackson, 1974, p.167)

Clearly then, the sea change in the structure of housing provision in the inter war period was in no sense a 'demand-led' process. This demand had been carefully created by the building societies.

The degree to which the cost of home ownership had been reduced is quite simply shown by the differential movement of housing costs in the two sectors over the interwar period. By 1930 the rents on a typical pre-1914 working-class house had risen by about 50 per cent for controlled lettings and between 85-90 per cent for decontrolled lettings. This meant that an average rent of 6s in 1914 had risen to between 9s (controlled) and 11s 6d (decontrolled) (Parry Lewis, 1965). For new houses being built in the mid 1930s, rent levels were estimated to be about 10s on average (Department of the Environment, 1977). In contrast, the net effect of the restructuring of mortgage lending practice and falling house prices was to reduce the average level of mortgage repayments from 15s in the 1920s to 10s in the mid 1930s. For a lower-value, unsubsidized house the equivalent repayment cost for a 70 per cent mortgage had fallen from roughly 12s in 1925 to below 8s in 1936 (Bowley, 1945). Thus the cost of buying a new house was little different from the cost of renting a pre-war, rent-controlled property. The implications of this are quite clear. When the private housing market responded at last to the pent-up demand for housing (there was an excess of 1 million households over dwellings in 1931) it was owner occupation which called the tune.

Notes

1 For a full discussion of the various Rent Acts and Rent Act Committees during the interwar period see Nevitt (1966), Robinson (1979), Murie, *et al* (1974), Greve (1965), Stafford and Doling (1981) and Balchin (1981).

2 For a full account of the development of state housing at this time see Merrett (1979) and Dickens (1977).

3 Up to a lump sum of £160 per house later increased to £260 in 1920 or a longer term annual payment.

4 Direct state support for home ownership can be traced back to 1899 when local authorities were given powers to borrow capital at favourable interest rates to be advanced as mortgages for owner occupiers. These powers were extended under the 1923 Housing Act (Merrett, 1982). By 1926–7 over £9 million per annum was being provided for such mortgages. The 1923 Act also allowed local authorities to guarantee mortgage repayments by house purchasers to building societies, effectively reducing the entry costs for home ownership. To what extent these guarantees were taken up has not been clearly established, however (Dickens, 1977; Pawley, 1978), although Merrett (1982) suggests that some 2,000 mortgages were being guaranteed annually by 1925–6.

5 Skilled labour was particularly in short supply. Consequently, the average bricklayer's wage of £2 2s 10d per week in 1914 had risen to £5 0s 7d by 1920 (Jackson, 1974). Similarly, wholesale building materials had doubled in price between 1914 and 1923 (Barnes, 1923).

4 From renting to owning: the tenure transfer process

Introduction

By the end of the 1930s owner occupation had largely displaced private landlordism in the production of new housing. But the changes which underpinned the transformation of the tenure structure of new housing production had a corresponding if more protracted impact on the existing rented stock. Ever since the 1920s investor landlordism has experienced a more or less steady decline. This has been reflected in the dramatic contraction of the rented stock, from 7.1 million dwellings in 1914 to 2.9 million in 1975. As Table 4.1 shows, the major source of this decline has been the transfer of rented housing into owner occupation, which accounted for 88 per cent of the overall net decline of the private rented sector between 1914 and 1975, and contributed no less than 41 per cent of the net growth of owner occupation. This chapter focuses specifically on the process by which this transfer has taken place and sets the context for the discussion of the flat break-up market in the following chapters.

Recapitalization and the development of the dual value system in residential property

The transfer of rented property into owner occupation was taking place on a limited scale in the years preceding the First World War (Jackson, 1974). In a period of falling demand by private housing investors there had been a move by builders towards the sale of new houses to home owners. The building societies had also become increasingly aware of this trend as a way of maintaining demand for their mortgages. But at the same time shrewder landlords realized that if housing could be built for sale then comparable rented housing could also be sold for owner occupation. The building societies were also favourably disposed to this move as an additional outlet for funds wherever the opportunities were suitable.

Table 4.1 *Components of change in the privately rented and owner occupier sectors, England and Wales, 1914–75*

	Private rented	Owner occupier
	(millions of dwellings)	
1914 stock	7.1	−0.8
Changes 19141–38		
Purchases from or sales to other terms	−1.1	+1.1
Demolition and change of use	−0.3	neg
New building and conversion	+0.9	+1.8
Net change	−0.5	+2.9
1938 stock	6.6	3.7
Changes 1938–60		
Purchases or sales	−1.5	
Demolition and change of use	−0.4	−0.1
New building and conversion	+0.1	+1.3
Net change	−2.0	+2.7
1960 stock	4.6	6.4
Changes 1960–75		
Purchases of sales	−1.1	+1.1
Demolition and change of use	−0.8	−0.2
New building and conversion	+0.3	+2.6
Net change	−1.7	+3.5
1975 stock	−2.9	9.9
Net change 1914–75	−4.2	+9.1

Source: Department of the Environment, 1977, Technical Volumes, Part 1, Tables 1.23 and 1.24; Part 3, Table ix.2.

By the end of the First World War these sales had become a distinct trend. As the Housing Policy Review states: 'contemporary comment indicates that sales for owner occupation were taking place on an extensive scale in the war and immediate post-war period because this was much more profitable than reletting' (Department of the Environment, 1977, vol. III p.65). The question is, then, why did it become more profitable to sell than to continue to let at this time? Wartime rent controls contributed to this trend. But the permitted rent increase over the 1919-23 period compensated landlords in line with rising costs and helped to maintain both levels of return and the value of the property as an investment. Controlled properties were therefore not unprofitable *in themselves*. Before 1914, of course, there were no rent controls to induce sales. To this extent, then, there would appear to be little evidence to suggest that landlords were selling to owner occupiers purely as a result of rent control.

There was, of course, another, more potent incentive to sell. Despite attributing the cause of sales to problems of delayed and extensive repairs allied to postwar rent control, Pawley makes the perceptive comment that

> *with the appearance of two sets of values for houses* - those with and without vacant possession - there were clearly opportunities for speculation. Rent controlled houses could be bought cheaply and sold expensively, provided the tenants could be induced to depart. (1978, p.62, our emphasis)

The Housing Policy Review makes essentially the same point. Referring to the increases in controlled rents allowed under the various Rent Acts up to 1923, the Review notes that these increases were allowed on the basis of 'preserving a return on the pre-1914 value, *not on providing a competitive return on the amount the house would fetch if sold*' (Department of the Environment, 1977, vol. III, p.65, our emphasis). Both these observations point to the fact that sales were predicated on the emergence of two values for existing rented property at this time, one reflecting its value as a tenanted rented investment, the other as a property with vacant possession in the owner occupied market. But this dual valuation system emerged, not as a result of rent control, but as a consequence of the development of an owner occupier market in which property values were higher than those of existing rented properties.

Explanations of the loss of rented housing have almost always overlooked this simple but crucial point. Rent control did not create the possibility of sales, although it undoubtedly increased the incentive for existing landlords to disinvest. Even so, there is no evidence to suggest that sales only took place within that part of the stock which came under control. In fact, both controlled and decontrolled rented property appear to have been equally affected by the transfer process. Given that the value of a property in owner occupation was clearly higher than its rented value, why were potential owner occupiers prepared to pay more for the vacant possession of a rented property than it was evidently worth to a landlord? Landlords who wanted to disinvest from the apparently troublesome and unprofitable business of letting property could have merely sold to owner occupiers for what it was worth to them as a rented investment, and the rationale for such action, that of disposing of a poor investment, would have been satisfied.

The point, of course, is that those landlords who sold to owner occupiers did not do so simply because their properties were unprofitable *per se*, or just to disinvest, *but in order to make capital gains by appropriating the difference between the capital values of their properties in the rented and owner occupied markets*. The opportunity for these gains was founded on the growing viability of owner occupation as a competitive form of housing realization and exchange during this period. For landlords who were able to effect the transfer of their property into the owner occupied market, this situation offered the possibility of substantial profit. It is a situation which has been exploited for well over half a century in Britain. But the basis of the dual value system and its consequences for the private rented sector is poorly understood.

Rents, values and the value gap

The emergence of owner occupation as the dominant structure of private sector housing provision in the early twentieth century and the dual value system which it created was reflected in a growing gap between capitalized property values in the two tenures. But there is no mystery as to how this *value—gap* has arisen: it is simply the net outcome of the different fiscal and financial structures on which the two tenures operate. The outcome of these differences has had a particularly marked effect on the ways in which properties are valued as items of exchange within the two tenures.

In order to clarify our arguments, we first need to establish the fundamentally different bases of property valuation in the two private housing sectors. Traditionally, privately rented property functioned as a source of long-term investment income and landlords' demand for such property reflected its attractiveness as an investment. As such, it should be viewed in the same light as other income-yielding investments – shares, bonds, Treasury bills, and so on (Harvey, 1981). As with those other types of investment, rental property which is used as a source of income is capitalized on the basis of its current and potential yield, i.e. its periodic rent. Consequently, investment property valuations are calculated as multiples of rental income, the exact multiple depending on the yield the landlord investor expected to derive from the income received from the property. The yield is equivalent to an interest rate and will itself vary depending on competing interest rates elsewhere in the financial system, as well as the rate of inflation, the risk involved in the investment, the potential for rent reversions, and so on.

The expected level of return on a property investment is also critically affected by financial constraints, in particular the real cost of finance, which in turn depends on such factors as general interest rates and inflation levels. As a simple example, a property on which a 10 per cent return is to be expected would be valued at 10 times its annual rental yield, or 10 years purchase (YP) of the rent. For a property yielding say, £1,000 per annum in rent, its value at 10 YP would be £10,000. This represents the amount of capital any landlord would be prepared to invest in the property to derive a 10 per cent yield. If the general interest rate level changes, or the required yield changes, then the amount the property is worth would also change. At an 8 per cent yield, the property would be worth 12.5 YP of the rent or, in the case of the above example, £12,500. Conversely, at 12 per cent the value falls to £8,333, or 8.3 YP of £10,000. Thus at any given level of rent, as yields fall, capital values rise and vice versa.

Two points can be drawn from this example. First, within the private sector, property values were traditionally determined by levels or expected levels of rental income. This was the basis on which rented property was valued and exchanged between landlord investors for the purpose of long-term capital investment. The resulting value can be termed the *tenanted investment* (TI) value. In a pure investment market, rented property has no independent capital value other than that determined by its potential rental yield. Second, given the inverse relationship between yield and capital value, in inflationary periods capital values deteriorate if rents are not increased. In the past, tenancies were assigned for periods of up to 7 or 9 years, or even longer. In a period where inflation was negligible such leases were designed to safeguard the landlord's investment, the rent being fixed and legally binding for the period of the lease. But during periods of inflation such leases are a liability for landlords, by restricting rents and eroding the capital value of the investment. Such lease arrangements have become less and less common during the twentieth century, being replaced instead by the rack-rent system which allows flexibility in rent levels for the landlord. Inflation, therefore, has increasingly focused landlords' attention on maintaining the capital value of their property. Where rents are unable to rise fast enough to keep up with inflationary pressures, then landlords will be tempted to withdraw from the market and invest their capital in higher-yielding investments.

The long-established method of property valuation in the privately rented sector and its implications for investment strategies can be contrasted to the fundamentally different method of property valuation in the more recently developed owner occupied market. Here property values represent a straightforward capitalization of effective household income mediated by the current structure of the mortgage market. In other words, in the owner occupied market, capital values are the dominant, if not sole, pricing mechanism. Since owner occupied property is exchanged on the basis of vacant possession, we can term this value a *vacant possession* (VP) value. An important consequence of the focus on capital values is that, in contrast to private renting, capital gains become the dominant source of investment income for the property owner. Consequently, inflationary pressures on capital values are positively welcomed by owner occupiers as a means of protecting their investment. Indeed, house price inflation and the capital gains which flow from it form a major attraction of home ownership.

Of course, property values in both markets are clearly related to final consumer demand in terms of the ability of households to pay rent or meet mortgage repayments out of income. But the manner in which this ability to pay for housing is translated into concrete property values is crucially mediated by the structure of the intervening tenure forms through which this demand is made effective. It is the differences in the organization of the various tenure forms, and in particular in their fiscal and financial structure, which determine the variation in exchange values between the different housing tenure markets.

What, then, are the determinants of these differential valuations? The impact of contrasting fiscal and financial structures becomes clear if we compare the evolving economic roles of the various agents directly involved in private sector housing consumption, namely landlord investors, tenants and owner occupiers. For this it is useful to differentiate between the dual aspects of housing as a commodity, that is its twin role as an investment and a consumption good. Landlords and tenants clearly represent the two sides of this duality, but owner occupation conflates the roles of investor (owner) and consumer (occupier). It is this conflation of roles which largely explains the economic domination of home ownership as the main tenure form and the emergence of the value gap. In effect, owner occupation allows home owners to out-bid both landlords and tenants for housing.

Pity the poor landlord: home ownership and the profitability of housing as a commercial investment

We have already discussed the impact of changes in the structure of housing finance on landlordism in relation to the costs of both a traditional private mortgage and the more recently developed building society amortized mortgage. The increasing reliance by landlords on the amortized loan as private mortgage capital was drawn away from landlordism into the building societies had a considerable impact on the costs incurred by landlords. Either rents had to be increased to meet the increase in loan-servicing costs, or the amount any investor landlord would pay for property yielding any given rent would be reduced, i.e. he or she would require a higher yield to cover the increased costs.

In the immediate post-1919 period, interest rates were high and therefore any increase in financing costs over and above that permitted under the Rent Acts (e.g. on the expiry of an existing loan) would have the effect of depressing TI values. On the other hand, the cost of owner occupier finance was steadily being reduced as the building societies consciously and systematically relaxed the terms on which mortgages were offered to home owners. As Nevitt (1966, p.36) observes: 'The competitive position of the building societies *versus* the landlord rests entirely upon the economic fact that the societies have quite intentionally made their loan terms competitive with those of landlords.'

Thus the percentage of property valuations advanced increased from 60-70 per cent typical in the nineteenth century to 90 per cent by the 1930s, and the repayment periods were lengthened from 10-16 years to 25-30 years. These were terms on which landlords simply could not compete. Nevitt (1966, p.36) concludes:

> The only reason why the societies have not utterly routed the private landlord from all sectors of the market is their refusal to give 100 per cent mortgages, which effectively debars a great many families from owner occupation.

Moreover, while the building societies allowed owner occupiers to borrow money at an increasingly subsidized rate, landlords, deprived of their sources of private mortgages, were increasingly forced onto the commercial money market. In the 1920s commercial interest rates were typically 1 per cent above base. They are now, of course, anything up to 5 per cent higher. This again increases the relative financing costs of landlordism relative to owner occupiers.

Thus, during the early decades of the twentieth century, while events were conspiring to push up the costs of finance for landlords, exactly the opposite was happening to the finance costs of owner occupation. Underlying this situation was the increasing importance of tax compositing on the ability of the building societies to attract investment capital and thereby provide cheap and, in effect, subsidized loans for home owners. The hidden subsidy to owner occupation through tax compositing has been one of the main fiscal disincentives to landlordism throughout this century. The net impact of these events on housing capitalization was to depress effective TI values and to increase effective VP values in real terms. This relationship has so far not been reversed—indeed it has become even more pronounced as inflationary tendencies have accelerated.

There have also been cumulative repercussions resulting from the costs which a landlord includes in his rent calculations compared to those included in the calculations of owner occupation. There are a number of points to note here. First, a landlord will expect to receive a current income on any capital of his own that is invested in the property he rents out. Not so the owner occupier. Again Nevitt sums up the situation: 'the great significance of owner occupation is that it is a form of finance which involves the investment of capital without the payment of interest' (1966, p.8). Thus in the immediate competition for housing, owner occupiers are only concerned about the costs of mortgage repayments. They do not expect an income from any capital invested to purchase the property. And although owner occupiers may well expect the capital invested to appreciate, this is a qualitatively different form of return and it does not affect current costs.

Second, gross rents have to include the cost of repairs, management, voids and, if prudent, an amount to meet depreciation in the form of a sinking-fund contribution. Few, if any owners include maintenance or depreciation costs when calculating the amount they can afford to borrow.

Third, rental incomes are subject to taxation. Before the abolition in 1963 of Schedule A taxation on the imputed rental income owner occupiers received from their property, this factor could be considered as having a marginal effect, and acted to reduce the subsidy provided through mortgage interest tax relief. However, owner occupiers tended to be taxed for this purpose on the historic rateable value of their property which was fixed only at infrequent periodic intervals. Landlords, of course, have always been taxed on the current rent levels they receive. Thus for the owner occupier the effect of this tax always tended to decrease over time, whereas it is constantly maintained for the landlord.

In any event, Schedule A taxation was a tax on the investment value of the property (i.e. its income-yielding potential). When the owner occupier became exempt from this tax the investment value of property for owner occupiers became effectively subsidized. While of relatively minor importance for the average household, this factor had definite attractions for the higher-income taxpayer and marked a switch in investment patterns amongst these households away from stocks and securities (income from which is still liable to taxation) and into house property. Finally, unlike landlords, owner occupiers have been largely exempt from Capital Gains Tax since it was introduced in 1965. Although this is only of more recent significance it again had the greatest impact on higher-income taxpayers who have subsequently diverted investment into houses in order to benefit from this undoubted investment subsidy.

Investor landlords have, therefore, suffered a long-term and cumulative disadvantage in comparison to home owners in relation to the costs of the finance required for the purchase of housing, the costs which are included in the calculations on which purchase is based, and by the long-term tendency for fiscal policies to favour owner occupation in terms of both taxes on rents (or imputed rents) and capital gains and through the building societies' tax-compositing arrangements.

Pity the poor tenant: home ownership and the consumption of housing

Owner occupation also places home owners in a much more favourable position in terms of their relative abilities to consume housing services. The main factor here has been the increasing level of tax subsidy flowing to the mortgaged owner occupier as opposed to the rent-paying tenant. While both landlord and owner occupier can offset interest payments against taxation of income, thus equalizing their position with respect to interest costs, the real impact of this factor is seen in the effective income which either the tenant or the owner occupier can spend on housing. The net effect of tax relief on interest repayments is to increase the amount owner occupiers can pay for the housing they consume. In theory this may be expressed in the purchase of larger amounts of space, but in practice it has been translated into a higher property value for any given property in owner occupation.

A simple example illustrates the effect that this subsidy has on the value of an existing rented property. Assume a house has prevailing market rent, net of all cost, of £1,500 per annum giving an expected gross yield of 10 per cent. The TI value of the house to the landlord is around £15,000. Now a householder capable of paying £1,500 per annum in rent will, on average, have an income of at least £6,000 per annum if he/she is not to be expected to pay more than 25 per cent of his/her income in housing costs (excluding rates). However, if the householder were to obtain a mortgage which cost, net of tax relief on the interest element at the standard rate of 30 per cent, the same as the rent (i.e. £1,500 per annum), his/her effective rent paying ability would increase to £1,950 per annum (£1,500 x 30/150). At a 10 per cent rate of interest, this represents a VP value for the property of some £19,500.

There is thus a notional 'value gap' of some £4,500 between the net TI value of the property rented out to a tenant at £1,500 p.a. and the imputed VP value which an owner occupier could 'afford' for no extra net cost as a result of interest tax relief. Given that building societies tend to lend up to two and a half times the gross income of a household, then a householder earning £6,000 per annum could actually afford a £15,000 mortgage. Moreover, given that the current long-term average ratio of house prices to income is around 3-3.5:1, then a household with an income of £6,000 per annum could be expected to be able to afford a house worth between £18,000 and £21,000.

In order to be able to capitalize this property on its imputed VP value, a landlord is faced with two options. The first option is to charge a rent which returns a 10 per cent yield on this value. This would mean a rent in the region of £1,950. But this would represent some 33 per cent of the householder's income of £6,000. The income needed to pay such a rent would normally be at least £8,500 per annum. But the landlord's problems are only compounded by this, for a household with this income would be capable of purchasing a house worth some £28,000. This represents a substantially better deal for the household than renting, for the same cost, the generally inferior standard of accommodation which the landlord is offering.

Thus, both the lower and higher income households would be unwilling to rent the property yielding its current economic rent. Only in conditions of housing scarcity, or in the absence of mortgage finance for owner occupier purchases (for either the property or householder), or where rent restrictions maintain rent levels which can compete with the advantages of mortgage-aided home ownership, could a landlord realistically expect to attract long-term demand for his housing. In the absence of these conditions a landlord can only take full advantage of the notional capital value of a property in a housing market dominated by home ownership by taking the second option: namely selling the property into owner occupation if and when the opportunity arises.

Tenants are not only disadvantaged against owner occupiers where house subsidies are concerned. Owners are only committed to paying for their accommodation for the period of the mortgage. After this time they become the outright owners of the property and only need to meet rates and repair costs. In contrast, tenants face a lifetime of steadily increasing rental payments with no capital asset to show for their expense at the end of the day. While this has no immediate impact on the initial economics of owning versus renting, it certainly has a long term influence in the relative costs of either tenure for the household. This is compounded by the fact that the home owner is in effect purchasing a capital asset, which during the course of the last 60 years at least has been constantly appreciating, thus giving the owner the added benefit of a capital gain, which is, of course, not subject to taxation. These capital gains are denied to tenants.

Finally, for those householders who have secure and structured career opportunities, the relative costs of ownership form a declining porportion of household income over time. This is compounded by the general inflation of incomes. Thus, mortgage repayments reflect the historic cost of the property which will not vary as the value of that property increases. Interest rate fluctuations aside, owner occupiers will still be paying the same in money terms for their property in 25 years' time as they did at the beginning of the mortgage. In large part the continual increase in rents which tenants have faced is in fact directly related to the development of owner occupation, which has not only added to the costs of landlordism but has switched attention away from a concern with investment income towards capital values. Since at least the 1960s, 'open market' rents have been increasingly based on current VP values for owner occupied property, which can be expected to keep pace with, if not exceed, average incomes.

Home owners, therefore 'benefit' in two major ways in relation to tenants. Tax relief on interest payments increases their effective purchasing ability, while the long-term attractions of an appreciating untaxed capital asset and declining real costs are clearly additional factors which reduce the costs of ownership over time. These attractions operate over and above any of the supposed 'psychological' attractions by which home ownership has been promoted since the 1930s.

House values and the cumulative disadvantages of landlordism

Although the relative importance of these various fiscal and financial factors has varied over time, the effect has been cumulative, with successive changes consistently operating to compound the cost disadvantage of landlordism. While the financial differences between the tenure systems were probably the major factor in undermining the landlords' position in the early part of this century, it is undeniable that taxation factors, particularly mortgage interest relief, and the building societies' composite rate arrangement, have played an increasingly important part in maintaining and indeed enhancing the value divergence since that time. Personal taxation has grown consistently from the First World War onwards, drawing more and more wage earners into the tax net and thereby creating an ever widening sector of the population who could benefit from tax relief on mortgage interest payments. Today the situation is such that

> Under our existing tax arrangements an owner occupier can *always* afford to pay a higher capital sum for his house than can a landlord who intends to let to a tenant with the same income as the potential owner occupier.' (Nevitt, 1966, p.20, our emphasis)

This is the key to understanding the reason why builders found it more profitable to sell direct to the household consumer using a building society mortgage and, equally, why it has proved increasingly profitable for landlords to sell existing rented property into owner occupation. The cumulative advantages for owner occupiers have only partially been translated into an ability to purchase more housing than they could if they were tenants. In practice this advantage is expressed in higher property values for owner occupied as opposed to rented housing. Rent control, which has helped to depress the capital value of existing property below its possible market level, and increasing house price inflation in the owner occupier market (a product of rising incomes coupled with increasing taxation subsidies), have both operated to widen the gap between the property values in the two tenures, but they did not create the gap. It was the basic fiscal and financial bases of owner occupation as opposed to landlordism which created this value divergence in the first place.

The development of the dual value system in the residential property sector since the interwar period in Britain has therefore led to a basic and unavoidable conflict for landlords of existing residential property. The resulting value gap has arguably been the principal underlying mechanism which has provoked the inexorable transfer of rented property into owner occupation. In effect, owner occupation has *recapitalized* existing private rented property. As Kemeny has perceptively put it: 'In a home owning society the market for dwellings is dominated by the home-ownership sector, and so the sale price of rented property is determined by the state of the home-ownership market' (1981, p.28). The pressure on commercial profit-maximizing landlords to capitalize their property on the basis of its potential VP value rather than its existing TI value has become overwhelming.

This process has had far-reaching effects on the privately rented sector. Not only has it prompted the sale of rented property into owner occupation but it has also distorted property valuation methods to the extent that the traditional basis of valuation for tenanted property has been totally inverted. It is now the general practice for most landlords to attempt to calculate their rental yield in relation to the (notional) VP value of their property. This is certainly the position currently taken by the British Property Federation (1977; also House of Commons, 1982). This inversion of property valuation methods experesses succinctly the real position of landlordism in relation ot owner occupation. Rather than rental income providing the basis of capital values, vacant possession values now form the basis for the determination of adequate return. In these conditions, remaining investor landlords calculate rents on the basis of the opportunity costs forgone of not being able to invest the notional VP value of their properties in alternative investments. This in turn creates tremendous pressure to increase rents well above their level under the traditional valuation system.

Rent controls and security of tenure, where they have applied, have helped to deflect this pressure and, in effect, acted to preserve the TI value of any rented property under control. In these cases the landlord is 'held in a vice' between the twin effects of control and vacant possession house price (Nevitt, 1966, p. 124). The incentive to sell such property to the sitting tenant, even at a considerable discount on the full VP value, or to effect a vacancy and then sell with vacant possession, is only too clear. But it is equally clear that it has not been rent control which created this situation. Rather it is the owner occupied VP value which offers the possibility of recapitalization.

Similarly, where security of tenure legislation is in force the incentive to sell upon gaining vacancy is considerably enhanced, for if landlords choose to relet they effectively deny themselves the possibility of realizing the capital appreciation for an indeterminate future period. In so far as their property has been tenanted for a considerable time at a controlled or regulated rent, reletting, especially for the larger, economically rational landlords, is unlikely to happen, as this would be to ignore the temporary 'window' of opportunity afforded by vacant possession through which landlords can escape.

In the absence of rent controls the situation is no better as rents set in relation to VP values would be unacceptably high for the majority of households. In any case, households would also be able to purchase similar property as owner occupiers at a much lower cost. Thus, the net effect of setting rents in relation to VP values is to drive households into owner occupation at a much faster rate. This helps to explain the apparent paradox that transfers to owner occupation speed up in periods of rent decontrol. When faced with the prospect of paying full 'open market' rents for their homes, now capitalized on VP values, tenants will be much more likely to appreciate the advantages of home ownership. Today the only sectors of the housing market where conditions allow these 'market' rents to be charged are the high-rent, short-stay furnished or luxury sectors. In Britain these are mainly concentrated in inner city areas, especially London, where the pressure of demand from mobile, high-income households or those unable to obtain mortgages can be successfully exploited.

Finally, in a private housing market dominated by owner occupation, inflation of owner occupied house prices, irrespective of the rate of increase in rental income, creates the possibility of a greatly enhanced rate of capital appreciation and the realization of even larger capital gains on eventual sale into owner occupation. As Kemeny (1981, p.28) points out:

> Whenever house prices in the home-ownership market rise rapidly, as happened in the early 1970s, renting suddenly becomes less profitable ... simply because large (potential) capital gains are being made by landlords who are then tempted to realize the gains on the home-ownership market if they are unable to increase rents in proportion ... the faster prices rise, the more landlords may be tempted to sell.

This in turn has created the situation where rental income constitutes a declining portion of what Prior (1980) has termed the *total returns* accruing to a landlord, the other portion being capital appreciation. It can be argued that, viewed from the perspective of total returns, the landlords' position does not necessarily worsen in a period of house price inflation. Indeed, it may even improve. Certainly, the rental return on current vacant possession values decreases as vacant possession values rise. But the important point is that the capital appreciation element increases proportionately, for as Kemeny (1981, p.28) notes:

> those who argue ... that private renting is unprofitable by pointing to the low rate of return in relation to current market values are misunderstanding one of the fundamental mechanisms in the private rented sector ... in a home owning society.

This misunderstanding is based, first, on the inversion of property valuation practices and, second, on the fact that few investor landlords today view their property solely in terms of its pure rental investment yield. Since the emergence of mass owner occupation, capital values, and specifically VP values, have come to form the major determinant of profitability of private rented property investment.

But there is only one way by which investor landlords can derive a full income on the recapitalized value of their property. It must be sold into owner occupation and the proceeds reinvested in alternative investments. But once achieved, the recapitalization of the property by sale into owner occupation is unrepeatable. The landlord has to kill the goose to obtain the golden egg.

The emergence of the residential property trader

The response of landlords to this situation of cumulative disadvantage has been far from uniform. The decision to disinvest is not a mechanical one and in reality will depend on the individual perceptions of landlords, their market position, their criteria for individual profitability, and so on (Allen, 1983). While many landlords have disinvested through a policy of direct sales to either sitting tenants or open market purchasers, others have sold out to landlords who were still willing to invest in rental property. Others were able to recoup their capital by selling out to local authorities who wished to redevelop or improve. This is especially the case in those submarkets where the properties were not mortgageable for owner occupation (in other words, where recapitalization was not possible).

But wherever the rental market has been subject to recapitalization pressures there is another possibility, namely that an intermediary will purchase the tenanted property with a view to effecting the transfer into owner occupation. The recapitalization process has therefore given rise to an entirely novel form of residential property ownership: the speculative residential property trader. Such traders do not purchase rented property for its rental potential. They buy it either to sell to the incumbent tenant or in the hope of obtaining vacant possession in the near future. For these property owners, the income derived from renting to a tenant and the resultant rent relation which this creates is an almost incidental byproduct of the real object of the exercise—that of exploiting the value gap and appropriating the locked-up capital gains. Residential property bought on this basis is therefore bought with a speculative 'hope value'—the hope that the tenant will buy, move or die.

The rise of the residential property tender has been one of the most significant and perhaps least recognized parts of the tenure transformation process since the 1920s. This form of property ownership is a specialized and distinct form of residential investment capital. The rationale on which the trading stock is held is the complete opposite of traditional investment landlordism. In the trader's case it is the capital element which is predominant in calculations of profitability rather than rental income. This is not to say that rents do not enter into the property trader's calculations. In many cases rents provide the necessary cash flow to meet current costs, particularly interest payments on the capital borrowed to purchase the property. Nevertheless, for the property trader, rents are a secondary consideration compared to the lure of speculative capital gains.

Although rental (investment) income has historically benefited from a taxation advantage over trading income, if the rate of sales of trading stock can be carefully controlled to minimize taxation liabilities, this form of business has provided a substantial long term basis for many property investors, be they corporate organizations or individuals. In fact, for many property traders, capital appreciation and rental yield represent varying components of total profitability, the exact proportions depending on changes in market conditions. During periods of rapid house price inflation the trading element may be the dominant source of profit, while in slump periods there will be a switch to the maximization of the rental element through, for example, systematic attempts to increase rents or to reduce maintenance expenditure.

The presence of the residential trader has also had a major repercussion on tenanted investment values in those parts of the rented market where they have been operative. Given the possibility of future capital gains to be made by sales into owner occupation, existing investor landlords who wish to disinvest have been increasingly reluctant to sell their properties to traders at 'pure' TI values. While fully aware of their property potential, many established landlords have either not wished to involve themselves directly in trading or have not possessed the specialized organization necessary to pursue a successful sales policy. On the other hand, they clearly have not been able to trade their tenanted properties at anything approaching its imputed VP value. Instead, such properties have been traded at what could be termed a *speculative tenanted investment* (STI) value which is considerably greater than its pure TI value but reflects a discount on the potential capital gain to be made through eventual sale into owner occupation. The actual level of the STI value varies considerably depending on the potential for sales, but currently such values can be expected to average about 40 per cent of the prevailing estimated VP value. In this way exising landlords are able to appropriate a proportion of the future gain to be made by the final property trader.

It is clear, however, that the role of the specialist residential property trader as a mediator in the tenure transfer process is essentially a transitional one. Their future is determined by the number of tenanted properties which remain to be sold into owner occupation. The bulk of house sales have already been accomplished and the flat sector represents one of the last major rented markets in which the process has yet to be fully exploited. The effects of the recapitalization process may take some time to work their way through what remains of the 'conventional' privately rented sector, but if the prevailing tenure relations continue, then these properties, too, will eventually move into owner occupation. When they have, the residential property trader will cease to exist.

Nevertheless, the current importance of this form of property ownership and its crucial role in mediating the transfer of rented property into home ownership cannot be understated. Nor has the role been merely a passive one. Residential property traders have played a key part role in initiating the transfer process by actively creating the conditions in which sales can be effected, particularly where they have been able to create a market for their property by the application of mortgage finance.

Creating the market: the role of mortgage finance

The value gap and the opportunities for capital gain depend on the availability of suitable mortgage finance, not only for the traders who purchase the property from disinvesting landlords, but, more importantly, for the households who are the eventual purchasers. As a result, the tenure transfer market can be closely related to developments in the structure and organization of the housing capital market since the 1920s. The mortgage lending policies of the major financial institutions and particularly the building societies have largely determined the speed and pattern by which the rented sector has been transferred into owner occupation. For the majority of house properties, particularly those in higher status suburban areas and for the middle income households and above, transfers have been in progress since before the First World War. But as lending policies have gradually been relaxed to expand outlets for the growth of deposits, mortgages have not only become increasingly available further down the income and occupational hierarchy, but have also been extended into other housing submarkets.

But the most important determinant of the speed of the transfer process has been the necessity for building societies periodically to find new outlets for mortgages during periods when the volume of capital receipts outstripped conventional sources of mortgage demand, or when alternative (and preferred) outlets were limited, usually during periods of recession in the building industry. During such periods, funds have flowed into the transfer market to soak up the excess supply of depositor's cash.

This was precisely the situation after the First World War. In the absence of demand from investors and the slump in new housing construction, virtually the only channel for the build-up of funds which had taken place in the period leading up to and during the war was into the tenure transfer market. Mortgage advances had risen from £7 million in 1918 to £25 million in 1920, largely as a result of this new market. By the late 1920s the pressure for suitable mortgage outlets 'had created a situation in which the only release for society funds was the business generated by transfers from rented stock to owner occupation' (Pawley, 1978, p.66).

This situation was repeated in the years immediatly following the Second World War, but with an added supply-side impetus. It is probably true to say that at no time during their 70 year history did rent controls have as much impact as during the 10 to 15 years after 1939, when they were reintroduced to cover nearly the whole housing stock. Strict rent controls, which had reduced the real value of rents by as much as 50 per cent by 1951 (Robinson, 1979), also held down TI values. For most landlords there was also little escape from the steady inflation in costs which continued into the 1950s. At the same time there had been a general inflation in house prices in the owner occupied market, reflecting both the general increase in average earnings and the lowering of taxation thresholds during the war. In combination, these trends had ensured that the notional value gap for many rented properties had grown appreciably. As a result:

> The inducement to sell as soon as possible was much greater than in the interwar years, and sales to sitting tenants at a large discount off vacant possession values appear to have been very common.' (Department of the Environment, 1977, vol. III, p.66)

Not surprisingly, this period saw an acceleration in the rate of sales to owner occupiers, which were now averaging 60,000 to 70,000 per year compared to 46,000 per year in the interwar period (Table 4.1).

But while these inducements all contributed to the increasing rate of transfers, it was the willingness of the building societies to fund suitable purchases, aided by a small but significant level of local authority lending (Merrett, 1982), which provided the necessary catalyst. Once again the societies had come through the war with virtually no new outlets for their depositors' investments. This situation continued well into the postwar period and the flow of savings was enhanced by the general increase in income levels. Moreover, new building had virtually ceased during the war and the postwar Labour Government was committed to a massive expansion of council building. There was little encouragement for the private housing market, and building and planning controls were strictly enforced.

The problem which the societies had faced in the 1920s—too much investment, too few mortgagors—was repeated in the 1940s and early 1950s. Again the solution was to channel funds into the purchase of previously rented property. The owner occupied market had by now become an established feature of the British housing scene and this made the estimation of current VP values for rented houses much more straightforward as there were many comparable houses, both rented and owner occupied. The role played by the societies in aiding the acceleration of sales after the Second World War can be judged from the fact that while new private sector housing completions were a mere 1,390 in 1945 and had barely reached 30,000 by 1950, building society advances leapt from 75,000 in 1944 to 207,000 in 1946 and had reached over 300,000 by 1950 (Merrett, 1982). While much of this boom in lending went to funding the remortgaging of exiting owner occupied housing, the Department of the Environment estimate of at least 70,000 transfers per year is easily accommodated by this level of advances.

The dependence of the tenure transfer process on mortgage finance has an important repercussion on property traders' marketing strategies. In a housing market characterized by an absence of freely available mortgage lending there is little or no effective basis for vacant possession valuations. However, in this situation, landlords who can *create* a vacant possession market for their property by arranging mortgage finance for potential home owners are then able to exploit a value gap of their own making.

This is precisely the practice used since the early 1920s by residential property traders to sell rented property successfully into owner occupation. As with the emergence of the owner occupier market for newly built housing, the transfer market had to be created and shaped. In earlier periods, property traders obtained suitable lines of credit from building societies or banks. More recently the larger-scale corporate traders and flat breakers of the post-1945 period have looked to the secondary and merchant banks and insurance companies for the necessary funding.

But whether a viable mortgage supported owner occupier market already exists or has to be actively created by the direct application of funding, adequate mortgage finance for the final consumers is vital for an extensive and successful transfer market. This partly explains why a number of remaining rented submarkets have so far not been subject to break-up – e.g. furnished rooms in shared accommodation. No one has yet been able to persuade building societies to accept such properties as security for mortgage lending. Consequently there is no mechanism by which these rented submarkets can be effectively recapitalized. This is precisely the point made by the Housing Policy Technical Volume III when commenting on the results of the Department of the Environment's 1971 National Movers' Survey: 'Roughly half the accommodation let to movers by companies or individuals (other than relatives) was probably unsaleable (or at least hard to sell) as a result of being without standard amenities or being only parts of houses' (Department of the Environment, 1977, vol. III, p.80). Of course, much of the remaining rental market is either a product of owner occupation itself (Kemeny, 1981; Forrest and Kemeny, 1982) or is still sufficiently profitable to maintain landlords' involvement. Nevertheless, landlords of properties which are mortgageable always have the future possibility of selling these remaining properties into the owner occupier market, either as single family dwellings or through the flat conversion market.

Creating the market: the case of the Bradford Property Trust

The emergence of residential property trading after 1919 and its close interrelationship with developments in the housing finance system at this time is well illustrated by the history of the Bradford Property Trust (BPT). The BPT is one of the most successful and long established of the many property traders whose existence is predicated on the recapitalization of the privately rented sector by the development of owner occupation. The foundation of the company's profitable involvement in property trading has been a close and long-standing relationship with building society finance. The official company history states quite unequivocally that 'As a pioneer in the movement from rented to owner occupied houses, the company grew side by side with the development of the building society movement' (Brennan, 1978, p. viii). Direct access both to building society mortgages to fund house sales and to clearing banks and insurance company finance to fund the acquisition of dealing stock has been vital to the growth and longevity of the company's activities. The BPT should therefore be seen as a direct product of the expansion of large-scale credit and finance systems which accompanied the development of monopoly capitalism during the earlier part of the century. Without access to the quantity of stable finance which this system offered, property trading in this form would have been impossible.

The BPT was incorporated in 1928, but its origins date back the early postwar period. It was during this period that one of the Trust's founder directors, Fred Gresswell, a Bradford estate agent, first realized that there were possibilities for profitable speculation emerging from, on the one hand, a situation where landlords were increasingly reluctant to maintain their investments as a result of the rapid inflation experienced in the years following the war and, on the other, his experiences in the developing owner occupied market. The opportunity which Gresswell perceived lay in being able to buy estates of houses cheaply from disinvesting landlords and then selling the houses piecemeal to sitting tenants or others. It is a situation which the BPT has exploited ever since: 'For fifty years the BPT has applied to housing the simple trading method of buying wholesale and selling retail' (Brennan, 1978, p.1).

Gresswell based his conclusions on two simple observations:

> One was that even for people receiving the dole, the first charge was the rent which had to be paid, and the second was that there was a vacant possession value—that is, the difference between the value of a house rented and one empty and for sale'. He adds: 'Building societies were also beginning to lend to owner occupiers of smaller houses' (quoted in Brennan, 1978, p.4).

Here the crucial link between the possibilities of residential property trading and the availability of building society funding is clearly exposed. Sometime in the early 1920s Gresswell purchased his first speculative investment of 16 houses for £95 each. The rents charged on these properties were 5s 6d per week, which represented a 15 per cent gross yield on purchase price. Such a rate of return might not be considered unreasonable even for that period. Nevertheless it provided no incentive for Gresswell to consider renting them.

The problem which faced him was to create a VP market for these houses when, quite evidently, none existed. Unlike other traders who preferred to wait for vacancy and sell at VP prices which exploited the full scarcity value of housing at this time, Gresswell's particular sales technique – 'Small Profits and Quick Returns' – was geared to a rapid turnover through sales to sitting tenants. This approach made the enterprise somewhat more of a gamble, but, if successful, it took correspondingly less time to see a return on the investment. However, in order to make the business viable, the sitting tenants had to be persuaded to purchase their houses.

Gresswell's marketing technique involved three main elements. First, an initial VP sale was effected in one of the houses which was empty. This established an 'open market' value for the other houses which could then be offered as 'bait' in the form of the potential capital gains for tenants should they also buy. It also provided an immediate flow of cash to help meet financing costs. The second element was to fix the sale price of the remaining tenanted houses such that the mortgage repayments costs were roughly comparable to the levels of rents the tenants were currently paying. After selling the empty property on the open market for £200, Gresswell then offered the rest to the sitting tenants for £135 each. The latter price was calculated to cost no more in mortgage repayments than the 5s 6d per week the tenants paid in rent. The value gap of some £40 between the TI value of £95 and their discounted VP value of £135 was equivalent to a potential trading profit of over 40 per cent, despite being a substantial discount on the full VP value of £200 established by the initial sale.

There was, however, a third element of the marketing strategy which was essential in making the whole exercise possible. The mortgages by which the tenants were to purchase their houses had already been arranged through Gresswell's contacts with a local building society and the sale price included all the legal costs as well as the mortgage survey fee. Tenants were thereby assured of a mortgage should they decide to buy and there were no extra costs to hinder the transaction. This was really the key factor in the success of the whole scheme. 'Self-financing' schemes such as these, where the property trader provides the necessary mortgage finance by prior arrangement with a lending institution, have been typical of the tenure transfer process from Gresswell's day to our own. In addition, building societies might have been reluctant to lend to the type of household purchasing the ex-rented property had they been approached on an individual basis. Quite simply, then, the market had to be primed by prearranged mortgages and a carefully pitched sales strategy.

Gresswell's sales drive met with resistance from an unexpected quarter, however. The mortgages which had been arranged amounted to 88 per cent of the full purchase price to be repayed over 12.5 years. But the tenants faced a very simple difficulty – they could not afford the deposit of some £10-11, for, as Gresswell notes with some incredulity; 'I found that none of the tenants had any money' (quoted in Brennan, 1978, p.5). His answer to this was to arrange an additional mortgage to cover the deposit, repayable at 2s a month. We noted in Chapter 2 the widespread practice of builders of providing additional mortgages to cover deposits on new houses for buyers with no savings. Gresswell appears to have simply used the same technique. Once this difficulty was overcome, all the houses were successfully sold and the completed transaction made a 20 per cent net profit on an total outlay of £1,520. Gresswell was apparently so surprised at the size and speed of this profit, some £300, that he states: 'I put it to one side until I could convince myself that it was a legitimate business' (quoted in Brennan, 1978, p.5).

After this early success Gresswell's trading business expanded. But the deposit problem continued to create difficulties. By the mid 1920s he appears to have been forced into a scheme similar to the 'builders' pool' arrangement. The Halifax Building Society, which had been supplying the mortgage for his house sales, found out that the deposits were being covered by second mortgages and insisted that a sum equivalent to the value of the second mortgages should be deposited with the society. This imposed an increasing burden on the profitability of the business, especially as the accumulated deposits tied up an increasing amount of working capital. Consequently, Gresswell adopted the idea, which had been developing elsewhere in the housing market at this time, that only a proportion of the full deposit capital need be retained to cover the small number of mortgage defaults that were likely to occur.

It was in fact from this early link with the local Halifax branch that the BPT would emerge; and it was the financial strength on which the company's business was based. When the company was formed in 1928, Gresswell's main partner, Algernon Denham, was by then a director of the Halifax Building Society from which the mortgages had been supplied. Denham was also the manager of the local branch of the Union Bank, later to be merged with Barclays Bank. By the time he died in 1961, Denham had been president of the Halifax Building Society—the largest building society in Britain—for 16 years and a long-standing director on the board of Barclays Bank—the largest British bank. The success of the company over the last 50 years owes a great deal to its long standing connections with these two major financial institutions.

The expansion of the Bradford Property Trust into one of Britain's largest and most successful residential property traders is almost a mirror image of the decline of the private landlord. The Trust's property trading technique has been the basic method which countless landlords and speculative house dealers have employed to sell rented property from the 1920s to the present day. It was essentially this same method which was used by the flat break-up dealers in the 1960s and 1970s. Although the BPT later developed its extensive property portfolio largely in and around London, including the purchase of some 300 properties in the Regents Park and Primrose Hill area from the Liverpool and Victoria Friendly Society in the late 1970s, a large proportion of its early business was built up by purchasing residential estates from major industrial landlords. These estates, which were built to house the particular firms' workforce, could be bought cheaply on the promise that the eventual prices at which the houses were sold to the sitting tenants, many of whom remained in the original firms' employ, would not be excessive. A list of some of the company's major purchases and their original owners is shown in Fig. 4.1.

In fact, the first purchase made by the company in 1928 was of this type. The 137 houses on the West Hartlepool estate of Furness Withy & Co. Ltd cost just £98 each. Subsequent purchases have been equally propitious: Saltaire Village (964 houses) and the 616 houses from the LNER, both in 1933, for £100 and £205 per house respectively; 257 houses from Dorman Long & Co. Ltd in Stockton-on-Tees for £177 per house in 1944; Lever Brothers' Port Sunlight estate, bought for £389 per house in 1953; and ICI's Billingham Estate in 1967 at £663 per house. By 1983 the company owned some 7,500 units – just over 0.4 per cent of all the remaining tenanted property in England and Wales at this time - and was still actively buying property for trading stock. Pre-tax profits stood at £7.29 million (£4 million net) on a property portfolio held at a total book cost of only £16 million, but with a directors' valuation of some £65 million at current prices.

But before we leave this particular example, it should be pointed out that the tenants played only a passive role in these property sales. If the example of Fred Gresswell's initial incursion into the market is anything to go by, then 'consumer demand' figured very little in the execution of the transaction. What tenants were faced with was a straightforward switch in the terms and conditions on which their homes were being supplied. Most importantly, the tenants were only offered the choice of owner occupation once the landlord had decided to sell to them. The decision to sell was not related to any perceived requests from the tenants. What determined the decision was the perception of the profit to be made from buying housing at its investment value and selling it in relation to a vacant possession value, or more specifically, at a value which was carefully priced to cost little more in mortgage repayments than current rent levels. The whole exercise was predicated on the recognition by the landlord that in switching the occupiers from paying a rent to paying off a

Date of purchase	Location	Vendor	Number of units
Apl 1928	West Hartlepool	Furness Withy & Co Ltd	137 houses
Sep 1932	Stocksbridge, near Sheffield	Samuel Fox & Co Ltd	640 houses
Mar 1933	Nottingham, Leicester Loughborough and Manchester	LNER	616 houses
Oct 1933	Saltaire Village, Shipley	Salts (Saltaire) Ltd	964 houses
Feb 1934	Sheffield and Scunthorpe	Thomas Firth and John Brown Ltd	145 houses
Jun 1934	Letchworth Garden City	Letchworth Garden City Tenants Ltd	300 houses
Nov 1934	Horsehay	The Horsehay Co, Wellington	120 houses
Feb 1935	Bacup, Rochdale, Shawforth, Preston, Summerseat & Wheelton	Joshua Hoyle & Sons Ltd	450 houses
Mar 1935	Elland, Old Lindley & Stainland	R & J Holroyd Ltd	65 cottages
Sep 1935	Dursley	R A Lister & Co Ltd	76 houses
Dec 1935	Denholme	W H Foster Ltd	108 cottages

***Figure 4.1** Some of the major early purchases made by the Bradford Property Trust. Source: Brennan (1978)*

mortgage, the capital value of the property could be substantially increased and the difference appropriated.

Clearly, then, the sales were the product of an actively mediated switch in the conditions of supply. Until the landlord had decided to sell, the tenants simply had no choice in the matter. This is not to deny that the tenants exercised choice once the initial decision to offer the houses for sale had been made or that, in the final analysis, it was the income of tenants, via their ability to meet mortgage repayments, which made the sales effective. But the point is that the framework within which the tenants made their choices was formed by the constraints imposed by the conditions of supply, not demand. These were set by the landlord. Of course, landlords also faced constraints stemming from the wider economic and political conditions which were restructuring the social relations of the housing market at this time. But the crucial determinant under which housing was offered for sale stemmed not from the needs of the consumers (tenants) but from the opportunity for a profitable transaction for the landlord/trader. It is this shift in the terms of profitability which formed the rationale behind the tenure transfer process. Privately rented housing was increasingly *unprofitable* for the investor landlord, but increasingly *profitable* for trading landlords.

Perhaps the true nature of the relationship between the property traders and their market is summed up in the following quote from Brennan's book, which was written to celebrate the 50th Anniversary of the Bradford Property Trust:

> In its early years the company provided an essential middle ground between landlord and tenant, enabling landlords to shed the responsibilities of low yielding residential estates, *and then convincing tenants that the novel idea of buying their own homes was both possible and sensible.'* (Brennan, 1978, p. viii, our emphasis)

This certainly does not suggest any widespread clamour for home ownership on the part of the tenants. On the contrary, the company had to work hard *creating* the necessary conditions of supply under which effective demand would be generated. Moreover, the emergence of residential property trading represents a classic reaction by entrepreneurial capital to the opportunities for profit which continually open up in changing market situations. The potential for a new opportunity for profit (based on capital gains) which the evolution of the value gap in the residential property market of the 1920s created was one that Fred Gresswell and his colleagues were not alone in appreciating – or exploiting.

5 The preconditions for flat break-ups, 1945-65

Introduction

The 1920s and 1930s saw the development of a dual system of valuation for house property in Britain and the emergence of a 'value gap' between the tenanted investment value and the vacant possession value of houses sold for owner occupation. The existence of this gap underpinned the tenure transformation from renting to owning. But as we argued in Chapter 4, the existence of the value gap did not automatically lead to the sale of rented property into owner occupation. The development of such a market was contingent on landlords and property traders perceiving the profitable opportunities presented by the value gap, their ability to persuade sitting tenants of the advantage of purchase, and the extent to which mortgage finance was readily available and could be arranged for potential buyers. The sale of privately rented houses for owner occupation was a process which was actively mediated by landlords and sharp-eyed entrepreneurs who were quick to perceive the profitable potential of sales.

Nor did the tenure transfer process proceed evenly across all sectors of the rental market. On the contrary, the sale of rented property for owner occupation between the wars was limited almost exclusively to house property where a dual value system existed. Because there was no owner occupied market for flats, there was no dual value system and no value gap. Just as the sale of rented houses was contingent on the development of a market in houses built for sale, so there was no owner occupied market for rented flats until after the late 1950s when the construction of the first blocks of flats for sale began. Before that, the idea of owning a flat was virtually unheard of outside Scotland and Gray (1947) estimated that only about 5 per cent of all flats in Britain were owner occupied in 1947.

The purpose-built flat sector also differs from the rest of the rented sector by virtue of its ownership structure which, as we showed in Chapter 2, was dominated not by individual landlords owning one or two properties, but by a relatively small number of large residential investment companies who each owned hundreds or even thousands of flats and adopted a strictly commercial profit-maximizing approach to the management of their residential flat investments. The implications of this ownership structure for the development of the break-up market were profound. Unlike the small housing landlords, many of the large landlords who dominated the purpose-built flat sector were quoted on the Stock Exchange and had to generate dividend income. They were therefore particularly sensitive to changes in the conditions of profitability and were constantly forced to evaluate the yields on residential property with those obtainable in other sectors of the property market. As we show in this chapter, the relative decline in the profitability of the residental flat market as a long-term investment initially led to the wholesale disposal of blocks by companies who used the proceeds to invest in other, more profitable sectors. Only later, when the building of flats for sale opened up the possibility of sales for owner occupation, did the sale of long leases commence.

Flats for sale: the development of a new form of housing tenure

The immediate post-1945 period saw little change in the size of the purpose-built flat sector. The interwar building boom had come to an abrupt end in 1939 and, despite the low cost of finance after the war, the strict building controls and rent restrictions were enough to deter the corporate investor. The main problem facing the sector was rising costs. These were particularly important for the the owners of blocks of flats because of the services which had to be provided for over and above the normal upkeep of the properties. Whereas for the house landlord, these costs were mainly related to maintenance, rates and management, block owners had to provide a much more elaborate range of services including such things as communal central heating, hot water, porterage and lifts. Postwar inflation seriously affected profitability in the sector because, unlike basic repairs, such costs were difficult to defer and rents for the smaller,cheaper properties remained fixed at 1939 levels until the advent of the 1954 Housing and Repair Act.

This Act permitted rents to rise to allow for increases in the cost of providing services and some large landlords managed to obtain substantial rent increases on their purpose-built flats. The Act favoured large corporate landlords because it was easier for such landlords to provide the information on costs and services required for rent increases to be permitted. Smaller, less professional landlords with less formal management practices may have found the bureaucratic safeguards a deterrent to rent increases. Nevertheless Allsop and Co.'s central London rental index (Figure 5.1) shows that the impact of the Act was limited even in central London where large landlords dominated the market. Rent increases were higher for uncontrolled property but they remained below the general rate of inflation regardless of whether or not rents were controlled.

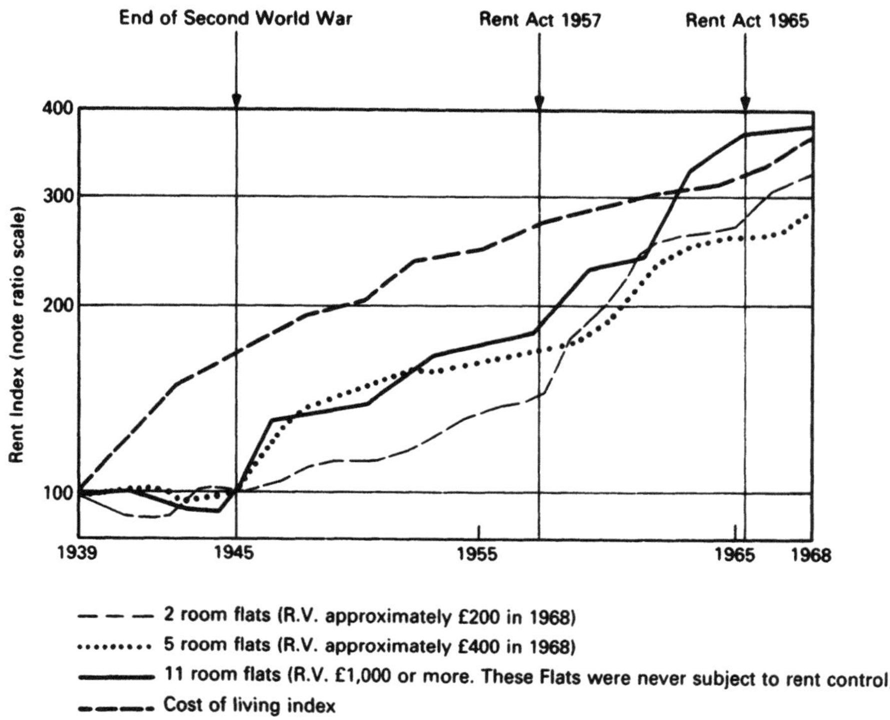

***Figure 5.1** Allsop & Co.'s Central London Rent Index 1939-1967*
Source: Allsop & Co. (1967)

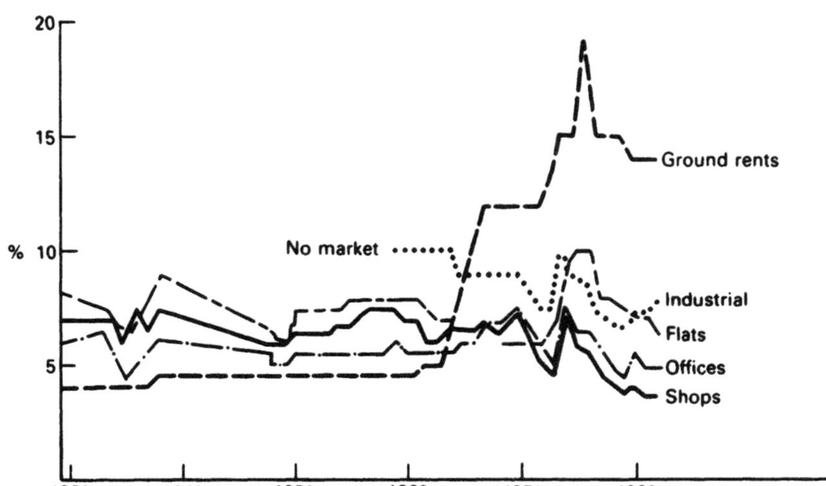

***Figure 5.2** Investment yields on real estate 1929-82*
Source: Allsop & Co. (1983)

In contrast, the 1957 Rent Act had a marked impact on rents, particularly for the lower-value flats it decontrolled. The effect in this part of the market was to bring rent increases much more in line with those prevailing in the rest of the sector (which had never been subject to controls). The case of London County Freehold, one of the largest owners of flats, is illustrative. Of their 8,500 flats, only 25 per cent were uncontrolled before 1957. After the Act, 70 per cent became immediately decontrolled and rents rose by 30 – 40 per cent, and rents in the controlled tenancies rose by 20 per cent. A year later the company reported that only 4 of their 2,000+ controlled tenancies had yet to accept a higher rent and only 4 per cent of their decontrolled flats had not received rent increases. In general, Figure 5.1 shows that while it took 15 years for rents to double after 1945, it took only another 5 years for rents to reach three times their 1945 level. The 1957 Act appears to have brought undeniable benefits to the rental income of companies in the central London rental market, and by the early 1960s rent levels of the highest value flats had outstripped the rate of inflation and restored profitability to its earlier levels.

There was a small but significant return to the building of flats to let in the middle to high rent sector by the early 1960s. Yields were favourable and the 1961 Housing Act had included measures which offered incentives for the building of flats to rent. With rising demand and little threat of rent control,several major companies were tempted back into the market at this time. Property Holding and Investment Trust began a small luxury flat development programme in central London in the early 1960s, including Kingston House South in the prestige Knightsbridge area. This block contained 47 flats, a quarter of which were let before completion and rents ranged from £1,300 to £1,800 per annum putting them well into the luxury bracket. In the more modest reaches of the market, Dorrington Investments, backed by Eagle Star Insurance, completed several blocks in the early 1960s. Bernard Sunley Investment Trust also began a substantial flat-building programme after the 1961 Act and by 1969, when they sold out to Freshwater, they owned 600 flats, the great majority of which were built after 1961. Freshwater was also actively developing flats in several suburban locations by 1962. One of the largest developments at this time was the Water Gardens complex, a 3 acre redevelopment in Sussex Gardens near Marble Arch. This ambitious 250 flat project, funded by the Church Commissioners and London Merchant Securities began letting in mid 1965.

Developments such as these were still profitable as sources of investment income in the early 1960s. But although returns on flat investments were favourable—and they appear to have been maintained at or about the 8 per cent level throughout the 1950s (Figure 5.2) – the main problem facing developers was finance. Not only was money becoming more expensive by the late 1950s, but finance for residential development had become more costly and difficult to obtain due to competition for funds from the booming commercial and industrial sectors. Much of the finance for both property development and investment was provided by large institutional investors who tended to eschew lending on residential building for rent or required an equity share in the development. The difficulty in obtaining long-term funding for new rental building led to the increasing attraction of building flats for sale and a growing number of new flat developments being sold on long leases.

Flat sale schemes had the advantage of absolving the developer from the problem of management and maintenance. They also only required short-term finance to cover the construction and sales period. Developers could quickly recover their capital and embark on new schemes. Rising land costs also contributed to the pressure to sell rather than rent new flats as the rental levels needed to make the development profitable were outpacing income levels. Most importantly of all, the value of a block to a developer where the flats would be sold to individual long leaseholders was significantly greater than the value of the block for rental investment. As Stacey (1959) commented at the time: 'For various reasons it seems possible today to realise a greater capital sum by the sale of individual leases to tenants than if the property is sold as a whole to an investor.' This is exactly the situation which house builders realized after 1920. Property capitalized in owner occupation (whether it be freehold or long leasehold) has a higher capital value than when it is capitalized as a rented investment. It was but a short step from the realization that development of new blocks of flats for sale was more profitable than for rent to the realization that existing blocks could also be sold for individual owner occupation. Stacey (1959) pointed out that the same logic applied both to new buildings and 'existing buildings where the age is not too great'. By the late 1950s it was coming to be recognized that the sale of long leaseholds in blocks of rented flats offered a way of exploiting the value gap. As Stacey (1959, p.5) suggested

> In a modern existing building partly fettered by controlled tenancies, the vendor can realise the maximum capital value of those flats of which he is able to obtain possession, and can bide his time on those where possession is difficult; thus, where capital is urgently needed (the owner) can obviate the necessity of taking a low price on account of certain restricted tenancies.

Stacey was also in no doubt where this advantage stemmed from.

> It must be remembered that the present system of taxation deals very much more lightly with one who invests his capital in a property, whether mortgaged or not, in which he lives than one who invests his capital relying on the income by way of interest to pay a rental'. (1959, p.6)

As with house property, a proportion of this tax advantage can be appropriated by developers and traders if the flat is sold to an owner occupier at value higher than its pure investment value.The financial logic of Stacey's argument was such that what he saw as a prudent long term course of action for landlords with controlled tenancies was to become within 10 years the basis of one of the more spectacular examples of short-term speculative activity. The emergence of the flat break-up market now only awaited time and finance.

Priming the pump: the provision of mortgage finance

There was one major barrier to the development of a flat sales market at the time and that was the non-availability of mortgage finance. There were simply very few sources of mortgage finance for individual flat ownership. Building societies did not lend on leasehold flats, partly because it was not a recognized market and partly because the traditional 7, 9 and 21 year lease lengths for flats were unmortgageable entities. No mortgagee would lend on the purchase of such a lease when standard repayment periods were commonly 20-25 years. Where mortgages were obtained for flat sale developments, they largely came from life insurance companies or private trusts at above average interest rates and the advances rarely exceeded two thirds of the flat's value. This presented a major deterrent to flat purchases,a situation directly analogous to the position in the 1920s and 1930s where, as we argued in Chapter 3, high entry costs were one of the principal constraints which had to be removed before widespread house ownership could develop.

The similarities do not end there. Commenting on "the enormous possibilities for expansion of life (insurance) business for the first company prepared to give mortgages on flats in a big way', Stacey pointed out that the risks could be greatly reduced as

> developers would be only too pleased to guarantee a certain percentage of the aggregrate sum made available by a mortgage company,so that in the event of one or perhaps two isolated cases of mortgagors failing, and the proceeds of the sale being insufficient to meet the debt to the mortgagee, he would not suffer any loss. I feel strongly that this should so increase the security,as to make the mortgage business sufficiently attractive for the necessary funds to become available'. (Stacey, 1959, p.9)

This was precisely the solution to the deposit problem that was successfully adopted in 'builders' pool' arrangements in the interwar years. Links with insurance companies were also important as endowment mortgages could be arranged by the developer for any prospective purchaser. The problem, therefore, was not one of the absence of consumer demand,but the absence of a mechanism to make the demand for ownership effective. While the sale of new flats was difficult given these circumstances, the sale of existing flats was even more problematic. Nevertheless, by the early 1960s the precedent for sales in new developments had been set, and the institutional and financial structures necessary for leasehold flats to become an accepted form of lending were slowly being developed.

A new lease of life

A further problem inhibiting flat sales was the complex issue of leases, lease lengths, premiums and ground rents. Although there were established procedures for leaseholds in the case of house property, the sale of leases in flat developments posed particular difficulties. The first sticking point related to the service and repair costs any would-be flat owner would have to pay, given that they would now be liable for upkeep of the communally owned fabric of the block. The problem, of course, was that residents had been used to not having to think about repairs and services.They were something the landlord took responsibility for. Indeed, during the 1930s one of the major advertising points of flat developments was that rents were inclusive of all major service and maintenance costs, partly as a result of competition amongst developers to maintain demand. Once tenants paid their rent the only other costs they were liable for were those of internal decoration and the gas and electricity directly consumed. Rates,services, maintenance and staffing costs were all met from the rental payments. When a lease was granted, often for up to 21 years, the tenant's sole responsibility in the agreement was the payment of rent for the period of the lease.These inclusive rents were subsequently to cause landlords major difficulties in the inflationary period after the Second World War.

There was usually one condition attached to these leases, however, and that was that increases in rates and water rates could be passed on. As service costs rose, landlords increasingly included clauses in new leases to make tenants liable for such increases. While tenants appear to have been unwilling to accept these sorts of changes at first, the impossibility of obtaining accommodation without such terms soon broke down consumer resistance. By the late 1950s new leases were regularly being granted which made the rent exclusive of both general and water rates and added charges for services, maintenance and management. Only long-term repairs remained the landlords' responsibility and a charge against rental income. In this way, the effect of rent controls on the tenancies could be minimized and profitability maintained. This trend helps to account for the rise in controlled rents in the period before the 1957 Rent Act (Figure 5.1) as well as the maintenance of yields at around the 8 per cent level throughout the 1950s (Figure 5.2). There was also a tendency for lease lengths to be reduced, first to 5 years; while after the 1957 Act, the 3 year lease became more widespread. This ensured more rapid rent reviews and increased potential rental income and yields.

This tendency to make rental leases exclusive of current costs had considerable significance for 'flat sale' developments. With rental leases increasingly stipulating that current costs had to be borne by the tenant,the net difference in terms of liabilities to the occupier of purchasing the lease rather than taking out a rented tenancy had become reduced to the cost of long-term major repairs. On a new development these were not considered to be too much of a deterrent, at least in the short term. Thus, changes in rental lease terms reduced the net differences between the costs of owning a leasehold flat and renting it. As Stacey (1959, p.3) noted: 'This is the first step towards getting flat dwellers used to the idea of buying a flat where they will be completely responsible for a share of all "outgoings"'.

The second feature of leasehold ownership which needed to be established before flat sales could become acceptable was the relationship between the premium and the ground rent. Here we can trace a consistent trend from the traditional short-term lease granted purely for rent and involving no premium, to a 'half way' stage where longer-term leases were granted in return for a lower rental and payment of a premium equivalent to 2 or 3 years' purchase of the gross rent, and the common situation today where a long-term lease is purchased for a large premium and the rental element has been reduced to a residual element in the form of a nominal ground rent of perhaps £100 per annum. There was no clear-cut progression between these different types of lease. Instead, there was a gradual movement towards the latter as market conditions changed and premium payments became more common. The final form that leasehold ownership has taken is partly a result of the need for mortgage institutions to lend only where lease lengths exceed 40-50 years. The sale of long leases also maximizes the premium and hence the capital gains from break-ups. It represents the triumph of capital gains over long term investment income.

Initially it was quite possible to find variations of the rent-premium relationship in the same block. Stacey quotes the example of two flats the basic rent (i.e exclusive of rates and costs) of which was £450 per annum each. In one, the rental was set at a nominal £15 per annum in return for a 'substantial premium', while the other was let at a reduced rent of £400 per annum and a premium of £1,000. In each case the terms were set to suit the particular circumstances of the occupiers. Peachey Properties were certainly operating this type of flexible approach to leases in their blocks by the late 1950s. They granted long leases at full market rents and on full repair and insurance terms in vacated and thus decontrolled flats. While they did not ask for a premium for these leases, due to the tax liability that would have resulted, the advertising point was that while the tenant was committed to a long-term market rent, he or she could sell the lease for a premium payment to the next occupant. The rent was fixed for the term of the lease and, given inflation, could be expected to fall gradually in real terms while premium payments would increase.

Between the mid 1950s and the mid 1960s the decision whether to build for rental or sale appears to have been a rather marginal one. If sales were slow then units could be offered for rent, but in some developments intended for rental, if potential occupiers wished to purchase a long lease rather than rent, the flats were sold. In 1965, for example, the Church Commissioners were offering a variety of lease types in their prestige Water Gardens project. Short leases (7 years) could be had for £525 per annum for a three room flat rising to £1,750 per annum for four rooms. Alternatively, longer-term leases were being sold for premiums of £22,000 to £55,000 and annual ground rents of £250 to £300 per annum. Service charges for both types of lease were set at £275 to £385 per annum.

By the early to mid 1960s sales were becoming increasingly common in the higher reaches of the market where demand was limited to the more wealthy group of higher-rate taxpayers. For high-income households the benefit of purchase on a mortgage with tax relief, especially where surtax was paid, was becoming more apparent in the face of escalating rents. In 1960 alone, rents rose between 15-20 per cent and it was becoming 'quite clear that there are now as many applicants willing to buy as there are willing to rent' (*Investors Chronicle,* 24 February 1961). This was particularly true in high-rent developments in central London where increasing land costs were pushing up market rents in new developments. The *Investors Chronicle* noted that 'The sale of flats has now become established and is usually on the basis of the tenant being responsible for a share of all outgoings as well as a ground rent'. The buyers of long leases were still referred to as tenants rather than owners at this time, and long leaseholders are still viewed as tenants under English property law. The sale of flats was viewed by developers and purchasers alike as a simple expedient and not as part of the ideological baggage of owner occupation. Developers saw sales as an ideal way of ensuring a quick return on capital during a period of inflation and expensive finance, and for buyers sales offered tax savings and protection from rent increases.

It is only during the past few years, as long leaseholds have come to be seen by buyers as synonymous with outright owner occupation (which they are not), that the problems of leasehold ownership have been fully appreciated by buyers. The problems are examined in detail in Chapters 9 and 10. It should just be noted here that English real property law distinguishes between freehold and leasehold tenure. Freehold ownership, which is outright ownership in perpetuity, is contingent on ownership of the ground on which the property stands. It is possible for a freeholder or ground landlord to lease property for a period of years (up to 999 years or even longer) in return for an annual ground rent and a premium payment. During the period of the lease, the leaseholder has the exclusive use of the property and can sell the lease to a third party, but at the expiry of the lease the property reverts to the freeholder without compensation. Although most house property is sold freehold today, and the 1967 Leasehold Reform Act permitted the long leaseholders of house property to purchase the freehold of their houses in certain circumstances, this was not extended to flats and long leaseholders have come to realize that they are no more than long term tenants. This has generated considerable pressure for leasehold enfranchisement to be extended to flats.

Inflation, taxation and politics: the recipe for disinvestment

While the sale of newly built flats was undoubtedly profitable wherever potential occupiers could be induced to purchase and where mortgage finance was forthcoming, existing flat investments were also still generally profitable. The 1957 Rent Act had helped increase yields in the flat market and well-managed companies had few problems with decontrolled rents. While the compactness and relative ease of management of blocks of flats compared to houses helped to maintain profitability, they also had the advantage of desirable locations and a middle-class and affluent tenantry who were reliable rent payers and could meet the higher rentals being sought. The profitability of such investments is reflected by the fact that a number of major landlords were actively expanding their residential portfolios by selective purchases during the late 1950s and early 1960s. London City and Westcliffe, London County Freehold and Alliance Property Holdings were acquiring property at this time, as were the Freshwater and Berger groups.

For most of the established residential companies, many of which had held property acquired before the Second World War, yields on historic costs were giving a more than adequate return. But there was a growing tendency towards disinvestment from flat properties. Although they were not unprofitable in themselves, they were becoming *relatively unprofitable* when the yields which were obtainable in the growing commercial and industrial property sectors were taken into account. This situation was a reflection of both inflation and the upward pressure on interest rates which had characterized the postwar period and which led to the breakdown of established patterns of investment yields.

After the financial crisis of 1949 following the cheap money policy of the postwar Labour Government, the previously low yield on government bonds began to rise, taking other investment yields with it. Until the war, investment yields had maintained a fairly regular relationship to each other. As Figure 5.3 shows,the yield on flats was usually some 3-4 per cent above the yield on consols and 2-3 per cent above that on ordinary shares. This reflected both the higher costs involved in residential property investment and the risks associated with it. After the war, this established relationship began to change as interest rates and the yield on fixed interest bearing assets started to rise. Throughout the 1950s the yield gap between government stock, shares and property investment was steadily narrowed and by the mid 1960s a 'reverse yield gap' opened as yields on fixed interest stock outstripped those on both equities and property. This reverse yield gap widened, and by the early 1980s had become an established feature of the investment market, in complete reversal to the situation in the pre-war period.

The reverse yield phenomenon is, of course, a direct product of inflation. In an inflationary period investors in fixed interest bonds such as

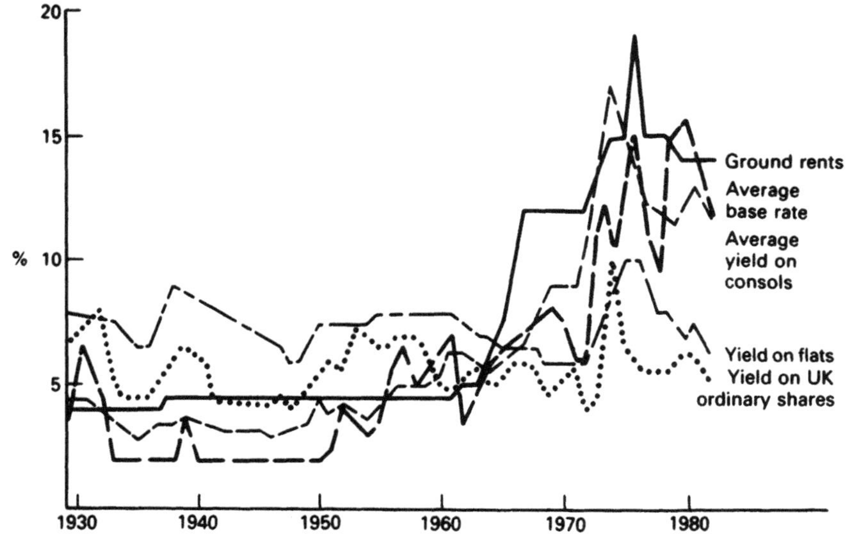

***Figure 5.3** Trends in investment yields 1929-83*

Source: Allsop & Co. (1983)

government stock require high yields to compensate for the decline in the money value of their investments. Property, on the other hand, offers an inflation hedge because its capital value can be expected to rise as rents rise with inflation. The owners of such investments are therefore much more willing to accept lower yields in return for future capital gains. Inflation, therefore, has the effect of focusing attention on capital values. Those investments which promise the greatest asset appreciation will be favoured because of the protection they offer against the decline of the value of money. The net result is that capital appreciation becomes the major determinant of long-term profitability. This has the effect of depressing yields as speculation on the future values of investments resulting from inflation in rent forces up the prices paid for investments. In these circumstances successful property companies have to shift their investment portfolio to take account of inflation on asset values and hence on long-term profitability. Those sectors which show the greatest asset appreciation are favoured over those sectors where asset appreciation is less certain.

This was the situation facing the property market by the late 1950s just at the time when Britain was experiencing its first major postwar commercial property boom. A number of factors had combined to produce this boom. Little commercial development had taken place since the 1930s, the postwar building controls and regulations were only removed in the early 1950s, and there was a major expansion of office employment and an associated demand for office space during the late 1950s. Finally, a major period of city centre redevelopment was taking place, partly as a result of wartime damage and partly of a tendency towards comprehensive town planning schemes in which property developers played a prominent role (Marriot, 1967; Barras, 1978).

The property development boom of 1957-65 saw the profitability of commercial development outpace the returns on residential investment as capital appreciation became the order of the day. The major institutional investors, such as life assurance and pension funds, had also begun to move into the property sector by the early 1960s, initially by way of equity holdings in property companies (Boddy, 1980). The channelling of investment funds into property development became an established feature of the property scene at this time and they helped to increase values and depress yields further. This in turn intensified the speculative pressure on capital values as the inverse yield gap widened.

As a result of the increased attraction of the commercial and industrial property sectors, for both development profits and their long-term investment potential, many corporate residential landlords began to switch their portfolios into these sectors. This was accomplished in two ways. Companies either expanded their non-residential holdings while retaining the residential element as a source of secure investment income, or they actively began to dispose of their blocks of flats and houses on a wholesale basis, reinvesting the proceeds in commercial property. While house properties found ready buyers in the specialist house trading market, blocks of flats were often sold as investment properties to landlords who were still attracted to the flat sector as a source of long-term investment income.

A number of the major property companies that emerged during the commercial development boom of the late 1950s were originally residential investment companies whose origins lay in the flat development boom of the mid 1930s and even earlier. Among those making the move into the commercial field during this period was the Beaumont Property Trust, which emerged from the war as owner of 2,500 interwar flats in London as well as a small number of shops attached to residential developments. Beaumont, controlled by Sir Cyril Black, a Conservative MP, building society chairman and public morality campaigner, was one of the first residential companies to move into commercial property. By 1959 Beaumont had sold over £1 million worth of blocks of flats and reinvested the proceeds in commercial and shop property. By 1963 residential properties contributed only 35 per cent of total company income and the blocks which were retained were the highest-value parts of the original portfio. By 1970 this proportion had been reduced to 10 per cent and by 1972 to less than 5 per cent.

London County Freehold's expansion into the commercial sector began even earlier. The company was almost entirely a residential landlord before the war but by 1956, 20 per cent of its portfolio was in commercial investments. But unlike Beaumont's, the remaining residential portfolio was not disposed of and LCF's 8,500 flats remained a mainstay of the company's investment income during the diversification process. Other major residential landlords who had begun to reduce their dependence on residential investments by the early 1960s included Peachey Properties, Property Holding and Investment Trust, Regional Properties and Artisan and General Properties (later Artagen Ltd). Artisan, which dated back to 1867, was one of the major remaining working-class estate developers in London. It owned 9,200 flats and houses at its 1930s peak and still owned over 8,000 when diversification began in the 1950s.

The impact of rent control and Corporation Tax

By the early 1960s diversification and disinvestment from flat blocks was growing as they became less profitable relative to the emerging commercial and industrial sectors where rents and hence capital values were increasingly rapidly. But at the time the economic pressures for disinvestment were growing, the political environment suddenly changed. In 1964 a new Labour Government was returned to office. In the wake of the Rachman scandal and the Milner Holland report on London's rented sector, the free market philosophy of the 1957 Rent Act was replaced by the introduction of rent controls once again: this time by Fair Rents.

The 1965 Rent Act is generally considered by landlords and their political allies to have been the principal cause of the general withdrawal of property companies from their remaining residential investments in the years after 1965. But while the Act undoubtedly added a further psychological impetus to landlord disinvestment from the rental market, it is far from clear to what extent the Act actually affected the profitability of rental investments by restricting rent increases. On the one hand the Act reimposed regulation on much of the flat property in central London and at least one estimate suggested that by 1968 rents for registered flats were 8-10 per cent below their open market level as a result of registration (Allsop and Co., 1968). But comments on the workings of the Act were by no means wholly unfavourable and the Investors Chronicle observed that 'Such evidence as there is to date suggests that rent officers and rent assessment committees are assessing rents on a basis which really is fair to the reasonable landlord as well as to the tenant' (25 March, 1966, p.xviii). And in their 1968 Annual Report, the directors of London County Freehold stated: "We are not dissatisfied with the levels of rents which have been fixed.' Other companies also reported their satisfaction with the rents being fixed, including New London Properties (Company Report, 1966) and House Property Corporation (Company Report, 1966).

Some, however, were not so impressed by the operation of the Fair Rent system. London City and Westcliffe thought that while rents set were fair at present, the rate of increase was likely to slow down as a result of the Act. And Regional Properties, the bulk of whose residential portfolio came under the Rent Act's provisions, suggested in 1967 that rent restrictions on residential property made further investment unattractive (*Investors Chronicle,* August 25 1967). Trafalgar House also concluded that while the Fair Rent system 'may appear to offer an adequate return on the historic capital cost, (it) hardly encourages us to persist in the policy of modernisation and will certainly not encourage others to provide accommodation for rent' (Company Report, 1966).

A very different view of the 1965 Rent Act and the rent regulation system was taken by William Stern, then at Freshwater. In an article commenting on criticism of the Act, he wrote:

> The long term investment value of residential properties has become strengthened as a result of the Act, first because of the likely end to all rigid control in the foreseeable future and secondly on account of the right of both landlord and tenant to seek a new determination of the fair rent every three years.... This three yearly rent review provides the best possible protection against the eroding effects of future inflation and makes good quality residential investments more worthwhile than commercial or shop lettings providing for rent reviews at 14 or 21 year intervals only.' (*Investors Chronicle,* 25 March 1966, p.lxiii)

Although inflation at the time was only 5 or 6 per cent, somewhat different from that experienced since, he went on to conclude that "the long term effects will, on the whole, benefit rather than harm landlords as a class'. Cynics may question the validity of his remarks in the light of Stern's spectacular crash in 1974 (an event probably due more to his highly personal style of business than any lack of acumen on his part), but his arguments represent the only attempt by a major landlord to analyse the housing market at that time in order to suggest practical policy measures aimed at stimulating continued investment in the sector. But most of his contemporaries did not share Stern's enthusiasm for the 1965 Rent Act and were, at best, content to maintain returns on their existing investments in the short term while looking to move out of the residential field in the long term. What is clear is that while the operation of the Act may not have been inimical to the interests of the 'reasonable' investment landlord, it provided an added psychological boost to the growing pressures for disinvestment which had been building up well before. There are parallels with the situation surrounding the introduction of the original rent-controlling legislation in 1915. As we showed in Chapter 3, rising inflation is the investment landlord's worst enemy. Rent regulation merely reinforced the perception that residential investment, even in flats, had become unsustainable in the prevailing economic conditions.

While landlord's explanations for the decline of the privately rented sector focus almost exclusively on the negative impact of rent controls, another piece of legislation introduced by the new Labour administration was to have a far more immediate and far-reaching impact on the property investment world. The Finance Act of 1965 introduced a new system of company taxation which was designed to shift the burden of taxation to distributed profits to encourage companies to retain a higher proportion of profits for reinvestment. The system was aimed at manufacturing industry but its ramifications for the property sector were dramatic and largely unforeseen.

The typical property company traditionally distributed the whole of its net rental income as dividend, and property companies had provided an essentially tax neutral vehicle by which private or institutional investors could retain interests in property while employing professional management. Before the introduction of Corporation Tax in the 1965 Budget, property companies were liable to income tax (at 7s 9d in the pound in 1964) and a 15 per cent tax on their gross profits resulting in a total taxation rate of 53.7 per cent. Shareholders were not liable for further taxation on the distributed earnings. Under the Corporation Tax system, these two taxes were replaced by a single tax initially set at 42.5 per cent and shareholders were made liable to separate income tax (including any surtax liability) on the distributed profits. In addition, Capital Gains Tax was charged at 42.5 per cent on the capital appreciation of any asset realized by sale over and above its value on the day the tax was introduced, or over the purchase cost of assets aquired after this date.

The most important of these two taxes on the property investment sector was Corporation Tax. For the average manufacturing company, new development was often funded internally through profits. But for a property investment company, nearly all finance was raised externally through mortgages and loans and the dividend was derived from the rental income which the properties generated. As one commentator remarked at the time: 'Alongside Corporation Tax, the other possible actions of the government affecting property companies pale into insignificance' (Svensson, 1965, p.50). Rent regulation was included in the list of comparisons. Corporation Tax had a number of crucial ramifications on property investment. First,it restricted the amount available for distributed earnings which had to be increased if net dividend payments were to be maintained. For the average property company Corporation Tax required an increase of some 24 per cent in pre-tax dividend in order to maintain current net dividend levels (Galvin, 1966). In some instances, the increased taxation left dividends uncovered by rent incomes. The short-term impact was therefore to stimulate the rationalization of investment portfolios, partly in an effort to maximize the higher-yielding elements and also to generate income through disposals of property in order to meet immediate needs for increased revenue.

The entry into the market for property by pension funds and other institutional investors at this time owed a great deal to the new tax situation. Involvement in the property sector through the acquisition of property directly rather than through property company shares was now an advantage for tax-exempt funds. While companies were only too pleased to maximize capital potential via such arrangements as 'sale and leaseback', the institutions were only too pleased to be able to oblige by purchasing the property on offer. Property investments of this sort were attractive to the institutions as long-term inflation hedges because capital values could be expected to be maintained despite inflation. In the longer term this move also favoured residential disinvestment because the greatest capital growth now accrued to the properties which the institutions found most rewarding. Residential investments were largely eschewed by the institutions because of their comparative lack of growth prospects and their uncertain political record. While asset values for prime commercial property accelerated as institutional buyers began to move in with their vast financial resources (Coakely and Harris, 1983), residential investment slipped even further back in relative attractiveness.

The whole process was given a shot in the arm by the 'Brown Ban' on new office development in London. In the years following 1964 demand for office space rose dramatically as employment in the office sector expanded (Barras, 1978). With restricted supply, office rents multiplied, compounding the inflationary pressures and the attraction of commercial over residential investments. The rise in yields on offices during the 1960s (see Figure 5.2) was not a function of falling capital values (the opposite was occurring) but of rising rents. The first major consequence of Corporation Tax was thus to increase the pressure to disinvest from those areas, particularly residential, which seemed to have the lowest prospects for future growth.

The second major consequence of Corporation Tax was that the 'double taxation' of property investments penalized the holding of property in corporate form. The effect was to depress property company share prices to levels which showed considerable discount on the underlying asset values. Because of higher tax liabilities a higher value of property was needed to produce the same level of net income than before the advent of Corporation Tax. This meant that property assets could be acquired cheaply by takeover or merger. The rate of takeover activity subsequently increased as companies attempted to exploit the weaknesses which the new tax revealed in some of their contemporaries. Takeovers enabled investment portfolios to be accquired at a much lower cost than would be the case if the properties were purchased on the open market. Alternatively, it allowed the successful bidder the chance to sell off unwanted or cheaply acquired assets at a good profit. This process of 'asset stripping' was to become a major aspect of residential property company takeovers by the early 1970s. Under capitalized companies could be bought cheaply and their assets realized piecemeal at a considerable profit. It became cheaper to buy property companies than to buy property. The effect of the new tax legislation was therefore to help widen the gap between the value of property investment companies and the value of the properties they owned. This created a classic speculators' market. Flat break-up fits squarely into this trend. Both asset stripping and break-up are exercises in recapitalization in the sense that companies and blocks of flats offer under-valued assets which are open to profitable exploitation—or getting markets to work more 'efficiently', as such exploitation is often described today.

The third consequence of the new tax was to encourage companies to increase their borrowing to asset (or 'gearing') ratios. Under the new system, loan stock interest was allowable as a deduction against Corporation Tax and income which was used to service interest payments on loans and debentures was less highly taxed. Not only did this favour high gearing (which was also encouraged by the general inflationary situation), but it additionally led to a spate of company reconstructions. By reconstituting a company's equity structure, principally by substituting unsecured loan stock for existing preference stock, Corporation Tax liability could be considerably reduced. A number of companies embarked on this process, usually by creating a holding company which acquired the existing stock, and then issuing shares in the newly reconstituted company. One of the earliest was Trafalgar House (February 1966), and others included Beaumont Property Trust (1967), London and European (1969), Regis Property (1966), Bampton Holdings (1966) and Central and District (1966), the latter through a partial reconstruction. The reconstruction of a company's capital in this way enabled a highly geared holding company to be imposed on the existing company structure. It also allowed investment property to be transferred into dealing stock for the internalization of dealing income (and hence lower taxation).

The transfer of investment property into dealing stock in this way was perhaps the most important direct repercussion of Corporation Tax where the development of the flat break-up market was concerned. It is also related to the fourth major impact of the changes stemming from the 1965 Finance Act. As Corporation Tax fell solely on distributed income it encouraged retention of earnings rather than their distribution. For property companies, the effect was to favour property trading rather than investment. As Nigel Broackes of Trafalgar House stated, Corporation Tax would: 'undoubtedly lead those companies with adequate management to explore the dealing and development for sale fields more thoroughly than hitherto' (Broackes, 1966, pp.x—xi). The optimum strategy for property companies under these conditions was be to be highly geared, using rents on investment property to service loan stock, to employ their equity capital to fund property dealing and then to retain the dealing profits for further property purchases for trading. Corporation Tax therefore broke down the long-standing differences between investment and trading companies. This gave a major impetus to the break-up process and led to the rise of the specialist flat-dealing company over the next few years.

Finally, the continued impact of inflation also contributed to the pressure building up on the residential investment sector. There was general reluctance on the part of institutions to lend long-term finance at fixed interest rates, which had been the main form of long-term funding for corporate landlords in the past. Finance became increasingly expensive and short-term as interest rates rose (mortgage interest rates rose from 7 per cent in 1967 to 9 per cent by 1969). The credit squeeze also reduced financial availability, and in 1966 the government instructed banks and insurance companies to refrain from lending to the property development sector. As a result, companies turned to the sale of lower-yielding residential properties in order to raise the necessary finance for expansion into commercial property.

These properties were typically sold on yields of 6-8 per cent compared to the 3 per cent yields on shops and offices. But they had lower growth potential and had probably shown less appreciation since the imposition of Capital Gains Tax. And finance raised on these terms was preferable to borrowing mortgage money at 9 per cent plus. In some cases it was even possible to sell a lower-yielding property and retain the existing fixed interest rate mortgage, financed in an earlier period of lower interest rates, to purchase a new and higher-yielding property. The high cost of finance also provided another incentive for takeovers and mergers. Properties acquired cheaply in this way could then be sold off to raise cash for expansion. Any preferential lines of credit the acquired company had with banks and other established funds could also be taken over. Companies with large residential portfolios, whose assets were capitalized in relation to their prevailing level of rental income rather than the break-up value of the flats, became prime targets. British Land was an example of a particularly successful company which funded the expansion of its commercial portfolio by selling its own residential investments and buying undervalued companies in order to asset-strip their residential properties (see Table 5.1).

The combined effect of the 1965 Finance Act and the acceleration of inflation after the mid 1960s therefore led to a fundamental restructuring of the corporate property sector. Quite apart from the effects of the Rent Act, these changes had a direct impact on the viability of residential property investment for corporate landlords. They prompted the move towards widespread disinvestment of the remaining residential investment portfolios and created the structure of opportunities favourable to the emergence of residential property trading, asset stripping and flat break-up. At the same time, the small but developing flat sale sector had created precedents, particularly at the top end of the market, for sales of long leases in new flats. The removal of Schedule A taxation in 1963 and the exemption of domestic property from Capital Gains Tax after 1965 only added to the attractions of flat purchase by higher-rate taxpayers. Coupled with the continuing demand for accommodation in central London and steadily rising incomes, the situation was ripe for exploitation. By the mid 1960s most of the conditions necessary for break-up were present. How the break-up market evolved, and the manner in which it was stimulated and developed after 1965, is considered in the following chapter.

Table 5.1 *British Land Company Limited: percentage of property by value per sector, 1965–78*

	1965	*1966*	*1967*	*1968*	*1969*	*1970*	*1971*	*1972*	*1973*	*1974*	*1975*	*1976*	*1977*	*1978*
Commercial	38	45	46	49	48	53	26	19	17	20	20	19	21	20
Offices	20	21	22	20	20	17	59	74	77	74	74	75	73	74
Residential	30	18	18	17	16	21	11	4	1	1	1	1	1	-
Industrial	10	13	12	12	14	9	4	3	5	5	5	5	5	6
Ground rents	2	3	2	2	2	-	-	-	-	-	-	-	-	-
Capital (£m)	14.5	15.3	16.3	16.2	18.3	32.9	85.9	121.9	207.2	274.6				

1966: Sold 2,200 Flats to Freshwater, £1.925m
1970: Bought Regis and Haleybridge Investment
1971: Sold 1,600 Flats, £5m
1976: Sold Fitzhardinge Hse, 65 Flats, £1.85m

6 The development of the flat break-up market after 1965

Introduction

Corporate restructuring and disinvestment

By 1965 the conditions were in place for the break-up and sale of blocks of flats to begin. The building of flats for rent had been replaced by building flats for sale, the necessary mortgage finance for purchasers was becoming more readily available, the commercial property sector was booming and changes in economic and financial conditions, particularly those brought about by the 1965 Finance Act, had made the holding of residential investment property increasingly unprofitable. It was also realized that the value of residential property as a long-term investment was lower than its potential value for owner occupation. The situation that traditional residential landlords faced at this time was summed up by the 1966 Annual Report from Trafalgar House Investments:

> We are considering the long-term future of our residential property investments. Private tenants of rented accommodation are now the only class of the community to receive no taxation benefits whatsoever in respect of housing: rent has to be paid out of taxed income but is taxable in the hands of a private landlord.Consequently,the point is reached where individual flats that can be purchased have a far higher capital value to their occupants than they have to the landlord.We may soon embark on a preliminary scheme to sell flats in one particular block.

As the Trafalgar House report makes clear, the gap between the tenanted investment value of flat property and its value to owner occupiers was becoming only too apparent as were the incentives for disinvestment. At this time Trafalgar House owned 631 flats in central London let at between £400 and £2,100 per annum, of which 532 were subject to rent regulation under the 1965 Act. The company had previously been active in the flat development and conversion for sale business and had recently extended the development side. Flat break-up, therefore, represented a natural progression from selling new flats to selling existing rented ones. A preliminary sales scheme was initiated in Campden Hill Court, a luxury block of 92 1930s flats in West Kensington, and by 1968 sales had been agreed for 21 flats producing a total of £229,000. In order to effect the sales, the block had been transferred to dealing stock from the investment portfolio at its current investment value and the subsequent surplus from sales was treated as trading income for tax purposes. The surpluses produced by these sales could then be retained for reinvestment in alternative and presumably higher-yielding assets. The sale of flats in Campden Hill Court was apparently successful, for by 1969 sales had grossed £0.5 million and the sales policy was extended. The company report for that year stated that: 'We now propose to convert almost all our remaining holdings of residential investment property to the same technique which should give rise to sales of a further £4 million over the next few years.' The capital gains this represented can be judged by the fact that in 1968 the investment value of the residential protfolio had been put at only £2.643 million.

By 1970, Trafalgar House had moved into the business of buying blocks in order to carry out break-ups and this policy continued into 1971. Properties acquired included the 57 flat Abingdon Court in West Kensington at a cost of £0.5 million, and purchased from a trustee vendor in spring 1970, and a more substantial purchase of 110 flats in six blocks in Marloes Road and Allen Street for over £1 million in summer 1971. This portfolio was acquired from British Land's subsidiary, the Clarendon Property Company. All these flats underwent modernization before sales were carried out and both purchases were from established residential landlords who were disinvesting from the residential sector. (British Land had initiated a policy of residential disinvestment in 1965 with a £2 million sale to the Freshwater Group and, after acquiring Regis Properties in the late 1960s, reinstated its disinvestment policy in 1970. In 1970-1 alone, British Land sold some 1,600 flats for over £5 million.) Trafalgar House also purchased Alexandra Court, SW7 for £600,000 in early 1971. After the common areas were modernised, the 45 flats, some of 7 rooms each, were put on the market for £35,000 to 40,000 apiece. This represented a £21,500 mark-up on the average purchase price of £13,000 for each flat and shows that the tenanted investment value of the flats was only 40 per cent of their vacant possession sale value.

By 1972 Trafalgar House had expanded into the industrial, civil engineering, oil exploration and shipping sectors and the company's shares were now quoted on the industrial section of the Stock Exchange. The transformation of the residential development and investment company which was first floated in 1963 into a major industrial conglomerate was undoubtedly helped by the realization of its flat portfolio by break-up. The shift in the policy of the company in the mid 1960s from a strategy based on investment into one based on trading was a reaction to the fiscal and financial changes heralded by Corporation Tax and higher interest rates. The rationale for this shift was that it had become impossible to maintain, let alone increase, earnings per share if borrowing had to be made at interest rates significantly above the prevailing yields on investment, a problem compounded by the increase in taxation on distributed profits.

Trafalgar House responded to this situation by restructuring its share capital in order to increase its borrowing capacity,and to acquire investment companies with a high earning potential but with a low borrowing in order to boost its earning power. It then switched to a policy of active trading both to maximize returns on asset values and to generate income for reinvestment at higher yields. This was a rational response to the situation facing the company at the time and similar decisions were being made in numerous other property company boardrooms, most of which had the same result. Residential investments were either sold *en bloc* or a policy of direct break-up was adopted.

London Housing and Commercial Properties provides another example of the policy of disinvestment from residential property. When shares in the company were first floated in 1960,the company was still known as the London Housing Society, a long-established residential investment company whose flat holdings included a leasehold estate of 494 artisan flats in Judd and Thanet Streets in the King's Cross area of Camden, and freehold blocks in St John's Wood, Chelsea and Wembley totalling some 730 flats in all (of which 427 were still rent controlled). By 1962 the name was changed and the company moved into the commercial and shop sectors through a policy of selling its 'inferior' residential properties. Residential investments had been reduced to only 50 per cent of all property assets by 1964 and had fallen to 40 per cent by 1967. Initially, sales were confined to house properties but in 1966 it was decided to extend sales into the flat sector. The company report for 1966 announced: 'During the year several of our leasehold flats held as investments were not re-let when they became vacant but were modernised and sold individually.' The rationale for the sale of flats in leasehold properties where the head lease had only 46 years to run, was straightforward. 'In this way we convert a wasting asset into a permanent investment.' The proceeds from the sales were reinvested in freehold shop and commercial property.

More fundamental changes were afoot. In 1969 London Housing and Commercial Properties became London Housing and Commercial Holdings through a company reconstruction where the newly formed holding company bought out the existing one. This reconstruction followed the normal pattern and £456,000 plus 10 per cent loan stock was substituted for part of the original equity, thereby considerably boosting the gearing ratio. At the same time all the residential property portfolio was transferred to dealing stock so that all the profits from the enlarged flat sale policy flowed into the profit and loss account rather than into the capital reserve as previously. Although this profit was now taxable as capital gains, it was available for distribution to shareholders, whereas previously it could only be reinvested elsewhere. In 10 years, an established and sleepy residential investor landlord had been transformed into a highly geared and asset-rich property trader. By 1972, 45 per cent of the company's total pre-tax income came from trading (the rest was from rents) and half the £113,000 earned from trading came from the profit on the sale of property which would previously have gone into the capital reserve.

The final transformation of the old London Housing Society took place in 1972 when LHCH bought the London and European Finance and Investment Company Ltd, a banking and finance company, for £1.5 million. This move was made possible as a result of a link-up with Eagle Star Insurance which took a £0.5 million share on LHCH's equity and provided a £2.5 million loan to fund property dealing acquisitions. By this move, and another change of name to London and European Securities Ltd, the company became a joint property and merchant banking group. With all funding internalized, the group was ready for further expansion into the commercial development and property trading sectors. As with Trafalgar House, London and European Securities' rapid expansion and diversification were carried out with the help of residential property dealing which provided capital for reinvestment, profits for distribution (hence maintaining share prices) and, as break-up values escalated, an appreciating asset base for high gearing.

For those companies which disinvested *en bloc* there was a growing number of entrepreneurs who were only too willing to take up the challenge and opportunities break-up offered. For this new breed of residential trading specialists the change in the tax laws provided the ideal vehicle for the break-up operation. The early break-up speculators often worked through the medium of small private companies which were in fact no more than partly or wholly owned subsidiaries of the secondary banks providing the finance for the deal. The profits were taxed at the lower Capital Gains Tax rate, passed through the profit and loss account and became available for distribution. For these companies, trading status had the advantage of allowing trading stock (i.e. the flats) to be written down to the lower of cost or net realizable value, thus dramatically reducing taxable profits. This was not a possibility if the flats were held as investments. In this way capital losses as a result of sales could be set against rented income because they are treated as trading losses. But, unlike break-ups conducted by established landlords, specialist break-ups necessarily involved deficit financing as the low yields on which the properties were purchased were exceeded by the interest rates on the finance. In these circumstances, trading status gave a greater degree of tax flexibility. With careful accounting, any liability for tax could be deferred until the original purchase cost had been recouped. An added advantage for the private property trader was that directors' salaries and allowances were more generously allowable against tax. The small, privately run property trading company was therefore eminently suited to the business of buying blocks of flats wholesale and selling them retail.

First National Finance Corporation, the activities of which we examine in more detail in Chapter 7, was one of the first non-property companies to become involved in break-up, with an initial purchase in 1966. Many of FNFC's early break-up operations were carried out via 'one-off' private trading companies, formed specifically to break a particular property and then be liquidated. Other specialist break-up schemes were carried out by Fordham Investments Group, run by David Rowlands. Major shareholders in Fordham included Slater-Walker, Jessel Securities and the ICI Pension Fund. Fordham was steadily buying and breaking blocks in the late 1960s, including blocks disinvested by Metropolitan Estates and Property Company (MEPC) and Central and District Properties. Soon after Rowlands sold his interest in Fordham in 1970, it was bought by Ralli International which asset-stripped it, including a large sale to the Freshwater Group.

The objective of these flat dealers was not to generate income to protect share values or surplus capital to reinvest in higher-yielding commercial property, but simply the generation of trading profits for distribution. The benefits flowed to the shareholders, who tended to be limited to the directors and the backing finance company. The flat breakers' game was quite simply the maximization of speculative profits by residential asset-stripping through the sale of residential investment property for owner occupation.

Other established companies which followed the trend set by Trafalgar House and LHCP included Aquis Securities (which began to break in 1968), Property Holding and Investment Trust (1966), Grovewood Securites (1968), London County Freehold (1968), New London Properties (1969) and Apex Properties (1970). Although these companies did not undertake major reconstructions, the end result was the same. The surpluses from flat dealings funded a shift out of residential investment and into the commercial and industrial investment and development markets. While some companies, such as London County Freehold, failed to survive the pressure from more vigorous rivals and eventually became the victims of takeover bids, the switch into break-up frequently created considerable and in some cases long standing financial benefits for the companies concerned.

Not all companies responded in precisely the same manner or at the same time to the prevailing conditions in the property market and there was no wholesale and simultaneous movement into dealing. As one commentator noted in 1968: 'Decisions to purchase or sell property investments at any particular time will turn upon a variety of circumstances both ... general ... and particular to the fund or individual concerned' (Preston, 1968). Some companies, such as London, City and Westcliffe and Freshwater, did not move into large-scale break-up until well into the 1970s. None the less, the writing was clearly on the wall for the corporate residential investor. Most companies were faced with the choice of breaking up their property themselves, selling to those willing to break-up or, if they were a quoted company, suffering the consequences of holding substantially undercapitalized assets during a period when the fiscal and financial conditions favoured takeovers and asset-stripping. The position in 1972 was summed up by Plender (1972, p.1047)

> If inflation continues, the time is fast approaching when the management of all but the strongest blue-chip companies will be obliged to take all possible short-term capital profits at the expense of long-term earnings growth to avoid the attention of the aggressive operators.

The response: creating the market

By the mid 1960s most of the conditions favourable to development of flat breaking had emerged. But as with most emergent market situations, the development of the market took some time to become established as a major feature of the central London residential scene. This was partly due to the variable response shown by the owners of residential investments to changes in market conditions. But it was also a function of the lack of large-scale demand for owner occupied flats. This lack of overt demand, except at the top end of the market, meant that a market had to be created if break-up, and the profits to be made from it, was to get off the ground. The evolution of the small flat sale development sector since the early 1960s had pointed the way, but it also highlighted one of the problems. As the Investors Chronicle (Walton, 1968, p.327) remarked: 'In London and certain other areas of the country where there has been a steady market for the sale of new flats there are signs that pre-war blocks, if they satisfy certain conditions, can be saleable piecemeal to the tenants. The key to this operation may be the provision of the finance for individual purchasers'.

This is exactly the same problem which faced the house traders in the 1920s. Without adequate mortgage finance at reasonable cost a large-scale shift into owner occupation is impossible. The building societies were still reluctant to lend on leasehold flat property and sources of alternative finance were limited. But there was one section of the market where mortgage finance was less problematic. Higher-income households had fewer difficulties obtaining access to finance from family trusts, insurance companies and banks.The principal form of mortgage used by these households was an endowment mortgage from a life insurance company. The maximum benefits from an endowment mortgage accrue to the higher-rate taxpayer. As Table 6.1 shows, in 1968 the net, after tax, costs (premium + interest – tax relief) to households of a with profits endowment mortgage of £10,000 varied from £912 per annum for a standard rate taxpayer to £539 for the highest rate of tax. This latter figure was little more than the average registered rent for a flat in central London in 1968.

As with flat sale developments and house trading, the trick was to set the price of the flat at a level that resulted in repayment costs not greatly

Table 6.1 *House buying by Insurance:the cost of borrowing £10,000 for 20 years and repaying loan through an endowment policy for £10,000 plus profits*

	Borrower pays top slice of tax at standard rate	*Borrower pays top slice of tax at 12s 3d*	*Borrower pays top slice of tax at 16s*	*Borrower has sufficient unearned income to pay entire interest gross, and pays tax at 16s*
Annual premium less tax at standard rate[1]	£385 1s 8d	£385 1s 8d	£385 1s 8d	£385 1s 8d
Annual interest on loan of £10,000 at 7¼% fixed rate for 20 years	£775	£775	£775	£775
Annual cost of interest after tax relief	£527(a)	£400(a)	£295(a)	£154(b)
Total of interest plus premiums over 20 years	£18,241	£15,701	£13,601	£10,781
Proceeds of policy (includes) £3,700 profits)	£13,700	£13,700	£13,700	£13,700
Cost of loan over 20 years	£4,541 i.e. £227 p.a.	£2,000 i.e. £100 p.a.	£99 profit to borrower	£2,919 to borrower

[1] Tax relief on endowment policy premiums is only made at standard rate, regardless of the amount of surtax paid. (a) Tax relief is on 7s 9d of the interest at the top rate paid by the borrower. (b) Tax relief is made on the total interest at the top rate paid by borrower.

Source: Reproduced from Investors Chronicle, 28 March 1968, p.58

dissimilar to the rent which the prospective owner, whether a sitting tenant or an open market purchaser, would expect to pay for the flat. Rent payments could therefore be converted easily into mortgage payments net of tax. The manner in which a sale value could be arrived at for a sitting tenant was set out by Gordon Dashwood, then joint managing director of London County Freehold, writing in the 1969 edition of the Investors Chronicle Property Review. It is worth quoting his example in full as it clearly sets out the relationship between rents, mortgage costs, investment and vacant possession values prevailing at the time when break-up was becoming established in central London. The figures are based on properties which LCF began trading in 1968.

> Take, for example, a flat of six rooms, kitchen and bathroom. This is let to a tenant for a three year term at £930 per annum inclusive of rates and services. These rates and services amount to £387 yearly, leaving £534 as 'pure rent', out of which the landlord must pay for repairs, insurance, management, ground rent (if any), and sinking fund and taxation (if any), leaving a net return of, say, £443 per annum. Revalued in 1969 on a current investment basis, the flat is worth, say, £5,500 to the landlord. This flat empty should sell on long lease for some £10,000, but to encourage the sale to the existing tenant, the landlord agrees to sell it for £9,000. Because the price is £1,000 below market price the tenant obtains a mortgage for 89 percent of the purchase price (i.e. 80 percent of the market valuation) at, say, 8 percent over 20 years and has only to find £1,000 himself. The tenant pays £620 per annum interest, plus premiums of, say, £255 per annum, on a with profits endowment assurance giving repayment in 20 years time. In addition to a tax allowance of ²/₅ths of the premium (giving a net premium of, say, £230), he will be allowed income tax relief at 6s 5d in the £ for the standard rate taxpayer, more for the higher taxpayer. The interest net of all tax, will amount to £310 per annum for a taxpayer paying tax at the rate of 10s in the £. Taking this particular example, the tenant, instead of paying an inclusive rent of £930 per annum with the likelihood of increases over the years will be paying:

Net interest	£310
Rates and services (including maintainence and insurance)	£453
Endowment assurance premiums	£230
Ground rent (say)	£50
	£1,043

> He will therefore be paying an additional £113 per annum plus possible interest on his own money, but against this he will own his own flat which should appreciate in value over the years and the only increase he will have to face will be in rates and services.' (Dashwood, 1969, p.22)

Dashwood's example shows that the cost of buying a flat plus service charge could be set at little more than the current inclusive rent. In return the tenant received an appreciating asset which was exempt from Capital Gains Tax and free from any future rent increases. For the landlord, a capital asset worth £5,500 as an investment was transformed into one worth £9,000. Several points are worth noting about these figures. First, the investment value of £5,500 represented 12.5 years' purchase of the 'pure rent': in other words, the flat returned an 8 per cent yield as an investment. This was the standard yield at which landlords had traditionally valued residential property since the nineteenth century and it suggests that flats still maintained their rate of return. Indeed, Dashwood (1969) stated that 'Flats let on short leases have for many years, in spite of parliamentary interference, provided good reversions often in excess of rising costs'. But selling the flat to a mortgagor created an entirely new value for the flat and, as Dashwood pointed out 'The landlord must balance this against his new investment prospects following the sale of flats'. In other words, landlords had to take the opportunity cost forgone of their investment into account. Measured against this, pure rents provided a notional yield of only 4.3 per cent. This was a situation which was clearly dangerous to any company in a competitive market and, as we discuss in Chapter 7, LCF failed to avert takeover bids from other companies bent on exploiting the considerable differential between the actual and potential asset values of their residential holdings.

In order to match the opportunity cost forgone of selling the flat at £9,000, LCF would have to set a pure rent of £800 to give an 8 per cent yield on the vacant possession value. This represents an increase of 80 per cent on the existing rent. If the rates, services and other costs are added on, an inclusive market rent for a flat worth £10,000 comes to £1,287, or £250 more than the cost to the tenant of buying the flat. This rent would be expected to rise in line with VP values. Between 1968 and 1986 London house prices rose by approximately 800 per cent (Nationwide Building Society, 1986). The implied rent on such a flat in 1986 would therefore have reached well over £10,000 per annum, or £200 per week, which would put it out of range of all but the very well off. Although rents at or above this level were being charged for flats in central London in 1986 the market was largely limited to company lets, embassy staff and short-term overseas visitors (Chartered Surveyors Weekly, 15 January, 1987).

With break-up operations yielding approximately 80 per cent gross profit over current investment values, let alone historic costs, the financial benefits of flat sales to landlords were clear. As Dashwood (1969, p.24) also pointed out, flat sales provided a landlord with 'a source of cheap money, enabling him to operate in the highly competitive investment and development market.' The key point is that renting flats was not intrinsically unprofitable in itself. Rather, investment in rented flats at prevailing rent levels was unprofitable in relation to the vacant possession sale value of flats and the potential return on the alternative uses to which the capital realized could be put.

The fly in the ointment remained the shortgage of mortgage funds. As Dashwood (1969, p.24) put it: 'From all points of view, a difficulty in buying and selling individual flats is undoubtedly the shortage of mortgage funds.' During the mid to late 1960s, the credit squeeze was affecting the supply of domestic mortgages just as much as company finance. Mortgage rates had reached 8 per cent by 1966 and remained there. Nevertheless, the flow of mortgages to the high-income market was not seriously affected and flat sales in this sector appeared to have been less problematic. In the rest of the market, a number of companies got around the problem by arranging mortgages for sales themselves. This 'pump-priming' activity was an important feature of the market when the usual sources of mortgage finance were unavailable. It was vital to assist the creation of a market so that flats could be sold from renting to owner occupation and the value gap appropriated.

A good example of this sort of 'self-financing' scheme was one operated by Property Holding and Investment Trust (PHIT) when it embarked on a policy of flat sales in early 1967 in some of its high-rent central London blocks. The provision of mortgages here was principally aimed at the problem of selling flats to elderly residents who were unlikely to obtain finance from normal sources, and also to guarantee flat purchase finance for flats in blocks where PHIT held only the head lease and where only limited term leases could be sold (some for under 40 years). The role of the secondary banking sector in such financing was particularly important and the First National Finance Corporation was able to self-finance its own break-up activities in this manner in the 1966-70 period. The importance of providing mortgages for purchasers was noted by Anthony Margo, senior partner in central London estate agents, Keith Cardale Groves. He stressed the necessity of 'providing purchasers with ... information concerning the availability and cost of mortgages, the details of tax concessions resulting therefrom and wherever practical, arranging for finance to be available' (Margo, 1973).

Providing buyers with mortgages and explaining the benefits of tax relief were not the only ways in which the benefits of sales were brought home to the potential purchasers. Successful flat break-up operations were usually carried out by a coordinated and determined sales drive to maximize the rate of purchase among the sitting tenants of the block. We are not talking here of consumer demand. Most sitting tenants had probably not given flat purchase a second thought until the landlord's agent arrived on their doorstep to extol its virtues. As one central London agent commented: 'Remember, sitting tenants are normally passive purchasers: *they have to be convinced* that to buy is right' (Tyler, 1971, p.663, our emphasis). This point was also stressed by Brett (1972, p.135, our emphasis): 'the breakup operator depends for his profit on his ability to *persuade* the tenants either to buy their flats or to move out'.

The sales technique was straightforward and well-planned, and usually followed the same sequence. First, the landlord decorated the common parts of the block (stairs, hallway, etc.) to improve the general tone of the building and bring it up to a marketable condition. Any vacant flats would be extensively modernized. The details of the leases, service charges, discounts and negotiating margins would be drawn up and finalized. The next step was to secure the sale of one or more of the vacant flats to establish current market (VP) values. The idea was to achieve as high a price as possible in order to maximize the potential returns from the sales to sitting tenants. In blocks where there were no vacancies it was worthwhile for the breakers to obtain one. There was no pussy footing about the technique. Tyler's advice was to the point: 'A handsome offer to a tenant of a typical flat for the surrender of his lease should do the trick' (Tyler, 1971, p.666).

It was only after market values had been established through the sale of modernized vacancies that the sitting tenants were approached. The approach would typically be made by letter which would inform the tenants that their landlord had decided to offer them the opportunity of purchasing their homes on attractive terms' (Tyler, 1971, p.666). The same letter might also explain that no more short term leases would be granted in the block and the letter was often accompanied by a judicious application to have the rent registered and/or increased. Then came the hard sell. Tenants would be paid a visit by a negotiator, usually one of a small team from the estate agent carrying out the sales drive. The purpose of the visit was clear. 'The negotiator wants to get into the flat so he can apply personal salesmanship to the tenant or the passive purchaser, as we have called him' (Tyler, 1971, p.666).

Once inside, the benefits of ownership would be firmly spelt out and the personal situation of the tenant assessed. After the visit, the next stage was to make a formal offer to the tenant to purchase at a specific price, setting a deadline for the offer to be accepted. Normally a discount on the full VP value established by the initial sale of vacant flats was included in the offer. The size of the discount varied depending on a number of factors. If the current tenant's lease was due shortly, or if he or she had no specific lease, then the discount would be low. Tenants renting with a long lease period left would need a larger discount. More generous discounts were given if the flat was in poor condition or if the mortgage advance was low compared to the flat's valuation, since the larger the discount, the greater the proportion of the full market value that would be covered by the mortgage advance. Finally, flats outside the provision of the Rent Act could expect small discounts compared to those given on protected tenancies. The actual proportion discounted might vary from as little as 2.5 per cent for an unprotected shortlet to 25 per cent for a fully protected tenant on a longer lease and in a less desirable flat.

The early sales were, therefore, very much the result of flat breakers creating a market where one did not previously exist. Fortunately for the breakers, the pressure for accommodation in central London was rising, and soon flat values began to escalate, which increased profits and further encouraged tenants to buy early before prices went beyond their reach. In fact, if the tenants had only realized it, the success of any break-up operation was largely dependent on the rate of vacancies and sales to sitting tenants. This put them in a potentially very powerful position had they decided to resist sales and jointly hold out for a much lower sale price. This was rarely appreciated, however, and it was only when sales drives became increasingly highly pressured during the early 1970s that tenants' organizations actually

Table 6.2 *The economics of a typical flat break-up in 1973*

VALUATION				
Proceeds				
5 flats VP @ £17,500	£ 87,500		Plus ground rents @ £75	£ 375
45 flats tenanted @ £14,000	£630,000		Plus ground rents @ £50	£2,250
			Total ground rents	£2,625
£2,625 x 7 YP	£ 18,375			
Therefore total proceeds:	£735,875			
Costs				
Purchase price, say	£450,000	or £425,000		
Stamp duty	£ 9,000	£ 8,500		
Buying costs, including agent's & solicitor's costs	£ 9,000	£ 8,500		
Selling costs, including legal & agent's fees, plans, etc.	£ 20,000	£ 20,000		
Improvements (including) modernising vacant flats)	£ 15,000	£ 15,000		
Shortfall	£100,000	£ 95,000		
	£603,000	£572,000		
Therefore profit:	£132,875	£163,875		
	or	or		
	22%	28.6%		
	of total financial commitment			

Source: Margo (1973)

became a force to be reckoned with. In general, tenants who could afford to were often willing to take the offer they were being made.

For the break-up operator, a number of considerations had to be borne in mind when embarking on a scheme. To begin with, the market into which the flats would be fed had to be established. This would determine the general price of flats, the extent of the modernization needed, the orientation of the sales drive and so on. Failure to get this right would result in either too few sales or too low a profit margin. In general, breakers approached the problem by fixing the level of profit which they expected to achieve and then working out the level of prices and rate of sales necessary to achieve the desired result. Having done that, the assessment of the operation's potential was quite straightforward. 'If one is unable to forecast at least 25 percent sales in the first year of trading there is probably something radically wrong with the marketing approach' (Tyler, 1971, p.666). The major problem the specialist breaker faced was to predict accurately the cash flow rate in order to minimize the immediate shortfall between the return on the property and the cost of finance which would normally cover the full cost of purchase. Invariably, the price paid for the block was such that the level of rented income failed to to meet the costs of purchase. The level of yields on which purchase was made, as low as 2 per cent in some cases, was well below the current costs of finance, with loan interest at 9 per cent plus. 'Deficit financing' of this sort had to be carefully managed to avoid the risk of running up high interest charges or failing to meet repayment deadlines. As Prior (1980) has put it: 'To be successful, a break-up operator must win the race against cash flow.'

A typical balance sheet of the sort a break-up specialist would draw up to estimate likely cash flow is shown in Table 6.2. The figures relate to average prices in central London in 1970–1. The importance of establishing the initial VP valuation is clear. All other calculations stem from this figure, including the price the breaker would be willing to pay for the whole block. As Margo put it, once the total proceeds had been estimated 'The remainder of the valuation really consists of fixing the level of profit which one is setting out to achieve and then adjusting the various figures to produce this result' (Margo, 1973, p.352). The point to note about these calculations is that rented income only plays a part to the extent that it helps to defray interest charges. The valuation of the block in this example rests solely on the estimated VP values of the individual flats. This brings home the point that flat dealers are 'reluctant landlords' in the sense that their primary concern is with vacant possession value rather than rental income.

These examples show that the break-up market was not a haphazard and spontaneous reaction to changes in impersonal 'market forces' which were prevailing in the mid to late 1960s. On the contrary, break-up was a carefully conceived and actively mediated response to changing opportunities by profit-maximizing intermediaries who saw the possibilities of substantial capital gains opening up. Although the origin of these opportunities lay in the wider economic and political changes of the time, the break-up market did not just 'happen'. It had to be made to happen. It was only when the market for flats had been created and VP values were established that an open market in flats emerged. Once the market had become established, flats rapidly became a more acceptable risk for the traditional mortgage lenders and break-up began to take off under its own steam.

Take-off into the 1970s

Throughout the late 1960s the break-up market gathered momentum, but it was not all plain sailing. A major threat emerged in 1967 with the passing of the Leasehold Reform Act. Section 39 of the Act was thought to have brought flats sold on long leases into the scope of the Act where the ground rent and the service charge exceeded two thirds of the rateable value. This would have permitted long leaseholders to purchase the freehold of their flats. When this anomaly was retrospectively removed in the 1969 Housing Act, the way was clear for break-up to begin in earnest. The Estates Gazette and the Investors Chronicle frequently drew attention to the way in which the break-up market was developing between 1969 and 1971, pointing to the increase in the volume of sales, the rise in prices and the growing shortage of rental accommodation:

> Much residential property is being eliminated from company portfolios via sales of flats to individual tenants or via sales of complete blocks to the break-up market. (IC, March 1970)
>
> During the last 18 months long leases have been offered to rent-restricted sitting tenants on terms advantageous to both sides, resulting in a dearth of rack rented property. (EG, February, 1971)
>
> We have experienced a very active market in central London flats - both in selling and letting. Selling prices are continuing to harden and rent levels are also increasing, this latter being, in some measure, due to the diminishing number of blocks where flats can still be rented. (EG, January, 1971)
>
> The market for residential investments has been extremely active and most of the sales have been effected with subsequent trading in mind. The creditibility of some of the transactions is difficult to assess, however, even allowing for inflationary factors over the trading period. (EG, January, 1971)

By the early 1970s the central London residential property market had changed dramatically from the earlier staid and static investment market. There were now several more or less distinct groups of residential landlords in the market. First, there were the established corporate landlord investors who had adopted wholesale disinvestment strategies by selling *en bloc* and who were gradually releasing their residential portfolios onto the market. (See Figure 6.1.) This group included several major insurance companies which had now also joined the disinvestment trend. The main difference between them and the residential property companies was that they did not engage in break-ups themselves. This was partly due to their unwillingness to saddle themselves with the management problems associated with break-up and partly a result of their desire to avoid the growing opprobrium surrounding the break-up market. Insurance companies could not afford to tarnish their socially responsible image by such activity. They were, however, willing to cash in on the growing value of their investments by allowing others to do the work for them.

The second major group were established landlords who had entered the break-up market themselves during the previous 5 years by adopting trading disinvestment strategies. While most of these companies had merely turned to trading the flats they originally held as investments, a few also began to acquire blocks to break them. The principal objective in both cases was to use the revenue to switch into the commercial property sector. The third major group were the speculative traders who had moved into the residential property market purely for its break-up potential. These dealers had a symbiotic relationship with the wholesale disinvestors, for while the latter provided the property for the dealers to exploit, the activities of the breakers generated the incentive (through higher block values) for the established landlords to disinvest.

***Figure 6.1** Auction advertisement for a large central London block*

Many of these specialist breakers had links to the financial institutions, particularly the growing secondary banking sector. These 'fringe' banks had received a boost under Section 123 of the 1967 Companies Act which exempted such companies from some of the more stringent controls introduced by earlier legislation regulating money-lending activity. Although not banks as such, their business of supplying finance to the corporate market was considered to be banking by both themselves and their clients. The secondary banks relied on the money market to raise their banking capital and to this end they became heavily involved with the insurance and pension funds for support (Plender, 1982). For example, the ICI and Electricity Supply Industry pension funds both provided backing for Dalton Barton. London and County Securities was 22 per cent owned by the United Drapery Stores Group Pension Fund and the property dealing side of London and County's activities was funded by money from the Leek and Westbourne Building Society. FNFC received support from the Electricity Pension Fund and the Crown Agents, and in the early 1970s Prudential Assurance financed Keyser Ullman's rapid expansion. All these secondary banks were active in the break-up business, either directly or through closely related companies.

These links were to become a vital factor in the rapid growth of the break-up market in the early 1970s. It was the secondary banking sector in particular which benefited from the relaxation of credit restrictions following the election of a Conservative Government in June 1970 as bank and institutional funds sought new investment outlets. The cheap money policy ensured an almost unlimited supply of mortgage finance not only for breakers but also for those tenants and other others who now bought individual flats. The building societies were playing an increasing role in funding flat purchase and they helped to jerk the process into top gear. The result was a rapid increase in both the speculative trading of blocks and prices as the demand for blocks increased and the supply of available property began to diminish as some landlords began to break their own blocks. As the Estates Gazette commented in its review of the year 1970:

> The market for residential investments has been extremely active and most of the sales have been effected with subsequent trading in mind. The credibility of some of the transactions is difficult to assess, however, even allowing for inflationary factors over the trading period'. (Estates Gazette, 16 January, 1971)

Like most speculative booms, the process rapidly began to gather its own momentum as speculation forced block prices up to higher and higher levels and rapidly rising prices attracted new buyers into the market. In the 2 years after 1970 a large proportion of blocks in central London changed hands, some several times in the course of just a few months. The price of blocks continued to escalate throughout 1971 and 1972, fuelled in part by the rapid increase in speculative demand and in part by the rapid increase in owner occupied prices in general, particularly in London where the average price of dwellings mortgaged to building societies rose by no less than 50 per cent in 1972 and a further 30 per cent in 1973 (Hamnett, 1983). The demand for blocks by dealers pushed the yields on which properties changed hands down to new lows—2 to 3 per cent was commonplace. Comments in the property press at the time reveal the extent of the speculative spiral. The Estates Gazette annual review stated of the residential property sector in central London in 1971 that

> The year seems to have been an amazing one; yet on reflection,the active market and rapid rise in values were only the continuation of existing trends. The market began a noticeable improvement in the late 1960s and had hit a new peak in 1970, assisted by the change of government and plenty of mortgage finance. A growing confidence, particularly where property values were concerned, the emergence of the break-up of flats and the countrywide policies of home-ownership all pointed to another boom'. (Estates Gazette, 29 January, 1972).

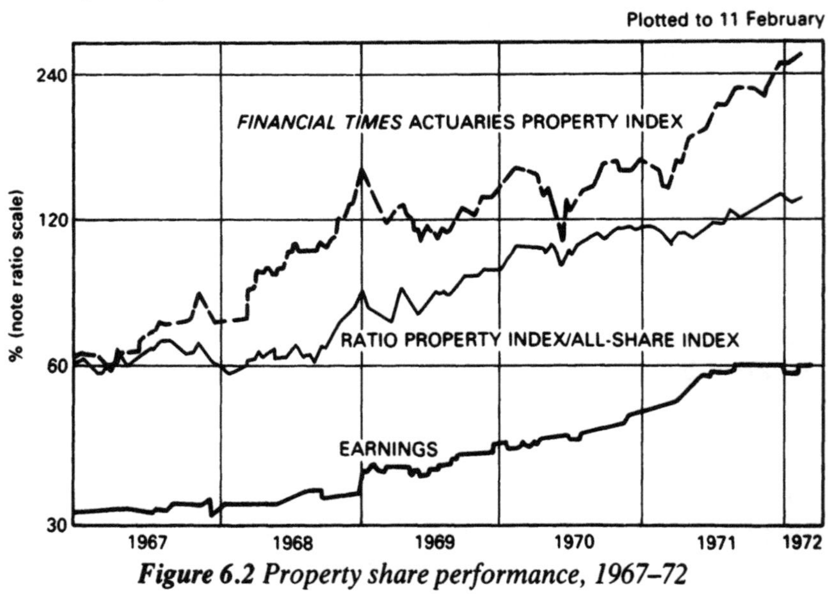

***Figure 6.2** Property share performance, 1967–72*

The impact of the Tories' 'quiet revolution' on the property world was given an added boost by the reduction of the Corporation Tax rate from 45 to 40 percent in the 1971 Budget. At a stroke, this measure increased distributed share earnings by 9.1 per cent and gave a tremendous boost to share prices, especially for those of property companies (see Figure 6.2). In 1971 alone the FT Actuaries Property Share Index rose by 61 per cent from 160 to 254 (Heath-Saunders, 1972). Companies with substantial residential holdings figured prominently among the market leaders. Cornwall Property, a newly emerged Slater-Walker subsidiary, was the market's 'star' performer with a share price rise of over 230 per cent. During 1971 Cornwall had successfully bid for Alliance Property Holdings, a major residential landlord, whose investment portfolio included 6,000 to 7,000 flats in London and the South East. Other notable events during the year included the sale of nearly 8,000 flats by MEPC in two parts, to Wallabrook and FNFC (see Chapter 7).

By early 1972 the market for blocks had reached unprecedented levels. This period also saw a marked switch in the character of the specialist flat dealers who were coming into the market.There was a trend towards the public flotation of trading companies in order to take advantage of the bull market in property shares. A trader with a public quotation could use its inflated paper assets to purchase properties cheaply through takeovers. The directors of these companies also stood to make considerable gains through speculative share dealings and sales of their own holdings. The Stock Market saw a series of 'off the peg' property trading companies come to the market in 1971 and 1972, several floated in 'shell' operations. All received heavy backing from the secondary banking sector. One of the best-known of these was Regalian Securities, created from the shell of a defunct Midlands-based finance company and refloated in March 1972 specifically to take FNFC and David Goldstone's £22.7 million flat-dealing portfolio. In a similar manner, Peureula Investments — an ex-Malaysian rubber company—was refloated in June 1972 with backing from Keyser Ullman, Dalton Barton, and the Burston and Texas Bank with an immediate £12 million injection of residential property from Town and City. These properties represented the residential portfolio of Charlwood Alliance Holdings, taken over by Town and City from the Davidson group in January 1971 with backing from London and County Securities. Stonegate Securities, another FNFC backed company also entered the break-up market in April 1972, with £4 million of blocks from the Co-operative Insurance Society. Buckingham Properties, another Slater-Walker subsidiary, was founded in October 1971 and by April 1972 it had bought £8 million of residential property. Finally, the Woodmill Property Group was formed in 1972 from the reverse take-over of the private Woodmill Estates by the publicly quoted shell of yet another ex-Malaysian plantation company, Perak Rubber Plantations Ltd. Backing for Woodmill came from The Burston Finance Group.

As a result of the activities of these and other companies, the central London flat market was transformed within the space of 5 or 6 years from genteel decline into one of the most dynamic and aggressive sectors of the property market. The share price of any company with sizeable residential holdings (especially the break-up companies) inflated rapidly as their potential underlying asset values soared. But the activity on which these profitable events were based, the buying and selling of people's homes for profit, was running into mounting criticism from those directly affected. Tenants were becoming increasingly vocal in their objections to the sales methods some of the more aggressive dealers were using as well as the confusion and uncertainty generated as whole blocks of flats were traded from speculator to speculator. The main source of complaint from the buyers centred on the terms of the leases on which the flats were being sold, rapidly rising service charges and gazumping. From the tenants, there were widespread accusations of 'winkling' (where undue or even illegal pressure was put on tenants in an effort to make them vacate), harassment, and general disturbance as gangs of workmen descended on the blocks to carry out cosmetic modernization.

The reaction to these tactics almost resulted in a revolt of the middle-class tenantry of central London. The issue even reached Parliament, leading to a temporary defeat for the government in April 1972 over the question of rapidly rising service charges. Problems were particularly acute in the older blocks where long delayed repairs were leading to considerable costs for new long lessees. In other cases the problem was the reverse, as long leaseholders were unable to get landlords to do any essential repair work at all once the flat had been sold. There was also a growing realization among some tenants that there was no need to be panicked into buying, despite rapidly rising property prices. There was no legal way a tenant could be evicted and they could afford to drive a hard bargain. For the break-up operator whose profitability depended on selling flats quickly, resistance in the form of a well-organized tenants' association could spell disaster. There was undoubtedly a growing resistance from sitting tenants, in the main drawn from the articulate middle classes to break-ups. FNFC in particular was the subject of considerable criticism, largely as a result of the size and vigour of its flat-breaking operation, and this was a major factor in the company's decision to dispose of its flat portfolio to Regalian and other breakers in mid 1972.

The flurry of speculative activity began to generate financial fears as well as political disapproval. As one leading central London valuer commented in 1972:

> Prices (of blocks) recently achieved in the open market make theoretical valuation principles and years of experience virtually irrelevant. We are seeing many examples of individual blocks being sold and resold up to 6 times within 6 months at ever increasing prices like the proverbial 'barrel of herrings'. In my view, this is a very dangerous market situation'. (Krieger, 1972, p.31)

The rapid appreciation of the shares in any company with a sizeable residential interest also drew cautionary comment. These inflated share prices reflected the potential break-up value of the residential portfolio, but often ignored both the substantial tax liabilities that any sales might incur and the costs inherent in the flat break-up operation. As one prophetic commentator pointed out: 'This is an unrealistic situation and one which must be corrected in due course' (Read Hurst Brown, 1972).

Most importantly, it was realized within the more cautious parts of the City that the property boom in general, and 'flat busting' in particular, was rapidly reaching unmanageable proportions and was threatening to unbalance the banking system. An injection of sanity was needed to restore the market to a more sensible level of activity. As a consequence, in August 1972 the Bank of England issued a directive to the banking sector asking them to restrain lending to the speculative property sector. This move was widely recognized to be aimed at the flat breakers and their backers. The directive had the desired effect of letting the steam out of the system and the key event marking the end of the boom period was the auction of eight large blocks by Regional Properties in early September 1972. All but two of the blocks failed to reach their reserve price and were withdrawn. But the fact that the remaining blocks were sold privately shortly afterwards, and for only a fraction short of their reserve price, showed that, far from halting the boom, the Bank of England's directive had temporarily defused a situation which could easily have proved disastrous for all concerned. It set the scene for a steadier level of break-up activity and it also drove the activity 'underground'.

From late 1972 onwards, deals involving blocks of flats became much more secretive as dealers adopted a low profile in order to limit the attention from Parliament and the media. But the peak of the market had passed. By late 1972 there were signs that the house price spiral was slowing down. Mortgage rates began to rise and tenant resistance was becoming increasingly noticeable. Some of the longer-established companies which had embarked on a break-up policy in blocks which were held at low historic costs and which were also affected by the prevailing adverse publicity began to scale down their sale programmes and sit tight. At the same time, there was a move towards the transfer of vacant flats into furnished accommodation which increased the returns and permitted sales to be deferred.There was no security of tenure on furnished lettings until the 1974 Rent Act. But for the break-up specialist with large borrowings, the burden of interest payments dictated that flat sales policies be pursued as vigorously as ever. They had to sell flats or lose the cash flow race and go under.

From boom to bust—and back

These difficulties were nothing compared to what was to follow. Disaster struck on 8 November 1973—Black Tuesday as it later became known—when the Bank of England raised the bank rate from 8 to 13 per cent in one jump. Interest rates on property finance, generally 4-5 per cent above Bank Rate, soared to 17-18 per cent. The effect on breakers was catastrophic. High gearing and deficit financing resulted in a severe cash flow crisis for most of the specialist companies. Very few escaped, and within months most of the breakers and their fringe backers had either crashed or were in grave difficulties. At the same time,the factor which had spurred break-up in the early 1970s—the widespread availability of mortgage finance for individual buyers—effectively dried up. Companies were faced with a situation where, at the very time that they needed to boost sales to cover finance costs, the market for flats had collapsed. Although most of the established companies were able to weather the crisis, many of the specialist breakers collapsed.

The crash of Stern Holdings (which did not pursue a break-up policy but was highly geared—see Chapter 7), owing over £100 million was the most spectacular of the period, but there were many others, and the Bank of England had to organize the big clearing banks in a £3 billion 'lifeboat' operation to save many of the fringe banks and prevent the whole banking system from crashing as a result of bad debts. The extent to which the flat break up market contributed to the collapse of the property and secondary banking sector in 1973-4 is still not fully appreciated. In the 2 years following November 1973, the market for both blocks and individual flats was extremely slack and cash flow problems were intensified by the rent freeze of 1974. Most of the survivors were forced into either extending break-up where possible or, as with London City and Westcliffe, initiating flat sales for the first time in order to try to clear debts.

Ironically, the wreckage of the crash was to provide the raw material to fuel the second boom from 1976 onwards. With a return to financial stability,the release onto the market of residential property from companies which had either been liquidated or run into difficulties was to prove a cheap source of blocks. Many of these blocks had either totally escaped break-up or had been only marginally broken. Between 1976 and 1980 there was a return to

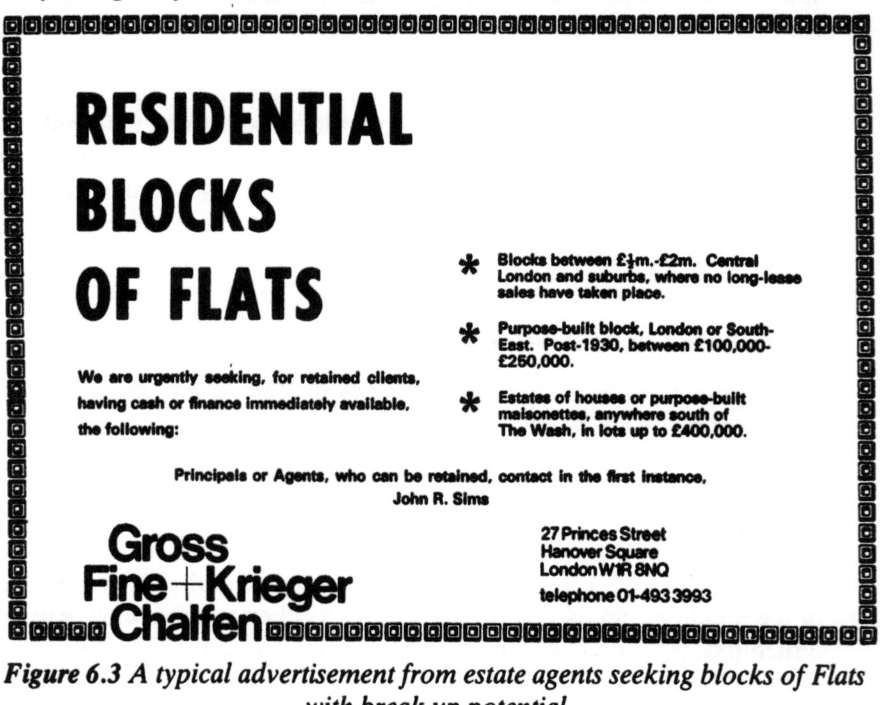

Figure 6.3 A typical advertisement from estate agents seeking blocks of Flats with break up potential

Figure 6.4

the sort of conditions which had prevailed in the early 1970s as blocks began to change hands again, but without the speculation that characterized the earlier period. (See Figures 6.3, and 6.4) The period since 1976 has seen the majority of blocks broken and flat sales completed, and the creation of a new set of fortunes for those who bought blocks at the right time.

By 1977 many of the breakers whose public property companies were crippled or severely affected by the crash were back on the break-up scene, though more often than not on a private basis. Jack Dellal, ex-Keyser

Ullman deputy chairman; John Black,ex-FNFC property director; Michael Rivkin, ex-Argyle Securities; and Jim Slater's Lonrho backed Strongmead, were all active in this period. Much of the finance for these dealings came from abroad, a great deal of it from the Middle East as the growing oil revenues were recycled into the Western property market. Middle Eastern buyers also figured prominently among those purchasing flats, especially at the top end of the market. In some cases funding was also made available by pension funds in the form of long-term financing. At the same time the large institutional landlords who had not sold during the previous boom now began to dispose of their remaining residential portfolios. The BP Pension Fund, the Liverpool and Victoria Friendly Society, the Legal and General Assurance Company, the Church Commissioners and the Prudential Assurance Company all sold property during this period. These institutions held many of the remaining prime unbroken residential blocks in London and the value of the blocks inflated as competition intensified. Legal and General's £15 million sale of 1,200 flats in 20 blocks to a consortium of private dealers headed by Bernard Sunley via its Tannergate subsidiary is particularly interesting. Legal and General had been preparing to sell in 1973 but was caught by the crash and decided to sit tight until conditions improved. Owing to L and G's scruples about the sale of its residential blocks over the tenants' heads, the deal involved a 'gentlemans agreement' that there would be no early break-up.Three months later the portfolio was being offered for break-up by its new owners. Some of the consequences for the residents are traced in Chapter 9.

The years immediately after the crash also saw an increase in the role of both local authorities and tenants' associations in the market. The London borough of Camden was particularly active in purchasing blocks in this period and tenants' groups bought out a number of blocks from the liquidators. But, as the market for blocks reasserted itself and prices began to escalate once again, both local authorities and tenants found themselves priced out of the market.

Prices and rents in 1980

By 1980 the break-up market had once more established itself firmly in central London. Following the house price boom between 1978 and 1980, flat prices rose to new highs. The influx of buyers from overseas, especially the Middle East, was an added factor in pushing prices up. Indeed, the central London flat market had now become increasingly international, with values reflecting the purchasing power of a wealthy international clientele, many of whom were looking to residential property in London as a safe haven and good investment for their money. London has become an increasingly important centre for the new 'global' economy, and its residential property prices reflect this position.

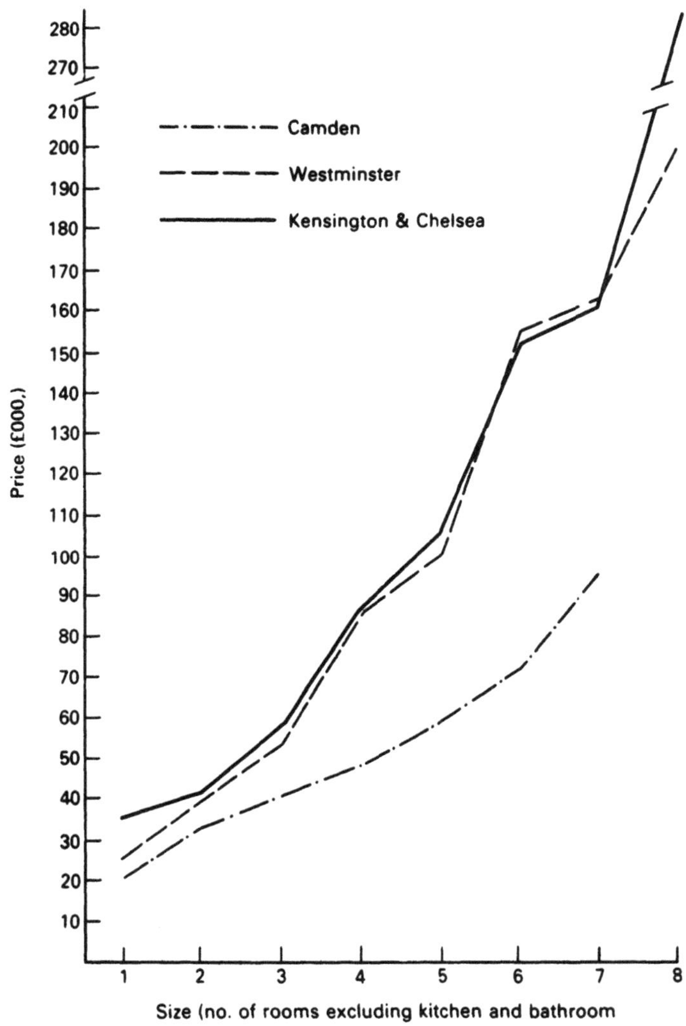

Figure 6.5 *Average prices of central London flats, first half 1980*

An analysis carried out in mid 1980 in the three central London boroughs clearly illustrates the level to which rates of return in the traditional rental market had fallen when measured against prevailing vacant possession values. The magnitude of the value gap which had opened up represented an opportunity no property investor could ignore. Figure 6.5 shows the prices of a sample of 320 purpose-built flats in the first half of 1980 using data taken from the lists of central London estate agents. The figures are average prices for each size of flat, from one roomed 'studio' flats to large flats of seven rooms or more. At this time a studio flat in Westminster or Kensington could be bought for around £30,000, and prices increased steadily to £200,000 and

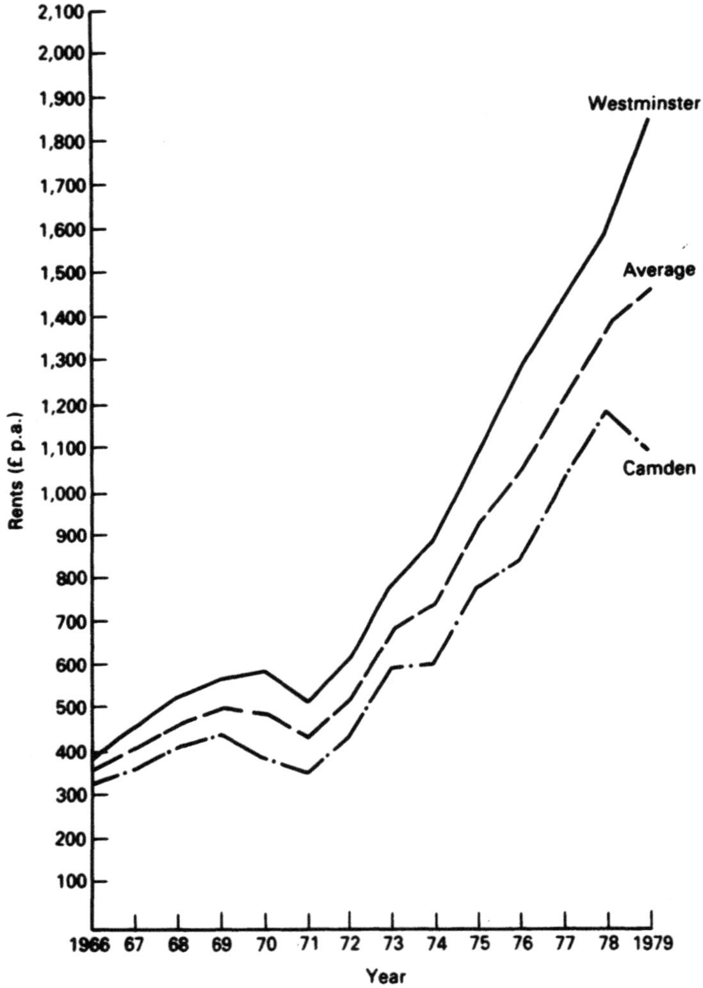

Figure 6.6 *Average registered rents for unfurnished flats, Westminster and Camden, 1966–79*

over for the largest flats. In Camden, prices were significantly lower, ranging from £20,000 for a studio to £90,000 for a seven roomed flat.

The average registered rent levels for unfurnished purpose-built flats in Westminster and Camden from 1966 (when rent registration was introduced) until 1979 are shown in Figure 6.6. The data were collected from the rent registers of the Rent Officer Service in these two boroughs. Data from Kensington and Chelsea were not in suitable form for analysis but are likely to have closely matched those in Westminster. Over this period rents rose from an average of £350 per annum in 1966 to £1,500 per annum in 1979—an increase of almost 320 per cent in 13 years. It is also clear that rent inflation in Westminster was much higher than in Camden. In 1966 average rents in Camden were 15 per cent lower than in Westminster, but by 1979 the gap had widened to 30 per cent. The dip in average rent levels between 1969 and 1972 is almost certainly a reflection of the large increase in registrations following the 1969 Rent Act which allowed the decontrol of controlled tenancies if the rent was registered. This resulted in a large number of lower-value flats being registered for the first time, pushing the average down.

Interesting though these two sets of figures are, what is most revealing is the relationship between them. Where data allowed, a comparison was made between registered rents and corresponding vacant possession sale prices prevailing in 1980 for flats in the same blocks. This showed that the level of investment yield calculated against VP prices ranged from 1.3 to 4.3 per cent in Camden and from 0.6 to 5.0 per cent in Westminster. The overall average for the two boroughs was 2.8 per cent. Given that these are gross figures, the average net return was probably as low as 1 per cent. Yields from the few furnished flats let on registered rents were higher, averaging 5.2 per cent, but this hardly represented a viable long term yield on vacant possession capital values.

A few examples give some idea of the exact relationship between rent and VP values at this time. In Portsea Hall, Marble Arch, the registered rent for a two room flat was £1,630 per annum unfurnished or £3,200 furnished, while similar flats were on the market at £57,000—representing notional gross yields of 2.9 and 5.6 per cent respectively. A four roomed flat in St Mary's Mansions, W2, commanded an open market value of £47,000 but had an unfurnished registered rent of £1,560 per annum, giving a notional yield of 3.3 per cent. Even in Berkeley Court, NW1, where rents reached £6,750 for an unfurnished seven roomed flat, the prevailing market price was £175,000—a notional yield of 3.8 per cent. Such levels of return were clearly unattractive compared to yields on alternative property investments of 6 to 10 per cent.

The value gap waiting to be exploited in these circumstances was substantial. Given that the average unfurnished rent in 1979–80 in Westminster and Camden was £1,500 per annum, and assuming that an investing landlord would expect a return of 12.5 per cent gross, or 10 per cent net, then the tenanted investment value of the average flat at this time was £12,000. But the data collected on sale prices suggested that the corresponding average vacant possession value for flats in the two boroughs was £52,000 at this time. The level of rent necessary to yield a gross return of 12.5 per cent would be £6,500 or £125 per week, well over four times the rents actually paid. And the notional value gap in this situation was no less than £40,000, over three times the pure investment value of these flats. The incentive to sell rented flats into the home ownership market was overwhelming.

Since the early 1980s the break-up market has continued to erode the remaining unfurnished rental stock, although the rate of new transfers has

Figure 6.7 *Vacant blocks of artisan flats of the type depicted here have been in demand by investors*

Figure 6.8 *Substantial sums have been invested in the flat break-up market*

fallen significantly as the bulk of the flats have been sold. The supply of unbroken blocks has virtually dried up, except for the growing number of disposals by government agencies such as the police, health authorities and armed forces, which have recently been disposing of blocks under the privatization policies pursued by successive Conservative governments. The most enterprising flat breakers have now turned their attention to the council sector with high hopes that the trickle of council blocks currently finding their way into the hands of property traders for sale to ower occupiers will grow into a new and potentially huge source of profits, especially under the current Conservative Government's proposals for the break-up of the local authority housing stock. Barratt's refurbishment of Myrdle Court in Liverpool was among the first schemes, but recently Regalian Properties (see Chapter 7) have made most of the running in London with several schemes in Docklands and Wandsworth where local councils have sold blocks to the private sector. Apart from their low prices, the great advantage of the purchase of publicly owned blocks over private sector ones is that they come already emptied of tenants. There is no race against cash flow to persuade tenants to buy or quit and sell the vacancies.

Meanwhile, within central London itself, there has been a small return to a rental investment market, this time to tap the demand from foreign visitors and company executives keen to avoid sky-high central London hotel charges of up to £150 per night. This is exclusively a furnished market and the clientele are unlikely to quibble at the rents being asked. The levels which rents and property values had reached in late 1986 can be seen from Table 6.3. Rents ranged from £135 per week for a studio apartment to £950 per week for a five bedroomed flat in a prime location. The yields on the equivalent open market values range from 8 to 13 per cent with an average of 10 per cent.

Table 6.3 *Rents and values in Mayfair, Belgravia and St James, November 1986.*

Type of property	*Long leasehold (£000s)*			*Let furnished (£s per week)*		
	Typical location	*Prime location*	*Prestige location*	*Typical location*	*Prime location*	*Prestige location*
Studio	65	50	100	135	175	250
1 bedroom	95	150	195	200	300	400
2 bedroom	150	250	360	350	600	800
3 bedroom	250	365	475	450	750	950
4 bedroom	345	500	685	550	850	1100
5 bedroom	450+	650+	850+	700	950	2000

Source: Chartered Surveyors Weekly (1987)

But the key attraction of this sector lies not in the rent levels which can be charged, useful as these now are in meeting finance costs, but in the capital gains to be made by holding residential property. Given the rapid escalation in property values in central London in the 2 years to early 1987 of up to 100 per cent in some cases (Campaign for Homeless in Central London, 1986), these capital gains can be substantial. Indeed, returns in this market are now as high, if not higher, as those from other sectors of property investment. The new type of landlord, many of whom are from overseas, may own a small number of individual flats scattered throughout the central area. This form of investment landlordism, with its emphasis on capital gains rather than long-term investment income is a very different affair from the one it has replaced. And so too are the tenants.

In these last two chapters we have described and analysed the development of the break-up market from its earliest days in the late 1950s through to the mid 1980s. In little over 20 years, the established private rental market has been almost completely replaced by a solid home ownership market, with only the limited number of exclusive furnished lettings representing what is left of a functioning rented sector. In tracing this history, however, we have touched only briefly on the principal actors involved. In the following chapter we aim to trace the history of the break-up market through the events surrounding the disposal and eventual sale of one of the largest portfolios of rented flats ever owned in Britain, the Key Flats empire of London, County Freehold and Leasehold Properties Ltd. The break-up of their prestige portfolio epitomizes, perhaps more than any other, the manner in which the central London rental market met its end.

7 The biggest break-up of them all: the rise and fall of London County Freehold's 'Key Flats' empire.

Introduction

The London County Freehold and Leasehold Property Company Ltd was probably the most prestigious of the residential investment companies which emerged in the inter war period. It was certainly one of the longest lived, tracing its history back to the revealingly named Middle Class Dwelling Company which built its first block of flats, Buckingham Palace Mansions, SW1, in 1888. It was also one of the largest, owning at its peak almost 10,000 medium to high rent flats under the 'Key Flats' banner. Moreover, the residential empire of London County Freehold (LCF) represents perhaps the largest single portfolio of flats which has undergone break-up in central London since the mid 1960s.

Consequently, the events surrounding the development of LCF, the demise of the company among a welter of take over bids and the saga of the subsequent break-up of the company's extensive residential holdings, provide an excellent illustration of the manner in which long-established investment companies were forced out of the lettings business in the face of the cumulative effects of changes in the investment climate of the postwar period. The fate of LCF and the activities of those to whom its properties have subsequently passed typify, albeit on a grander scale, the numerous other instances where residential investors have sold out to or been acquired by others more concerned to exploit short-term capital appreciation than long-term investment income. The key 'actors' involved in this particular episode have also been active in effecting the break-up of other large portfolios, and with essentially similar results.

The scale of LCF's central London residential investment can be traced from a number of sources, including company reports and press articles. But the most comprehensive information on this long-lost empire is hidden in the rent registration records of the three boroughs concerned. In all, some 50 blocks containing approximately 4,100 flats were identified as having been owned by LCF in central London (Table 7.1). These flats represented almost half of the residential holdings which LCF had owned since before

Table 7.1 *The ownership history of LCF's Central London blocks, 1966–80*

	No. of Flats	Flats registered in 1980	1966-69	1970-71	1972	1973	1974	1975	1976	1977	1978	1979	1980
Cumberland Mansions	32	23	London County Freehold and Leasehold Property Company	Metropolitan Estates and Property Corporation (MEPC)	First National Finance Corporation Swallow Securities					J Management*			
Harvard Court	92	66								Jesso Management Services*			
Lyncroft Mansions	51	25										Atabel*	
Abbey Court	26	6								Atabel*			
Yale Court	88	33						Enmark Estates*					
Neville Court	87	22									Enmark Estates*		
Witley Court	86	34								Enilworth Investments*			
Bryanston Mansions	24	8							Enilworth Investments*				
Clifton Court	128	0							Enilworth Investments*				
Fairhazel Mansions	8	0								Evanley Investments*			
Antrim Mansions	82	56							Evanley Investments*				Swallow
Carlton Mansions	90	45							Evanley Investments*				
Morshead Mansions	104	47						Evanley Investments*					
15 Portman Square	119	8				Evanley Investments*							
Wymering Mansions	160	0						Montim Estates*					
Cunningham Court	31	17							Spiritville Investments*				
Furzecroft	73	14							Jesso Management*				Swallow
Grove Court	60	8							Evanley Investments*				Swallow
Avenue Mansions	44	7				Metropolitan Property Holdings						Capital best	
Iverna Gardens	47	2				MPH			Iverna Gardens Residents' Assoc.				
Albert Court	62	31				MPH				Hailbury Investments			
Albert Hall Mansions	82	55				MPH				UAE Investments			
Clive Court	154	84				MPH				Beleggings NV Corvan Prop.			
Grosvenor Court Mansions	36	15				MPH				Gaingold			
Rodney Court	95	60				MPH				Princecliff			
Sandringham Court	52	24				MPH				Church Commissioners			
Southwold Mansions	61	31				MPH					Biskeep Nominees		
Buckingham Mansions	49	1				MPH						Tenants' Assoc.	
Cleveland Mansions		0				MPH					Biskeep Nominees		
Phillimore Court	32	8				MPH				Jamboree Holdings Electromech			
Bedford Court Mansions	20	0				MPH				Unknown			
Leinster Mansions	9	0				MPH				Unknown			
Marlborough Mansions	95	0				MPH						Tenants' Assoc.	
Cheyne Court	79	34						Regalian Securities					Swallow
North Gate	122	4						Regalian Securities					Swallow
86 Portland Place	41	8						Regalian Securities					Swallow
Bickenhall Mansions	230	117			Wallabrook Properties								
Montague Mansions	169	77			Wallabrook Properties								
Montrose Court	87	10			Wallabrook Properties								
Portman Mansions	126	61			Wallabrook Properties								
York House	28	12			Wallabrook Properties								
Biddulph Mansions	117	46		Church Commissioners									
Castellean Mansions	238	84		Church Commissioners									
Delaware Mansions	167	44		Church Commissioners									
Lauderdale Mansions	270	81		Church Commissioners									
Gordan Mansions	76	0				Smarden Properties					Camden Council		
Elm Park Chambers	15	2		Southwestern and County					Salcombe Investments				
51 South Street	25	2							Tillington Securities				
Wellesley House	15	2				Oxford Street Properties			Worthmore				
Ridgemont Gardens	130	0		Wallabrook Properties				Trustees of the Bedford Estates					
Total	4,114	1,314		(current = 33%)									

*Subsidiaries of the Berger Group

the Second World War. It is to the history of LCF and the subsequent owners of these flats which we now turn.

London County Freehold: 1888 to 1970

LCF was very much a 'blue chip' residential property investment company par excellence. The company's 70 year history, which covered the heyday of this form of corporate landlordism, saw it expand from a modest central London residential landlord to a major international property company with a mix of residential, commercial and industustial investment properties valued at £62 million when it was acquired by Metropolitan Estates and Property Company (MEPC) in 1969. The company prided itself on its stable management – there were only two managing directors over the whole period 1924 to 1969 – and good tenant relations, reflected in a company-wide tenants association and the company's telex address of 'Pampered, London'. But it was this conservative management style which eventually led to the company's undoing. It was simply unable to adapt quickly enough to the asset-stripper mentality which emerged in the late 1960s.

Formed from the amalgamation of three smaller companies in 1909, LCF went public in 1924 and soon became a major force in the central London residential investment market where the majority of its properties were located. It built its business on 'top class management, sound finance, steady progress and the determination to offer the City a fundamentally good opening to the investor' (Company Report, 1965). As a result, the company benefited from the backing of major institutional investors, with the Prudential Assurance Company acting as trustees of the debenture stock.

The interwar period saw a major expansion, with rent revenues growing from £43,000 in 1925 to £297,000 by 1935. By 1939 LCF's holdings were valued at over £10 million, a large capitalization for a property company at that period. By the outbreak of the Second World War, LCF owned over 9,000 flats in 114 blocks in London, the surrounding suburbs and the south coast, catering for a predominantly middle-class, white collar clientele—or 'black coated workers' as the company referred to them. The central London blocks included some of the most prestigious residential properties in the country in some of the prime locations.[1]

But the war abruptly halted expansion, and in the postwar period there were nothing like the opportunities which had existed before 1939 to expand the residential lettings business successfully. Added to this, the company's property had also suffered some £1.5 million worth of war damage and the inability to deduct lease amortization or replacement costs before tax (a large proportion of LCF's properties were held on head leases, especially on the Church Commissioners' estate in Maida Vale) was becoming a major drain on profitability.

As a result of these problems, rents were barely covering repair and replacement costs by the early 1950s. Despite a rent roll of almost £2 million in 1949, LCF was undoubtedly finding its income growth impaired. The 1939 Rent Act notwithstanding, the company launched a concerted policy to increase rental income from its residential portfolio. For existing tenancies, rents were renegotiated in excess of the controlled level wherever possible, especially when the leases fell due. Where vacancies occurred, the flats were relet on rents exclusive of rates.[2]

But the other consequence of the company's profit squeeze was an active diversification into commercial and industrial property development in order both to expand the investment portfolio and to increase rental income. LCF was also one of the earliest British property companies to expand into the overseas development market, notably in Canada, Australia and Rhodesia. By 1956, commercial developments represented 20 per cent of LCF's assets, while the residential portfolio, 75 per cent of which was still rent controlled, had not been expanded since 1939.

The 1957 Rent Act gave a major boost to profitability through a rapid uplift in residential rental income, although all but 2,300 flats remained under control. Between 1957 and 1959 rents for the decontrolled properties increased by over 50 per cent, while controlled rents rose by some 20 per cent through permitted increases.[3] Decontrol also restimulated investment activity and by 1964 the company had spent some £1 million on improving and modernizing its residential properties. More importantly, the 1957 Act boosted asset values by almost a third and led to a rapid growth in company income, which rose from £22.5 million in 1958 to £33.45 million in 1962, while the dividend increased 1.5 times.

But it is significant that the income derived from decontrol under the 1957 Act did little to prompt LCF to increase investment in new residential property. Rather, the profit boost it stimulated was channelled into the company's move into the commercial and industrial property sectors. In 1959-60 alone, LCF invested some £3.25 million in industrial property and the overseas development policy was also expanded. Consequently, by 1963 the residential portfolio represented only 50 per cent of the company's assets. In fact, the bulk of the expansion of the non-residential portfolio over the next decade was to be funded by income derived from these rent decontrol measures rather than through increased borrowing. If the 1957 Act had been aimed to stimulate new investment in the private rental market, then it clearly failed in the case of LCF. Instead, the Act had precisely the opposite effect. It merely aided LCF's move out of the residential market.

Although the 1965 Rent Act brought almost all of LCF's flats into the new framework of rent regulation, by 1966 the company was able to report that rents had risen faster than had been anticipated. But it was also claimed that costs had risen some 20 per cent during 1965 and 1966 alone and, while these costs would eventually be recouped, it would take several years before they could be fully passed on to tenants. The following year costs had reportedly risen by a further 15 per cent and by 1968 for every £1 received in rent 7s went on management and repairs and 3s in rates and water rates. By now, however, the residential portfolio represented only 43 per cent of the company's total assets.

However, it was not rent regulation which was to prove too much for LCF, but an altogether different consequence of the return of a Labour Government in 1964, namely the advent of Corporation Tax under the 1965 Finance Act. LCF was particularly badly affected by this new tax, and by 1967 income was severely reduced as the company's taxation burden increased sharply. The net effect was to restrict the dividend severely, and this had an immediate impact on share prices. By 1968-9 only 85 per cent of the dividend was being met by income and it had been short-earned ever since the advent of Corporation Tax. LCF desperately needed a rapid source of additional income.

There was little alternative for LCF but to capitalize on the growing value of its residential portfolio and plunge into the rising tide of the flat break-up market, no matter how murky the water. Flat sales, to meet the immediate income shortfall as well as for reinvestment in higher-yielding investments, had become an acute necessity. The move was portentous. As a contemporary report stated: 'When a company the size of London County Freehold starts to sell flats, it has important implications for the future of rented accommodation in the country as a whole' (Investors Chronicle, 5 July 1968). Moreover, the tax changes which had led to the necessity for sales also meant that the cash they raised would be treated as trading profit rather than investment income and would therefore escape Corporation Tax. Instead, only Capital Gains Tax, by now the lower of the two, would be charged on the relatively small difference between sales prices and the notional value of the flats at 5 April 1965 when the Finance Act came into force.

Even for LCF, the rationale for flat sales was clear and an initial sales drive was initiated in 9 of the 70 blocks considered suitable for the process. Flats were offered to tenants at substantial discounts on the notional vacant possession value and second mortgages were made available in some cases to enable sales to go through. By the standards of the more aggressive break-up operators, LCF's marketing policy was decidedly low key. But such was the attractiveness of the offer that by the end of the first year of sales 40 per cent of tenants in these blocks had agreed to buy. Flats in the remaining 61 blocks were to be gradually released for sale up to 1971, when the company predicted that full cover for the dividend would have been restored.

Whether or not this prediction would have come true will never be known. Uncertainty caused by the 1967 Leasehold Reform Act concerning the sale of long leases on ground rents delayed the completion of the initial sales. By the time this confusion had been removed (under the 1969 Housing Act), the benefits of the income from these sales had arrived too late to save LCF.

Quite clearly, the dead weight of LCF's still substantial residential portfolio was dragging its income and hence its share values down.

With hindsight, the outcome was predictable. In November 1969 MEPC put in a £42 million bid for LCF. At the time, LCF had a book value of £62 million and the low bid by MEPC clearly reflected the discount at which LCF's shares stood on their underlying asset value. Although the residential portfolio offered considerable speculative opportunities given the developing break-up market, MEPC was attracted to LCF more for the commercial elements of the portfolio, which it saw the possibility of buying cheaply. This situation was also evident to others, and counter-bids soon arrived from Star (GB) Holdings and Minster Assets whose eyes were more firmly fixed on the large break-up potential of LCF's flat blocks.

At £28 million, LCF's own valuation of its residential portfolio was undoubtedly a conservative estimate, based on the standard residential investment yield of 8.0-8.5 per cent. In fact, the yield on a prevailing break-up basis was probably as low as 4 per cent, suggesting a potential break-up value in excess of £50 million for these properties alone. Clearly, LCF was going cheap by any stretch of the imagination. In the event, MEPC fought off the counter-bidders and, in early January 1970, LCF accepted the final bid of £47.5 million. The key factor in the outcome of these events was the behaviour of the institutional shareholders who held over 40 per cent of the company's equity. The attraction of an LCF-MEPC merger for these investors lay in the size of the enlarged MEPC which would emerge – combined assets would exceed £200 million—and the fact that LCF's shareholders would see their gross income rise by 20 per cent.

The takeover of LCF was perhaps the single most significant event in the overall demise of corporate residential landlords in the late 1960s, in terms both of the size of the property assets involved and of the nature of the company and its history. Although the sheer size and quality of LCF's holdings had insulated it from the changing economic climate of the post-war period, enabling it to maintain its traditional attitude to rented property well after many of its smaller contemporaries had fallen to speculative acquisition or had embarked on disinvestment policies, the company's conservatism eventually led to its undoing. Other, less substantial residential investors were more able to adapt to the rapid changes that had overtaken the sector by the mid 1960s and were more willing to take advantage of the potential for speculative asset realization, both to enhance income growth and to avoid the under-utilization of assets which spelt disaster for LCF and heralded a new and uncertain future for its 'pampered' tenants.

From pampered to protest: the arrival of the flat dealers

The acquisition of LCF brought MEPC's residential holdings from below 5 per cent of its total assets to 15 per cent. In fact MEPC had been actively disinvesting its existing residential portfolio throughout the mid to late 1960s through the selective sale of blocks and their remaining housing estates. These had been fed into the developing break-up market and blocks had been sold to flat dealers such as Fordham Investments, Amalgamated Investments and City and Municipal Properties. MEPC continued the flat sales policy belatedly inaugurated by LCF, and by May 1970 some £5.5 million worth of sales had been made or contracted.

The funds generated by these sales were directed into the property development and investment programme which MEPC was actively expanding. At the time MEPC was investing over £1 million a month in the commercial property sector and had substantial development interests abroad, principally in Canada and Australia. LCF's residential portfolio did not fit easily the company's structure and, as block values were rising, MEPC decided to realize an immediate profit on this part of the LCF purchase by disinvesting the bulk of its residential portfolio and reinvesting the proceeds in higher yielding commercial property.

This was not the only reason behind the sale, however, for in July 1970 MEPC found itself the object of a £120 million take-over bid by Commercial Union Assurance which was looking for a suitable vehicle with which to move into direct involvement in the burgeoning property sector. This move was part of a wider trend towards mergers and link-ups between the financial institutions and the property sector which were becoming a prevalent feature of the early 1970s (Barras, 1978; Boddy, 1981). For the institutions, property offered a stable and appreciating asset base for their business and provided a lucrative and expanding outlet for their ever growing financial resources. There was also the taxation advantage of investing in property directly rather than via property company shares.

The bid by Commercial Union coincided with a £55 million bid MEPC was making for merchant bankers Hill Samuel for very similar reasons. Under the prevailing tax situation, the prospect for property investment had been curtailed, but if property assets were used as a base for financial operations their potential could be greatly increased. At the same time, the potential asset growth of the property would provid security for long term borrowing. And naturally, a merger with a merchant bank would ensure a constant and guaranteed source of finance. In the event, both the Commercial Union bid and the proposed Hill Samuel merger failed to materialize. But meanwhile, the bulk of MEPC's residential holdings were put on the market.

In November 1970, an initial tranche of 1,532 flats in 11 blocks was offered for sale. Ten of these blocks were ex-LCF properties. The price asked was £10.5 million (or £6,850 per flat) which reflected a yield of less than 4.5 per cent. The blocks were sold to the Wallabrook Property Company, a break-up company formed specifically for the operation by a consortium of institutional investors and headed by Harold (now Lord) Lever, Chancellor of the Duchy of Lancaster in Harold Wilson's Government. Six of these blocks, representing half of the flats, were located in central London, while a further block involved in the deal, Ridgemont Gardens, appears to have subsequently passed back to the freeholder of the land, the Bedford Estate.

Wallabrook's flats present a cameo of the fate of much of the rest of the central London flat market in the last two decades. By 1980, only some 277 of the 640 ex-LCF flats owned by Wallabrook in the central London area were still registered at local rent offices. This suggests that well over 50 per cent of the flats in these blocks had been broken by this date. The remainder represented a potential sales value of over £13 million at average 1980 prices—well over the original price paid for the entire portfolio in 1970 and considerably more than the £2 million or so these 277 flats costs Wallabrook.

Using data from the registration records it is possible to compare the relative increases in rents and capital values which took place in the following decade. For example, the registered rent for a typical three room flat in Bickenhall Mansions, W1, was £640 per annum in 1970. Given that the flats were bought on an average yield of 4.5 per cent, this suggests an investment value for these flats of about £14,000 at that time. By 1980, three room flats in Bickenhall Mansions were selling for £72,000 for a 119 year lease, while registered rents for such flats had risen to £1,700. The comparative rates of increase in rents and values, 165 per cent and over 400 per cent respectively, clearly shows how rental yields have lagged behind the appreciation on vacant possession values. Despite these ample rewards, the break-up of these blocks was not without its problems for Wallabrook. In common with many of its contemporaries, Wallabrook only managed to remain solvent after the 1974 crash by a timely loan from the Bank of England's 'lifeboat', in their case to the tune of £30 million.

But what of the fate of the other LCF blocks taken over by MEPC in 1970? The subsequent history of these flats is much more convoluted, and much more revealing, involving as it does some of the key events in the break-up process. Following the successful disposal to Wallabrook, MEPC concluded its disinvestment policy in April 1971 by selling the rest of the ex-LCF portfolio, plus a few of its own remaining blocks, in a deal worth £33.5 million to a joint partnership formed by the First National Finance Corporation (FNFC) and William Stern, then still with Freshwater. In all, MEPC is reputed to have made 10 per cent net on the sale of the ex-LCF flats it bought a year earlier, which was not a bad return by the standards of the time, but distinctly modest compared to what was to follow. Half of the flats went to Swallow Securities, jointly owned by FNFC and Stern, and formed specifically to carry out a break-up operation. FNFC took a quarter for its own thriving break-up trade, and the remaining quarter, including some of the most prestigious blocks, were taken into the Freshwater organization for investment purposes. This situation did not last long, however, and from here on LCF's ill-fated flats took increasingly divergent paths into the break-up trade. But few of the new owners were to gain much pleasure or profit in the long term from the acquisitions which promised them such riches. We will deal with the separate paths of the three portfolios in turn.

William Stern: last of the residential magnates

William Stern, a Harvard trained lawyer and son-in-law to Osias Freshwater, had been responsible for guiding the Freshwater Group from a modest but essentially down–market operation into a major property empire in the 10 years since he had joined the group in the early 1960s (see Chapter 8). By 1971, however, he had decided the time was right to set up on his own and he broke with the Freshwater organization. Stern took with him some £36 million worth of the better-quality Freshwater residential portfolio, including the 18 ex-LCF blocks (worth £16.75 million) bought from MEPC.

Stern intended these blocks to form the investment core of his private property, insurance and banking group, Stern Holdings. The 'Key Flats' logo inherited from LCF was resurrected and Stern moved his head office into the old LCF head office in the prestigious Albert Hall Mansions, Kensington Gore. Stern held something of a unique place in the property world, for he was still arguing that, under conditions of steady inflation, a well-managed middle-class residential portfolio could be made to pay as a long-term investment. He saw the fair rent provisions of the 1965 Act as an opportunity rather than an obstacle, given that the tenants of his quality blocks were getting good value for money and a sought-after address and that they could be persuaded to pay regular rent increases using the fair rent procedure. This would ensure a steady growth in investment values, giving a good long-term return and a basis for his banking activities. It would also allow rapid equity growth as the initial purchases were made entirely on borrowed money.

The technique which Stern used to maintain the investment values of his blocks was one which he had successfully adopted during his period with Freshwater and was relatively straightforward. Once a flat became vacant, the rent asked for a new tenancy would be considerably higher than that which had previously been charged, despite the fact that the latter was the maximum legally permitted rent under the provisions of the 1965 Act. Often rents were doubled. New tenants were generally willing to pay such a rent due to the shortage of rented accommodation elsewhere in central London, itself partly the product of the emerging break-up process. The new tenants also tended to be both younger and wealthier than the previous occupants and, by flat sharing, the rent an individual would pay could be kept reasonably low.

There was nothing actually illegal about charging these higher rents, although if the tenant became aware that the previous (maximum permitted) rent was lower than his/her present rent, then a full rebate of the excess paid could be demanded. In practice, most tenants simply did not know, or did not complain. The technique, therefore, relied on implicit compliance by the new tenants, which could usually be relied on given the shortage of alternative accommodation.

New tenants were also usually asked to sign a tenancy agreement which stated that the new rent had been mutually agreed by both parties. Although not legally binding in the sense that it replaced the permitted maximum rent for the flat, the new 'unofficial' rent could then be used to back up applications to the rent officer for substantial increases in the registered rents for existing regulated tenancies. Furthermore, once a flat had been let at the higher rent and subsequently vacated, this higher rent then became the recognized 'fair' (i.e. maximum permitted) rent, and the whole process started again.[4]

The effect this policy had on property values and equity can be illustrated by an actual example quoted by Stern in 1972 concerning a property bought by Freshwater in 1962 in north-west London (Hillmore and Raw, 1972). Although predating the rent regulation procedures introduced by the 1965 Rent Act, the mechanisms of the process are identical. The block in question cost £72,000 for which the company raised a £55,000 mortgage and contributed £17,000 of its own equity. The gross rent roll at the time of purchase was £5,480 per annum, representing a yield of 7.6 per cent. By 1966 the rent roll had been increased to £9,026 per annum and the block was revalued at £115,000 on a yield of 7.8 per cent. A new mortgage was then negotiated for £76,000 which not only allowed the existing mortgage to be repayed, but also released £21,000 in cash for further investment. At the same time, Freshwater's original equity had been more than doubled to £39,000 (£115,000—£76,000) in only 4 years.

In itself, this was not a particularly novel technique: it is essentially the basic modus operandi of most property investment operations. But it was the particular way Stern used the fair rent process which made his style unique. The rent registration records of the three central London boroughs give testimony to the systematic manner in which Stern used the rent registration procedures to boost rents and hence property values in his blocks throughout the early 1970s. In many cases rents fixed by the rent officer were challenged through the rent assessment committees, and in a clear majority of cases the rents were further raised to the benefit of the landlord. Table 7.2 shows examples of this technique from two of Stern's central London blocks in 1972.

By concentrating his investments in the high-status end of the market in large, easily managed properties, Stern clearly hoped to maintain a profitable long-term lettings business in a period when the overwhelming pressure was for such residential assets to be fully capitalized on their sale value. To his credit, Stern fully recognized the social costs which this sort of policy placed on his tenants and played an instrumental role in the

Table 7.2 *Typical rent increases awarded by the rent assessment Committee (RAC) on appeals by Stern Holdings, 1972*

Phillimore Court, Kensington, W8: rents registered June 1972

	RO registration			*RAC appeal*	
Rooms	*Rent*	*Service*	*Rent*	*Services*	*% increase*
3	725	315	900	318	28.6
5	900	374	1,100	378	22.2
6	885	374	1,000	378	13.0
3	675	315	850	318	25.9
4	800	374	1,000	378	25.0
3	650	315	800	318	23.0
3	700	315	850	318	21.4

Iverna Gardens, Kensington, W8: rents registered May 1972

	RO registration			*RAC appeal*	
Rooms	*Rent*	*Service*	*Rent*	*Service*	*% Increase*
7	920	255	1,300	255	41.3
7	910	238	1,100	238	20.9
6	940	238	1,400	238	48.9
6	920	255	1,200	255	30.4
7	900	193	1,000	193	11.1
6	920	238	1,100	238	19.6

Note: in all these cases it is the rental element, not the service charge element, which is substantially increased by the rent assessment committee's decision. The committee's increases ranged from 13 to 49 per cent and averaged 22 per cent for the flats in Phillimore Court and 29 per cent for those in Iverna Gardens.

introduction of a national rent rebate scheme for tenants of unfurnished property in the 1972 Housing Finance Act. This scheme was specifically designed to give financial support to those tennants who were unable to meet the sort of rent increases landlords like Stern were demanding. Clearly, Stern saw no long-term future for private renting without state subsidies or tax shelters.[5]

However, the major problem inherent in Stern's operation was that it entailed deficit financing, at least in the initial stages, with rental yields of 4-5 per cent and interest rates at 9 per cent plus. This was a perfectly normal situation at the time, but whereas Stern's flat-dealing contemporaries such as FNFC aimed to cover this shortfall by rapid flat sales, Stern's policy was either to 'subsidize' the investment side through other property dealing and development, or to roll up the interest until the regular 'fair rent' reviews raised income to meet the changes. In the euphoria of the 1971-3 period and the general appreciation in property values, Stern was able to refinance short-term loans as they became due with little difficulty, purely on the basis of personal guarantees.

But it was this personal involvement that led to his spectacular bankruptcy in mid 1974 when his property and finance empire crashed in the wake of the financial crisis of 1973. The sudden 5 point increase in bank rate in November 1973 was not matched by rental income and, with others, Stern experienced a massive cashflow deficit. His personal debts totalled £118 million and creditors included the Crown Agents (owed £40 million), National Westminster, Barclays and Lloyds banks as well as Keyser Ullman, FNFC, International Credit Bank and many others. In March 1974 Stern's ex-LCF blocks had been valued at £17.4 million. But outstanding debts on these totalled £16.5 million at interest rates of between 12 and 17 per cent. As Table 7.3 shows, the bulk of these debts were owed to FNFC and MEPC.

Table 7.3 *Valuations and outstanding debts of Stern Holdings' ex-LCF blocks in central London, May 1974*

Property	*No. of flats*	*Valuation at March 1974*	*Estimated value per flat*	*Creditor*	*Debt £M*	*Rate of interest*
Avenue Mansions, NW3	44	£636,000	£14,455			
Iverna Gardens, W8	47	£940,000	£20,000			
Clive Court, W9	154	£1,619,000	£10,513			
Grosvenor Court Gardens, W2	36	£730,000	£20,278			
Rodney Court, W9	95	£931,000	£9,800			
Sandringham Court, W9	52	£207,000	£3,980			
Southwold Mansions, W9	61	£558,000	£9,148	MEPC/FNFC	£5.378	12.5%
Buckingham Mansions, NW6	49	£676,000	£13,796			
Phillimore Court, W8	32	£1,487,000	£46,469			
Bedford Court Mansions, WC1	20	£202,000	£10,100			
Leinster Mansions, NW3	9	£20,000	£2,222			
Marlborough Mansions, NW6	95	£1,441,000	£15,168			
Cleveland Mansions, W9	32	£184,000	£5,750			
Albert Hall Mansions, SW7	82	£2,470,000	£30,122	FNFC	£8.614	17.0%
Albert Court, SW7	62	£3,483,000	£56,177	MBFC/KU	£3.480	15.0%
Total	870	£15,584,000	£17,913		£16.072	

MEPC – Metropolitan Estates and Property Company
FNFC – First National Finance Corporation
MBFC – Midland Bank Finance Corporation
KU – Keyser Ullman

Source: W. H. Cork Gully & Company, Proposals for a Moratorium, the Stern Group of Companies, 1975

The vultures descend

Exactly how much MEPC ever received in payment for the blocks is unknown. The valuations given in Table 7.3 represented nowhere near the price received for the blocks when they were eventually disposed of by the liquidators Cork Gulley in the following 3 or 4 years. For example, Albert Court was valued at almost £3.5 million in 1974. It was sold for just under £2 million within 2 years to David Tannen's Hailbury Investments. Tannen had been active in the break-up business in the early 1970s and was not alone among the speculators who re-emerged from the wreakage of the property crash, which they had done so much to create, in order to pick up residential properties at bargain basement prices which their more unfortunate colleagues such as Stern were now being forced to sell.

Tannen bought Albert Court at an estimated average of £30,000 to £32,000 per flat. In 1977 registered rents in the block ranged from £2,200 for three rooms to £3,000 for four rooms, giving a creditable 8-10 per cent return gross. But capital gains were much more rewarding. By 1980 flats in the block were on the market for between £130,000 for an unmodernized five room flat and up to £335,000 for a fully modernized six room flat inclusive of fittings, on 117 year leases. Phillimore Court, Kensington, went for a similar bargain price of £810,000 to Jersey based Jamboree Holdings via its subsidiary Electromech Properties Ltd. Jamboree had every reason to celebrate - the flats cost it about £25,000 each and by 1980 were fetching £120,000 for five rooms on a 97 year lease. This figure can be contrasted with registered rents of between £2,000 and £2,450 per annum in 1980 for flats in the block.

The other beneficiaries of Stern's bankruptcy were a varied collection of speculators, tenants and institutions. The break-up dealers who, like Tannen and Jamboree, cashed in on the domestic property inflation of 1977-80 and Stern's misfortune, included the Liberian registered UAE Investments and the aptly named Gaingold Ltd. Beleggings Company NV, registered in Curacao in the Dutch Antilles, purchased Clive Court, Maida Vale, for a reputed £1.4 million in 1977 (Figure 7.1). Beleggings was controlled by another established flat breaker, Michael Rivkin, ex-boss of the property dealing company Renslade. Unlike Stern, Rivkin was able to walk away from the debts incurred by his companies during the property crash under the protection of limited liability. Clive Court was one of several purchases of blocks he made during this period, paying just over £9,000 per flat in a block where registered rents in 1978 ranged from £580 for one room to £3,000 for five rooms. By 1980 these five room flats were fetching £85,000 for a 76 year lease, representing a staggering 800 per cent profit in 3 years.

Two blocks eventually passed to Biskeep Nominees, the National Westminster Bank's trustee vehicle for Westgrove Securities' break-up property trust operations. Run by Arnold Hagenbach of Arndale Shopping Centre fame, Westgrove offered an anonymous method of attracting

FOR SALE
BY TENDER
THESE TWO EXCEPTIONAL LONG LEASEHOLD
RESIDENTIAL INVESTMENTS
ALBERT HALL MANSIONS KENSINGTON
34 Flats Vacant
CLIVE COURT
MAIDA VALE
24 Flats Vacant
For further particulars apply:-
Keith Cardale, Groves & Co.
Chartered Surveyors
43 North Audley Street, Grosvenor Square, London, W1Y 2AQ
Tel: 01-629 6604

Figure 7.1

institutional funds into break-up situations. Westgrove was to founder in similar circumstances to Stern during the interest rate increase instituted by another Conservative Government, this time in the early 1980s. The Church Commissioners took the opportunity of Stern's liquidation to buy in the head lease of Sandringham Court on their Maida Vale Estate, adding it to the four ex-LCF blocks they acquired in a similar manner in 1970. The Commissioners began to break-up these blocks in 1979 in line with a policy of disinvesting and rationalization of their large-scale residential portfolio which had been in progress for some years. The move to a direct involvement in break-up marked a change in disinvestment policy for the Commissioners. Previously they had been selling blocks wholesale to flat breakers.

Finally, at least three of Stern's central London ex-LCF blocks were bought by residents' associations—Iverna Gardens, Buckingham Mansions and Marlborough Mansions. The successful tenant buy-outs were dependent on the presence in the block of articulate, well-organized and, in most cases, professionally qualified residents who were able to draw on their expertise and self-motivation to push the deals through. In blocks where these qualities were missing, there was little opportunity for residents to benefit from the opportunites tenant buy-outs presented. In all, some 15 of Stern's blocks passed into residents' control through the liquidators.

Stern's vision of a viable middle class residential investment sector collapsed in the face of the inexorable pressures facing the sector, pressures which themselves had aided the expansion of the property values this vision was based on. In the event, Stern had underestimated the extent to which the property market had undermined its own viability during the mad scramble for speculative profit in the early 1970s. A little inflation may be a property investor's best friend, but it has a tendency to bite back if provoked!

First National Finance Corporation: bringing the game into disrepute

If LCF was the epitome of the established residential investment company which went to the wall in the 1960s, then the activities of FNFC and its property-dealing subsidiaries epitomize its mirror image, the specialist speculative flat breaker who emerged in the 1970s to take its place. Put simply, FNFC was to flat breaking what LCF was to flat investment. It was one of the earliest in the field, and certainly one of the largest. Unlike LCF, however, its involvement in residential property was far shorter lived. Whereas LCF fell foul of the adverse investment climate of the 1960s, FNFC caught the full force of the mid 1970s property crash, caused in no small way by its own heavy involvement in flat break-up.

FNFC's involvement in flat breaking dates back to 1966 when Trust House Ltd decided that its block of 138 'service' flats at Marsham Court, Marsham

Street, SW1, were no longer compatible with the group's hotel operations. FNFC, through its property-dealing subsidiary, First National Developments (FND), formed Allisday Properties and bought Marsham Court for £750,000. FND spent £40,000 refurbishing the common parts and the flats, along with their ground rents, were sold within 3 years for a profit of well over £250,000 after costs. This might not seem a great deal given the initial £790,000 outlay and a 3 year wait, but FND's equity stake in Allisday was a mere £50. On this basis, the leverage was quite phenomenal!

The structure of Allisday itself is interesting in that it typifies the many break-up companies which followed as the market developed. Most importantly, it illustrates the close links these companies had with the secondary banking sector. These were to prove the crucial channel through which the finance for flat breaking was funded in increasing quantities. Allisday was a £100 company, formed by FND in partnership with the British and Continental Banking Company and Hambros Nominees, two other secondary banking houses which each took a quarter share. Hambros also owned 13.3 per cent of FNFC's equity and was a consistent source of financial support for FNFC throughout this period. Allisday's finance was provided jointly by the partners and the proceeds of the operation were split proportionally.

As with its later break-up operations, FNFC provided the purchasers of the flats, mostly sitting tenants, with 90 per cent mortgages on its properties through its own banking facilities. Thus the whole exercise, from the initial acquisition of the block to the sale of the flats to tenants, was entirely self financing. There was no need for purchasers to seek outside mortgage funding, an important factor during a period when flats had yet to become an acceptable risk for building societies, and also in a property in which tenants were mostly only on moderate incomes (average rents were about £460 per annum at the time). Once the operation was completed Allisday was wound up.

In the following 3 years FND embarked on a series of these one-off break-ups, on its own account as well as in conjunction with other heavyweight backers (Table 7.4). There were also a number of joint companies with David Goldstone, a rising star of the break-up fraternity, again on a profit-sharing basis. The Goldstone-FND partnership created 11 companies between May 1967 and July 1971 to break 1,100 flats in 17 blocks, mostly in central London. FNFC provided the full finance for the operations and, by December 1971, some 350 of these flats had been sold. By mid 1969 FNFC was itself involved in breaking 2,000 flats in 30 blocks worth about £10 million at break-up value, again mostly in central London, and all purchased from established disinvesting landlords. This total had increased to an estimated 50 blocks by the end of 1970 after a major purchase from the Co-operative Insurance Society. By this time FNFC was probably the front-runner in the break-up field.

Table 7.4 *First National Finance Corporation: break-up subsidiaries, financial partners and properties purchased, 1966–9*

Company	*Partners*	*Properties*
Allisday Properties (1966)	British and Continental Banking Co. Hambros Bank	Marsham Court, W1
Du Cane Court Ltd (1967)	British and Continental Banking Co. Suez Finance Co. Hambros Bank Ionian Bank	Du Cane Court, SW12
Mandtail Ltd (1967)	Anglo-Israel Bank	Maitland Court, W2
Perlevere Properties (1968)	British and Continental Banking Co. Ionian Bank Hill Samuel Rothschilds	Moreland Court, NW2 Wendover Court, NW2 Lancaster Close, W2
Shortlands Properties (1968)	Commercial Credit Trust	Sloane Avenue Mansions, SW3 Strathmore Court, NW8
Keston Securities (1969)	Robert Fleming	Campden Hill Court, W8

Source: Milner (1969)

However, even these dealings were to pale in comparison with the events of 1971 when FNFC acquired the major share of the 6,000 or so ex-LCF flats from MEPC. This deal brought FNFC's total involment in the break-up market to almost 10,000 flats. But the low yield on which the properties were bought, 4–5 per cent, meant that FNFC faced a financing shortfall of at least 4 per cent. To accommodate this, MEPC agreed for the payments to be made in instalments over the following 6 years, thereby considerably reducing the immediate financing requirements. Nevertheless, the deal was only feasible if a steady rate of sales could be maintained.

FNFC instituted a high-powered sales drive in the newly acquired blocks, but its sales methods soon began to run up against increasing protest from tenants. Ironically, much of this protest came from the well-organized and middle-class Federation of London County Residents Associations, the London-wide tenants' association inherited from LCF. As one observer noted, 'Hell hath no fury like the middle-class scorned' and the articulate tenants FNFC found itself with certainly proved an embarrassing thorn in its side. The complaints were not about rents but rather the leases on which the flats were being offered, the level of service charges, which were increasing dramatically, and also accusations of large price increases if would-be purchasers were slow to buy.

Nevertheless, FNFC was unrepentant and Viscount De L'Isle, company chairman and noted free marketer, claimed FNFC's activities had been misrepresented. In a statement issued by FNFC to answer those charges, De L'Isle denied culpability for the consequences of his company's policies, commenting: 'We have not been responsible for the rise in the price of residential property. This is an economic factor outside the control of private individuals or commercial organizations' (Financial Times, 6 June, 1972). This is a revealing statement. The mysterious 'economic forces' De L'Isle invokes to explain the events surrounding his company's activities are simply those which compel assets to be exploited in their most profitable form. Flat breaking was the most profitable utilization of these blocks during this period and in this respect FNFC was only responding to the wider profit imperative.

But what the statement fails to mention is that the conditions in which flat blocks could be broken, and therefore put to their most profitable use, had to be actively created by the companies involved. Without the secondary banking sector to funnel money into the break-up market there would have been no effective demand, no value gap and no profit. The point, of course, is that while FNFC and companies like it were indeed reacting to 'economic forces' not specifically of their making, they were nevertheless able to mediate those conditions in order to exploit them to their best advantage. Contrary to De L'Isle's opinion, FNFC and its compatriots were very much responsible for the speculative boom in residential property prices which they were exploiting – and for the social costs they imposed on the residents.

However, the increasing criticism that the company's activities were generating attracted the attention of the media and the growing anger of the tenants eventually reached Parliament, not least due to the sizeable population of MPs housed by the central London flat market. At the same time, FNFC had just acquired full banking status from the Department of Trade and the row over such contentious sales activity was clearly not the sort of thing the newly emergent bank wanted to be involved with. FNFC probably also realized the rapid price spiral might end soon and this was as good a time as any to get out, at or near the top of the market, and realize the capital gain which had accrued to the flats. FNFC's answer was therefore to sell off its entire flat dealing portfolio in one go. The 10,000 or so flats were sold in June 1972, grossing over £76 million, and an estimated profit of £24 million spread over the next few years. This represents well over £2,000 for every tenant involved. At the time only £5 million of the monies owed to MEPC had been repayed and FNFC had probably made a net profit of 50 per cent on their half of previous year's deal.

Of the 10,000 flats, probably 6,000 comprised the Key Flat element of the MEPC purchase, representing something like £45 million of the total. Thus, in 2 years the value of this share of the LCF portfolio had more than doubled, despite being partly broken. Reflecting this, the yields on which the properties were reputedly traded fell progressively from the 8.0–8.5 per cent on which the LCF—MEPC takeover was valued in 1970, to 4–5 per cent for the 1971 deal between MEPC and FNFC/Stern, and to 2.0–3.0 per cent for FNFC's sale in 1972. This certainly suggests at least a doubling of capital values between 1970 and 1972.

The blocks, including at least 22 of the ex-LCF properties in central London (see Table 7.1), passed to Regalian Securities, Fairview Estates and a host of private companies owned by the Berger Group. Of the total properties sold by FNFC, Fairview took four blocks worth £3.4 million, while Regalian acquired £22.25 million of property, representing the bulk of FNFC's own dealing stock and totalling some 3,000 flats in all. The blocks acquired by Berger appear to have been those jointly owned by FNFC and Stern through Swallow Securities, and in general comprised much of the lower value end of the ex-LCF portfolio.

In fact, FNFC's sales to Regalian and Fairview actually amounted to little more than a piece of deft profit taking and financial manoeuvring. FNFC not only owned a 30 per cent share of Regalian and held the controlling interest in Fairview, but also provided all the finance on which the flats were purchased at a variable interest rate set at a very lucrative minimum of 9.25 per cent. The repayments were to be deferred for 3 years to obviate the immediate shortfall problem and to coincide with FNFC's repayment deadline to MEPC. Thus at least a third of FNFC's so-called sale was entirely self-financed. FNFC therefore stood to benefit not only from the interest repayments on the finance lent for the deal but also from a slice of the trading profits through its share holdings in the two companies. At the same time, by disposing of its flat dealing portfolio in this way, FNFC had sufficiently distanced itself from the now tarnished activity of flat breaking to pursue its banking pretensions with a cleaner image.

Fairview was a small London based property development company which had been backed by FNFC since 1964 and the principal activity of which until mid 1972 had been building blocks of flats for sale in suburban London. Regalian was altogether different and in many respects much more interesting as it typifies the type of break-up specialists that were launched in the 1970s during the property boom.

Regalian Securities: from boom to bust in two years

Regalian's immediate history dates from January 1971 when an FNFC subsidiary, First National Industrial Trust, bought 60 per cent of a run-down Midlands based holding company called Yarm Investments and Finance Ltd at 20p a share. The main attraction of Yarm was that it had a quotation on the Midlands and Western Stock Exchange, and shortly after acquisition

David Goldstone became chairman and managing director. Yarm's remaining assets were stripped out and in October 1971 the shares were suspended to allow the private property-dealing interests of Goldstone and FNFC to be injected into its inert shell. This operation was completed by March 1972 and the company renamed Regalian Securities.

The objective of this shell operation was to provide a public vehicle for the flat-breaking activities of Goldstone and FNFC without the trouble of seeking a quotation themselves, and it provided for the continued partnership of Goldstone's dealing 'expertise' and FNFC's administrative and financial resources. FNFC made £5 million immediately available for dealing activities. Regalian was 30 per cent owned by Goldstone and 31 per cent owned by FNFC, but all the company itself owned was a string of minority stocks in Goldstone's property-dealing companies which were brought in.

The majority shareholder in these companies was, of course, First National Developments, and FNFC also derived at least 50 per cent of the profits accruing from the company's activities. This posed problems, for the Midlands Stock Exchange was reluctant to restore the public quotation for a company which only owned minority shareholdings in subsidiaries where the other partner (FNFC) had voting control. Before the quotation was restored capital restructuring was required in order to give voting control to Regalian rather than FNFC. This still left FNFC as the major shareholder in Regalian and the beneficiary of over half the profits of the main subsidiaries in its own right. This complex structure ensured that FNFC retained the major share of any profits to be made from the flat breaking the new company would be involved in. As one source noted, Regalian represented 'a 5 year profit bank from the flats it owns, with an unspecified chance to strip assets' (Sunday Times, 26 March 1972).

When the shares were refloated in March 1972 they soared immediately to 134.5p, reflecting not only FNFC's heavy backing but the prevailing euphoria surrounding property and especially flat-dealing activity. The extent of the faith city investors had in the Goldstone/FNFC partnership can be judged from the fact that the asset backing was only 13.5p per share and the share price was 40 times the forecast earnings. The great advantage for Regalian was that the high share price would allow takeovers in exchange for paper rather than money. This was a popular activity at the time (cf LCF) and was a further incentive for established property investors to capitalize assets in terms of their short-term capital profitability at the expense of long-term income in order to deter the acquisitive attention of more aggressive competitors.

Within 3 months of its reflotation Regalian added its £22.25 million share of FNFC's flat sale to existing property assets worth only £6.25 million. Repayment of the 100 per cent mortgage finance provided by FNFC for the purchase was to be delayed until June 1975 and even then payments, including interest, would not be enforced until individual blocks of flats were completely sold. Therefore, the deal gave FNFC the major stake in a flat trading subsidiary and neatly avoided the cash flow deficit which would have arisen on property purchased on a 2 - 3 per cent yield. Regalian merely took over the break-up of the blocks where FNFC had left off: the operation was exactly the same, only the name of the company selling the leases changed. The efficiency of the FNFC/Regalian break-up operation can be judged from the fact that in mid 1980 only 19 per cent of the 242 flats in the three ex-LCF blocks owned by Regalian in central London had current registered rents.

In the event, Regalian and FNFC were to suffer the fate which befell most of the other inflated property speculators and traders whose activities had contributed so much to present the 'unacceptable face of capitalism'. The interest rate rise of November 1973 coupled with the mortgage famine and the collapse of the market caught both companies with equal force. The mysterious 'economic forces' which had so benefited FNFC in 1971 were to lead to its downfall in 1974. Of course, FNFC was as much culprit as victim. By 1975 FNFC had made provisions of £110 million against losses in the preceding year and in all some £289 million in loans from the Bank of England 'lifeboat' operation were needed to keep the company afloat.[7]

Regalian's crash was nothing if not spectacular. By May 1975, the shares had plummeted to 7p and in desperation the company was even contemplating negotiations for the sale of some of its partly broken blocks to the GLC, a somewhat paradoxical move given Viscount de L'Isle's free market views. In the event, the state was to provide an alternative salvation, in the form of the Bank of England's 'lifeboat', which allowed FNFC to renegotiate its outstanding debt and Regalian to restructure its repayments to FNFC. In 1976, the completion date for the 1972 deal was deferred to 1982 with the debts being effectively transferred to subsidiary companies. This enabled Regalian to resume earning management fees and trading those flats which had not been part of the 1972 FNFC sale. As a result, by the end of 1976 Regalian had become in all practical senses a quoted estate agent.

However, this restructuring allowed Regalian to benefit from the resurgence of the break-up market during the late 1970s, and the company was able to embark on further property acquisitions from 1978 onwards in order to replenish its depleted property portfolio. This was becoming a problem, for as it continued to sell property it was losing its principal revenue source at the same time. This, of course, is the classic problem of any property trading company and Regalian was now looking for alternative sources of profitability in the commercial and industrial property sectors.

During this period Regalian was to discover a novel, and state aided, source of break-up stock. In 1981 five blocks of 290 flats were bought from the London Borough of Wandsworth for £3.5 million as part of the council's privatization policy. The blocks had been emptied by the council and

Regalian set about investing £2.5 million in renovation, modernisation and landscaping. The flats were put on the market at between £30,000 and £60,000, and by early 1982 only 13 flats of the original 162 put on the market were reputedly unsold (Fielding, 1982). Again, an essential element of the sales strategy was the provision of 100 per cent mortgages for prospective owners. Regalian is now the market leader in the break-up of ex-council estates with a growing portfolio of blocks purchased cheaply from disinvesting local authorities. The skills developed in the speculative boom of the early 1970s are now being profitably used to help the current Conservative Government pursue its dismantling of public housing. Of course, in many ways Thatcherism merely represents the political triumph of what was once the 'unacceptable face' of capitalism, typified by the asset stripper and financial speculator.

But what of the flats, including the ex-LCF blocks, derived from the FNFC sale? These flats had effectively been in limbo since 1976, with Regalian acting as manager, but not as full beneficial owner. The renegotiated completion date for the sale – 31 July 1982—arrived with Regalian no nearer to repaying the outstanding loans. The original principal of £22.5 million had by now accrued rolled-up interest charges of some £25 million. But by this time Regalian was capitalized at a mere £3 million. Consequently, the 3,000 or so flats simply reverted to FNFC. Of these, some 800 were still tenanted or held vacant, with a potential sales value of perhaps £26 million. This nevertheless represented a poor return for FNFC given Regalian's outstanding debts of almost £50 million. For Regalian, however, the good times were just beginning again.

Berger: the secret empire

A more or less similar series of events appears to have befallen the £20 million worth of blocks which FNFC sold to the Berger Group. A large proportion of LCF's central London blocks (at least 18 and possibly 20), comprising over 1,300 flats, were sold to Berger companies. It is almost certain that this deal was also self-financed by FNFC, for by the late 1970s Berger was facing a debt-rescheduling problem on these properties similar to Regalian's. But by the time Berger took on its share of the ex-LCF portfolio from Swallow Securities, it was already an old hand at flat breaking.

Berger had been actively selling flats since the early 1960s and was an early leader in the field. Like the Freshwater Group, Berger's property empire was built on the basis of high gearing during a period of steady inflation and using the expanding equity to remortgage existing properties in order to buy new ones. By the late 1960s Berger was well used to deficit financing, using rents to pay interest charges and relying on trading to generate profits. It was also adept at self-financing its own sales by arranging mortgages for would-be buyers. As early as 1964 the annual report of one of its two publicly quoted subsidiaries, Reliable Properties, noted a scheme which the company ran to provide mortgages for buyers in flats it was trading in north-west London.

By the early 1970s the Berger Group was going through an expansionary phase helped by the enormous break-up potential of its existing investments. In 1972 Reliable claimed to be making 70 per cent profit over the book value of its flats and the Berger Group clearly looked forward to a comparable level of profit on the new purchases from FNFC. But while Berger undoubtedly continued the break-up of the ex-LCF blocks, which by then had been in progress for some 2 years, it is by no means clear to what extent this policy was pursued by the individual companies involved. This is partly due to the group's notorious secrecy as to the nature of its activities and to its highly convoluted company structure. But it is also a result of Berger's approach to the management of its property portfolio which is typified by a degree of parsimony not generally adopted by its contemporaries.

The success of the Berger property empire is based on a closely controlled balance between trading and investment which minimizes taxation and maximizes long-term capital appreciation. And the balance between these two activities varies considerably, not only between the many private companies controlled by the group, but also within each company at different times. Thus while in some cases sales may have been pursued with sitting tenants in certain of the blocks or at certain periods when sales needed to be speeded up, at other times only those flats vacated by tenants would be offered for sale. There is no way of telling which of these approaches was adopted in the ex-LCF blocks Berger acquired in central London.

That sales were pursued in these blocks is quite evident, however. By mid 1980 only 400 or so flats had current rent registrations, approximately a third of the total. During the 1974-6 period Berger had been forced into selling flats at depressed prices due to the need to generate income in order to meet the interest charges it faced after the events of 1973. Although the group survived this period, both the publicly quoted companies went into the red and it is probable that a large number of its private companies did so as well. It is almost certain that the Berger companies involved in the ex-LCF purchase were forced into a policy of rapid sales, but with little long-term effect. In late 1979 it had become clear that Berger would not be in a position to meet the deferred repayment deadline which, like that of Regalian, had been rescheduled to 1980. The flats simply passed back to Swallow Securities in lieu of payment.

The move was shrouded in some mystery, however, for in 1980 Swallow's accounts showed a deficit of £1,033, the company being technically insolvent. FNFC explained this apparent anomaly by claiming that Swallow merely held the properties as a trustee, although it refused to name the ultimate owner. This was not surprising, for the residents of the blocks were pressing for £5 million worth of repair works to be carried out, a legacy of Berger's notorious non-maintenance policy. Of course, Swallow was not the only company with problems. In 1982 FNFC was itself also still technically insolvent, supported only by the outstanding £170 million in loans on 7 days' notice from the Bank of England's 'lifeboat'. Ironically, by this time it was being suggested in the City that FNFC could itself be subject to a break-up operation which would undoubtedly benefit the shareholders and, moreover, 'rid the City of the uncomfortable memories inherent in the FNFC name' (Sunday Times, 23 June 1982). In the case of FNFC, the cycle of competition had come full circle.

Postscript

In little more than 10 years, London County Freehold's prestigious Key Flats empire, which for the most part had been held since well before the Second world War, had passed through a bewildering series of ownership changes. Some blocks changed hands five or six times. The break-up policy which London County Freehold had itself put into effect in 1968 had reduced the rented proportion to perhaps a third by 1980, when only 1,136 flats out of the 4,100 referred to in Table 7.1 remained as registered unfurnished tenancies. Even so, at average 1980 prices, these represented well over £50 million of potential break-up value still to be extracted from the rump of the Key Flats portfolio in central London. This compares to the 1969 valuation of £28 million for the entire 8,000 or so flats originally acquired by MEPC.

Precisely where the profits from the break-up of these blocks has gone is a matter for conjecture. Some individual directors of the companies involved have certainly derived considerable private fortunes from the activity. For those whose operations were protected by limited liability, the events of 1974 were unfortunate, but essentially harmless in the long run. And the property crash made opportunities which were to prove eminently profitable for those able to take advantage of the 'knock-down' sales of Stern's blocks. For the Berger Group, flat sales helped to maintain the many charities it devoutly supports. For MEPC the bulk sale aided the expansion of the company into large-scale commercial and industrial development programmes both at home and abroad. And a large proportion of the money generated by the break-up of the blocks accrued, in the form of interest payments, to the banks which supplied the financing for the various deals. The extent to which the various banking interests involved in the sale of these London County Freehold blocks have ever received their repayments in full remains an open question, however. Benefits will have also been derived by the various shareholders in the public companies involved, while the stipends and upkeep of numerous Church of England parishes will in some part have been derived from the sale of flats resulting from the Church Commissioners' break-up activity. Last, but certainly not least, the Inland Revenue will have taken its share of the capital gains generated by sales through the flat dealings of all these varied interests.

But what is certain is that little, if any, of the profits which have flowed from the break-up of these blocks have been reinvested in new housing provision. The whole process has been characterized by, and indeed is predicated upon, the systematic extraction of capital gains from the ownership of residential property through the tenure transfer process. Not one extra house or flat has been added to the housing stock of central London. The profits derived from this process have invariably accrued to or been directly reinvested in sectors which have had nothing to do with housing. The sale of these flats into owner occupation has simply proved the most profitable use of this particular investment commodity during the current period.

Notes

1 Typical of its properties were Cheyne Court in Chelsea (79 flats), Harvard and Yale Courts in West Hampstead (190 flats) and the large concentration of flats in Maida Vale - Bickenhall, Castellain, Delaware, Lauderdale, Southwold and Wymering Mansions among others (1,200 flats in all).

2 LCF also had the distinction of being the first landlord to bring a case before the Rent Tribunal under the provisions of the 1954 House Repair and Rent Act, which allowed rent increases to cover increased service costs.

3 Rent levels at this time ranged from £200 to £4,000 per annum. Typical examples included £320-540 per annum for three or four rooms in Richmond Hill Court and £540-930 per annum for four to eight rooms in Wildcroft Manor, both in Putney Heath (Key Flats *City Press Supplement*, September 7th, 1962).

4 This process is illustrated by the rent increases which were being negotiated in Buckingham Mansions in 1972. A vacant flat with an existing registered rent of £580 per annum was offered to a new tenant at £1,250 per annum. This the new tenant agreed to pay. At the same time an application was being made to the rent officer to raise the rent of an existing regulated tenancy from £638 per annum to a new 'fair' rent of £950 p er annum. The 'open market' rent was then used as a comparable rent to persuade the rent officer of the reasonableness of the proposed 'fair' rent. The difference between the two rents represented the scarcity element which the rent officer would discount (Hillmore and Raw, 1972).

5 Stern's attitude to the investment potential of a well- managed, higher-value residential portfolio, and the possible form of state intervention needed to stimulate it, is discussed in a series of articles he wrote in the late 1960s and early 1970s. See 'Magna Carta for tenants - and landlords', *Investors Chronicle*, 25 March 1966; 'Residential development for letting', *Investors Chronicle*, 29 March 1968; 'Rented accommodation—a continuing scarcity', *The Financial Times*, 5 May 1971; 'Flats to Rent', *Investors Review: Housing and Urban Renewal Survey*, 28 July 1972; also J. Morton, 'The Marks and Spencer of London housing', *New Society*, 15 October 1970, and P. Riddell, 'How to provide new homes to let', *Financial Times*, 29 August 1972.

6 The second block FND purchased was Du Cane Court in Balham, a development containing 735 flats and one of the largest private blocks in the country. The acquisition was completed in March 1967 and cost FND about £1 million. The seller was Central and District Properties which was actively disinvesting its extensive residential portfolio at this time. Again, a £100 company, Du Cane Court Ltd, was set up to break the block. This time a partnership was formed by FND and four other secondary banks which provided the finance for the purchase, with FNFC again providing the mortgages. Prices for the newly marketed flats ranged from £1,100 for a one roomed flat to £5,500 for six rooms on 69 year leases. The average selling price of over £2,000 per flat compared to an average cost to FND of only £1,300. This suggests at least a 50 per cent profit on each flat sold (Milner, R., 'First National turns the £10m flat key', Sunday Times, August 3, 1969).

7 This operation cost £12.8 million in interest charges in 1975/6 alone. By summer 1976 the accumulated interest deficit was of the order of £58 million, and a major proportion of this related to loans on residential property, principally through FNFC's trading satellites. Active disinvestment followed, and in 1976 Fairview was sold to a number of institutions.

8 Varieties of landlord response: investor and trading landlords

Introduction

As the preceding chapters have indicated, the existence of a 'value gap' between the tenanted investment value and the vacant possession value of privately rented residential property has resulted in the transfer of the majority of the sector into owner occupation since the early 1920s. It is significant, however, that the purpose-built flat sector remained almost untouched by this process until the mid 1960s. The recapitalization of the privately rented sector did not manifest itself equally and evenly in all sectors of the market. On the contrary, the exploitation of the value gap was highly uneven both between type of property and type of owner. The mere fact that the economics of continued renting *vis-à-vis* sale for owner occupation had generally favoured sales for half a century did not necessarily ensure that sales would take place.

Similarly, the fact that conditions became increasingly propitious for flat break-up and sale in the mid to late 1960s did not necessarily mean that break-up occurred at the same rate or at the same time across all parts of the sector. In other words, market response cannot simply be 'read off' from changes in the general underlying conditions of profitability. One reason for this, of course, is precisely that the changes in the general conditions of profitability are general. They do not necessarily manifest themselves in exactly the same way or at the same time to individual companies. As Harvey and Chatterjee (1974) observe: 'professional landlords make their decisions in terms of a structured decision environment and closely gear their operations to the characteristics of sub-markets *as they perceive and experience them*' (p.30, our emphasis).

It can be argued that landlords who fail to perceive and react to changing market conditions may, like other entrepreneurs, lose market share, experience declining profitability, fall prey to other more aggressive competitors or even go out of business altogether. But changing market conditions can affect different companies in different ways according to the type of owner, the form of property relations involved, and the different market position and orientation of different owners. The constraints of continued profitability are quite wide and there is often a large degree of variability in both the speed and the accuracy with which individual owners perceive changes in external conditions and the conditions of internal profitability, and hence in their response to changes in external conditions.

There are, for example, likely to be considerable differences in response to market changes from institutional owners such as insurance companies and pension funds which need to generate steady long-term income to meet their obligations, property companies with stock exchange quotations which are under shareholder pressure to maintain dividend income and share prices and which could face the possibility of a takeover bid, private companies with a long-established portfolio acquired at low historic costs and with limited borrowings, and companies with a high debt to asset ratio facing the need to generate income as quickly as possible to repay substantial debts. There is, therefore, likely to be a considerable *variability of response* to changes in market conditions.

The process by which rented flats have been transferred to owner occupation has also varied considerably. While some landlords were actively disinvesting from a long term commitment to residential property, other landlords were often investing in the very same properties for very different reasons. Within a process which appears to reflect declining commercial profitability, we in fact discover quite the reverse. But the rationale on which this new-found profitability is based is quite different from that which prevailed before. The conditions which created a situation of declining profitability for one form of residential property ownership actually created profitable opportunities for another. As one City tax consultant, discussing the impact of the 1965 Finance Act, remarked: 'anomalies ... create opportunities and while the last generation of property developers are licking their wounds, a new generation may be buying into cheap situations and laying down the basis of new fortunes' (Chown, 1967). Not only will the rationale and motivations of existing landlords change as conditions of profitability change, but the rationale and motivations of new landlords entering the market will mirror these changes and the nature of their operations will differ radically from those of their predecessors.

This shifting pattern of responses is reflected very clearly in the changes in the attitude and behaviour of existing landlords towards their residential investment portfolios during the past 20-30 years, as well as in the behaviour of landlords who have entered the market during this period. Although, at one level, there were as many responses to the changing general conditions of profitability as there were landlords, it is possible to distinguish a number of general trends in landlord policy towards residential investment in the purpose-built flat sector since the 1950s. These trends reflect various combinations of the two main bases on which residential property has been held over this period, namely its traditional role as a source of medium to long term investment income and its more recent role as a source of short term capital gains.

The shift in ownership rationale

The main trend in ownership rationale has been the long-term withdrawal from investment landlordism and the more recent rise of residential property trading or trading landlordism. But these should not be seen as exclusive categories and the policy of any given owner may reflect a combination of ownership rationales and may change over time as conditions of individual profitability change. In reality, rental income and capital gains are likely to play a part in the calculations made by almost every landlord, but the important point is that the role of rental income and capital gains in the purpose built flat market has shifted fundamentally since the 1950s in favour of capital gains. Those landlords whose principal orientation is towards investment for long-term rental income have ben reduced to a residual presence in this sector of the residential market. They are mainly confined to a few private trusts and estates which have owned their property for some time, who may not fully appreciate the changes in the market, may lack the appropriate entreprenurial skills or who still emphasize the importance of a steady rental income.They are essentially passive owners who are not susceptible to the attentions of predators or to the demands of shareholders. Even so, many of them have sold as a result of approaches made to them by breakers or their agents. Easy capital gains have their attractions, even to passive owners.

For the purposes of this analysis, however, we have concentrated on changes in the pattern of corporate and institutional ownership since the 1960s. The dominant position of commercial landlords in the purpose-built rented flat sector, discussed at the end of Chapter 2, means that changes in ownership policies in this group will, to all intents and purposes, also dominate the trends in the sector as a whole. Using the framework provided by these two types of ownership rationale—investment income and capital gains—and their corporate expression—investment and trading landlordism—it is possible to construct a typology illustrating the shifting structure of landlordism in the central London flat market over the past 30 years.

The first group of landlords we can identify were those whose principal rationale for holding residential property was solely for its investment yield.They included the established residential property landlords who had held their properties for some time, often since well before the Second World War. This group of more or less 'pure' investor landlords evaluated the rental yields on their residential portfolios in relation to those to be obtained elsewhere in the property sector, especially in the commercial property sector during the late 1950s and early 1960s. The major characteristic of this group was the tendency to disinvest *en bloc* by selling off their blocks of flats to whoever was willing to buy them. These companies were not, therefore, interested in generating dealing profits by breaking their own blocks and many of them were actively disinvesting well before break-up took off after 1965. Their residential operations were simply not providing an acceptable yield in relation to the possible alternative uses to which the capital could be put.

This pure disinvestment strategy was characteristic of the early reaction to declining relative yields in the purpose-built flat market and was the general attitude taken in the early 1960s by most major established landlords. It was the first stategy adopted by such companies before flat break-up became both possible and acceptable. Beaumont Properties, British Land, Berkeley Properties, Alliance Property Holdings, Central and District, Bernard Sunley and Artagen are all examples of companies which were quick to appreciate the decline in relative yields. The proceeds from sales were almost invariably reinvested in commercial property, particularly in office and industrial development. Sales of residential property freed such companies from an increasingly troublesome and low-yielding investment and provided a source of capital in a market where interest rates and finance costs were increasing steadily.

To this group we can also add most of the major insurance company landlords such as the Norwich Union, the Pearl, Sun Alliance, the Prudential, the Co-operative Insurance Society, the Liverpool and Victoria Friendly Society and Legal and General which also disinvested in a similar manner. As with the commercial property companies, the insurance companies' principal concern was with relative investment yields. Where they differed was in the timing of their disinvestment. Although some insurance companies such as the Co-operative and the Norwich Union disposed of much of the residential property in the early 1970s, most of the others did not begin disposal until later. In the case of Legal and General this was because the 1974 property crash forced the postponement of their original plans. But in most cases the delay was because many insurance companies take a longer-term view than publicly quoted or privately owned companies, which are in business to maximize profits for themselves or their shareholders. Also their constant stream of new premium income can be channelled into new investment opportunities, and the balance of their portfolios changed, without the necessity either to borrow or immediately to disinvest from other areas.

Insurance companies were also keen to preserve their respectable public image and it was not in their interests to be seen to be directly involved in breaking blocks of flats in the face of a growing shortage of privately rented accommodation and the furore over break-up. By the late 1970s there were still several major institutional landlords in the rental market though, with the resurgence of the flat break-up market, they too began to sell off their remaining blocks. (See Figure 8.1.) In the case of the Sun Alliance this did

By Direction of Eagle Star Insurance Company Ltd.
Two freehold blocks of mansion flats in central London
MANOR HOUSE,
Marylebone Road, NW1
57 Flats - 6 Vacant
Currently producing a gross income of about £72,000 p.a.
WINSFORD HOUSE,
Luxborough Street, W1
13 Flats
Currently producing a gross income of about £13,000 p.a.
For Sale by Tender
Closing Date: 30th July 1981
Full Tender Documents available from the Vendors agents
KFR
Knight Frank & Rutley
Knightsbridge 01-730 8771
152 Sloane Street, London SW1X 9DB

Figure 8.1

not take place until 1983 when it belatedly sold off a number of blocks to Aylmer Square Investments, a Jersey-based offshore break-up company owned by David Kirch, a well-known breaker from the early 1970s. It should be emphasized that it was a direct result of the decision by these landlords to disinvest that released onto the market the blocks which fuelled the break-up market. By selling their residential holdings these companies provided the opportunity for other, less scrupulous landlords to enter the market and exploit its trading potential.

The second major group consists of those established landlords such as New London Properties, Grovewood Securities, Property Holding and Investment Trust, Peachey Property Corportion, London County Freehold and London,City and Westcliffe who did not sell *en bloc*. Instead,they held on to most of their portfolios and subsequently started to break the blocks themselves. These companies, therefore, shifted their policy orientation from investment to trading. But not all companies in this group reacted at the same time or for the same reason to the potential opportunities for sales. Some began to break-up blocks at the very beginning of the trend, while others did not become active until well into the 1970-3 boom period or after. Yet others began by disinvesting *en bloc* before recognizing the profits in breaking themselves.

While some of this group were actively engaged in stimulating the break-up market as part of a deliberate sales strategy, others were forced into break-up either to ward off potential predators or to generate income during periods of company crisis. Companies engaged in this type of 'defensive disinvestment' obviously have very different goals and motivations from those who entered into break-up of their own volition. Landlords who moved from *en bloc* disinvestment to break-up obviously comprise a very diverse group. To misquote Malvolio in Twelfth Night, 'Some are born breakers, some become breakers and some have breaking thrust upon them.' The profits generated by flat sales were also put to a wide variety of uses. While the more active breakers invested profits in alternative property sectors or elsewhere, those who were forced into break-up tended to use the income to meet debts or in attempts to fend off potential takeovers.

The third major group of landlords are those companies and individuals who entered the market specifically to exploit the value gap and whose principal business was the purchase of blocks of flats solely for break-up. Their strategy was based solely on property trading rather than investment and they actively mediated the market from the beginning. While some of the earlier break-up specialists were independent companies which relied on the secondary banking sector to fund acquisitions and sales, the traders who appeared as the market developed were often little more than the property trading subsidiaries of secondary and merchant banks. Apart from the payment of interest, a good deal of their trading profit often found its way back to the financial shareholders.

Early trading companies included the publicly quoted Dorrington Investments, the various private subsidiaries of First National Finance Corporation and Fordham Investments. But as the break-up market developed, companies were formed solely as vehicles for speculative flat trading. They included Regalian Securites, the Wallabrook Property Company, Peureula Investments, Audley Properties (part of Bovis Construction), Consolidated Securities, Renslade Investments, Buckingham Properties (a Slater-Walker subsidiary) and the Woodmill Property Group. While many of these earlier breakers fell victim to the 1974 property crash, the more recent tendency has been for traders to form private companies, often registered in tax havens such as the Channel Islands or the Dutch Antilles.

The final group of landlords consists of the property empires of the Freshwater and Berger families. Although their involvement in blocks of flats dates back well before the 1960s, they do not fit particularly well into any of the three groups outlined above. During the 1950s and early 1960s, Osias Freshwater and Gerson Berger were purchasing blocks of flats from other disinvesting landlords and they bought much of their property cheaply. The two men seem to have adopted essentially similar investment policies based on rapid asset expansion and high gearing in a period of steadily rising inflation. While Berger has been selling flats since the early 1960s, Freshwater only entered the break-up market in any quantity after 1974 when financial difficulties prompted an active flat sales policy. The blocks comprised a strong asset base which were used, via continued rent increases and consequent capital appreciation, as security to finance further purchases. Both Freshwater and Berger moved from an investment to a trading strategy over the post-war period but the rationale for investment itself was rather different from that of most residential investment companies which looked to their blocks for rental income rather than as an asset base to boost borrowing potential and expansion.

Although the net effect of policy decisions taken by different owners has been the sale of rented flats to individual leasehold owner occupiers, the underlying reasons have often varied widely from active disinvestment to improve investment yields and growth potential to active investment by companies seeking to exploit the break-up potential.Other landlords have varied their policies between these two poles, depending on the external state of the market and their internal conditions of profitability. While some responded positively to favourable market conditions to implement sales, others have been forced into sales as a defensive reaction to adverse conditions. What appears at first sight to be a simple and uniform pattern of investment can be seen to be the result of a wide range of specific reactions to a variety of causal factors reflecting both internal and external conditions of profitability. As Massey and Meegan (1982, p.97) argued in the case of industrial disinvestment:

Table 8.1 *Trends in investment policy, 25 largest central London residential landlords, 1966-69.*

Company	*Flats*	*Blocks*	*Policy 1966*	*Policy 1969*
London County Freehold	3,760	46	I	IT
Freshwater Group	1,556	28	I	I
Regis Property Holdings	1,388	8	IT	IT
Peachey Property Corporation	1,072	6	IT	TI
New London Properties	1,008	12	I	IT
Church Commissioners	978	8	I	I
Legal and General Assurance Society	868	13	I	I
Property Holding and Investment Trust	841	13	I	TI
London, City and Westcliffe Properties	800	28	I	I
Clarence Estates (Camden Town)	707	3	I	I
London Housing and Commercial Holdings	706	7	I	IT
Norwich Union Insurance Group	689	11	I	I
Charlwood Alliance Holdings	629	13	I	I
Trafalgar House Investments	618	16	I	T
Regional Properties	607	10	I	ID
Prudential Assurance Company	604	14	I	I
Metropolitan Industrial Dwellings	595	12	I	u/k
Central and District Properties	556	7	I	D
First National Developments	555	10	-	T
Cooperative Insurance Society	428	5	I	I
Berger Group	411	7	I	IT
Beaumont Property Trust	405	5	ID	DI
Capital and Counties	370	12	I	D
Berkeley Property and Investment	353	4	I	DI
Grovewood Securities	345	4	I	TI
Total	20,859	229		

Key: Prevailing policy towards residential portfolio.

I—Residential property held for investment (rental) income.
D—Disinvestment of residential properties by selling en bloc.
T—Residential property held for trading (break-up) income.
u/k—unknown

In those cases where more than one policy was held, the principal policy position is placed first.

Source: Policy positions derived from company reports and press coverage. Flat and block numbers derived from rent registration records in Camden, Kensington and Chelsea and Westminster rent offices.

> It would be wrong to try to establish empirical 'rules' of behaviour, of ways of responding to different comparative rates of profit, for different kinds of company. What is clear however, is that behaviour may vary substantially: it is not a question of some immediate and automatic response as might be predicted by theorists of perfect market situations.

This is exactly the point we wish to make here. Even within an apparently homogeneous subsector such as the central London flat market we find a diversity of conditions,attitudes and behaviour. However, the dominant influence which has underlain this variety of corporate response has been the growing pressure to capitalize the vacent possession value of residential investments. The shift from investment to trading has taken place within both companies remaining in the market and those entering or leaving it. This in turn has restructured the pattern of ownership within the sector as a whole. Without the possibility of sales to owner occupiers, existing block owners would either have remained in the market, deriving a steady income from rents, or have sold to other companies which were willing to continue letting. The specialist speculators would not have had the opportunities of capital gains and would not have entered the market. The trend towards flat break-up was not inevitable. It was contingent on a range of economic, social and political changes.

Investment to trading: an empirical analysis

In order to illustrate these general points and to explore in more detail the range of corporate responses to the changing conditions of profitability over the period from 1965 to 1980, we analysed the changing orientations of the largest 25 corporate landlords in the central London purpose-built flat market at the beginning and end of the period. The analysis was restricted to these companies for practical reasons—the sheer number of landlords identified precluded a detailed analysis of them all—and also because these large landlords dominated the market.

Tables 8.1 and 8.2 show the largest 25 companies ranked in terms of their holdings of flats in the three central London boroughs in both 1966-9 and 1977-80.The information on their holdings was derived from the rent registration data kept in the borough rent offices and provides a reasonably reliable estimate of the size of the flat portfolio of each of the companies in the central boroughs during these periods. Where possible, these figures have been cross-checked with alternative sources of information and these have been incorporated where appropriate. The figures refer to the maximum determined size of company holdings during the two periods including flats which may have been sold to individual owner occupiers but where the company owns either the freehold or the head leasehold of the blocks concerned. The figures, therefore, represent the number of flats from which rack and ground rents were derived. Where blocks were transferred between companies in the same list during either period, the ownership of these blocks has been assigned to the company which owned them for the major part of each period. Each company or institution was classified according to the dominant policy towards flat ownership in each time period as determined from interviews, company records and the specialist property press.

Several important points emerge from these tables. First, the concentration of ownership by large landlords is shown by the fact that, in both periods, the largest 25 landlords owned over 40 per cent of the total number of flats identified in the three boroughs. Second,it appears that ownership became more concentrated in the hands of the largest landlords between the two periods. The four largest owners in 1977-80 accounted for no less than 51 per cent of the total number of flats owned by the largest 25 owners, compared to 37 per cent for the largest four owners in the earlier period.But beyond the largest owners, block ownership became more fragmented. By the late 1970s there were many companies which had acquired single or small numbers of blocks once held by large-scale established owners the portfolios of which had been split as a consequence of sale. While all the owners in the 1966-9 listing owned several blocks, in the 1977-80 period, three were owners of single large blocks and the proportion of medium sized owners fell from the late 1960s. Given that the figures probably understate the size of landlords' holdings in the early period as rent registration was not applied as systematically as it was in the late 1970s, the fragmentation of holdings since the late 1960s is probably greater than the figures in the tables indicate.

The third and most important point is that the rationale for ownership changed markedly over the 1966-80 period from a concern with investment considerations to an emphasis on trading. Thus 22 of the 25 1966-9 landlords began the period with more or less 'pure' investment policies. Of the other three, First National Developments, formed in 1966, was the only pure trading landlord, while the two owners operating trading policies in some form by 1966 – Peachey and Berger – still had predominantly investment oriented strategies with respect to their central London flats. By 1969, the proportion of the 25 landlords with trading policies had increased to 8, of which at least 3 were predominantly concerned with break-up. Of the remaining 15 landlords, at least 6 were actively disinvesting blocks wholesale, using the income to reinvest in commercial property. Even those companies holding on to their blocks were actively increasing their non-residential property portfolios.

By 1977 the dominant policy orientation of the largest 25 owners was totally the reverse of that in 1966. Only three owners still had a predominantly investment oriented portfolio. There were no fewer than 11 companies in the list which had entered the market as break-up specialists, mainly during the early 1970s. A large proportion of the properties held by the breakers in the 1977-80 listing were previously owned by investment companies which were in the 1966-9 listing, but which had subsequently disappeared from the market. The remaining 11 companies were established property companies which had transferred part or all of their residential investment portfolios to trading stock since the mid 1960s. Some of these had also disinvested by selling whole blocks, especially after 1974, in order to meet short term debts incurred during the property crash. The majority of these companies had adopted trading policies either during the early phase of the break-up market in the immediate post-1966 period or during the 1971-2 boom in property prices once the market had been established and the economics of flat breaking had become too great to ignore.

In 1980 it appeared that only 1 landlord from the largest 25 still held residential property for investment, and this was the sole pension fund. The remaining institutional landlords had either disinvested or, in the case of the Church Commissioners and the Prudential, switched to trading. Of the four major insurance companies present in the 1966-9 listing, only two remained by 1977. The additional institutional landlord which had entered the list, the BP Pension Fund, had in fact acquired its residential interest as part of a much larger purchase of a mixed residential and commercial estate from Capital and Counties in 1977.

This analysis of changing ownership patterns among the largest 25 landlords clearly illustrates the basic trend in corporate policy from the mid 1960s to the late 1970s away from investment and towards trading. But it says nothing about the actual decisions that led to the break-up or the variety of ways in which owners reacted and responded to the changing market conditions. In order to illustrate the variety of corporate response to these changes, the rest of the chapter presents a number of detailed studies of selected companies. These examples should not be taken as being in some way 'typical' or 'representative' of different types of response. Rather, they have been chosen to reflect the wide variation in attitudes and decisions concerning residential investment.

Underpinning all these decisions was the eventual necessity for the companies concerned to evaluate the potential of residential property in the light of competing returns on the investment capital they represented and the need to maximize profitability in a competitive market situation. Those which were reluctant or hesitant to adopt profit-maximising strategies towards their residential holdings often found themselves the object of acquisition by others who were not so hesitant. Companies whose experience and tradition prompted them to view residential properties as a troublesome and low-yielding investment found ready buyers in companies which recognised that the market was changing and saw the profitable opportunities. In the remainder of this chapter we look in detail at the development of a number of major residential property companies, the circumstances and problems they faced or perceived themselves to face, and

Table 8.2 Trends in Investment Policy, 25 Largest Central London Residential Landlords, 1977-80.

Company	*Flats*	*Rents registered mid 1980*	*Blocks*	*Policy 1977*	*Policy 1980*
Freshwater Group	3,775	1,717	61	TI	TID
Regalian Securities	2,381	619	33	T	T
Church Commissioners	2,196	1,154	21	I	TI
Berger Group	1,763	595	34	TI	TID
Property Holding and Investment Trust	813	65	13	T	T
New London Properties	781	95	5	TI	TI
Peureula Investments	759	180	19	T	T
Wallabrook Properties	652	281	6	T	T
London and European Housing Group [1]	644	202	7	TI	T
Peachey Property Corporation	601	117	8	TI	TD
London, City and Westcliffe Properties	563	161	16	TI	T
European Housing Corporation	546	60	1	-	T
Prudential Assurance Company	534	402	10	I	D
Dorrington Investments	483	85	9	T	T
Convestor Establishments	450	180	1	TI	TI
Westgrove Securities	418	147	8	T	T
Regional Properties	389	110	5	T	T
London and Cleveland Property Co.	280	36	8	TI	TI
BP Pension Trust	262	115	8	I	I
Trafalgar House Investments	249	22	11	T	T
Swallow Securities [2]	247	80	4	n/a	T
Tannergate	233	172	3	T	T
Town and General Investments NV	232	50	2	T	T
Berkeley Hambro Properties [3]	218	9	3	TI	T
Correga SA	211	77	1	-	T
Norwich Union Insurance Company	190	181	4	ID	D
Total	19,510	6,912	302		

Notes:
[1] Was London Housing and Commercial Holdings.
[2] Subsidiary of FNFC (see Chapter 7).
[3] Was Berkeley Property and Investment Ltd.

Key: Prevailing policy towards residential portfolio.
I—Residential property held for investment (rental) income.
D—Disinvestment of residential properties by selling en bloc.
T—Residential property held for trading (break-up) income.
n/a—not applicable

In those cases where more than one policy was held, the principal policy position is placed first.

Source: Policy positions derived from company reports and press coverage. Flat and block numbers derived from rent registration records in Camden, Kensington and Chelsea and Westminster Rent Offices

the various policies they pursued towards their residential investments.

The Peachey Property Corporation

The history of the Peachey Property Corporation is an interesting one not only in terms of flat break-up, but also in relation to the decline in the rented sector as a whole. In Peachey's case, house trading formed the basis of a rapid expansion during the 1950s, and the company's subsequent shift into the property investment market, which it achieved both by moving up market in the residential sector and by diversifying into the commercial sector. However, the company held onto most of its highest-value flats until well into the 1970s when it used them as a source of ready revenue to help rescue the company from financial crisis, following the property slump, and to fund further diversification. In fact, for over 20 years Peachey used the residential property it acquired in the 1950s and early 1960s as a major profit bank to aid in its restructuring into a major commercial property company.

Peachey's involvement in both residential investment and trading for almost the entire postwar period (it is still active in the house-dealing field) is perhaps its most valuable feature for an analysis of the residential disinvestment process. The company provides an excellent example of the way in which a major corporate landlord, active in the central London market, continually reassessed the value of its residential assets in the light of changes in the investment climate over this 40 year period and the alternative uses to which the capital they represented could most profitably be put.

The Peachey Property Corporation started life as a small building firm, A. Peachey & Company, which was bought in 1947 by two south London estate agents, C.W. Huntley and G.F. Farrow. Like Fred Greswell some 20 years earlier, Huntley and Farrow saw the possibilities in purchasing residential estates wholesale and selling individual properties retail when the opportunity arose. Under their control, Peachey rapidly expanded from a very modest base (assets in 1947 amounted to 131 houses, 7 shops, a debit balance sheet and substantial tax losses) into a major company. By 1963 it was one of Britain's largest private residential landlords, owning some 7,500 houses and maisonettes, 4,000 flats, 3,000 freehold ground rents (the product of house sales) and 400 shops in many parts of the country. In the process it had absorbed Bell London and Provincial, one of the most prestigious interwar developers of central London flats, the Gunter Estate, which owned The Boltons in Kensington and other prime property, as well as several other smaller property companies. It had also forged important links with the London Assurance Company (later Sun Alliance), Hambros Bank and the Royal Liver Friendly Society, among other heavyweight backers.

Peachey's rise was based on exploiting the situation which arose after the Second World War in which the profitability of landlordism had been further eroded by rigid rent control. Many established residential investment landlords were ready and willing to disinvest. At the same time, the building societies were more than receptive to the idea of putting funds into the tenure transfer market. Demand for mortgages was low due to the low level of new private house building, while incomes, and hence building society receipts, were steadily rising. As in the 1920s, the building societies had a lot of money but relatively few outlets.

In such a climate, Peachey gained a reputation as an active property trader, buying out established landlords and selling on to tenants at between one half and two thirds VP value, inclusive of legal costs and stamp duty. To encourage sales, Peachey arranged 100 per cent mortgages for the purchasers through insurance companies and building societies. Where possible, the company had a policy of offering inducements of up to £300 to sitting tenants to vacate their controlled tenancies. This enabled the house to be sold on at full vacant possession value. The 1957 Act gave a considerable boost to the house-trading activity, for it meant that discounts on houses decontrolled under the Act could be reduced to only 15 per cent (the average sale price of a Peachey house at this time was £2,140).

However, by the mid 1950s the company was beginning to shift its policy, perhaps unusually, from residential property trading towards residential property investment. This diversification was underpinned by the profits from house trading and was directed at acquiring companies with high yielding block of flats. This involved several major property purchases and take-overs, most notable of which was the merger with the Bell London and Provincial Property Company in a reverse take over in 1958. The joint value of the newly renamed Peachey Property Corporation was £8.8 million, of which £4.2 million represented the value of Bell's blocks of upmarket flats. Included among these was the prestigious Park West, a block of 550 flats at Marble Arch valued at almost £3 million in 1960, and the Etons, a complex of 380 flats in three blocks just north of Camden Town. These blocks were part of an extensive portfolio of some 1,300 houses and 1,800 flats which Bell had developed in the interwar years, mainly in London and South East England. Bell appears to have been in the process of selling property at the time Peachey took the company over (including a major disposal to Berkeley Property and Investment Ltd, later Berkeley Hambro) in an attempt to raise cash to cover outstanding maintenance and war repair work.

Peachey soon set about increasing the income potential of the blocks it had acquired in order to improve their investment value. At least a quarter of the flats in Bell's blocks were kept vacant while a move was made to replace the existing furnished 'service' lettings (which were not subject to rent control and were let on a day-to-day basis) with unfurnished tenancies to be let on long (21 year) leases at full market rentals and on full repairing and insuring terms (i.e. where the tenant agreed to meet all the repair and insurance costs for the flat). The rents therefore represented a much higher net return to the company.

In many respects, these 'long' leases represented a half-way position between the short (3 to 9 years) rented lease where the rent was inclusive of all costs and the long (21 years and above) lease system which is typical for flats today, where all costs are met by the resident. As we saw in Chapter 5, this was a major obstacle to the sale of flats. This mid-way strategy probably constituted the optimum solution for a company aiming to maximize its profitability in the period before mortgages for the purchase of individual flats were available. It was an attempt to enhance the long term investment value of its flats by increasing the net return. Such was the scale of the operation that the 1959 Company Report noted 'substantial temporary reductions in income' as a result of 'our policy of seeking a very large number of vacant possessions'.

The 1957 Act undoubtedly aided this shift in policy, especially where vacant possession was obtained. In 1959, the company calculated that rents for its controlled houses and maisonettes were equivalent to only 34 per cent of their full open market potential. The situation on the lower-value flats was even less satisfactory, rents here being estimated at only 22 per cent of their market level. Given this situation, there was a very clear rationale to pursue these new tenancy arrangements and the policy was soon extended to the rest of the flat portfolio wherever vacancies occurred. Peachey also offered cash incentives to existing tenants to move out in order to allow further units to be relet on these terms. By 1961 the company estimated that some £774,000 had been spent in buying tenants out and refurbishing their vacated flats for reletting on long leases.

The new long leases, it was claimed, would allow the tenants to sell the lease on at a substantial premium or to sublet the property if they wished. Peachey did not itself ask for premiums for these new tenancies simply because of the greater taxation liability that income derived in such a manner would incur. For Peachey, the benefit came in the form of greatly enhanced investment values for the blocks and was thus fully in line with its new emphasis on property investment.

By the early 1960s Peachey had successfully established a solid investment base for its activities. The move into investment appears to have been a response to the inherent instability of a business based purely on property trading. In particular, there was increasing competition on the part of property traders for the remaining unbroken tenanted estates as sales activity had gathered momentum during the 1950s. Portfolios of tradeable houses were simply becoming scarcer and therefore more expensive to buy. Profits were consequently being squeezed, and profitability was being further undermined by the shift in building society finance away from the tenure transfer market and into the private house building boom which was under way. In any case, trading activity had always been viewed as a secondary concern in the property world, after the primary business of generating secure investment income. Peachey's shift into property investment was therefore only a move towards the norm. Moreover, it is impossible to expand into a major force in the property world on property trading alone. However, it does provide a very profitable base from which diversification into other sectors can be achieved. This is precisely what Peachey was using its trading potential for. The shift towards investment would also ensure a more stable dividend payment over the longer term, which in turn would protect the share price and the company's independence.

Peachey's newly established investment portfolio was to form an additional foundation for further expansion in the residential market. To begin with, the stability it brought to the company's earnings potential made it much easier to attract institutional backing. In 1960 a major debenture issue was underwritten by Hambros Bank, allowing the complex system of short-term loans which had prevailed to be successfully refinanced. Additional long-term finance was obtained from the Royal Liver Friendly Society which put up £2.5 million in loans in 1963. The diversification into property investment provided the security for an injection of long-term capital that trading could not, and the move into high-value flats for investment purposes was extended. For example, in late 1962 Peachey bought Viceroy Court, a block of 84 prestigious flats overlooking Regent's Park, for £1 million.

The result of this move into residential investment was that, by January 1963, while over a half of Peachey's residential portfolio was still subject to rent control, these properties contributed only a third of total residential rental income. There was also a shift into residential development in some of the earliest flat blocks to be built for sale in central London, including one at Baker Street and one at Harley Street. And the trading portfolio was further strengthened by the purchase of several large portfolios of mainly residential property (over £2.5 million worth between 1961 and 1962 alone). Throughout this expansionary period, house trading continued to represent a major source of the company's profits.

But like most of its contemporaries, Peachey also began to diversify into the commercial property sector. During the latter half of the 1950s and the early 1960s the company had built up a sizeable portfolio of shops in addition to its residential investments. But events were to trigger a major reorientation of investment activity. In particular, by 1963 the threat of a new Labour Government and a return to stricter rent control had begun to hit the shares of companies with substantial residential holdings. Consequently, the expansion of Peachey's residential portfolio came to an abrupt halt, and in 1964 a major disinvestment policy was initiated. By July 1964, some 4,500 lower-yielding residential properties had been disposed of, worth between £6 million and £7 million, including some of the company's smaller suburban blocks of flats.

Furthermore, in January of that year, the Holly Lodge Estate, an imposing Mock Tudor development of 668 mansion flats at Highgate, north London, all let at controlled rents, was leased to the then St. Pancras Borough Council (now part of the London Borough of Camden) for 150 years at an average rent for the first 40 years of £107,000 per annum. In a statement which undoubtedly expressed the apprehension with which Peachey faced a possible Labour Government, the company announced the deal to be 'gilt edged' and 'completely out of the reach of any political threats that may exist, however unreal such threats may be, and it is our view that any threats are much exaggerated' (Company Report, 1964). Exaggerated or not, they were enough to persuade Peachey that residential property had become too problematic to rely on for the bulk of its income in the future and the switch into commercial investment began in earnest.

The rate of restructuring was rapid. By 1965, the commercial portfolio represented 50 per cent of Peachey's total assets and some £7.7 million had been invested in commerical property since 1963 alone. The sale of residential property had provided the lion's share of the capital for this expansion. By 1967 the bulk of the company's remaining rent-controlled property had been sold for upwards of £0.5 million. In less than 5 years, Peachey had reversed its investment policy from one of rapid residential expansion (albeit largely for trading) to one of disinvestment from bulk residential ownership. Only the high-value blocks of flats (including those inherited from Bell) and the non-controlled houses were retained. It is likely that most of the readily saleable part of the rent-controlled stock had been traded on to sitting tenants and others, and the 'rump' could be sold at a healthy profit over its book value. The imposition of Capital Gains Tax almost certainly added further impetus to these disposals.

The trading potential of the remaining high-value flats in the developing break-up market soon began to make an impression. Between 1966 and 1970 Peachey abandoned the policy of reletting vacant flats on long leases and switched to selling long leases instead. Sales do not appear to have been made to sitting tenants and Peachey may well have taken a much more long-term view of the returns to be made from this type of activity than some of the more aggressive break-up operators at this time. Having bought the blocks some years earlier and with no real urgency to effect a rapid rate of sales, this would seem a perfectly logical approach. The company could look forward to many years of steady income for what was becoming a rapidly appreciating asset.

The late 1960s saw Peachey extending its commercial and development activities, aided by the income generated from flat and house sales. However, the freer availability of capital during the property boom of the early 1970s was increasingly based on short-term loans. These, coupled with the controversial activities of Sir Eric Miller, who had moved to a position of dominance in the company after Huntley's death in 1961, were to contribute considerably to the difficulties in which the company found itself in when the crash came. Miller, former treasurer of the Socialist International and prominant Labour Party supporter, had presided over a hugely inefficient company, including 450-odd subsidiaries, with very little clear financial control. Quite apart from the extravagant entertaining of politicians and others at the company's expense, he was accused of using Peachey more or less as a personal bank. By the time the Department of Trade's inquiry into the management of Peachey for alleged breaches of the Company Acts finally reported in 1977, the company was firmly in the red and the share price had plummeted.

Following Miller's dismissal as chairman in the same year (and subsequent suicide), John Brown, the ex-chairman of Artagen Properties, was brought in to restructure and rationalize the ailing company. Brown immediately embarked on a major disposal of unwanted low-yielding property, including the residential portfolio which still represented 40 per cent of the company's total assets. It was Peachey's remaining blocks of flats which were the prime target of this policy, however. In the following 5 years all of Peachey's remaining blocks of flats were sold, earning some £31 million, much of which was eventually reinvested in commercial property.

The most important of these disposals was the sale of Park West for £10 million early in 1979 to the European Housing Group, a property dealing subsidiary of Gulf and Western. Gulf and Western was also forced to pay a further £2 million to the Church Commissioners for the freehold of the site, a remarkable price given that the Commissioners were receiving only £12,500 per annum for the lease from Peachey. What the Commissioners and Peachey were able to cash in on, of course, was the immense break-up potential of the block. By the time it was finally sold (two earlier deals, one involving Kuwait businessman Mubarak el Hassawi and the other Westgrove Securities, having fallen through), some 215 of the 540-odd flats in the block were vacant. After spending £1.5 million on refurbishing these and the common parts, European Housing intended to put them on the market. At the time of the sale, the flats could be expected to fetch an average of £50,000 each, giving an immediate value of almost £10 million for the vacant flats alone and a potential of nearly £20 million for the block as a whole. Gulf and Western could confidently expect this to rise with domestic property inflation.

The sale of Park West benefited Peachey in a number of ways. First, £5.9 million went to paying off short-term bank loans. As a consequence, interest charges were reduced by over 40 per cent from £1.2 million to £0.7 million in one year during a period of increasing interest rates. Second, Peachey was able to place the remainder on deposit to take advantage of these rising rates while it considered the most profitable long-term use for the money. Finally, the sale resulted in considerable savings in management and administration costs.

Despite this series of disposals, Peachey's residential portfolio still stood at 15 per cent of its total assets. This comprised predominantly houses and maisonettes, the remnants of the original house trading stock built up during the 1950s. In 1980, some 1,650 of these remained on Peachey's books. The intention was to retain these for future trading as and when they fell vacant, thus providing a useful source of cash flow. Indeed, commenting on these houses, John Brown was quoted as saying, 'I would like to have more of these, because you get both capital appreciation and income' (Estates Times, 26 February 1982). At the time, each year some 100 houses were falling vacant and being sold. The fact that these houses were bought for perhaps less than £1,000 apiece in the 1950s and would sell for 25 times that by the early 1980s meant that they represented a virtually cost-free profit bank underpinning future growth. Owning tenanted houses in this situation is clearly highly profitable. In addition to the houses, some 4,000 ground rents were owned, a clear legacy of its 30 years of house trading. These were disposed of in the following year.

Peachey's history since the late 1940s therefore provides a very clear picture of how residential property, both houses and flats, not only provided a firm base from which the company could expand into non-residential sectors, but also provided a much needed resource to fund a defensive restructuring programme to stave off a major financial crisis. Moreover, in Peachey we have an example of how a property company perceives and responds to the changing opportunities and constraints it faces in order to maximize those opportunities (or minimize the constraints) with the assets at its disposal. The initial concentration on house trading, the move into the residential flat investment market in the late 1950s, the subsequent disposal of low-value residential investments in the mid 1960s, the switch to flat sales in the high value invesment blocks in the late 1960s, the disposal of these remaining blocks in the late 1970s and the retention of the house portfolio for its remaining trading potential in the 1980s, are all aspects of the changing use to which residential property assets have been put over the 40 or so years by property companies such as Peachey. While Peachey's long-standing involvement in all aspects of the residential market and its multiple shifts in policy may well be unusual compared with the activities of most of its contemporaries, these policy changes are typical of the reactions shown by many other companies involved in the residential investment market over this period. Each change in policy has reflected both the specific changes in the fiscal and financial climate that this market has experienced over this period, the varying values that flats have held in this market and the particular market position of the company.

Regional Properties

The example of Regional Properties encapsulates a number of the main uses residential assets were put to over the period since the mid 1960s. But in particular, Regional stands out for two main reasons. First, the company's disinvestment policy, introduced in two large auction sales in 1972, represents one of the key events in the break-up story (see Chapter 6). Second, and more importantly, Regional's rapid switch out of residential investment and into commercial development fell foul of the property crash, prompting an equally rapid sales campaign to break-up the company's remaining residential assets as fast as possible. Like many other similar companies, Regional was forced into sales as a defensive measure to help pull the company back into the black during the mid 1970s.

Regional Properties Ltd was one of the more prestigious residential investor landlords to emerge during the 1930s property boom. Although a publicly quoted company, Regional, in common with a number of residential companies that dated from this period, was in fact closely controlled by a single family interest. When the King family relinquished control in 1972, Regional abruptly switched course into a large-scale commercial development programme. Up to 1972 Regional had been slowly expanding its non-residential portfolio, but even in 1971 residential properties, principally quality flat blocks in London, made up 50 per cent of the company's total property assets. Moreover, the dominant policy orientation was still towards investment and relatively few residential holdings had been sold. Neither had any large-scale development programme been implemented and borrowings were only 6 per cent of total assets, well below the usual proportion contemporary property companies were prepared to entertain. In other words, until 1972 Regional had pursued a low-key investment strategy and had made little attempt to sell off its residential investments. There were a number of reasons for this. First, as the King family controlled up to 78 per cent of the voting share capital, Regional was virtually immune from the threat of takeover which would almost certainly have succeeded with a less closely controlled property company with a similar proportion of undercapitalized, high-quality residential properties. Under the control of the King family, Regional was able to maintain an traditional investment policy long after other companies had been forced into sales or been acquired by predators.

Second, the flats owned by the company were concentrated in the medium to high rent end of the market where returns were sufficiently secure to ensure the continued viability of the investments. The company had concentrated its investment portfolio in this sector of the market since the early 1950s by adding to its existing portfolio of blocks through the acquisition of both companies and single properties. Examples of the former included the take-over of London Midland Associated Properties in 1950 and Atlas Properties in 1951. The strategy of concentration had been helped by a policy of selling the existing house property portfolio which the company had owned since before the war. Estates of houses acquired during take-over activity were also sold off *en bloc* during the 1950s and the proceeds invested in both offices and high-value blocks of flats. The 1950s, therefore, saw a concentration of Regional's residential holdings into high-quality flats, the sale of house properties, and a limited expansion into the commercial sector.

By the early 1960s, when the expansion of the residential portfolio appears to have ceased, Regional owned 2,800 flats comprising 60 per cent of the company's assets. The effects of the 1965 Finance and Rent Acts appear to have had little impact on the policy towards these flats and, as Table 8.3 shows, while profits fluctuated between 1963 and 1966, due in part to the taxation changes over this period, the mid to late 1960s was a time of steady growth. A number of lower-yielding blocks were sold in mid 1969, realizing some £348,000, which was immediately reinvested in commercial and industrial property. This brought the balance between residential and other property assets to about 50:50.

Table 8.3 *Regional Properties: company statistics, 1962–79*

Year	*Net Profit (loss) £*	*Residential property as % of total*	*Residential sales £m*	*Rented flats owned*
1962/3	226,210	n/a		2,800
1963/4	220,100	n/a		
1964/5	268,859	60.0		
1965/6	263,100	60.0		
1966/7	360,042	57.0		
1967/8	397,126	57.0		
1968/9	429,267	57.0	0.35	
1969/70	453,334	50.0		
1970/1	526,480	50.0		
1971/2	532,874	45.0		
1972/3	589,419	28.0	16.41	508
1973/4	504,951	15.0		
1974/5	265,978	15.0	2.20	478
1975/6	(777,702)	16.0		223
1976/7	(44,527)	8.4	6.4	
1977/8	597,241	5.4	2.6	
1978/9	701,110	4.2	1.9	100

Source: Regional Properties' Company Reports

However, the main interest from the point of view of this analysis came in January 1972 when Neville Conrad, late of the central London estate agency Conrad Ritblat, was appointed chief executive after buying 35 per cent of the company's share capital from the King family for £1.5 million. Conrad immediately set about radically restructuring the company's business, the object of which was to reduce the residential portfolio to a minority holding, consisting of the highest-value blocks. This was to be carried out by a wholesale realization of the residential portfolio, investing the proceeds into central London office properties and embarking on an ambitious development programme. The residential portfolio was to provide the financial basis on which the shift in policy was to be undertaken. As Bernard Sultan, the chairman, explained: 'The residential market was at a point where it was advantageous to effect these sales.... There is no doubt that the proceeds ... when reinvested will produce a greater net income than that derived from the properties hitherto'. (Financial Times, 13 May 1972). Conrad was undoubtedly taking the opportunity of cashing in on the escallating break-up value of Regional's flats to fund this dash for growth. During the summer of 1972, Regional attempted to dispose of the majority of its flats in two major auction sales, the results of which represented key markers in the progress of the break-up market. The first sale, in April 1972, consisted of five of the lower value blocks located in the suburbs of south and west London and comprised 275 flats and 47 shops. Rents totalled £107,000 per annum and the blocks fetched £2.735 million (some 40 per cent above the expected price), giving a yield of 3.9 per cent. In fact, the blocks had been valued at only £772,000 in March 1971 at a pure investment yield of 12 per cent.

This successful sale was followed in August 1972 by a further auction of 8 higher-value blocks, comprising 1,213 flats and 11 shops and a yearly rent roll of £500,000. Unfortunately for Regional, this second sale coincided with moves by the Bank of England to damp down the speculative fever in the property market, especially that surrounding the London flat market. In the event, only two blocks were sold at the auction, these being the two smallest blocks on offer, Sherwood Court, W1 (37 flats) and Tudor Close, SW2 (105 flats), fetching £800,000 and £530,000 respectively. These two blocks sold on yields of 5.0 and 4.7 per cent respectively, a good point higher than the April sales. The purchaser was William Stern's Metropolitan Property Holdings.

The failure of the sale was generally taken to represent the end of the rapid spiral in block prices which the previous 2 years had witnessed. However, within 2 weeks, the six remaining blocks were successfully sold to a private consortium for break-up. The price, £9.83 million, was only £120,000 less than the total bids during the auction, suggesting that the Bank of England's initiative had simply driven the breakers underground rather than seriously impeding their activities. And a week after this, Regional sold Russell Court, a block of 500 flats in Holborn, for £3.775 million. The purchaser was Metropolitan Property Holdings. The sales of blocks during 1972 were reputed to have grossed some £14.1 million net of Capital Gains Tax. The proceeds were immediately channelled into the commerical property sector, including £2.225 million spent on purchasing the freeholds of Ibex and City House in the City. The remaining residential portfolio consisted of 8 high value blocks in central London: Inver and Riven Courts, WC2 (65 flats), Duchess of Bedford House, W8 (45 flats), Stockleigh Hall,

NW8 (61 flats), Apsley House, NW8 (80 flats), Wellington Court, NW8 (84 flats), Porchester Gate, N2 (69 flats), and Arlington House in Mayfair, SW1 (104 flats), the latter considered to be one of the most exclusive blocks in the country. Some 500 flats remained in all, valued at a conservative £13.4 million.

So far, Conrad's expansionist plans had been eminently successful and in 1973 a large scale commercial development programme was launched. This was funded from both the proceeds of the block sales and a rapid growth in bank lending which by now had reached £21 million (compared to £2 million in 1971). It was this rapid increase in gearing which was to cause problems for the company in the following year.

There was also a further change in policy concerning the remaining residential portfolio. In 1973 Regional began to break-up these last eight blocks, but only for those flats which became vacant and where full market value could be obtained. This sales policy would ensure that the maximum capital value of these blocks would be eventually realized over the long term.

However, within months the whole situation had changed. The rise in bank rate landed the newly geared-up Regional with a severe cash flow problem. Regional's shares crashed in November 1973. From a peak price of 239p, the shares had fallen to just 27p by January 1975. Interest charges rose from £0.386 million in 1973 to £2.214 million by mid 1974 and asset values were falling. Conrad's gamble had failed. As one commentator noted: 'Basically it looks as if the group came onto the scene late and with no institutional lines of credit, geared up to fast and too short' (Financial Times, 30 August 1974, p.12). All the borrowing had been on 5 to 7 year loans at floating rates.

As far as Regional was concerned, the blame for its predicament was only too clear. As the 1974 Company Report stated:

> Just as government measures greatly contributed to the euphoric market of 1972 and 1973, so they have helped create conditions in 1974 which at one point destroyed any market in property. It is important not only for the property industry, life assurance companies and pension funds, but also for industry and the economy as a whole that a strong and well balanced property market should exist. This must be based on rational criteria and not, on the one hand, on blatant opportunism, nor, on the other hand, controls and restrictions. Until political parties stop using attacks on property as pegs on which to hang promises for electoral gain, your company will take an entrenched and consolidating position.

They could hardly do much else, given the parlous financial state they were now in. The statement, containing more than a hint of righteous indignation, fails to mention that the 'entrenched and consolidating position' the company had been forced to adopt was in no small way directly related to the 'blatant opportunism' they had displayed during the height of the break-up boom. Moreover, this opportunism was based on fully 'rational criteria', those of maximizing speculative capital gains.

By mid 1975 Regional's cash flow deficit had reached £2.7 million (on a capitalization of £50 million) and profits had fallen from a high of £589,000 in 1972/3 to a loss of £777,000 in 1975/6. Clearly, Regional was in trouble. Luckily, however, most of the property inherited from the King family was owned outright rather than on mortgage or in partnership with financial institutions. The most 'rational' course of action was therefore to sell as much property as possible to meet the financial deficit and reduce the crippling level of borrowings. A major property sales programme was launched, and as part of this programme the flat sales policy, until now confined to vacant flats, was extended to all sitting tenants. This change in policy was announced in the 1975 Company Report which stated quite bluntly: 'The proceeds will help to reduce the Company's indebtedness.' By this time, 478 flats remained rented, representing 15 per cent of the company's assets. Whereas sales of flats had totalled £2.196 million between 1973 and 1976, some £6.4 million worth were sold in 1976/7 alone. This figure included the value of Arlington House, sold for an undisclosed price to Cubcall Ltd, a company controlled by 'interests in the Arabian peninsular' (Financial Times, 17 July 1976).

The enforced property sale programme managed to pull Regional back into the black. Some £15.8 million worth of property was sold in 1976-7 alone, allowing borrowing to be cut back to £14.5 million by 1978. By 1980, £11.9 million worth of flats had been sold, representing perhaps a quarter of the proceeds of all the property sold by the company over this period. Clearly, Regional's remaining residential portfolio had contributed a disproportionate amount to the company's return to profitability. Yet even in 1979, some 100 flats, worth perhaps over £5 million at prevailing prices, remained to be sold off over the longer term.

For Regional, then, the residential investments built up in the 40 years prior to 1972 not only provided a major source of the funding on which the ill-timed expansion into commercial property development was launched in 1973, but, as with the Peachey Property Corporation, they played a significant role in the defensive restructuring that brought the company back into solvency in the period after 1975. In both periods, of course, it was the recapitalised value of these residential properties which provided the basis of the profits which Regional was able to exploit to advantage.

Central and District Properties Ltd

The various stages in the transformation of Central and District Properties from a substantial residential landlord, owning up to 4,500 flats and houses at its peak in the early 1960s, to an international commercial property development and investment company by 1970, and its subsequent merger with a major merchant bank in the early 1970s, provide an illustration of a number of key tendencies in the use of residential property as an investment asset during the postwar period up to the mid 1970s. Over this period, Central and District's residential holdings were subject to a series of major changes in policy, from active investment to active disinvestment (in order both to reduce taxation liability and to fund the move into commercial property), then to direct flat break-up and finally to wholesale portfolio speculation as the company itself was subject to takeover and systematically stripped of its assets.

The company also provides an example of the way in which established landlords fed the evolving break-up market, benefiting from the increase in the value of their properties in the process. Disinvestment was not simply a reaction to poor profitability, but was a means of capitalizing on the higher value of the blocks in the break-up market. Furthermore, the company's strong links with the Prudential Assurance Company illustrate the increasing importance of the institutional sector in guiding property company policy since the 1950s. At various key stages in Central and District's history during this period, the Prudential emerges as an underlying force. And finally, Central and District's merger with Keyser Ullman and its subsequent sale to Town and City Properties at the height of the property boom typify the close ties that built up between the property market and the banking sector during this period, and the repercussion these had on the property market and the banking system.

Central and District Properties dated back to the pre-war period when it built up a portfolio of blocks fo flats in and around London. By 1952 the residential portfolio consisted of 8 freehold and 28 leasehold blocks. Most of these were subject to rent control under the 1939 Rent Act, including all of the blocks owned by its principal subsidiary company, Regor Properties. By 1953, the company was complaining of low operating margins due to the combined effects of rent control, rising maintenance costs and increased taxation liability. Nevertheless, 5 more leasehold blocks of flats had been purchased, bringing the total owned to 41. The 1957 Rent Act had a major impact on the income potential of the company, for some 950 flats of the 1,352 owned became decontrolled. As a result, the policy which had been adopted for some years of converting unfurnished lettings to furnished, in order to evade rent control and increase rent income, was abandoned.

Despite this, in 1958 a major reorientation of investment policy was set in motion following the acquisition of Central and District by the Unicos Property Corporation in a reverse takeover bid. Unicos, controlled by two property entrepreneurs, Jack Rubens and Barney Shine, was a private company looking for a publicly quoted vehicle for expansion into the wider property field. The new enlarged company retained Central and District's name, but the merger led to a rapid diversification into a much more broadly based property investment concern. Initially, the newly reconstituted

Central and District embarked on a series of expansionary acquisitions of other residential property companies. Among the most important was the Orion Property Trust, bought in 1959, which owned a well run portfolio of first class flat blocks in London, including blocks at Abercorn Place (180 flats) and Cumberland Court (65 flats) in Westminster and Chatsworth Court (197 flats) and Mountborough Court (60 flats) in Kensington. This purchase was quickly followed by the acquisition of the James Hartnoll Estate of 80 shops and 400 flats in the Grays Inn Road and Roseberry Avenue area of Holborn, and General London and Urban Properties, purchased in January 1960, whose major holding comprised flats and houses in south-west London. General London's principal investment properties were the 750 flats at Du Cane Court in Balham, one of the largest private blocks in the country, and The Grove in Twickenham, a high-rent block of 60 flats. The latter was valued at under £40,000, or less than £700 per flat.

At the same time, a major long-term loan of £6.75 million at 6 per cent interest was arranged with the Prudential Assurance Company. The objective of this loan was to rationalize the company's existing mortgage structure by substituting outstanding short-term loans with long-term finance, and to provide a surplus for further expansion. The solid investment value of the residential portfolio provided much of the collateral on which the loan was raised. However, the expansion which the blocks helped to secure was now directed entirely towards commercial property and the company also moved into the international market with developments in the USA and Australia. Diversification rapidly changed the structure of the company's investments and by 1960 the rent roll was almost equally divided between residential and commercial sources. As the commercial portfolio expanded, the proportion of total company income derived from the residential side fell further—to 40 per cent in 1964 and to 30 per cent a year later.

The decline in the importance of the residential side was accounted for entirely by the expansion of the commercial portfolio rather than by the sale of residential properties. In 1965 the number of flats held had changed little from the 4,000 or so owned in 1961. There was also a limited move into the residential development market with the building af 56 flats on a site leased from the MCC adjoining Lord's Cricket Ground. This formed part of the Lord's Ground redevelopment scheme and most of the flats at the top of the 12 storey block, Century Court, had a clear view over the wicket. Central and District paid £150,000 for the lease and the flats were marketed for £10,000 plus.

This foray into residential development was a short-lived move, however. In 1967 a new policy was adopted involving the selective disposal of blocks into the emerging break-up market. The reasons for this shift into disinvestment were clearly stated in the company's reports of the time. The 1965 Company Report stated of the 1965 Rent Act: 'The legislation dealing with the residential premises is not expected to cause any difficulties. We have always enjoyed a good landlord-tenant relationship and our rents are considered fair and reasonable.' The pressure for disinvestment came from other sources. Corporation Tax became effective in the year 1966/7 and it was in this year that the first major sale, that of Du Cane Court, Balham, was effected. The block was sold for £1 million to FNFC for the latter's second break-up operation (see Chapter 7). By 1968 block sales to the value of over £3.2 million had been completed. These properties had produced rents of £170,000, giving a speculative break-up yield of 5.3 per cent. This suggest sales values were at least 50 per cent in excess of the company's 1965 valuation of the blocks on a traditional 8 per cent yield basis.

The 1968 Company Report gave the rationale for this sales policy. The cash received was used to pay off outstanding short-term bank loans on which recent commercial developments had been funded and which were now incurring high interest rates. It should be remembered that under the 1965 Finance Act, interest on development costs was no longer chargeable against income for taxation purposes, but against profits. Although the block sales had the net effect of reducing the profit available for distribution, by allowing these expensive loans to be redeemed, they actually resulted in a considerable reduction in the amount of Corporation Tax payable. The proceeds from the block sales, therefore, allowed the interest burden to be reduced, thus increasing the proportion of distributed profits under the new tax arrangements. The company was also able to negotiate the retention of the existing low-interest mortgages on which these properties had been held and thereby to substitute new commercial developments in their place. Thus block sales not only provided the company with a measure of relief from Corporation Tax, but also served as a source of cheap finance for new developments.

This disinvestment strategy had an immediate impact on the proportion of income received from the residential portfolio. By 1968 this had fallen to 20 per cent of total income, and between 1968 and 1971 residential blocks worth a further £9 million had been sold. The proceeds were reinvested in commercial property development and other commercial acquisitions. In 1971 the income from residential property stood at 8.5 per cent of the total and the remaining blocks consisted of the highest-value part of the portfolio, worth some £6 million according to a 1970 property valuation based on prevailing rents.

Judging by the hands into which the blocks which were sold fell, it seems clear that the company was quite deliberately selling blocks to exploit their break-up value, albeit at one remove. Other than Central and District itself, the principal beneficiaries of the sales were the growing band of flat breakers. A number of well-known dealers obtained blocks from Central and District during this period. As well as FNFC, David Rowland's Fordham Investments picked up 226 flats in three blocks for £750,000 in

1969, including Melford and Hermitage Courts in Woodford, Essex, an average of £3,300 per flat. Whitehall Court Holdings, run by John Salfield, bought Barons Keep in Kensington in December 1969. The Davidson Group acquired Princes Court (25 flats and 2,000 square feet of offices), Treborough House (12 flats) and Brendon House (17 flats), all in W1, also in December 1969, for about £350,000. Other suburban blocks were sold to Freshwater. Each block was sold for a much higher value than that implied by its rent-yielding capabilities.

In September 1970 a new influence arrived at Central and District in the form of company chairman Edward Du Cann, Conservative MP and then chairman of the influential 1922 Committee of backbench Tories. Du Cann's accession to the chairmanship coincided with a further shift in policy. In 1970 Central and District began to break-up the remaining blocks itself rather than selling them to others to break. The remaining blocks were revalued at an estimated break-up value of £12 million after expenses and the costs of improvement had been deducted. Clearly, Du Cann had a better grasp than his predecessor of the profitability of the flat break-up market, and the potential value of breaking the flats retail rather than wholesale. The process also strengthened the company's asset base during a period of mounting takeover activity.

Central and District's days as an independent company were drawing to an end, however. In April 1972, merchant bankers Keyser Ullman made a successful takeover bid which valued the company at almost £70 million. This can be compared to Keyser's own market value of only £53 million (and under £20 million at the beginning of 1972). For the second time, therefore, Central and District was subject to a reverse takeover by a company looking for a vehicle to expand into wider property investment. This takeover was not wholly unsurprising, however, given that Central and District and Keyser Ullman shared a common chairman in Du Cann. In any event, Central and District did not appear to resist.

The reasons behind the merger were fairly straightforward. Keyser Ullman was undergoing a period of rapid expansion. Central and District gave Keyser a greatly increased capital base on which this expansion could be carried out. Most importantly, the Prudential Assurance Company (Central and District's old backer) had subscribed to £7.5 million of Keyser Ulman's shares in January 1972. This move greatly enhanced Keyser's share price, which rose from 150p in January 1972 to 375p by early April. The rapid rise in Keyser's paper value enabled the takeover offer to be made on the basis of an exchange of shares rather than cash. Crucially, the whole inflated deal (Keyser Ullman shares had an asset backing of only 82p at the time) was underwritten by the Prudential, allowing those shareholders who accepted the bid to sell their Central and District shares for cash rather than accept Keyser's shares. Jack Rubens, who had been a partner in the previous reverse takeover and who was still a major shareholder, took the cash.

The story of Central and District's residential portfolio did not end here, however. In March 1973, William Stern's Metropolitan Property Holdings agreed to purchase six of Central and District's remaining high-quality (but presumably part-broken) blocks in west and south west London for over £9 million. The 450 flats in the deal were sold on a yield of only 3 per cent, clearly well below the cost of the finance Stern borrowed to make the purchase.

Whether this marked a further shift in policy is difficult to say, for this deal was little more than a prelude to the sale of the whole of Central and District to Town and City Properties for £97 million in July 1973. This represented a monumental piece of bulk speculation by any stretch of the imagination. Central and District was producing pre-tax profits of only £3 million and Town and City expected to have to pay over £10 million more than this in interest alone on the finance raised for the purchase. No less than £95 million had to be borrowed for the deal, mainly from Town and City's enthusiastic backers, Barclays Bank and N.M. Rothschilds (Plender, 1982).

The deal netted Keyser Ullman in excess of £20 million profit over the price paid for Central and District a little over a year earlier, and provided almost £100 million to reinvest, which Keyser did in a series of poor quality speculative property deals, for which it was to pay dearly in the subsequent property crash. Within 2 years Keyser Ullman was making provision against £119 million of bad debts and had received £84 million in loans from the Bank of England's 'lifeboat' operation. For its part, Town and City was later forced to sell much of its portfolio to repay its massive debts, including an agreed sale of £20 million to the Prudential.

By the time of the 1973 deal, most of Central and District's residential portfolio had been disposed of and Town and City was left with little of the original company's residential holdings. Perhaps the final major disposal concerning Central and District's residential property came in December 1978 when Town and City negotiated the sale of the remains of the James Hartnoll Estate, purchased by Central and District in 1959, to the St Pancras Housing Association, aided by a loan from Camden Council. Nine blocks were sold in all, comprising some 300 flats plus shops and some offices, for a price of around £1 million. Town and City no doubt made good use of this help from ratepayers and taxpayers to repay some of the crippling debt charges run up as a result of their unwise speculation 5 years previously.

The transformation of Central and District from a mainstream residential investor into a commercial property developer and its subsequent demise through wholesale speculative acquisition, provides a fairly typical illustration of the manner in which such landlords used flat blocks to their best advantage as market conditions changed during the 1960s. Feeding blocks into the flat break-up market in this way was the most straightforward method of participating in the recapitalization process stimulated by the possibility of selling flats on long leases. Profits might be lower than by breaking the blocks directly, but then the risks were lower and, more importantly, Central and District needed an immediate injection of cash to cover its increased taxation liability. In addition, the disposals provided cash for investment in the higher-yielding commercial property sector and also allowed the exisiting low-interest mortgages on which the blocks were held to be used to fund commercial development in a period of rising interest rates. The events surrounding and following Keyser Ullman's takeover of the company are also typical of the wild speculation which developed during the property boom and the close involvement of the banking and institutional sectors in stimulating the boom and, of course, their responsibility for the subsequent crash.

Property Holding and Investment Trust

Property Holding and Investment Trust (PHIT) represents an example of a successful adaptation by an established residential investment landlord to the problems and possibilities of the 1960s. Unlike many of its contemporaries, PHIT was quick to perceive the need for changed attitudes and actively set about creating the conditions in which full advantage could be taken of the possibilities for increased profit by adopting policies which would maximize the full potential of its residential assets, in this case by breaking its own flats. PHIT therefore provides an opportunity of examining how an established residential landlord actually proceeded to create a break-up market for its flats, the problems it encountered, the economics of the process, and the benefits it derived.

The example of PHIT also provides important evidence as to the role of rent control in the break-up process, and indeed in the tenure transfer process in general. PHIT was a leader in the break-up market, but it operated at the top end of the market where the effects of rent control had been minimal. Indeed, as we shall see, the company launched its first sales drive in a block which had never been subject to control. Quite clearly, rent control played no part in the decision to sell these particular flats.

PHIT emerged as a public company in 1947 following the amalgamation of seven private property companies which were all controlled by Claude Bullock, a London solicitor. The basis of PHIT's business was medium to high rent residential investments located largely in central London, although even in 1947 some 40 per cent of the company's £3 million capitalization was in non-residential property, mainly offices and shops. Nevertheless, in the following decade, the company expanded further into the residential market and at least 10 blocks of luxury flats were added to the portfolio.

The 1957 Rent Act resulted in the freeing of all the company's rent-controlled flats and the resultant income growth enabled a modernization

Table 8.4 *Property Holding and Investment Trust: Sources of rent income 1951-75 (percentages)*

Income source	*1951*	*1964*	*1965*	*1966*	*1968*	*1969*	*1970*	*1971*	*1972*	*1973*	*1974*
Residential	60	58	60	60	47	45	38	31	18	12	7
Commercial	31	42	40	40	50	52	58	66	79	88	93
(offices)					28	30	37		55		
(shops)					22	22	21		24		
Industrial	9	—	—	—	3	3	4	3	3	—	—

Source: PHIT Company Reports

and improvement policy to be implemented in its inter-war blocks. This income growth also helped PHIT to embark on further expansion through the acquisition of several smaller property companies in the early 1960s. As Table 8.4 indicates, these acquisitions did not fundamentally alter the portfolio structure of the company, which had changed very little since the late 1940s. Nevertheless, the company had a keen eye on profitability and while a modest development programme for new luxury residential lettings was inaugurated, three lower-yielding blocks of flats were disposed of during the 1960-4 period. There was therefore a clear policy to concentrate the residential portfolio on the highest-yielding investments in the more prestigious locations, and the 1,100 or so flats owned by the company at this time included some of the highest-rent blocks in London.

Even so, despite the secure and unfettered returns to be derived from these properties, there were clearly opportunities for enhancing profitability, especially when the company, like so many others, was faced with the increased taxation introduced in 1965. PHIT's decision to begin selling its flats in mid 1966 sheds an interesting light on the oft-repeated argument that apportions blame for break-up on the rent regulation system introduced by the 1965 Rent Act. While this Act brought about half of PHIT's flats back into the scope of rent control, only a quarter of the company's residential income was derived from these properties, and this represented only 15 per cent of total company income. Furthermore, perhaps to reassure shareholders, the 1965 Company Report concluded that rent regulation would not have an adverse effect on the company.

Significantly, the decision to launch a sales policy was made for Berkeley Court, a prestigious block of 128 flats in Baker Street that had a rateable value which lifted it well above the scope of the various Rent Acts. Clearly, rent control played no part in the decision to sell these flats. Quite simply, it was the pressure to capitalize residential assets on their trading value rather than their investment value which was the overwhelming rationale for these sales and this in turn was based on the possibility of exploiting the gap between their tenanted and vacant possession values.

The initial sales proceeded modestly and by March 1967 more than a quarter of the Berkeley Court flats had been sold, principally to sitting tenants, and the sales policy had been extended to two other blocks. The sales drive was supported by an innovative scheme in which an 'independent' third party management company, Holding and Management Ltd, was created for the life of the leases to manage the property on the tenants' behalf. This was a laudable attempt to create an attractive marketing situation to induce purchasers from the high-income tenants who characterized the blocks. However, too many of the tenants who had been approached were either reluctant to commit themselves to the purchase of a commodity for which there was no established market or, more seriously, were finding some difficulty in raising the required finance, particularly those tenants who were retired. Consequently, a further scheme to encourage more rapid flat sales was introduced under which purchasers would be supplied with mortgages on favourable terms. The scheme was clearly aimed at removing two substantial barriers to the flat sales, namely the inability of the high proportion of ageing tenants to obtain mortgages, and the more general difficulty of mortgaging flats in blocks for which PHIT only held head leases of limited length.

Whether PHIT funded these mortgages itself or in association with a financial institution is unclear, but the scheme provided for 10 year mortgages of £10,000 for applicants between 35 to 65 years old in flats valued at an average of £15,000 with 40 year leases. On flats with longer leases—67 years or more—mortgages of up to 25 years were provided. Tenants aged between 65 and 85 years could obtain a mortgage on security of their leasehold or, in some cases, on unencumbered personal assets of stocks and shares. The promotional literature accompanying the offer stressed the value of purchasing for tenants paying a high rate of surtax and gave an example of an 82 year old tenant with an endowment mortgage of £10,000 who then put £2,500 of her own savings into the scheme and ended up with a tax-free income of £240 after all mortgage payments had been met. The economics of the sales shows the level of profit derived. The flats were sold on 20 years purchase which indicates an average rent of about £750 per annum for the properties concerned. It also suggests that at an investment yield of, say, 8 per cent, the tenanted investment value of these flats was about £9,000 at this time. Of course, the historic cost was well below this, but it suggests that there was a surplus of at least £6,000, or 40 per cent over prevailing investment values, to be derived from sales. Interestingly, the fact that the sales prices quoted were expressed in terms of a notional multiple of annual rent, the traditional manner by which investment property was valued, is a reflection that there simply was no established vacant possession market for these flats on which they might be independently valued.

By March 1968 some £1.3 million worth of flats had been sold, representing perhaps 80 or so units, and PHIT expanded its sales drive into 7 more blocks, 4 of which were in the lower rental range where rents had been regulated under the 1965 Rent Act. Prices ranged from £5,150 for a small flat in Greville Hall in Maida Vale to £39,000 for the largest luxury flat in the recently (1964) developed Kingston House South in Knightsbridge. By now, the established lettings policy had stopped, and from 1969 a policy of not reletting vacant flats was adopted.

This marked a significant turning point, for whereas before this sales had been overwhelmingly directed at sitting tenants, from this time onwards it seems clear that PHIT felt confident that it could sell the flats on the open market with full vacant possession. In other words, a market had been created for the flats which no longer relied on preferential discounts to sitting tenants to stimulate demand. Rented flats could now be considered to have a full open market vacant possession value independent of their investment values. The long-leasehold owner occupied flat had become an accepted commodity for both open market purchasers and mortgage funding sources.

From here on flat sales escallated and, as Table 8.5 shows, sales peaked in value terms in 1972/3 by which time flats worth some £10.6 million at book value had been traded. This total had reached £16.8 million by 1979. The actual value derived from these sales was undoubtedly far higher than the book values shown in these figures. The revenue the sales policy generated was destined for reinvestment in the commercial property sector, particularly office development. In 1972 alone, some £13.5 million was invested in the development programme, of which £9.7 million came from the sales of residential property. Naturally, the switch into higher yielding commercial property had a significant impact on the balance of the investment portfolio. The proportion of total company income coming from residential income fell from 60 per cent in 1966, the year the first sales were made, to 38 per cent in 1970 and to only 7 per cent in 1974 (Table 8.4).

Table 8.5 *Property Holding and Investment Trust: value of flats sold, 1966–79 (£ million at book value)*

	Year											
	67/8	*68/9*	*69/70*	*70/1*	*71/2*	*72/3*	*73/4*	*74/5*	*75/6*	*76/7*	*77/8*	*78/9*
Value sold	1.3	0.8	2.0	2.1	2.0	2.4	1.0	0.9	1.0	1.5	0.8	1.1
Total	1.3	2.1	4.1	6.2	8.2	10.6	11.6	12.5	13.5	15.0	15.8	16.8

Source: PHIT Company Reports

The events of 1974 were to cast something of a shadow over PHIT's activities, reflected by the slump in the value of flat sales in the 1974/5 period. Although the company survived the property crash with relatively little apparent damage, it was forced to abandon a residential development and improvement policy which had started in 1971/2 in two of their older blocks. Both these blocks were sold in late 1974. Nevertheless, sales had begun to pick up again by 1975 and a policy of negotiating the extension or purchase of head leases in their leasehold blocks was pursued. This improved the sales potential of the remaining unsold flats, especially in those blocks which only had 40 year leases left when flats were first marketed in the mid 1960s.

The recovery in sales continued into the late 1970s, by which time the bulk of the original portfolio had been broken. In 1976, the company reported that a net profit of 50 per cent was being made over the book value of the flats being sold. In March 1978, the remaining unsold flats were worth some £877,000 at book value, but an estimated £2.7 million at current sale prices. By 1979, sales had been in progress for 13 years and, of the 1,150 units held in 1960, only about 80 remained tenanted.

PHIT represents one of the more successful of the established residential landlords who entered the break-up market on their own account. This success may well be partly a result of the high value of the properties PHIT owned, but it is also due to the company's early and purposeful action in responding to the emerging opportunities for recapitalizing its residential stock through the tenure transfer process. As we have seen, the transfer of PHIT's flats from renting to long-leasehold owner occupation was not a simple matter, but required a concerted programme which included special financial arrangements to sell otherwise unmortgageable flats. Even at the top end of the market in which the company operated, the conditions in which the potential value gap could be exploited had to be arranged and demand carefully nurtured. Clearly, even among the wealthy clientele of PHIT's flats, for whom the tax incentives for investing in domestic property were the most rewarding, there was no such thing as a 'natural' owner occupier.

Freshwater: Swimming against the tide

Freshwater was, and probably still is, London's largest private landlord. At its peak in 1970, Freshwater owned 23,000 flats and houses, most of which were concentrated in London and the South East (Morton, 1970). Even as recently as 1977, Freshwater owned some 20,000 properties (The Economist, 29 October 1977). The sheer size of the company alone makes its response to the changing conditions of profitability of some interest, but what is fascinating about Freshwater is that the company's strategy was almost diametrically opposed to that of most other traditional investment landlords during the 1960s. While most other landlords were busy divesting themselves of their residential investments, both Freshwater and the rather similar Berger group of companies were busy acquiring residential property as quickly as possible.

This strategy of residential investment may appear 'irrational' given the prevailing conditions; but when examined in the context of Freshwater's strong commitment to residential property, coupled with the group's close control of a largely privately owned property empire and its analysis of the evolving financial conditions, the strategy can be seen to be an astute and rational response to changing market conditions. The key lay in their realization that inflation was likely to prove a long-term phenomenon which could be profitably, if rather riskily, exploited to advantage. Freshwater recognized that the long-term inflation of rents, and hence of investment values, could be used as a basis for a policy of large-scale acquisitions and long-term capital growth using borrowing rather than equity backing. While the interest on borrowing would often exceed the immediate rental income from the property, Freshwater evolved twin solutions to the problem of deficit financing. First, it increased the rents, frequently using the new rent registration procedures introduced in the 1965 Rent Act. Next, it had the property revalued on the basis of the higher rents. It then remortgaged the property, using part of the new mortgage to pay off the existing one and part to fund deposits on new purchases (Hillmore and Raw, 1972). The second solution was to engage in selective sales of its lower-quality properties to help cover the interest charges on borrowing until rents could be increased yet again. The blocks of flats owned by Freshwater played a key part in this strategy, providing a high-quality and appreciating asset base to underpin mortgage borrowing for new acquisitions.

Such a policy necessarily involved a very high gearing ratio as the growing empire was founded on a growing mountain of debt, but it enabled the group to maintain close control of its companies without recourse to the traditional solution of raising cash via share issues. As a result, the majority of the Freshwater empire remains privately controlled and the only publicly quoted company in the group—Daejan Holdings—is 65 per cent owned by Freshwater family interests. Indeed, it can be argued that it is this close control that enabled the group to pursue its idiosyncratic investment strategy at a time when most publicly quoted residential property companies were being forced into a more conventional response to the pressures of market forces. Unfortunately, the private nature of much of the Freshwater Group's interests and the complex way in which these interests are organied makes systematic analysis of the group's policies difficult. We will therefore limit our discussion to Freshwater's general policies and analysis of its quoted property company—Daejan Holdings (see Figure 8.2).

The Freshwater empire was founded in the early 1940s by Osias Freshwater, a Jewish emigre from Nazism, who bought lower-quality residential investments in the London suburbs during the 1940s and 1950s which other landlords were keen to sell. The rapid growth of the group dates from the appointment of his son-in-law William Stern as joint managing director in 1964. Freshwater's attitude to residential investment was in many ways the exact opposite of that of most of their contemporaries. Where most corporate landlords saw residential investment as an area of low and

e Freshwater family
plified version, main companies only

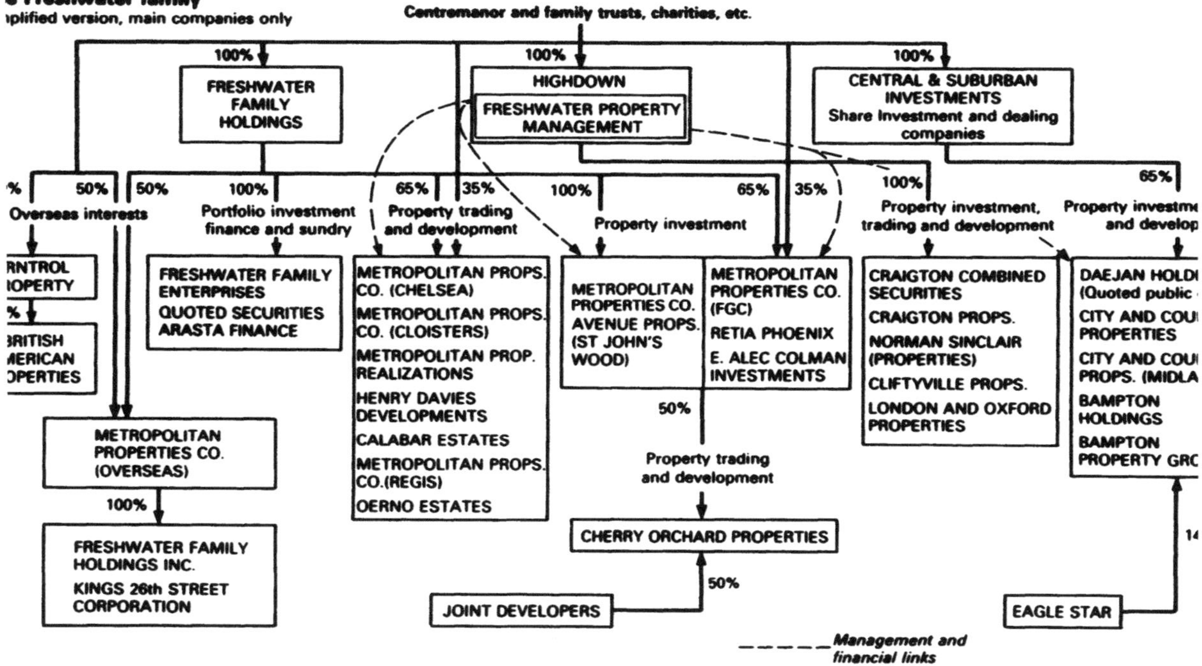

declining relative profitability, Stern saw opportunities for greater profitability. Not being constrained to maintain short-term share dividends, the group was able to take a long-term view of residential investment, using deficit financing to fund rapid growth. In 1961 the company was worth £10 million but by 1971 it had grown to £100 million and to £150 million by 1975. The most rapid growth was between 1967 and 1970—when most other companies were disinvesting rapidly. In 1967 the total flat portfolio stood at around 12,000 but by 1971 it had doubled to 23,000. During this period Freshwater acquired 2,200 flats in 18 blocks from Regis Property Holdings in 1968 for £6 million, 600 flats from Bernard Sunley Investment Trust in 1969 for £2.1 million and 3 quoted property companies—the E. Alec Coleman Group, City and Country Properties and Lockes Estates, the latter bought for the trading potential of its portfolio of houses and maisonettes.

The early development of Daejan provides a clear example of how Freshwater expanded. Daejan was floated in 1959 in the shell of a defunct Malayan rubber plantation company with a Stock Market quotation. It was 60 per cent owned by Osias Freshwater and funded by Eagle Star Insurance. The property portfolio consisted of £3.18 million of investment property and a further £1 million of trading property. From the outset, therefore, Daejan adopted the classic Freshwater profile with a substantial proportion (30 per cent in the first year) of gross revenue from trading in order to cover dividends. Initially, the company was not highly geared and total mortgage borrowing was only 33 per cent of the value of investment properties in 1960. This conformed to usual practice in the residential property sector as high borrowings usually meant that interest took a high proportion of rents and reduced shareholder dividends. But this degree of financial constraint did not last long. Consistent with the investment strategy outlined above, Daejan's gearing ratio (the ratio of borrowing to assets) rose rapidly, to 38 per cent in 1962 and reached 70 per cent by 1964.

Such rapid growth based on deficit financing and remortgaging generated the problem of interest charges which could well exceed the rental income of the properties. Freshwater's solution to this problem was to adopt an active trading policy. As Osias Freshwater stated in 1969:

> "Despite the unprecedented rise in the rates of interest, yields of good quality properties have remained unchanged. In the field of commercial properties, pension and other gross funds have continued to pay prices reflecting yields as low as 5% and sometimes lower, whilst in our own field of good class residential properties, yields remained unchanged at about 8%. With long-term interest rates ... at 10% and more ... the choice facing an expansion minded group such as ours was either a halt to all new purchases or, (the) alternative we favoured, a 'subsidy' to the investment side of our business by means of a vigorous and sustained trading policy." (quoted in The Economist 29 October 1977)

This sales policy was carefully controlled to minimize taxation liability. Sales were limited to units which fell vacant and could be stepped up or down according to current requirements. In this way the balance between rental income and trading profits could be maintained at any desired level. The benefits of this policy were particularly marked after the 1965 Finance Act, for while rents could be set against interest charges, thus minimizing Corporation Tax, the surpluses derived from sales were liable for the the lower rate of Capital Gains Tax. Houses and maisonettes and lower-value flats in smaller suburban blocks formed the bulk of the trading stock while the investment portfolio was made up of the larger, more valuable, centrally located blocks of flats which, because of their size and geographical concentration, also minimized the unit costs of maintenance and management.

The cost advantages of holding a geographically concentrated investment portfolio of large blocks of flats were also enhanced by a series of other policies designed to maximize the long-term capital growth of the assets. First, Freshwater was particularly keen to purchase blocks from institutional and other established owners where rents and block values were relatively low, but which offered considerable scope for improvement through application of the 3-yearly rent increases under the 1965 Rent Act. For a group such as Freshwater, which did not have to worry about maximizing the short-term capital potential of its assets, the Fair Rents system offered considerable scope for steady and guaranteed growth. Second, the rent registration policy was exploited to the full. When new lettings were made, tenants were encouraged to submit a joint application to the rent officer for a rent to be registered. This was invariably set at a full 'market' rent, including any scarcity element, but, as the application was from both parties, the proposed rent was usually accepted regardless of what the previous rent for the flat had been. Even where a registered rent already existed, new market rents were asked and generally agreed to by new tenants who had little option given the growing shortage of flats to rent, and, perhaps, only a limited understanding of the Fair Rent system.

A loophole in the 1965 Rent Act meant that this was not actually illegal under the Act, although the legal rent was meant to be that charged on the day the Act came into force or subsequently set by a rent Officer. As Harloe *et al* (1974, p.115) commented: 'The company considered that the absence of legal penalties for charging a market rent, even where the property in question had a registered rent, could only have been intentional.' Even if tenants subsequently discovered the registered rent and appealed to the rent officer, only 2 years' excess rent could be reclaimed, and by the time tenants became more aware of the provisions of the Act in the early 1970s, the company had ceased reletting most property. The third element of Freshwater's strategy was brought into play if and when rent officers failed to award sufficiently high rents. They systematically appealed to the rent assessment committees in an attempt to get the rents increased and analysis of such appeals indicates that they were successful in about 60 per cent of cases. Appeals were clearly a worthwhile policy.

The creative use of the Fair Rent scheme was accompanied by a dynamic tenant management policy introduced by Stern with the aim of reducing tenants' grievances and fostering good landlord-tenant relations. This included a full-time PR representative; an in-house magazine, *Freshview,* for tenants; discounts on purchases of furniture and cars; a team of social workers to look after the needs of tenants who fell into difficulties; free holidays in company flats on the south coast for the needy, and, importantly, a decentralized management system which permitted rapid response to maintenance, repair or service problems. This policy earned Freshwater the uncritical accolade of 'The Marks and Spencer of London housing' (Morton, 1970), but, worthwhile as the policy was, it was introduced in the name of good business. A contented and well looked after tenantry should be less resistent to the regular rent increases which Freshwater needed in order to meet interest charges and generate appreciating asset values.

Stern believed that blocks of flats comprised a profitable long-term investment which offered yields and capital growth comparable to those of commercial property, if they were properly run and managed using the provisions of the 1965 Rent Act to the full. As he stated in 1969: 'We have prepared ourselves for such types of residential properties, which is now a highly specialised occupation, so we can go against the trend' *(Investors Chronicle,* 25 January 1969). It was a conviction which Stern took with him to his own property empire when he split from Freshwater in 1971. Unlike Stern, however, the Freshwater Group managed to withstand the property crash of 1974, largely due to the fact that it had built up a large portfolio of cheaply acquired residential property in the years before the property boom and because it had ceased investing in residential property in 1972. The problems were more intense on the private side of the group than they were in Daejan because most of the higher-yielding properties had been channelled into Daejan in order to generate adequate shareholder dividends.

The Economist (29 October 1977) report on Freshwater revealed that the 1975 accounts for Freshwater Family Holdings (FFH) showed borrowings of almost £50 million against properties valued at £50 million—a gearing ratio of almost 100 per cent. The pace of expansion is shown by the fact that FFH's total stock of trading properties grew by nearly 60 per cent to £19 million during 1973 and 1974 while Daejan's stock of trading and development properties grew by 50 per cent in 1974 alone. The accounts also revealed that FFH's interest payments of £6 million in 1974 were almost double the net rents received. *The Economist* also revealed that Daejan purchased several blocks of flats from private companies in the Freshwater Group between 1975 and 1977 and money was lent to the private companies by Daejan at a lower rate of interest than they would have had to pay in the market. Freshwater maintain that the flats were a good buy and provided Daejan with valuable dealing stock, but the inference is that Daejan helped bail some of the private companies out of difficulties.

The Freshwater Group also got into difficulties in the early 1970s as a result of a misjudged commercial property acquisition. Keen to diversify out of residential property, the group bought Alec Coleman Investments. But, as *The Economist* revealed, the new £21 million portfolio consisted of recently developed speculative offices in less fashionable parts of London that seemed resistant to early letting, a provincial shopping centre—the Tricorn development in Portsmouth—in which too few people wanted to set up shop, and an uncompleted office development in Baltimore. The Baltimore scheme was the biggest problem and the American holding company was eventually declared insolvent, owing over $6 million to various Freshwater interests. A second source of problems for the Freshwater Group was the involvement in property development. Various private companies became involved in developing a 5 acre site on the Thames adjacent to Southwark Bridge and a 170 acre site near Bristol. Both projects became embroiled in planning wrangles and interest charges rose. Finally, Freshwater borrowed £10 million in 1973 in Swiss francs to purchase the Strand Palace Hotel. Unfortunately for Freshwater, the decline in the value of the pound against the Swiss franc led to mounting foreign currency losses on this and other overseas loans, and from 1973 and 1977 Daejan lost over £5 million.

The impact of these losses on Freshwater's residential holdings was clear-cut. The group was forced into a programme of large-scale disposals of individual flats and, increasingly, of whole blocks in order to meet the rising interest charges and losses and to pay Daejan's dividends. The pace of disposal increased rapidly after 1974 and numerous blocks were sold to breakers. But by 1977, as the break-up market was beginning to take off again after the crash, Benzion Freshwater asserted that the rapid increase in prices could only benefit the Freshwater empire. 'We stand before particularly explosive growth.' In the space of just 5 years, Freshwater made the transition from rapidly expanding investment landlordism to property developer and, like Regional Properties, to enforced sales in order to pay off debts. Even Freshwater could not resist the tide.

The other impact of the property crash and Freshwater's subsequent difficulties with the group's residential holdings was in the management of the stock. In 1976 Freshwater announced that maintenance and repairs would be cut to a minimum while the company attempted to extract itself from its financial crisis. The group also initiated a policy of applying for rent increases of 100 per cent or more with appeals to rent assessment committees where the increases awarded were not deemed large enough. Together these policies created considerable tenant protest and destroyed Freshwater's image of a responsible and 'caring' landlord. Care was clearly an expendable commodity when the survival of the company was at stake.

Peureula Investments

Peureula Investments, a specialist property trading company reformed from the shell of a defunct East Indian plantation company in 1970, had all the trappings of the new breed of speculative flat dealers who came to prominence during the 'bull' market of the early 1970s. Like Regalian Properties (see Chapter 7), Peureula, and the various companies it controlled, was little more than a vehicle for the speculative asset-stripping activities of the fringe merchant bankers who funded it. The rapid rise of Peureula in the 1970-3 period and its almost as rapid fall from grace in the succeeding 2 years is a fully representative example of the numerous flat-breaking enterprises and their backers in the secondary banking fraternity who leapt onto the 'block-busting' bandwagon at this time.

Peureula's initial transformation into a flat break-up company was carried out to provide an outlet for the property-dealing talents of the brothers David and Peter Kirch. The Kirches had been active in the Earls Court and West Kensington property market since the mid 1960s (and indeed still are), buying up tenanted property, removing the tenants, converting the flats and renting them out furnished at high rents, or, more latterly, selling them off. Peureula formed one strand in a web of inter-related public and private companies concerned primarily with residential property dealing, including Matlodge Ltd, Nessdale Ltd, Mountrise Properties Ltd, Swordheath Ltd, Hillflight Ltd, Crown Lodge (Surbiton) Ltd and Cityland and Property Holdings Ltd, among many others.

There were also close links with a number of fringe banks, including Dalton Barton, headed by property entrepreneurs Jack Dellal and Stanley von Gelder (Peureula and Dalton Barton shared the same Knightsbridge address); the Burston and Texas Bank, run by Edward Burston; and Keyser Ullman, the major City merchant bank headed by Edward Du Cann. Dalton Barton, itself only recently floated as a public company in 1970, could boast heavyweight financial backing from the ICI and Electricity Supply Industry Pension Funds and the Trade Development Bank. Peureula was able, therefore, to draw on considerable financial resources from the booming secondary banking sector.

The company's fortunes really began to take off in April 1972 when Keyser Ullman sold Peureula a substantial portfolio of West End ground rents worth £400,000 per annum for £8.1 million which Keyser had recently purchased from the Royal Liver Friendly Society. The deal was financed by a share issue worth £5 million and a loan from Keyser for the remainder. This gave Keyser a 34 per cent stake in the expanded equity of Peureula. At the same time Keyser advanced an additional £1.2 million for further property-dealing purchases. The investment by Keyser Ullman in Peureula was far from coincidental, for almost immediately Keyser announced a £58 million merger with Dalton Barton, Peureula's original merchant banker. As Dalton Barton already held a third share in Peureula, the merger made

Keyser the major shareholder in both Peureula and its related companies. By this time, Peureula was capitalized on the Stock Market at around £22 million.

With its financial backing secure, further expansion followed rapidly. For example, in June 1972, the company bought some 3,000 flats and houses from Town and City Properties for £12.2 million, funnelling them into its Swordheath subsidiary. This deal included almost all the remaining residential portfolio of Charlwood Alliance Holdings which had been taken over by Town and City in February 1972 for £16.6 million. Charlwood Alliance, originally known as the East End Dwelling Company, was founded in 1884 to provide houses, and later flats, for working-class tenants at low rents and had been controlled by the Nisbet family since that time. Charlwood owned residential properties in Bayswater, Notting Hill, Maida Vale and other areas of north-west London, as well as the Lambeth Estate next to Waterloo Station. In 1971 about half these properties were still let at old controlled rents, although Charlwood had reluctantly initiated a sales policy in the late 1960s as part of a belated attempt to diversify into the commercial sector. This move was too late to save the company and, being severely undercapitalized in relation to its break-up potential, it succumbed easily to Town and City's predatory attentions.

The deal with Peureula was a highly profitable one for Town and City. These residential properties had been valued at only £5.5 million when Town and City had acquired them along with the rest of Charlwood Alliance just 6 months earlier and yielded only £150,000 per annum in rents. Town and City therefore made a 120 per cent profit in 6 months and Peureula bought the property at a yield only marginally over 1 per cent, hardly enough to cover basic management costs! Not that Peureula was too concerned about management. The objective was simply to break the portfolio as fast as possible.

Given that all the property Peureula had bought was financed with short-term bank loans, resulting in sky-high gearing and a substantial financing shortfall (e.g. Matlodge paid £1.2 million interest on its £12 million borrowings in 1972 alone), a rapid turnover was essential. By all accounts their sales methods were certainly effective. Peureula could boast trading profits of well over 25 per cent at this time. It was this high level of profitability which appealed to Keyser Ullman, which was keen to benefit from Peureula's high-earning assets to balance its low-yielding purchase of Central and Disrict Properties earlier in 1972. The profitability of Peureula was also the principal reason why Keyser Ullman, with financial backing from the Prudential, went ahead with the merger with Dalton Barton (Plender, 1982).

Keyser Ullman's heavy involvement in Dalton Barton and Peureula was to contribute greatly to its downfall 2 years later, however. As a report on Peureula at the time noted,

> Investors in Peureula should realise that they are backing personal dealing qualities rather than ascertained asset values. And they should not be too greedy. The shares of companies with a narrow equity base have a tendency to plummet at the end of a bull market.' (Investors Chronicle, 2 June 1972, p.1012)

The immediate benefits to Keyser were too appealing to warrant caution, however. As the same article continued, with only a thinly veiled reference to Keyser Ullman, 'Peureula's bankers are obviously doing well at each stage of the operation, providing straight finance, effectively controlling the associated companies and, perhaps least important to them, holding substantial stakes in Peureula itself.' In the event, Keyser Ullman had no one to blame but itself when the bull market eventually came to an end with a bang in 1974. Although the money loaned to Peureula represented only part of Keyser Ullman's £119 million provisions against bad debts in 1974-5 (and the £65 million of the Bank of England's 'lifeboat' support needed to keep Keyser afloat in 1976), the debt was nevertheless typical of the millions outstanding on loans for speculative flat-dealing activities which played such an integral part in the financial collapse during this period.

The rise and fall of Westgrove Securities

Westgrove Securities was one of the new generation of breakers which emerged in the mid 1970s to cash in on the resurgent break-up market. It was founded by Arnold Hagenbach who, with his earlier partner Sam Chippendale, changed the face of many British cities by developing their Arndale shopping centres. Hagenbach wanted an investment vehicle for his retirement, but money to finance break-up was in short supply and expensive, and mortgage interest rates reached 15 per cent in 1977. The 1974 crash had also shown flat break-up to be a risky business. Hagenbach and the managing director of Westgrove, Clifford Smith, therefore hit on the ingenious idea of financing break-up by bringing in investors keen to profit from the break-up market but lacking the expertise and the money to get directly involved. They initiated unit trust break-ups and purchased property by obtaining half the finance from banks and half from unit investors.

With the backing of the National Westminster Bank as trustee and Panmure Gordon as brokers, they established a unique series of unauthorized property unit trusts, one for each break-up, and set out to find investors willing to invest a minimum of £2,000. Using the name Biskeep Nominees, a £5 nominee company operated by National Westminster, they quickly obtained institutional finance and purchased their first two blocks from Guildhall Properties for £883,000 in mid 1977. After limited cosmetic refurbishment, flats were sold totalling almost £1.5 million. After legal expenses, estate agents' fees, interest charges and management fees—the major source of profit for Westgrove—£210,000 was distributed to the unit holders: a return on their investment of almost 25 per cent in under a year (*Sunday Times,* 6 August 1978).

With this start Westgrove had no difficulty in attracting more finance even though it was not permitted to advertise, and it expanded rapidly, purchasing the 100 flat Boydell Court in St John's Wood from St John's Wood Park Investments for £1.6 million, and Marlborough and Chatsworth Mansions, previously owned by Town and City Properties. Westgrove also bought Merton and Grosvenor Mansions and Ham House. The returns on the unit capital invested in these schemes varied between 25 and 38 per cent and by 1979 Westgrove had embarked on a total of 16 such schemes. Flushed with success, Westgrove then embarked on its most ambitious scheme to date,the purchase of the 550 flat Park West block from Peachey Properties.

Peachey had previously attempted to sell the block to a wealthy Kuwaiti businessman for £9.9 million but the Church Commissioners who owned the freehold withheld their consent to assignment of the lease on the grounds that it could prove impossible to hold an overseas company to the repair and maintenance covenants in the lease. Peachey asked the court to rule that the Commissioners were acting unreasonably in withholding their permission but lost (*Guardian,* 27 July 1978). At this stage, Westgrove bid £9.4 million for the 117 year lease and agreed to pay a further £2 million to the Church Commissioners for the freehold. This figure—far in excess of the capitalized value of the ground rent of £12,500 per year—was the price the Church Commissioners were able to exact for break-ups to proceed (*Evening Standard,* 7 April 1979).

In the event, the Westgrove purchase failed at the last moment because one of the investment groups 'in' for £1 million of units withdrew half an hour before contracts were due to be signed and Westgrove had to withdraw. Despite the failure, the arithmetic of the proposed break-up operation demonstrates the profitability of such operations. In addition to the purchase price, Westgrove would have had to spend a further £400,000 on acquisition costs and £1.3 million in capital expenditure including refurbishments - a total expenditure (including administration costs and contingencies) of £14 million. Westgrove would then have raised a bank loan for £8 million in addition to the £6 million of investors' equity. The companies estimated that the sales of the 150 plus vacant flats and sales to sitting tenants would have raised just over £12 million, sales of the commercial elements of the block £4 million, and sale of the rump of the headlease with ground rents £2.7m. Total projected income was therefore £18.7 million. After conveyancing and estate agents' fees, Westgrove estimated a gross yield of £4.17 million, 60 per cent of which would have gone back to the investors and 40 per cent to Westgrove (Estates Gazette, 18 November 1978).

Park West was subsequently sold to the European Housing Group, an offshore-funded operation, in early 1979 and the group immediately

PARK WEST
The biggest address in town
Studios, 2-3-4-& 5-room luxury apartments
from £32,500
Exceptional value
125 year leases and low ground rents
Situated on the Hyde Park Estate
Fully modernised
TV Security system and Entry phones
24 hour uniformed porterage
Magnificent entrance halls
New fully-equipped kitchens and bathrooms
Wall-to-wall carpets
Swimming pool and Squash courts
Car-parking available
Mortgages available
Model apartments designed and furnished by Robin Anderson
Selling agents
Keith Cardale Groves
PARK WEST
MAYFAIR
HYDE PARK
BELGRAVIA
PARK WEST The Hyde Park Estate, London
Open 7 days a week – 11am to 7pm. Phone: 01-262 7733

Figure 8.3

THE SPECIAL OPPORTUNITIES FUNDS

1. PURPOSE OF FUNDS

Within the framework of the Universal Bond we have introduced the first of the Special Opportunities Funds which will enable the discerning investor to take advantage of special investment opportunities wherever they may occur. The objective of each fund will be to seek out these special opportunities, whether they are found in the equity market, in the property field, or in any other authorised investment medium. For many reasons, such opportunities are often missed by other more traditional funds, or are thought to be unsuitable for the average investment bond holder.

We at NZI, however, firmly believe that such opportunities should not be denied to the more discriminating investor, who will be alive to the implications of the nature of the fund, and can recognise the potential for considerable financial reward.

Certain of these opportunities will be short term in nature but investors should consider their investment in the Universal Bond through the Special Opportunities Fund as long term. Each fund will be kept open for as long as the Company considers that there are suitable investment situations available.

2. CURRENT INVESTMENT POLICY AND CONCEPTS

There are certain specialised investment opportunities currently available within the property sector. Some fall under the heading of commercial and industrial enterprises, but one exciting yet relatively unknown opportunity exists in the field of residential property. This involves subdividing large blocks of tenanted flats into owner occupied homes.

In general terms these blocks have proved to be unattractive investments to the current owners, many of whom inherited them during the collapse of the property market in the early seventies, because of the various rent acts which have given a high level of protection to tenants.

The concept is essentially straight-forward. A suitable block is carefully appraised and a purchase price negotiated in the region of 35-40% of its vacant value. One basic requirement is that the property should be a purpose built block in a good state of repair requiring minimum refurbishing and maintenance. Then, as a matter of policy, the standards of accommodation and decoration are improved, since the modest additional outlay has been shown to enhance the return to investors.

Any vacant flats are sold at market value. The remaining flats are then offered to sitting tenants at an attractive discount or vacant possession is negotiated in return for a sizeable disturbance allowance.

No pressure is applied to tenants to buy or vacate and, in evaluating each project, it is anticipated that only 50% of tenants will take advantage of either of the options. The success of transactions to date results from the fact that tenants have recognised the advantages to themselves of accepting one of the alternatives offered.

These ventures are financed by bank loans to the extent of approximately half of the expenditure involved. In this way the returns to investors have been substantially increased.

The New Zealand Insurance Co. (U.K.) Ltd. now offers investors in the Special Opportunities Fund a means of participating in profits from this type of project, whilst at the same time enjoying the tax protection and life assurance benefits afforded by a single premium life assurance policy. Each project is planned to run for approximately twelve months.

1

Figure 8.4

An extract from a brochure for the New Zealand Insurance Co.

KINGS GARDENS NW6

STATEMENT OF PROJECTED NET SALE PROCEEDS

This statement forms an integral part of, and should be read in conjunction with, the projection of increase in unit value.

INCOME:		**£**	**£**
(i)	**Estimated Vacant Sales**		
	1 x 2R @ £27,500	27,500	
	1 x 3R @ £35,000	35,000	
	1 x 4R @ £38,000	38,000	
	2 x 7R @ £55,000	110,000	210,500
(ii)	**Sales to Tenants**		
	2 x 3R @ £24,500	49,000	
	1 x 4R @ £26,500	26,500	
	1 x 7R @ £38,500	38,500	114,000
(iii)	**Sale of Garages**		
	26 @ £3,000	78,000	78,000
(iv)	**Sale of Residual Interest**		
	1 x 2R @ £ 9,500	9,500	
	4 x 3R @ £12,500	50,000	
	3 x 7R @ £18,500	55,500	
	Ground Rent @ 6 Years Purchase	27,500	142,500
			545,000
EXPENDITURE:			
	Conveyancing Costs	6,250	
	Agents Fees	18,750	25,000
	TOTAL PROJECTED NET SALE PROCEEDS		520,000

Figure 8.5

commenced selling individual flats in what was heavily advertised in the press as 'The biggest address in town' (see Figure 8.3). Having missed their chance of big profits, Westgrove teamed up in 1979 with the New Zealand Insurance Company (UK) Ltd to establish a series of 'special opportunity funds' for investors. The first of these was Westminster Mansions, near the Houses of Parliament, and the second was Kings Gardens, West Hampstead. The brochure (see Figures 8.4 and 8.5) sent to potential investors was very revealing about both the economics of break-up and the company's policy towards them. It stated:

> The concept is essentially straight-forward. A suitable block is carefully appraised and a purchase price negotiated in the region of 35–40% of its vacant value. One basic requirement is that the property should be a purpose built block in a good state of repair requiring mimimum refurbishing and maintenance. Then, as a matter of policy, the standards of accommodation and decoration are improved, since the modest additional outlay has been shown to enhance the return to investors. Any vacant flats are sold at market value. The remaining flats are then offered to sitting tenants at an attractive discount or vacant possession is negotiated in return for a sizeable disturbance allowance. No pressure is applied to tenants to buy or vacate and, in evaluating each project, it is anticipated that only 50% of tenants will take advantage of either of the options.

The basis of the Westgrove operation was to get in and get out as quickly as possible, selling as many flats as it could within 12 months and selling on the unbroken 'rump' of the block to yet another buyer. Nor did it see itself having a permanent presence in the break-up market. In October 1978, just before the collapse of the Park West deal, Smith stated that Westgrove would leave the market by the end of 1979. It is possible that Smith was already aware of a slowdown in the rate of sales, and saw Park West as Westgrove's swan-song. But in early 1980 Westgrove launched its twenty second trust, to buy Drayton Court in Drayton Gardens, Kensington, for £1 million. The usual 24 per cent profit was forecast but Westgrove had failed to get out of the market in time and the slump in the residential market in 1981 caught Westgrove exposed with too few flat sales and high financing charges. It had also bought some blocks which had already been part-broken and where the potential for further sales was extremely limited. In June 1981 Westgrove was forced to put seven blocks, totalling 550 flats, up for auction. But given the depressed state of the market, only one (totally unbroken) block of flats was sold and the remaining blocks all failed to meet their reserve price. Of the 28 flats in Westminster Mansions, bought in 1979, only 11 flats had been sold before the auction took place, and only a handful of flats in Drayton Court had been sold by October 1981. Westgrove then, unsuccessfully tried to sell the block 'at a price which will give a satisfactory return to unit holders' (*Sunday Times,* 2 May 1982).

Westgrove had come unstuck. The sale of the rumps had been envisaged as providing the icing on the profits cake. But potential buyers were well aware that all the breakable flats had been sold and they were only willing to purchase on the basis of the tenanted investment value or a little above to allow for a trickle of vacancies. Selling the rumps for a good price had become the difference between success and failure. By the end of April 1982 the value of the units in Drayton Court had fallen well below the purchase price and Westgrove presented the option to unit holders of selling the block at any price or putting in more cash to extend the life of the trust. The investors were up in arms, but National Westminster stated that it was confident of Westgrove's ability to continue managing the trusts.

In July 1982 Westgrove resigned as manager of the trusts and went into liquidation, leaving 13 trusts uncompleted and unlikely to return to investors the original value of their units. Westgrove had not filed any accounts for 3 years and those for 1978 indicated that it was technically insolvent (*Sunday Times*, 18 July 1982). Investors turned on National Westminster, arguing that they had put considerable faith in the bank acting as trustee. But worse was to come. By September 1982 it was revealed that Drayton Court (and possibly other blocks) was bought via a string of nominee companies at an inflated price. The *Sunday Times* (26 September 1982) stated:

> In May 1980 Rooff Estates sold the block for £635,000 to Chartwell Investments which immediately sub-sold, via nominee Grandkemp Properties, to Biskeep Nominees.The price had now leapt to £800,000. Chartwell is an Isle of Man company with its shares held by Liberian and Jersey interests. That makes ultimate ownership virtually impossible to discover. Chartwell also passed a resolution in May this year that it should be voluntarily wound up and decreed that all its books and papers should be destroyed six months later.

Unit holders were suspicious that Westgrove may have purchased at a deliberately inflated price in order to channel off profits to beneficial intermediate owners before break-up, but they were unable to prove this, and they subsequently took unsuccessful legal action against NatWest on the grounds that the bank had been negligent as trustee. Westgrove's attempt to spread the costs and risks of break-up over a number of investors had succeeded in the sense that they were able to walk away unscathed from the crash. Arnold Hagenbach retired to live in Spain. Meanwhile, residents of Fitzgeorge and Fitzjames Avenue in Fulham were fighting to get urgent repair work on their blocks completed. They had already successfully taken Biskeep Nominees to court for failing to fulfil their legal obligation to maintain the block. But they were still waiting for Biskeep's 24 per cent share of the repair costs when Westgrove resigned as manager of the trust and went into liquidation (Sunday Times, 25 July 1982). Once again the breakers and investors took the profits and left the residents to pick up the pieces.

Conclusions: disinvestment, break-up and the corporate experience

In this chapter we have attempted to show, through a variety of examples, how the disinvestment process and the flat break-up market developed as a result of the policy decisions of those landlords involved. As we have seen, these responses represented reactions to changes in the general investment environment in which corporate residential landlords found themselves over time, as well as to the particular structure of the companies themselves which greatly affected the way they perceived and responded to these general conditions. No two companies responded in the same way and at the same time to the overall changes which affected them.

Despite this variety of response, the overall trend has been been quite straightforward. There was an initial period during the 1950s when there was still a considerable level of investment in flats for their rental potential, albeit at a time when house property was being rapidly traded into owner occupation. This was followed by a period in the early 1960s when the move into commercial and other property sectors really got under way, while flat portfolios tended to be consolidated. From the mid 1960s onwards, disinvestment, to flat break-up specialists and also through self-breaking, became the dominant trend, although there was considerable latitude in the timing of this move, and variations in the motivations which lay behind it. The emergence of the specialist flat dealer in the late 1960s and early 1970s paralleled the gowth of the house traders who had been active since the interwar years. Thus, the flat breakers were simply one more link in the slow decline of the privately rented sector over this century.

By the late 1970s there were no companies investing in the flat market for anything other than its break-up potential. In the process, the entire flat market had been transformed and, with it, the characteristics and orientation of the landlords who own it. But the disinvestment and break-up of the sector has also had a profound impact on those living in the properties. The next chapter explores the effects that flat break-up has had on them.

9 The social costs and consequences of break-up

Introduction

We have argued in previous chapters that the major underlying cause of flat break-ups was the falling profitability of private renting compared to the opportunity cost of sale for owner occupation. Although different landlords sold at different times for different reasons, it is clear that break-ups have generated substantial profits for both traditional landlords and the new generation of flat breakers. The focus so far has therefore been almost entirely on the financial determinants of landlord decisionmaking. The residents of the blocks have only entered into the analysis in a rather passive and indirect way as rent payers or lessees. In our view, this is entirely appropriate, given the predominantly supply-led nature of the process. The residents are merely players in a financial drama where the principal actors are landlords and financial institutions.

Although, as we argued in Chapter 1, the sale of flats for owner occupation relies upon the existence of a pool of potential buyers, be they sitting tenants or the open market purchasers of vacant flats, it would be wrong to assume that all these potential buyers are necessarily willing buyers in the sense that the purchase of a flat is an expression of their free and unconstrained choice. The relationship between the suppliers and consumers of central London's purpose built flats has been, and remains a highly asymmetrical one in which landlord decision making has been dominant. Although some tenants have clearly welcomed the opportunity to buy, their desire to buy could only be realized if and when landlords decided to sell. If landlords had continued to consider renting as more profitable than selling, there is little doubt that any desire to buy on the part of tenants would have come to nought. The reverse is also true, in that once the decision to sell was made, most potential residents had little choice but to buy or look elsewhere. Renting ceased to be a feasible option for all but a small minority of affluent, short- term corporate or overseas renters. And while sitting tenants had the option of continuing to rent, rapidly rising rents have forced many of them either to buy or to quit. The residents of central London's private blocks of flats have been the financial fodder for large speculative profits.

Although resident choice and preference have played little part in the *causes* of flat break-up, the point we wish to stress in this chapter is that it is the residents who have borne the social *costs* of the search for greater profitability on the part of landlords and speculators. The break-up of the central London flat market has had major consequences both for the residents themselves and for the social composition of the sector as a whole, and the purpose of this chapter is to examine these impacts. We will look at the changes in the social composition of the sector in central London, and then examine the nature, scale and incidence of the considerable problems generated for both existing and new residents by the break-up process. First, however,it is necessary to spell out our approach to the determinants of social change in residential areas.

Social change in residential areas

Social change in residential areas can occur as a result of *insitu* change in the characteristics of residents or as a result of differential in- and out-migration. Migration is commonly viewed as 'the most important direct determinant of the stability or transformation of the demographic and social composition of urban neighbourhoods' (White, 1984, p.134). But migration does not take place in a vacuum. While differential migration is capable of rapidly reshaping the social character of residential areas, it is not the product of unconstrained preference and choice on the part of individual migrants. Migration always takes place within the context of the structure of opportunities and constraints afforded by the nature and distribution of the housing stock, the operation of the housing market and the differential structure of housing accessibility and migrant purchasing power. Migration can therefore be seen as the outcome of the changing relationship between the demand for and the supply of housing differentiated by size, type, price, quality, tenure and location mediated by the decisions and policies of financial institutions, landlords and others. As Short (1978, p.546) has argued:

> The differentially priced housing market, the unequal distribution of income and the policies of housing finance institutions all affect the response of households to new housing needs. These factors structure the decision-making framework of households and broadly outline the type and location of housing available to different households. The decisions of individual households are more adequately explained as a form of adaptive behaviour in relation to the housing system, which in turn is shaped by the nature of the wider society, than by consumer preference arguments.

Although migration generally operates to maintain and reinforce the social character of different areas (Adams and Gilder, 1976; Short, 1978), changes in the structure of housing supply have a major effect on both migration flows and social structure. To the extent that migration can be seen as a major 'direct determinant' of the social composition of residential areas, changes in the supply of housing constitute the major indirect determinant. Such changes can take various forms in different areas at different periods. They may involve the clearance and redevelopment of older, predominantly privately rented housing in inner city areas for public housing,the construction of new, owner occupied housing on peripheral green field sites, the sale of council housing for owner occupation, the conversion of large older houses into flats or the sale of rented property for owner occupation. But given that *access to housing* is is primarily structured by tenure, income and price and that the distribution of housing is socially stratified by tenure (Payne and Payne, 1978; Bourne, 1981; Hamnett, 1984) changes in the tenure and price structure of housing supply play a major role in the transformation of the social composition of residential areas. Because housing tenures are not distributed at random across urban areas, unequal access to housing tenures also implies unequal access to residential space and the geographical structure of the housing market plays a major role in 'orchestrating' both migration and residential social change in general (Bonnar,1979).

Flat break-ups and the social restructuring of central London

When the large aristocratic landowners set about developing their estates in central London in the eighteenth and nineteenth centuries they specifically set out to attract the well-to-do. Consequently, they excercised considerable control over the quality of development—and thus the nature of the tenants—through the use of building leases and restrictive covenants (Summerson, 1978; Thompson,1974; Prince, 1964; Jenkins, 1975). Although some areas have subsequently declined, central London has remained a predominantly high-status residential area for over 200 years (Hamnett, 1983). If anything, the desirability of central London as a residential area has increased over the past 20 years as the number of office-based professional and managerial jobs has grown along with London's role as a major international centre of business and finance (Coakely and Harris, 1983). London has also acquired a justifiable reputation as a haven for the international rich looking for a safe and desirable place in which to invest in property.

The purpose-built flat sector in central London is no exception to this pattern. As Chapter 2 showed, most of the blocks were originally developed for those members of the middle and upper classes who could afford the high rents associated with a highly accessible and prestigious central London address. Although many of the blocks built in inner and outer London during the 1930s were constructed for the growing army of junior white-collar workers, most central London blocks have tended to retain both their social cachet and their exclusiveness. A glance through the rent or electoral registers readily reveals a good sprinkling of members of the aristocracy, peers of the realm, titled figures and Members of Parliament as well as a variety of well known public figures ranging from industrialists to actresses and even the odd bishop or two. Even Lady Diana Spencer occupied a flat in a large Kensington block prior to her well-publicized marriage.

Such impressionistic descriptions are useful, but a much more rigorous picture of the social composition of the blocks just prior to the onset of large-scale flat break-up in the 1970s is provided by the 1971 census of population. The analysis of enumeration district (ED) data for the 100 large blocks in central London which possessed comparable ED boundaries in 1971 and 1981 revealed that no less than 72 per cent of economically active and retired household heads in these blocks in 1971 were, or had been, in non-manual occupations. This figure can be compared to 55 per cent of such heads in the three central London boroughs and 43 per cent in Greater London as a whole. The predominantly non-manual character of the blocks is quite apparent, but when the figures for the professional and managerial categories alone are examined, the distinctive character of the blocks is shown even more clearly. Whereas 20 per cent of economically active household heads in Greater London and 24 per cent of heads in the three central London boroughs were in professional and managerial occupations in 1971, the figure for the 100 large blocks was 40 per cent. It is also significant that the largest single group of manual workers in the blocks comprised the self-employed (Table 9.1).

Table 9.1 *The socio-economic characteristics of economically active and retired household heads in 100 large blocks, 1971–81*

	1971	%	*1981*	%	*1971–81*	%
Managerial	304	28.3	232	30.6	−72	−23.7
Professional	129	12.0	80	10.5	−49	−38.0
Other non-manual	336	31.3	288	37.9	−48	−14.3
Self-employed	47	4.4	44	5.8	−3	−6.4
Skilled manual	40	3.7	28	3.7	−12	−30.0
Semi-skilled and service workers	60	5.6	43	5.6	−17	−28.3
Unskilled	26	2.4	20	2.6	−6	−23.1
Armed forces and inadequately described	132	12.3	25	3.3	−107	−81.1
Total economically active and retired	1,074	100.0	760	100.0	−314	29.2
Never active	133		223		+90	+67.7
Total	1,207		983		−224	−18.6
		35.7		33.2		−31.1

What effects has the advent of large scale break-ups had on the social composition of the purpose-built flat sector? The first point to stress is the very considerable reduction in the number of enumerated 'usually resident' households in the sector between 1971 and 1981. In the 100 blocks for which we have comparable data (Table 9.1), the number of usually resident households fell by almost 29 per cent over the 10 year period. This large decline has two contributory causes. The first is that the decision not to relet flats on vacancy but to sell them or to hold them vacant pending sale has resulted in a considerable increase in the number of vacant units. It cannot be too strongly emphasized that the increase in vacancy rates is *not* the product of a fall in demand for such flats. The demand is as strong as ever. It is the supply that has changed. The second cause is that a substantial but unknown number of flats have been bought by companies for use by their employees or by overseas buyers who may live abroad and may only use the flats for 2 or 3 months a year. Such flats have no 'usually resident' households. Given that there was a very low level of sharing households in the sector in 1966 and that very few blocks have been demolished, we would argue that the demolition of blocks and the 'thinning out' of sharing households have made virtually no contribution to the decline in the number of usually resident households. The loss of such a large number of households is a direct product of the tenure change brought about by break-ups and not a result of a fall in demand or a change in residential preference.

Although it is impossible to categorize the data on absent and other non-resident household spaces by tenure, the 1981 census results for the two central London boroughs of Kensington and Westminster revealed that of the total number of household spaces in *both* public sector *and* private sector purpose-built flats, some 11 per cent were 'absent household spaces' and some 15 per cent were classified as 'other', and presumably vacant, non-resident household spaces. In addition, another 2-3 per cent of household spaces were enumerated as containing 'persons present on census night but with no usual residents'. If this group is taken to include transitory corporate residents or foreign owners, the total number of non-resident household spaces totals exactly 29 per cent. On the assumption that these figures are not unduly distorted by the presence of public sector blocks in the totals, they can be taken as providing an approximate estimate of the relative importance of the two principal causes of the decline in the number of usually resident households. Although the impact of vacancies on the usually resident population is likely to be only temporary, it can be argued that it has played a considerable part in the sharp reduction in the size of the usually resident population of central London during the 1970s. The population of Kensington fell by no less than 26 per cent 1971-81 (Hamnett and Randolph, 1983).

We have dealt with the decline in the number of usually resident households first as the magnitude of the decline makes it important to analyse other changes in relative rather than absolute terms. Looking first at the socio-economic composition of the blocks, it might be expected, on the basis of the known national relationship between tenure and occupation, that the sale of flats would result in a marked increase in the proportion of higher occupational groups.The 1981 census showed only limited evidence for this. Table 9.1 shows that the total number of usually resident household heads in the blocks fell by 19 per cent as a result of the processes discussed. Within this overall decline, the proportion of 'never active' household heads doubled from 11 to 23 per cent while the proportion of economically active and retired household heads fell from 89 to 77 per cent. This probably reflects the death of elderly previously economically active or retired male household heads and their replacement by never active female heads. Looking just at the changing composition of the economically active and retired, the proportion of professional and managerial heads rose from 40 to just 41 per cent while the number of other non-manual heads rose from 31 to 38 per cent. But, although the total proportion of non-manual heads rose from 72 to 79 per cent between 1971 and 1981 this was largely a reflection of the decline in the proportion (from 12 to 3 per cent) of household heads classified as 'occupation inadequately described'. When this group was removed and the figures were recalculated, the proportion of non-manual household heads remained stable at 82 per cent in both years.

Several explanations can be advanced for this. First, the central London flat sector was already high in status prior to break-up. Second, a substantial proportion of flat sales were to existing sitting tenants. A postal questionnaire survey by the authors of a random sample of 150 residents in a random sample of 24 blocks in central London, undertaken in spring 1981, found that 25 per cent of owners had been sitting tenants. Third, as many overseas buyers are not enumerated, the data on the social characteristics of residents are likely to be skewed towards longer standing tenants and sitting tenant buyers. Finally, the process is still far from complete and it may be that when the remaining vacant flats are sold the proportion of professionals and managers will increase.

These are aggregate figures, however, and evidence from the 1981 census on the socio-economic group of residents by tenure in the 100 ED blocks revealed the existence of distinct differences between owners and renters (see Table 9.2). While both groups were predominantly concentrated in non-manual occupations, almost three quarters of owners had professional, managerial or intermediate non-manual occupations compared to just over half of tenants. Evidence from the random sample survey of residents confirmed these differences. While break-ups appear to have reinforced the existing high socio-economic status of the blocks, they also seem to have resulted in a growing occupational division between owners and renters.

This division is even more marked where incomes are concerned. Our

Table 9.2 *The socio-economic characteristics of economically active and retired household heads in 100 large blocks, by tenure, 1981*

	Owner occupied	%	*Unfurn-ished*	%	*Other rent*	%	*All tenures*
Managerial	94	35.1	77	31.9	61	24.3	232
%	40.5		33.2		26.3		100
Professional	48	17.9	17	7.1	15	6	80
%	60.0		21.2		18.8		100
Other non-manual	91	33.9	102	42.3	95	37.8	288
%	31.6		35.4		33.0		100
Self-employed	11	4.1	23	9.5	10	4	44
%	25.0		52.3		22.7		100
Skilled manual	6	2.2	5	2.1	17	6.8	28
%	21.4		17.9		60.7		100
Semi-skilled	11	4.1	7	2.9	25	10	43
	25.6		16.3		58.1		100
Unskilled	0	0	2	0.8	18	7.2	20
%	0.0		10.0		90.0		100
Armed forces and inadequately described %	7 28.0	2.6	8 32.0	3.3	10 40.0	4	25 100
Total economically active and retired %	268 35.3	100	241 31.7	100	251 33.0	100	760 100
Never active	83		85		55		223
%	37.2		38.1		24.7		100
Total	351		326		305		982
	35.7		33.2		31.1		100

survey revealed that whereas 46 per cent of tenants said their gross household income was less than £5,000 per annum, only 9 per cent of owners said they fell into this category. Conversely, while 41 per cent of owners said their gross household income exceeded £12,000 per annum, only 13 per cent of renters fell into this category. The modal income band for renters was £3,000-5,000 and the modal band for owners was £8,000-12,000. When incomes were compared for sitting tenant and open market buyers significant differences were found. Some 31 per cent of open market buyers said they had incomes of less than £8,000 per annum (none was less than £5,000), but 46 percent of sitting tenant buyers and 62 per cent of unfurnished tenants fell into this category. It therefore appears that, in terms of income, sitting tenant buyers occupied an intermediate position between renters and open market buyers. It is not unreasonable to infer that the higher incomes of sitting tenant buyers compared to unfurnished renters was a major factor in enabling them to buy their flats.

The sharp income polarization of owners and tenants which has emerged as a result of break-ups is paralled by another distinction: that of age. The age distribution of central London residents is distinctive. There are a large proportion of individuals aged between 20 and 34, and relatively low proportions of adults aged 35-54 and children aged 15 years or under (see Figure 9.1). This type of age structure is common to the central areas of most large cities as young childless adults are attracted to live there and families in the child-rearing stage of the family life cycle often tend to move out if they have the financial resources to do so (Rapkin and Grigsby, 1960; Abu-Lughod, 1962; Bell, 1968) and the age structure of the three central London boroughs reflects this. But, as Figure 9.2 shows, the age distribution of residents in the 100 large blocks is more unusual still in that it exhibits a clear bi-polar distribution. In 1971 the blocks had a large proportion of residents in their 20s and 30s and of residents aged 55 and over. This second peak is quite distinctive, and while the first peak was simply replicated in 1981 for the 25-34 age group, the second peak shifted from the 55-64 age category in 1971 to the 65-74 category in 1981. While the proportion of the population aged 75 and upwards increased by 3 per cent in the 3 central boroughs it increased by 27 per cent in the blocks.

How can these age distributions and their changes be explained? The existence of twin peaks in the age distribution could be interpreted as reflecting the attraction of block residence for both young and elderly households, and the fact that the 25-34 peak was replicated in 1981 seems to indicate that households in this age group tended to move out by their mid 30s to be replaced by an identical age group.This is explicable in terms of movement within the family life cycle, but the elderly residents appear to have simply aged *in situ* without being replaced by a younger age cohort. We suggest that both the replacement of the 25-34 age group and the non-replacement of the 55-64 age group can be interpreted in terms of the changes wrought by flat break-up. More specifically, we would argue that because rented flats are not relet on vacancy, young renters have moved out to be replaced by young buyers,while elderly renters have simply hung on, to be eventually replaced by younger buyers rather than by the dimished cohort of middle-aged renters. Eventually, this group of elderly renters will simply die out to be replaced younger buyers. This, of course, is partly the aim of the whole exercise—hence the attraction to breakers of blocks with a high proportion of elderly sitting tenants. Two sources of evidence support this age-tenure polarization argument. First, the 1981 census figures for the 100 large blocks in central London show that only 32 per cent of owner occupiers were pensioner households compared to 53 per cent of unfurnished rented tenants. The figures for the much smaller furnished rented sector are quite different. Because it is almost exclusively a high-rent sector for short-stay lets to overseas diplomats and business people, the residents tend to be much younger: only 17 per cent of households were of pensionable age.

The second source of evidence is the survey. The results showed that 72

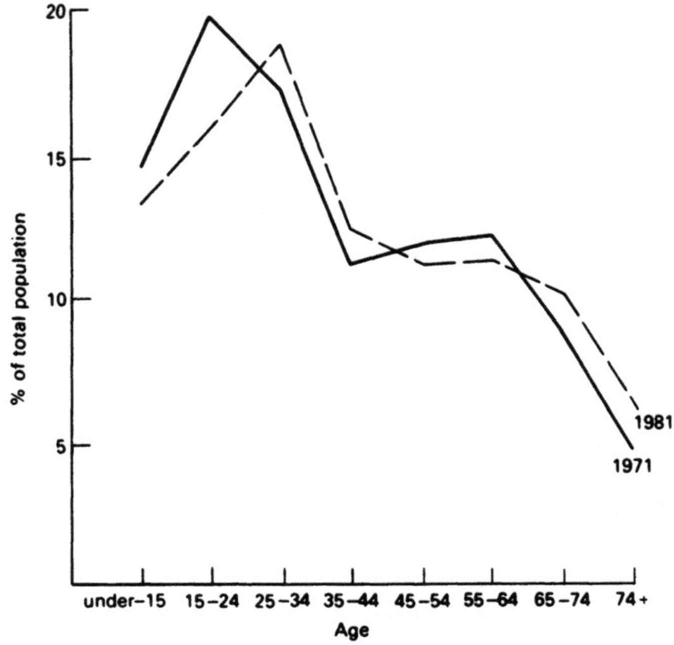

Figure 9.1 *The age distribution of all residents in central London, 1971 and 1981*

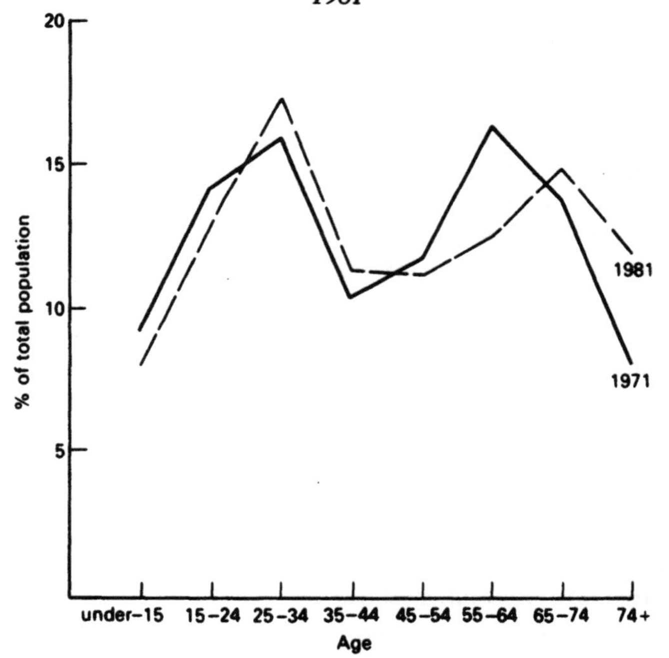

Figure 9.2 *The age distribution of residents in central London blocks of flats 1971 and 1981*

per cent of household heads in the unfurnished sector were aged over 60 years, and 63 per cent of all household heads aged 60 or over were unfurnished tenants compared to only 18 per cent of household heads aged 40 years or under. The average age of heads renting unfurnished was 64 years compared to 34 years for furnished heads, 43 years for open market buyers and 62 years for sitting tenant buyers. Not surprisingly, a large majority of unfurnished tenants had retired or were economically inactive heads of household. The survey results also showed that whereas 75 per cent of all owners had moved into their flats since 1970, only 31 per cent of tenants had done so. Indeed, when unfurnished tenants are considered by themselves, only 17 per cent had moved in after 1970. Conversely, none of the furnished and short-let tenants had moved in *before* 1980. The largest proportion (49 per cent) of unfurnished tenants had moved in during the 1960s and a further 20 per cent had been resident since before 1950. Looking at those residents who entered the sector after 1970, 12 per cent were unfurnished tenants, 14 per cent short-let or furnished tenants and 72 per cent were owner occupiers.

Taken collectively, these results confirm that the advent break-ups led to the replacement of elderly tenants by younger, more affluent, buyers. While many of the new generation of buyers are relatively young, affluent professionals or business people, the average age of the tenant population has steadily increased. A large and increasing proportion of rented tenants are now elderly and retired and many of them now live on fixed incomes. As a result, the population of the blocks has become increasingly polarized into a relatively youthful and affluent group of owner occupiers and an increasingly elderly and relatively poor group of tenants. There has also been an ethnic dimension to the changes as the original tenants—some of whom were Jewish emigres from Nazism in the 1930s—have been gradually replaced by overseas buyers from Africa and the Middle and Far East with the money and the inclination to buy into central London's steadily inflating residential property market. These changes are difficult to document precisely, not least because many such buyers will not usually be resident. What is clear is that flat break-ups are increasingly rendering the central London purpose-built flat sector the preserve of young, wealthy owner occupiers.

The consequences of flat break-up for residents

That flat break-ups have generated problems for residents is hardly suprising. The reasons are largely self-evident and stem directly from the nature and economics of the break-up process, the ownership changes involved, and the social changes within the blocks. Up until the mid 1960s the purpose-built flat sector was controlled by traditional residential investment companies. For these companies blocks of flats represented a long term asset and source of rental income. They thus had a vested interest in both the repair and the maintenance of their blocks and in reasonably good landlord- tenant relations. In order to minimize management problems and costs and to keep an effective control over their properties, most larger companies had a two- or even three-tier management system. First, many companies maintained their own experienced in-house management department.Some companies,such as LCF and Freshwater, also had an established decentralized system of local area managers. Finally, most larger blocks generally had one or more resident porters to assist residents and to deal with any immediate problems. Taken collectively, these arrangements tended to result in effective and efficient management. Some companies, such as LCF prided themselves on the quality of the management and on their ability to deal with tenants social and financial problems (Morton, 1970) and the telex address of London and County Freehold — 'Pampered, London' — was chosen to reflect the image of the landlord-tenant relationship the company fostered.

This is not to argue that all repairs were done immediately, that the management was free from defects or that the tenants lived in a privately rented paradise. To do so would be quite unrealistic although, when measured against what was to come, this era can be seen as something of a 'golden age' for the tenants of these blocks. The point is rather that there was a substantial degree of congruence between the requirements of continued profitability for landlords and the maintenance of both the blocks and good landlord-tenant relations. The maintenance of the one was assisted by the maintenance of the other. Put simply, good estate management was essential to maintain the value of the blocks as profitable long-term investment assets.

With the advent of break-ups both the structure of landlordism and the goals,orientation and background of the landlords changed dramatically. Although some traditional residential investment companies transformed themselves into residential traders and adopted a 'self-breaking' strategy of selling their own flats, the dominant tendency has been the sale of entire blocks or holdings to specialist flat breaking companies.It is this process which has been the major source of problems. The new breed of speculative breakers tended to have very little backgound in residential property and their motivation for entering the sector was the maximization of short-term capital gains.Not suprisingly, their attitudes and orientation to both their blocks and their tenants were quite different from those the investor landlords they replaced. The blocks were regarded as a source of short-term profits and tenants were an unfortunate but necessary prerequisite for the generation of capital gains. As we have argued previously, the term 'landlord' is something of a misnomer for such owners— some with such revealing names as Specmore and Gaingold. They can more accurately be categorized as 'residential asset- strippers', attracted into flat-breaking by the promise of quick high profits. Consequently, residents have faced an interrelated series of problems as the new owners have sought to realize the potential profits locked up in blocks of flats as rapidly as possible.

Break-ups and the advent of the anonymous landlords

For many residents, their first exposure to the break-up market was the discovery that their block had been sold without them being either informed or consulted. The first residents knew of the sale was when they were notified of the change of landlord. Some were not even that fortunate. In the peak period of flat break-up between 1970 and 1973,the wave of speculative excitement was such that some blocks were sold repeatedly within the space of a few months.In some cases, particularly where blocks had been sold to overseas landlords or offshore based holding companies located in Jersey, the Dutch Antilles or elsewhere for reasons of tax avoidance and anonymity, tenants had little real knowledge of who their landlords were or how to contact them. Dealings were generally conducted through the landlords' managing agents in Britain. In the case of Northways, a block of 89 flats in the Swiss Cottage area of Camden, the Legal and General Assurance Company sold the block in 1976 to Bernard Sunley and Company and thence to Northways Properties Ltd (Channel Islands)—believed to be associated with the large building firm of Wimpey. The block was managed by Pegasi, and in 1979, at the height of a dispute with residents over rent increases and attempts to purchase the block collectively, a spokesman for Pegasi was quoted in a local paper, the *Hampstead and Highgate Express*, as saying: 'It must be obvious to anyone in the residential field today that one doesn't want the names of individual shareholders flaunted in the local newspapers' (Ham and High, 16 November 1979). It is unnecessary to ask why.

The problems faced by the residents of Northways are by no means atypical. As a result of large scale surveys into the scale and incidence of management problems in privately owned blocks of flats, the Nugee Committee of Inquiry, Department of the Environment, 1985, found that almost half (49 per cent) of current residents had experienced at least one change of ownership while they had been resident in their flat. Of those residents who had experienced a change of ownership, 50 per cent had had one change of ownership, 18 per cent had experienced two changes and 32 per cent had had three or more. Given that the surveys were undertaken in 1984 and included a large proportion of relatively recent buyers, many longer-established residents must have experienced far more changes of ownership.

The report also found that 15 per cent of those residents who answered the questionnaire had experienced major problems in establishing the identity of their landlord or lessor and that 31 per cent had had major problems in contacting them. In the case of the 6 per cent of respondents who stated that they had a landlord based overseas, the proportion of residents who had experienced major problems in either identifying or contacting their landlord rose to 44 and 58 per cent respectively. These problems were not confined to blocks owned by a minority of disreputable landlords. In the early 1970s, hundreds of blocks were sold by one landlord to another without the tenants' prior knowledge and informing the tenants was the exception rather than the rule.

Attempts to purchase

Even where residents had prior knowledge that their blocks were to be sold, relatively few were offered an opportunity to purchase their block collectively. The Nugee Report found that only a fifth of residents had been offered the opportunity to buy. The attitude of the owners generally seems to have been that sales to residents were a complex and time consuming business and that sales could be effected much more quickly and easily with outside buyers. There is a great deal of truth in this. Residents not only have to agree to buy their block collectively, they also have to get it professionally valued, take legal advice as to the form of ownership they should adopt and obtain the necessary finance. All these things can take considerable time and the process of collective decision making is not the best vehicle for making rapid decisions. Unless key members of a residents' association are given delegated powers to negotiate, it may be necessary to make frequent references back to the residents, not all of whom are likely to be either willing or able to buy. Not surprisingly, given the difficulties faced by many residents, the surveys for the Nugee Committee revealed that even in those cases where residents' associations were given the opportunity to purchase, bids were made in only just over half of the cases.

To acknowledge the very real practical problems associated with resident collective purchases, and the desire of many landlords to side-step them, is not to seek to legitimate the sale of blocks over the tenants' heads. There have been many instances where large institutional landlords with a reputation to uphold and who are under no immediate financial pressure to sell have sold blocks to speculative breakers without bothering to consult residents or offer them the first right of refusal. The Co-operative Insurance Society quietly sold off several of its London blocks to the breakers in the early 1970s, as did the Liverpool and Victoria Friendly Society, the Norwich Union Insurance Company, the Legal and General and the Prudential Assurance Companies. As late as 1983, the Sun Alliance Insurance Group were selling blocks on the open market (see Figure 9.3. Although residents had the opportunity to bid for these blocks, the bulk were sold to a break-up company owned by a well-known Jersey-based property dealer who was centrally involved in break-ups in the early 1970s (see Figure 9.3). Even the Church Commissioners have been guilty of attempting to sell over tenants'

By Order of Sun Alliance Insurance Group
A Residential Portfolio
of 5 Blocks of flats
Highgate, London, N6.
Hampstead, London, NW3.
Brondesbury, London, NW2.
Ealing, London, W5.
Comprising 201 Flats (29 Vacant)
& 72 Garages and Administrative Offices
For Sale by Private Treaty
ALLSOP
& CO
21 Soho Square, London W1V 6AX
Tel: 01-437 6977
Telex: 267 397

Figure 9.3

heads (*Ham and High*, 27 February 1976). The Church Commissioners were on the brink of selling a total of 322 flats in 58 large houses and 4 small blocks in the Belsize Park area of Camden to the Rossminster group of companies in 1976 when residents discovered what was happening. Fortunately, the prominent public position of the Church Commissioners makes them particularly wary of adverse publicity and the residents were able to persuade them to call off the deal and sell to an association of residents. Rossminster has subsequently attracted the attention of both the Inland Revenue and the courts for their tax avoidance schemes.

Not all residents have been so fortunate. The collapse of the Stern empire in 1974 and its subsequent liquidation created major problems for residents in the blocks affected.Because of the size of the collapse, the number of blocks involved and the highly depressed state of the property market in the mid 1970s after the collapse of the property boom, the liquidators proposed a 'scheme of arrangement' to Stern's numerous creditors. The essence of the scheme was that rather than selling off all the blocks as quickly as possible for relatively little, a slower and more controlled sales policy over a period of years would maximize the receipts for the creditors. Although the liquidators stated that they were willing to sell blocks to residents, they saw the maximization of creditor revenue as their principal goal and the residents were only successful in purchasing 15 of the 65 blocks. In at least two cases—Avenue and Park Lodges in St John's Wood—the blocks were only purchased by the residents in the face of opposition from potential speculative buyers anxious not to see their potential profits disappear into the hands of residents (*Ham and High* 27 January 1978). In early 1978, Jack Beauprez, chairman of the tenants' company which took over Sheen Court, Richmond, from the receivers of the Stern empire, contacted the Fraud Squad with allegations that tenants' attempts to buy their blocks had been hampered by rival bids from anonymous companies and financial inducements to withdraw tenants' association bids (*Ham and High*, 27 January 1978). There have also been charges of delay and substantial price escalation on the part of the estate agents responsible for the sales. In one case, that of Gloucester Court in Kew, the sale to residents was only effected after their MP stepped in to protest at the agent's handling of the sale (Estates Times 14 April 1978).

These residents were the lucky ones. As Chapter 7 showed, many of the Stern blocks were sold at knockdown prices to speculative breakers who subsequently resold individual flats at spectacular profits. In at least one case, that of Russell Court, a block of 500 one-roomed flats in the London borough of Camden, residents put in a bid of £1.5 million for the block. Camden Council then attempted to step in and purchase the block at an agreed price of £1.6 million. Under this joint council/tenants' association scheme, the 150 empty flats in the block would be taken over by a holding company and sitting tenants were to be given the choice of buying their flats at valuation, continuing to rent privately from the holding company or becoming council tenants. In the event, Camden Council was pipped at the post by a bid a few thousand pounds higher from an unknown company called Alapam Ltd which subsequently declared their intention to offer sitting tenants the option to buy their flats at 60 per cent of their open market valuation and to sell the vacant flats on the open market (*Ham and High*, 2 December 1977; 27 January 1978; 14 April 1978; 19 January 1979; *Evening News* 13 June 1978). This would have yielded Alapam a large profit, and the potential of these blocks for the generation of substantial capital gains makes it easy and profitable for speculative buyers to outbid residents and council.

Once a block has been sold to a breaker the prospect of substantial profits from sales often makes it very difficult for the tenants to try to buy their flats on anything other than an individual—and much more expensive—basis. Even where tenants have made a bid to buy, there is no guarantee of success. Tenants and landlords often disagree over the valuation of blocks. Either the residents place too high a discount on the fact that they are sitting tenants or the landlord sets an unrealistically high price. In some cases, residents have found that, having made a bid, they have then been out-bid by a matter of a few thousand pounds by a private buyer. This inevitably creates the suspicion that this was the landlord's intention all along and that the resident's bid merely served to jack up the price. The Northways case provides a good example of the difficulties faced by tenants who attempt to buy. Northways (in Camden) hit the headlines in early 1979 when the new owners applied for rent increases of between 100 and 200 per cent. The predominantly elderly, long-established tenants were angered and frightened by these proposals and by 'creeping hotelization' of the block—the letting of vacant flats to short-stay foreign visitors and companies on short lets.

Camden Council intervened to issue a Compulsory Purchase Order on the block with the aim of selling the flats back to the tenants in a 'back-to-back' deal. Although it was unlikely that the Department of the Environment would approve the CPO order, it had the effect of stopping the owners selling the 17 vacant flats in the block. The owners then retaliated by serving a writ on Camden alleging conspiracy between the council and the tenants' association. In late 1979 the council withdrew their CPO after the management company – now believed to represent Middle Eastern investment interests – assured them that they would sell the flats to tenants at a discount of one third of their vacant possession value. But early in 1980, the tenants' association alleged that, while the owners were quick to sell vacant flats, they were dragging their heels on their pledge to sell to the sitting tenants. The disagreement revolved around the purchase price. The tenants of 48 flats had their flats valued at just over £2.5 million. They then made a collective bid for the flats based on a one third discount plus an additional discount of just under 20 per cent for 'bulk purchase'. The owners refused to accept the bulk discount and insisted on selling to the tenants individually. By early 1981, nearly 40 vacant flats had been sold—mostly to Far Eastern and Middle Eastern buyers—and the owners once again applied for rent increases of 100 per cent on the remaining tenanted flats. The tenants' problems were compounded by the fact that the block was owned by an offshore holding company with no records at Companies House. The tenants therefore did not know the identity of their landlord and were unable to communicate except through the management company.

Even where the landlord's identity is clearly known, tenants are often faced by considerable uncertainty over their landlord's plans for the block. In August 1978 it became known that the John Lewis Partnership which owned the John Barnes department store in the Swiss Cottage area of Camden, was planning to sell the 150 flat St John's Court above the store. The tenants, many of whom were elderly, were concerned about the future of the block and by the large rent increases—of almost 100 per cent for some flats— being sought by John Barnes. The tenants' association chairman stated that many of the flats had already been left empty for some time to make the block a more attractive proposition for a buyer and wanted help from the council and the Housing Corporation to form a housing association to purchase the block. A John Lewis spokesman could not say whether the flats would be offered to the tenants either individually or collectively (*Ham and High*, 15 August 1980).

The race to maximise cash flow

Once a block has been sold over the tenants' heads, their problems are far from over. Because flat breakers buy tenanted blocks at their speculative tenanted value on money borrowed at several points above base rate, profitable break-ups depend on selling as many flats as possible as quickly as possible before rising interest charges, major maintenance expenditure and negative cash flow push the buyer into trouble (Prior, 1980).

This financial pressure on speculative buyers to maximize sales and minimize expenditure in order to maximize short-term capital gains frequently causes major problems for residents. Obtaining vacancies is particularly important to the new owner as the price fetched by the first few vacant flats determines the base line against which discounts are offered to sitting tenants. As Anthony Margo (1973), a major estate agent in the break-up market puts it: 'it is desirable to achieve as high a price as is possible, as it is these first vacant possession sales that will set the tone of price levels for the whole building'. This in turn generates pressure on breakers to undertake cosmetic improvements, such as the introduction of entry phones on the block prior to sales. As Margo (1973) comments:

> landlords should carry out as many improvements as can reasonably be

> supported by the size of the operation. Expenditure on improving surrounding grounds, perhaps by planting flowers and trees, and on raising the standard of the common parts, can often have a disproportionate effect on the value and saleability of...units.

Such cosmetic improvements are a source of frequent complaints from both existing long leaseholders and the majority of rental tenants who pay a variable service charge, as the cost of such improvements is often added to their service charge.

Rapidly rising rents

It is also common, as in the Northways case, for the new owner to make an immediate application to the rent officer for an increase in the level of registered rents. In some cases, such applications have been for increases of up to 200 per cent over a 3 year period. Rent increases have two advantages for breakers. First, they increase the cash flow to the new owner and help offset the cost of interest charges. Second, they provide an invaluable encouragement for tenants either to buy or to vacate the flat. The number of such cases is too large to document in detail. Suffice to say that between 1978 and 1981 numerous applications were reported in the *Ham and High* for rent increases of between 90 and 200 per cent over a 3 year period at blocks such as Northways, Regency Lodge and Brookfield, Homefield and Gilling Courts in Camden and Northways in Hornsey. In 1981 a rent assessment panel was told that the proposed rent increases of 185 per cent at Northways and nearby Regency Lodge in Camden would result in many elderly tenants having to leave or being evicted as they simply could no afford to pay (*Ham and High*, 31 July 1981). This did not worry the landlords of course. At a rent assessment committee hearing in 1979 a surveyor for Daejan Properties, an arm of the Freshwater Group and the landlord of Regency Lodge agreed that the proposed rent increases of 140 per cent would put the flats 'beyond the reasonable means of most of the population of London'. He added: 'that is as it should be. The best one or two per cent of housing will always be beyond the means of most people' (*Ham and High*, 16 March 1979).

Tenants are often placed in a difficult position when the rent officers award large rent increases to landlords. Although the rents are sometimes reduced on appeal to rent assessment committees, there have been a number of cases where the rents have actually been increased on appeal by residents (*Ham and High*, 4 July 1981) and many large landlords now appeal against rent officer decisions as a matter of course as they can often expect to see rents increased by 10 per cent or more. Disturbingly, rent officers and rent assessment committees are increasingly accepting the argument put forward by landlords (*Ham and High*, 9 March 1984) that 'fair rents' should provide a fair return on the vacant possession value of the flats and, to this end, rents have been allowed to increase at a rate far above inflation. This represents a major victory for landlords as it successfully challenges the traditional basis on which 'fair rents' have been set and reflects the growing dominance of vacant possession values in the privately rented sector.

As further encouragement for tenants to move it is common to offer them several thousand pounds to go. Measured against the potential capital gains to be made from selling vacant flats, such cash inducements represent a sound investment for the break-up operator. The case of South Grove House, a 1930s block of just over 50 flats in the middle of Highgate village, one of London's prestige residential areas, provides a good example of the process at work. Until the end of 1982 the block was one of several owned by the Sun Alliance Insurance Group. The block was then sold to Alymer Square Investments, a Jersey-based company, for around £1.6 million—an average of £32,000 per flat. Almost immediately Alymer Square applied to the rent officer for increases of up to 200 per cent on the existing rents. Simultaneously, it offered tenants the opportunity to buy their flats at discounts of 25 per cent on the vacant possession value or £4,000 to vacate their flats. In spring 1983 the rent officer announced rent increases of between 50 and 150 per cent for most flats. Over half of the tenants were over retirement age and, according to the residents' association, many were unable either to buy or to pay the increased rents. Some vacancies quickly ensued and in May 1983 a selection of modernized and unmodernized flats were put on sale on the open market at between £58,000 and £74,500. In November 1983 a further selection of flats was offered at prices between £74,950 and £135,950. Working on the generous assumption that the average unmodernized flat was offered for sale at £64,000, this would represent a gross capital gain of 100 percent on the purchase price. Measured against this figure, the £4,000 offered for vacant possession is a small price to pay.

Given the capital gains to be made by the sale of vacant flats, some landlords are none to scrupulous about how they get them and there are persistent allegations of landlord harassment despite Margo's (1973) rather high minded declaration that: 'the possibility of negotiating the surrender of a lease is...a very sensitive matter; very great care must be taken to avoid any suggestion of harassment'.

Falling standards and rising costs

Once a break-up is under way, the principal problem faced by tenants and long leaseholders alike is the tendency for many of the new speculative owners to cut back on maintenance and the provision of services such as lifts, porterage and hot water and/ or to raise the the costs of services to residents. Both tactics serve to improve the landlords'cash flow position. The Nugee Report found that no less than 56 per cent of residents surveyed said that they had experienced major problems regarding excessive delay on the part of landlords or agents in responding to or acting upon requests to carry out maintenance or repair works. A further 49 per cent said that they had experienced major problems in attempting to enforce the landlord's obligations and responsibilities under the terms of the lease or tenancy agreement, and 48 per cent noted major problems regarding both the level of service charges and the quality of services provided (see Table 9.3).

Examples of these problems are unfortunately only too easy to document. In July 1978 the *Ham and High* reported that tenants from The Eton's—three blocks of flats owned by Peachey Corporation in Hampstead—had mounted a clean-up campaign in protest at the 'disgraceful squalor' into which they said their blocks had been allowed to deteriorate since they had been transferred, without consulting the residents, from one managing agent to another. It was also reported that the agent's management fees were to be doubled (*Ham and High*, 14 July 1978). In January 1978, it was reported that the chairman of the residents' association at Northwood Hall, a 1930s block of 200 flats in North London, told residents that the rises in service charges of 400 to 500 per cent over the previous five years were totally unacceptable in view of the gross neglect of the property and advised them to pay only half the charges demanded. The chairman of the tenants' association—representing the tenants rather than the long leaseholders—did not recommend such action, although he felt that the residents had a good case on grounds of negligence, because the solicitor's letter which they would receive as a consequence would cause distress and worry to elderly tenants (*Ham and High*, 19 January 1979). In April 1979, the tenants claimed at a rent assessment committee hearing that the cost of services was far in excess of what the rent officer had previously estimated would be reasonable. The cost of boiler maintenance alone came to nearly £7,000 instead of £450 (*Ham and High*, 6 April 1979). At Southwood Hall in north London, the residents passed a unanimous vote of no confidence in their mananging agents in 1981 alleging that the service charges were excessive, that services were inefficient, that the managing agents did not answer letters and that they failed to send representatives to the residents' meetings to hear their complaints (*Ham and High*, 28 August 1981).

The problem of inadequate maintainence can be even more serious than that of rapid increases in service costs and the declining quality of services, not least because flats can rapidly become uninhabitable. As repairs and maintenance are the responsibility of the landlord, and the landlord can legally only pass on to the leaseholders a pro rata share of the costs and must bear the tenants' share of the costs out of rental income, residents of many blocks—both tenants and long leaseholders—have frequently found it extremely difficult to get the new breed of speculative landlord to carry out necessary work. Landlords refuse to answer letters, repairs are promised but delayed, and a variety of reasons and excuses are found to postpone the work as long as possible—preferably until the landlord has been able to take the profits from flat sales and sell the 'rump' block to a smaller breaker who

Table 9.3 *The incidence of problems experienced by respondents (percentages)*

	Major	*Minor*	*None*
(a) Imprecisions, ommissions or onerous clauses in terms of the lease/tenancy agreement	31	30	39
(b) Establishing landlord's/lessor's identity	15	12	73
(c) Contracting landlord/lessor	31	19	50
(d) Excessive delay on the part of landlord/ agent in responding to or acting upon reasonable requests to carry out maintenance or repair works or other failures to act	56	21	23
(e) Excessive delay on the part of landlord/ agent in responding to reasonable requests to provide information	49	20	31
(f) Enforcing the landlord's obligations and responsibilities under the terms of the lease/tenancy agreement	49	20	31
(g) The level of service chargesl	48	23	29
(h) The quality of services provided	48	29	23
(i) Unexpected bills	41	19	40

Source: Department of the Environment (1985), Vol.I, Ch.5, Table A

will have even less margin for repairs. Every pound spent on the maintenance of a block is a pound of profit forgone to the short-term breaker.

Cases are numerous. Throughout 1978 the *Ham and High* reported a long-running struggle on the part of residents in Hampstead Garden Surburb to get their landlord—the Freshwater Group—to carry out delayed but urgent repairs. Other landlords have a far worse reputation. The notorious Berger Group of companies has come under constant attack for allowing blocks to fall into disrepair and failing to heed residents' pleas to get them repaired. In 1982 the residents of Thurliegh Court, a delapidated block of 52 flats in Clapham, south London, owned by one of the many Berger companies, went to court to compel their landlord to turn on their heating and carry out essential repairs which had first been ordered in 1978 when Wandsworth Council placed 41 statutory repair notices on the block. At the time, the landlord argued in court that the flats were unfit for human habitation and that the repairs would be too expensive. The judge found that the landlord had let the building deteriorate in order to obtain vacant possession. At the hearing it was revealed that the landlord was in the process of selling the block to another landlord about whom the tenants could find out nothing. This is a common manoeuvre to avoid repairs, and the judge ordered that ownership documents be produced to establish clearly who was responsible for the block (*Observer Business News*, 14

November 1982; Wolmar, 1982). The evidence to the Nugee Committee from the Berger Action Group revealed many such cases.

The problem of getting necessary repairs and maintenance done when the identity and financial position of the landlord is uncertain can be a nightmare for residents. In Chapter 7 we referred to the case of the blocks of 'Key flats' bought by FNFC from MEPC and later sold via Swallow Securities on a deferred puchase agreement to the Berger Group. In 1979 the flats reverted to Swallow because of Berger's inability to pay the outstanding balance of the purchase price. According to FNFC, Swallow owns the flats as trustee. The problem facing the residents is that, because of 15 years of neglect, the blocks require some £5 million to restore them to their former state of repair. But because the 1980 Swallow accounts made no mention of the properties and revealed a net deficit, the long leaseholders in the blocks were unwilling to agree to their share of the repairs until they knew the identity of the ultimate beneficial landlord and found out whether there were enough funds to complete the work. Despite the fact that the 1974 Housing Act gave tenants and long leaseholders a right to know the identity of the beneficial owner, FNFC refused to disclose the identity of the beneficial owner until disputed service charge arrears from the Berger era were paid. The residents in turn refused to pay until they knew the identity and financial status of the real landlord.

A similar case occurred at the end of 1981 when the residents of the 187 flat Fitzgeorge and Fitzjames Avenue blocks in the London borough of Fulham, went to court alleging that their new landlords—Biskeep Nominees: the holding company for Westgrove Securities—had failed to fulfil their legal obligations to maintain the blocks. They won and Westgrove was ordered to pay up. Although Westgrove's share of the £500,000 bill was only 25 per cent (the rest was to be paid by the leaseholders), the full amount had not been paid to the residents association (which was organising the work) when Westgrove went into liquidation.

Where repairs are carried out, residents frequently face the problem of meeting large unexpected bills—often for several thousand pounds each—for such things as major roof repairs and lift and boiler renewals. Although the existence of a 'sinking fund'—to which residents pay a set sum every year to cover major items of expenditure—would ameliorate this problem, the Nugee Committee found that only a minority of blocks possess such funds and there were difficulties over their ownership and control. In a few instances, landlords have treated sinking funds as their own property and have taken them when they have sold the block.

In addition, residents frequently complain that repairs have been badly carried out and/or that the cost of the repairs is excessive. It is frequently alleged that landlords place repair and maintenance work with their associated or subsidiary companies or that they accept high tenders in return for large financial kickbacks. There are also frequent complaints regarding the inefficiency and unresponsiveness of the landlords' managing agents to residents' complaints over services and repairs and requests for action or information as well as over the excessive charges levied by agents. Where, as is common, such charges are on a percentage rather than a flat fee basis, residents argue that agents have a vested interest in maximizing costs—and hence their own fee income—rather than seeking to minimize them. This is a particular problem for long leaseholders who are only able to challange the 'reasonableness' of charges in the courts. This can be an expensive and time-consuming business and, even where residents have won their case, it is not uncommon to find the landlords legal costs added to the following years service charge (plus 15 per cent for the managing agents fee). It is scarcely surprising that residents feel a growing sense of powerlessness in the face of what they perceive to be systematic exploitation and neglect by landlords and agents who see them solely as a source of profit. The Nugee Committee received numerous complaints on this score.

The residents' problems are not over even where the majority of the flats in a block have been sold on long leases. They may even be intensified because of the tendency of the big breakers to sell blocks to smaller dealers once most of the easy vacancies and sales have been achieved. The new owners are likely to have even less resources and to try to extract every ounce of profit through the manipulation of service charges and undermaintenance.

Even where all the flats in a block have been sold on long leases, the peculiarity of English property law ensures that the freehold owner of the block has total control over the level of maintenance, services and service charges. Although the long leaseholders own the great majority of the equity in the block, they have no say in its management and they are virtually powerless in the face of the freeholders, some of whom are said to be currently purchasing freeholds not just for their long-term ground rent income, the traditional basis on which freeholds were bought, but for the possibilities they offer of extracting money from leaseholders for poor quality or non-existent services, and for insurance which is also the responsibility of the landlord.

Although major problems over insurance are fortunately few and far between, evidence to the Nugee Committee indicated that some residents did not know whether the building was properly insured, whether the premiums had been paid on time, whether competitive quotations had been obtained and what commission, if any, the landlord was receiving on the leaseholders' premiums. In addition, because the insurance contract is generally between the landlord and an insurance company, it is impossible for residents to force their landlords to file a claim even where major damage has taken place. There is also no guarantee, even where major damage has occurred, that a landlord will necessarily release the money for re-building to commence immediately. Some leases also state that in the event of it not being possible to rebuild that insurance monies are the property of the landlord! Such provisions are quite iniquitous and it is clear that, in the event of a flat or block being totally destroyed, some leaseholders could find themselves without a home and without any prospect of one or of compensation for the loss of their home. In such cases, leaseholders are completely powerless in the face of a difficult or intransigent landlord. Although they owned a long leasehold interest in their home, they may be unable to obtain financial recompense in the event of its destruction.

Even where residents have managed to purchase and manage their own blocks, there can still be conflicts of interest between the generally better off leaseholders and the often poorer renting tenants who may find that they have simply exchanged one landlord and on set of problems for another. In a report to the Nugee Committee, the London borough of Camden argued that the interests of leaseholders and tenants were often at variance. The report pointed out that because many renters are elderly, retired and disabled, they tend to be at home all day and to be heavy users of hot water and heating, while the leaseholders may wish to limit supplies to the early mornings, late afternoons and evening. More generally, the report argued that:

> The long leaseholders may wish to upgrade common parts, to install luxurious amenities and services (in one case there was an intention to install a swimming pool in the common grounds) and generally to ensure that their homes, acquired at a low concessionary price,would have an increased and increasing value....As the blocks became more attractive, the regulated rents were inevitably subjected to steep increases. In addition the service charges escalated dramatically and the luxurious items contained within those services were ineligible for...rent allowance....Thus, the poorest tenants in the blocks, who had been precluded from purchase in any event,were forced to seek accommodation elsewhere ...the resultant empty flats were a great asset to the joint freeholders since they could be sold off at market values and the profits gained therefrom ploughed back into the upkeep and improvement of the blocks, thus keeping down their personal maintenance charges. (Unpublished evidence to the Nugee Committee from the London borough of Camden).

Leasehold ownership: the time bomb ticking away in the flat world

So far, we have said nothing about what is potentially the greatest problem stemming from the break-up and sale of blocks of privately rented flats—the long leasehold itself. English real property law is based on ownership of land rather than buildings (hence the derivation of the term *landlord*, and there is no absolute right of property ownership independent of the land on which property stands. 'Freehold' owners own their property and the land on which it stands outright in perpetuity, and it is possible for freeholders to sell long leases (commonly for 99 years today) which give the leaseholder right of use and exchange of the property for a specified period of years in return for the payment of an annual 'ground rent' (the term itself is revealing) and a capital sum. Whereas most houses in England and Wales are owned on a freehold basis, the overwhelming majority of flats are purchased on long leaseholds. And while the leaseholder has to pay a substantial premium to purchase a long lease—usually only a little less than it would cost to purchase a similar property freehold—the freehold landlord or head lessor is still treated as the long-term legal owner of the property and is responsible for all major decisions regarding maintenance, repairs, services and insurance. Although leaseholders often own the great majority of the equity in a block of flats, they can find that they have virtually no control over the running of the block. And, when the lease expires, the ownership of the property reverts to the freeholder without any compensation to the long leaseholder.

This system has worked extremely well for the owners of large landed estates who have been able to sell long-term use-rights in property in the full confidence that the property will eventually return to them like some financial boomerang. While this system has proved acceptable in the commercial and agricultural property world, it is beginning to generate considerable resentment and anger on the part of residential leaseholders who can see their expensively purchased ownership rights trickling away like the sand in an hour-glass. Not only does the value of a long lease begin to decline sharply when it has less than 30 or 40 years to run, but building societies are generally unwilling to mortgage property with much less than 50 years less to run.

Because the break-up and sale of blocks of flats did not begin in ernest until the late 1960s and early 1970s,the great majority of long leases were granted quite recently and still have 70 or 80 years to run. But, as the Nugee Report pointed out, the short-lease problem will steadily grow in size and importance over the next 20 years or more. The political pressures for an end to the leasehold system and for extension of leasehold enfanchisement to flats (a right for leaseholders of houses to buy their freehold was granted in 1967) have already grown substantially and are likely to grow further as the number of leaseholders increases.

Conclusions

The problems we have outlined above have all occurred as a direct consequence of flat break-ups. The transfer of ownership from traditional investor landlords who had a vested interest in the upkeep of their blocks and good landlord-tenant relations to the new breed of speculative owners interested only in short-term capital gains has meant that both the blocks and their residents have been treated merely as sources of quick profits. In the past, the tenants of most blocks could expect a reasonable level of both maintenance and services and good management was crucial to maintain the long-term investment value of the blocks. Today, the value of the blocks lies not in their long-term investment value but in their short-term capital gains value and the style and quality of management has changed accordingly.

In addition, the expansion of leasehold ownership has created a growing group of second-class owners who have found that their ownership rights are limited and divorced from control of their blocks. The problem was neatly summed up by a report published by the Building Societies Association in 1984 entitled 'Leaseholds—Time for a Change' which was prefaced by the quote that 'An Englishman's home, if it is held on a leasehold, is his landlord's castle'.

10 The international parallels: a comparative analysis of Britain, the United States and Holland.

Introduction

The 1970s saw the rapid development of the flat break-up market in London. But, as we have shown in earlier chapters, the sale of rental property for owner occupation was not a new phenomenon. On the contrary, the tenurial transformation of the rental housing stock in Britain has been proceeding at a rapid rate since the opening up of the 'value gap' in the early 1920s first made sales for owner occupation a profitable possibility. Flat break-ups and the allied process of converting rental house property into owner occupied flats merely represent the extension of an existing tendency into a new and hitherto unexploited area of the rental housing market as market circumstances and opportunities changed.

Such sales are not peculiar to Britain. On the contrary, the sale of rental house property for owner occupation has been common throughout Western Europe, North America and Australasia for much of the postwar period (Grebler and Mittelbach, 1979; Bourne, 1981; Harloe, 1985; Paris, 1984). Similarly, the 1970s have seen the conversion and sale of rental apartment property grow rapidly in many Western capitalist economies.In this chapter we want to examine how flat break-ups fit into this wider transformational process and the extent to which *national differences can be seen as variations on a more general underlying process*. We shall argue three things: first, that there is a common underlying financial and economic logic to the sale of privately rented apartments for owner occupation which transcends national boundaries; second that the process is predominantly supply side led and is the outcome of the maximization of profitability by landlords and developers; and third, that the social and political reactions to the process vary from one country to another, depending on the precise form of national differences in the laws of real property, landlord–tenant law and the tax system among other things. We shall pursue these points by comparing the British flat break-up market to the essentially similar processes of *condominium conversion* in the United States and *appartementen-splitsing* in the Netherlands. Unlike in Britain, where the flatmarket has evolved on the basis of leasehold ownership, both the US and Dutch markets involve forms of condominium ownership. Consequently, it is necessary to begin by first identifying the key differences between condominium and real property ownership.

Condominium and leasehold ownership

The term *condominium* derives from the Latin *con* (with) and *dominium* (ownership), and refers to any block of apartments or multi-unit development in which *the owner of each individual unit holds an exclusive title to the unit coupled with a collective interest in the undivided common parts* such as stairs, lifts or grounds. This form of title was common in continental Europe as early as the Middle Ages when separate floors and individual rooms of a house could be separately owned, and so-called 'flying freeholds' have existed in Scottish tenement buildings for severalcenturies. Article 644 of the French Napoleonic Code (the Code Civil) of 1804 made express provision for this form of ownership and most civil law countries have subsequently adopted specific statutes detailing the title description and the rights and obligations of unit owners under this form of ownership. Holland did so in 1951.

In North America, however, the condominium as a form of real property title is a relatively recent innovation. Because the owner of a condominium unit holds absolute title to the individual unit *combined* with a collective interest in the undivided common parts, it is necessary to register a development as a condominium and to register separate title to all the individual units before a single unit can be sold. The development of both new-build condominiums and condominium conversions was thus contingent on the enactment of prior enabling legislation which permitted the registration of condominium title. As Ishino (1979) points out:

> A condominium conversion is a change in the form of ownership of an existing structure built for rental purposes from ownership by a single legal owner to ownership by many individual legal owners as a condominium project. Such a conversion involves both a change in the ownership of the entire development and a shift in the tenure of the individual housing units from rental to ownership status.

English property law, by contrast, allows of no absolute right of property ownership independent of the ground on which the property stands. Instead, it distinguishes between *freehold* title (absolute title to buildings and the land on which they stand) and *leasehold* title which confers the right to exclusive use and occupation for a specified period of years subject to the payment of an annual ground rent to the ground landlord or freeholder. When the term of the lease expires the property reverts in full to the freeholder without compensation. For this reason, even long leaseholders (usually with a lease of 99 years or more) are referred to as tenants under English law.

The implications of this system are manifold. First, although the majority of houses in England and Wales are owned freehold, the great majority of flats are purchased on long leases because it is impossible under English real property law to own property outright without owning the land on which it stands. Second, although long leaseholders pay a very substantial premium for their lease—usually little less than the equivalent for a freehold—they own what is little more than a wasting asset. Towards the end of a lease, the value of the lease falls sharply; there are great difficulties in selling, or obtaining a mortgage to purchase, leasehold property with much less than 40 years to run. Third, it is legally possible under the leasehold system to sell long leases on individual flats on a one-off basis. There is no necessity, as there is under condominium law, to register independent title to every unit within a condominium before a single unit can be sold. Finally, although the responsibilities of both landlord and tenant for maintenance and upkeep of the property are set out in the lease, it is the *land*lord (the derivation of the term is a revealing one) or freeholder who is responsible for the management and repair of the common parts of the property and its structural fabric.

These differences in real property law have given rise to significant differences in both the form of the conversion process and the resultant problems. Although, as in Britain, condominium conversions in the United States only began after the development of purpose-built new blocks, it is clear that in the United States both new-build condominiums and conversions were contingent upon the introduction of prior enabling legislation. In England and Wales, of course, the sale of long leases has been possible for centuries (Nevitt, 1966).

The development of condominium legislation in the United States

Condominium enabling legislation first made its appearance in mainland United States in 1961 and by 1968 all 50 American states possessed some form of enbling legislation (van Weesep, 1981a, 1981b, 1984). The development of condominiums in the United States and the enabling legislation which underpinned it did not suddenly fall fully fledged from the skies in response to some sudden outburst of enthusiasm on the part of potential condominium owners. On the contrary, as van Weesep (1984,1987) has convincingly demonstrated, once the potential of the condominium concept for the building, development and real estate industries was appreciated, the concept was systematically promoted and marketed by real estate interests. Although these interests realized that the post-war baby boom would result in a considerable upsurge in demand for low cost owner occupation, the legislative history of the condominium in North America is almost entirely a supply-led phenomenon. Indeed, van Weesep argues that it was appreciated very early on that both the real estate industry and potential consumers would have to be educated to accept the condominium and appreciate its potential advantages. There are some striking parallels with the promotion of the flat break-up market in Britain.

Condominiums first made their appearance in the United States dependency of Puerto Rico in the early 1960s and the importance of property development in lobbying for new legislation soon made itself apparent. As van Weesep (1984, 1987) has shown, although the initial promoters of condominiums in Puerto Rico had the Puerto Rican Horizontal Property Act of 1958 to go on, they soon realized that the potential of such developments was severely limited by the absence of Federal Housing Authority (FHA) mortgage insurance which would have allowed buyers to borrow up to 97 per cent of the value of a property on terms of up to 30 years at an interest rate of only 5 ½ per cent. Without this, potential buyers were faced with deposits of 30-40 per cent and interest rates of 7 per cent. This effectively put condos out of reach of most middle and low income earners-the bulk of the potential market. The developers therefore petitioned the FHA to extend mortgage insurance to condominiums. While they were sympathetic,they required statutory authorization, and this Congress was persuaded to introduce in Section 234 of the 1961 Housing Act.

The explicit purpose of Section 234 of the 1961 Housing Act was to provide an additional means of increasing the supply of privately owned dwelling units where, under the laws of the state in which the property is located, real property title and ownership are established with respect to a one-family unit which is part of a multi-family structure. But, although the principle of 'air lots' (the ownership of flats or apartments separate from the ground on which they stand) had been successfully pioneered in the United States early in the century, the successful introduction of the condominium concept to the American housing market first required that mortgage lenders be convinced of the value of condominiums as security for their loans.

Given the legal complexity of condominiums, the creation of this confidence required the preparation of draft statutes that individual states could adopt on a more or less uniform basis. Such draft statutes were promulgated by both the National Association of Real Estate Boards and the FHA itself. The construction and real estate industries then set out to influence state legislatures to enact legislation. They were remarkably successful in this. Within 2 years of the passage of the 1961 Housing Act, 39 states had recognized the condominium form of real property ownership. In some states, the legislation was actually drafted by lawyers representing real estate interests. Given this legislative history it is not surprising that the form of this first generation of condo legislation were very heavily biased towards protecting the interests of the real estate industry and its financial backers. Only later did the legislation embody a greater degree of consumer protection.

The enactment of enabling legislation, while crucially important, was still only a step along the road to acceptability and the promoters of condos continued to promote the concept in trade papers and at conferences of real estate lawyers and developers. Van Weesep (1984) quotes one advocate as saying:

> the condominium...because of its inherent value is destined to become universal, and yet the millions of people who ten years from now will own condominium apartment homes...are not aware of the fact. You builders and you realtors who are in the business know about condominium, and what is more important, you are in a position to occasionally guide the progress of condominium's growth....

Another is quoted as stating that 'the major job of condominium developers is to educate the public to accept this new concept of ownership' and van Weesep (1984) himself concludes:

> The developers and their allies have worked deliberately and purposefully to make the condominium a success. They disseminated information and assessed the potential profits and risks, lining up the industry behind the concept. They succeeded in creating legal instruments that at least provided for public acceptance. They learned, applied and experimented; in the process they created the condominium sector as it can be observed today.

The development of condominium conversions in the United States

As happened in Britain with the development of flat break-ups, the conversion of existing rental apartment buildings into condominiums in the United States was contingent upon the prior development and acceptance of purpose-built condominiums. Once these were in place in sufficient numbers and the financial conditions were right, condo conversions could take place. The 1970 Census recorded a total of only 70,000 condominium units, the great majority of which were concentrated in a small number of retirement areas in Florida and California. From 1970 onwards condominium construction increased rapidly until 1975 when a combination of overbuilding and the recession led to a sharp reduction in new construction. Between 1970 and 1975 just over 1 million new units were completed, predominantly concentrated in a small number of large cities in the growing southern and western states (van Weesep, 1981a and 1981b).

Up till 1975 only 85,000 or 8.5 per cent of the 1 million new condominium units arose from the conversion of existing rental stock; however, in the second half of the 1970s conversions rapidly overtook new building as the major source of condominium units. The number of converted units grew from 20,000 in 1976 to 145,000 in both 1979 and 1980 and conversions accounted for 80 per cent of the growth of the total condominium stock during the second half of the 1970s. Although only just over 1 per cent of the American rental housing stock had been converted by 1980, conversions were overwhelmingly concentrated in a small number of the largest Standard Metropolitan Statistical Areas, such as Boston, New York, Miami, Los Angeles, Washington DC, San Francisco, Seattle, Houston, Denver/Boulder and Chicago where they accounted for over 3 per cent of the total rental stock. In some cities the figure was much higher, rising to 5 per cent in Houston, 7 per cent in Denver and Chicago and 8 per cent in Washington D.C.

How did this rapid increase come about? The influential 1980 report of the US Department of Housing and Urban Development (HUD) on condominium conversions pointed to the existence of two distinct explanations. The first is that conversions are the products of a distressed rental market, where landlords sell for conversion as a response to declining profitability. The second explanation is that conversions are a response to a strong and growing demand for ownership, produced by rapid inflation (US HUD, 1980, chV, p.1). Although the HUD report pointed out that the two explanations are not necessarily contradictory, in that decreasing rental cash flows caused by operating costs increasing more quickly than rents, could be associated with an increase in ownership demand, it concluded on the basis of a correlation analysis of conversions and a number of other housing market variables that 'conversions are associated with strong housing markets characterised by increasing demand for home ownership. (US HUD, 1980, ch.V, p.3).

We would not disagree with this conclusion but we do disagree with the interpretation placed on this conclusion that 'Although the most visible cause of conversion is the profit realised by rental property owners and by converters, the availability of households willing to buy converted units represents the most direct cause of conversions' (US HUD, 1980, ch.V, p.3). Although an effective demand is clearly necessary if supply is to be sustained, such a conclusion reflects the traditional neo-classical belief that demand generates its own supply. We would argue that, as with flat break-ups, the evidence points clearly to supplier profitability as being the key determinant of and principal moving force behind, the development of condominiums and condo conversions in the United States. If the demand for housing could have been more *profitably* satisfied by the provision of rented accommodation, condo conversions would not have occurred.

In the final analysis, the decision to convert or to sell rental units for conversion rests with the landlord. If the financial benefits of sale and conversion are not greater than those of continuing rental, landlords will not sell irrespective of the level of demand. If sale and conversion are financially advantageous, landlords will seek to sell, irrespective of consumer preferences. If there is a shortage of available and affordable property of the desired type and tenure, potential consumers may be forced to buy irrespective of their preferences. Demand is not an autonomous product. On the contrary, most demands are expressed within and shaped by the constraints of available supply. If the structure of supply changes, so does the structure of demand. In other words, supply can generate its own demand as the history of both new build condominiums and conversions clearly illustrates.

Where condo conversions are concerned, the HUD study found that the metropolitan areas with the highest levels of conversion activity tend to be characterized by low levels of rental stock losses through abandonment or demolition. Such areas also tend to be characterized by low rental vacancy rates, higher than average rent levels, a high proportion of high-income rental households and a higher than average proportion of luxury units. Rent controls were not found to be a major factor, not least because few of the areas where conversions are concentrated have rent controls. And, although the report argued that rising operating costs have generally served to depress landlord profitability, there was no clear cut evidence that conversions took place as a direct response to reduced operating margins. On the contrary, the report quoted several sources to the effect that in some cities, just as in London, the better, more profitable, properties were generally converted first. The study concluded that, although the evidence on rental profitability was unclear

> In all cases, however, it is the greater market value of certain properties as condominiums or cooperatives than as rentals, that directly motivates the sale of rental property for conversion....conversion is more a sign of market strength and, more directly, a response to profit opportunities presented by healthy market conditions than worsening operating margins or declining returns on investment from rental operation". (US HUD, 1980, Ch.V, p.19).

The HUD study rightly identified the centrality of financial conditions in the explanation of conversions. This is as true for the unit buyer as it is for the converter/developer or the rental property owner. Where the unit buyer is concerned, a high rate of house price inflation may serve to increase the demand for owner occupation while simultaneously pricing single family, detached units out of the range of many buyers. For many potential buyers, condos may represent the only affordable option irrespective of their desirability. When the effects of inflation are combined with the allowance of mortgage interest against Federal Income Tax and the limited Capital Gains Tax on residential property, the cost of ownership is reduced and house prices are bid up. Whereas inflation raises interest rates which are deducted at ordinary tax rates, the capital gains thereby produced are not taxed. But, as the HUD report points out, landlords are not taxed on the same basis as home owners. Although they can both deduct mortgage interest and depreciation against tax, the depreciation is at historical rather than current prices and the value of this deduction is reduced as inflation increases. The result, says the HUD report, is that

> the price an owner-occupier is willing to pay for a unit rises relative to what the landlord is willing to pay for the same unit. Hence, as inflation increases, the demand for ownership increases and the pressure for condominium conversion rises. (US HUD, 1980, Ch.V, p.25/26)

As in Britain, the favourable tax treatment of owner occupiers has played a major part in the creation of a 'value gap' and, the greater the magnitude of the gap, the greater the incentive to sell rental property for owner occupation. Interestingly, the HUD report comments that if tax relief were given on real or inflation-adjusted interest rates rather than nominal interest rates, inflation would not reduce home owner costs and the fiscal impetus for conversion would vanish.

The profit-maximizing rental property owner will, in general, compare the returns to be gained from continued renting with those to be obtained from sale as a rental investment to another landlord and with sale for conversion. In comparing these returns such owners will take the cost of operating rental property versus the rental income (the cash flow) into account along with the general return on investment. The general return on rental investment is lower than that obtainable elsewhere and the HUD report notes that: 'a rental property as an investment is worth what the building can sell for as a rental plus any tax shelter advantages and depreciation benefits accruing to the owners' (US HUD, 1980, Ch.V, p.29). But, as the report goes on to point out

> no amount of allowable depreciation or expected appreciation can equal the return recieved on the sale of rental property to converters.. a combination of greatly increased values of rental properties as owned units and real or perceived constraints on operating margins provides strong inducement for property owners to sell and reinvest elsewhere.

The report also subsequently states that the market values of rental properties have been pushed up due to the possibility of conversion. Consequently, many landlords have sold to converters at speculative prices far in excess of the tenanted investment value of their properties. Thus,the speculative trading of blocks of flats which characterizes the flat break-up market in London is repeated in the American condominium conversion market.

It is clear from this analysis that there is a remarkable similarity between the forces propelling flat break-up in London and condominium conversion in the United States. The structure of tax relief on mortgage interest combined with inflation helps bid up the price of owner occupied units relative to rental units in both countries, with the result that the tenanted investment value of a building is considerably lower than the vacant possession value of the building for home owners or the speculative investment value of the building to potential converters. The attraction to rental owners of selling for conversion is enhanced by the fact that, regardless of its intended use, profits on the sale of an entire building are taxed at the lower capital gain rates rather than the higher earned income rates. But if rental owners undertook conversions themselves, the profits would be taxed as ordinary income. This is crucial in explaining why most rental owners sell to converters rather than converting the properties themselves, and it can be argued that the elimination of some of the tax shelter benefits of rental ownership in the 1976 American Tax Reform Act was a major incentive for the sale of rental property. As ever, the operation of the tax system is a crucial determinant of the precise form and timing of the tenure transformation process (Whinihan, 1984).

From the converter's perspective, conversion is undertaken for the simple reason that it is highly profitable. The convertor's aim is to appropriate as much as possible of the difference between the value of a building as a rental investment and its value as individual owner occupied units. Because landlords would be liable to much higher taxes if they undertook conversions, they are unable to realize the full ownership value of their rental investments. Converters are thus able to offer landlords the equivalent of a 'speculative tenanted value' for their buildings, which, although considerably in excess of their rental investment value, is far short of their converted ownership value.

The HUD report comments that converters aim to earn 30 per cent of gross sales as profits. In some developments the profits can be much higher, and if the converters own equity or 'exposure' is used as the base for calculation, the returns can be enormous. The principal financial constraint on conversions is the current rate of interest on the money borrowed to purchase and convert the property. If the rate of interest rises too much, converters are faced with high holding costs and potential buyers face high mortgage payments. It is not, therefore, surprising that conversion activity dropped off sharply in 1980 when American interest rates rose rapidly to reach 20 per cent. There are strong parallels with the collapse of the flat break-up market in London in 1974 when interest rates rose sharply.

It is a constantly reiterated assertion in the HUD report that: 'Conversions are driven by a shift of housing demand from renting to owning'. This assertion is highly questionable. Although both inflation and the tax structure favour ownership at the expense of renting, it can be argued that a good deal of the 'demand' for owner occupation may represent displaced demand from elsewhere in the housing market. Some, indeed, may arise from displaced renters themselves. In the final analysis, it is the landlords' assessment of relative profitability which is the key determinant of whether or not units are sold for conversion. It is also clear from the major uproar regarding the impact of conversions on existing rental buildings that many existing renters are not part of the enthusiastic army of conversion demand. Conversions are undertaken because they are profitable for landlords and developers not because they are desirable or because they fulfil a demand. When interest rates rose to 20 per cent in the USA in 1980, the number of conversions fell sharply as rising financing costs cut profits.

Condominium conversion in the Netherlands

The Netherlands introduced a Horizontal Property Act in 1951 but the Dutch equivalent of condo conversion 'appartementen-splitsing' - did not take off until after the 1974 Rent Control Act when the rental subsidy system was overhauled and subsidy payments to landlords in the first few years of operation were substantially reduced. This had the effect of making landlords and residential investors dependent upon subsidies and rent increases over a much longer period and, consequently, upon long-term political and economic circumstances (van Weesep and Mass, 1984). As a result, the long-term profitability of rental property became uncertain for investors. Maintenance costs also rose rapidly after 1974 and the prospect of long-term capital gains declined. On the other hand, owner occupiers' mortgage payments are tax deductible, imputed rent is hardly taxed and capital gains on owner occupied property is untaxed. Given the strong progression in Income Tax scales, owner occupation has become increasingly attractive. The result, according to van Weesep and Mass,was that investors began to follow individual landlords by selling their rental housing for owner occupation. Between 1947 and 1975 some 600,000 units were converted from rental to owner occupied status, but during the second half of the 1970s, the rate of decline increased and between 40,000 and 50,000 units were removed from the rental stock annually (van Weesep and Mass, 1984, p.1153). Although only a small proportion of these units were converted, this proportion was higher in the big cities. Some 6 percent of Amsterdam's total housing stock had been converted by 1982 and no less than 13 per cent of Rotterdam's total stock was converted between 1975 and 1980 (van Weesep and Mass, 1984, p.1150).

This increase in the volume of conversions was not the product of the unfettered expression of consumer demand. On the contrary, van Weesep and Mass argue that the severe shortage of rental housing and tight government controls on the allocation of private rental housing served to disqualify numerous potential renters, who were therefore forced into owner occupancy or induced to buy. From surveys of home owners in several Amsterdam neighbourhoods, it was found that the majority of condominium owners interviewed would rather have rented a dwelling than buy a unit; but they could not find or did not qualify for a suitable rental dwelling. Although van Weesep and Mass (1984, p.1154) argue that government housing controls played into the hands of converters by creating a captive market, the growing shortage of rental housing would probably have produced the same result even without government intervention. Indeed, it can be argued that without intervention, condominium conversions would have had an even more severe impact on low-income renter households. But, irrespective of the role of government, the importance of van Weesep and Mass's finding lies in the challenge it presents to the view that conversions are a demand-led process.

Conversions in the Netherlands has been concentrated in Amsterdam and Rotterdam, but there have been intriguing variations within the two cities. Prior to 1975, the majority of conversions in Amsterdam were in the older, nineteenth-century neighbourhoods. But the National Housing Act was amended in 1975 to permit cities to operate a licence system for conversions. These were generally denied in the older, urban renewal areas; consequently, converters shifted their activity to the interwar suburbs. In Rotterdam, by contrast, the historic inner city had been largely destroyed in the war and conversions had always been concentrated in the interwar residential areas.

The pace of conversion activity in Amsterdam and Rotterdam fell sharply after 1978 as a result of the sudden downturn in the owner occupied housing market. As a result of rapid price inflation and mortgage overlending in the early and mid 1970s, owner occupied house prices began to fall sharply in the Netherlands from 1978 onwards, and by the early 1980s prices were still some 40 per cent below their previous peak. In addition, Amsterdam and Rotterdam introduced municipal occupancy regulations—in 1978 and 1980 respectively—which effectively restricted the sale of converted property in the privately rented sector to owner occupiers. Although this legislation was successfully challenged in the courts, the threat of further controls has proved a considerable deterrent to further conversion activity.

Although a substantial proportion of the stock in Amsterdam and Rotterdam has been converted into condominiums, only a relatively small proportion—between 20 to 30 per cent—of converted units have been lost to the rented sector (van Weesep and Mass, 1984). The reason lies in the strong tenant protection legislation which has been in force in the Netherlands since the war and which has effectively prevented converted units with sitting tenants being sold for individual ownership. Mass and van Weesep (1985) stress that it is important to distinguish between the *conversion of a property title* from 'fee simple' where the owner of a unit owns either the freehold or leasehold of the whole property to a 'horizontal property regime', and the actual *sale of the separate units* to new owners.They point out that although sales and profit maximization are the object of the conversion excercise, the existence of tenant protection legislation means that the two parts of the process may be far apart in time. The implications for tenant protest of this delay between conversion and sale are explored in the following section.

The social and political impact of condominium conversions and flat break-ups

The timing and underlying financial rationale of flat break-up, condominium conversion, and appartementen-splitsing have been similar in each of the three countries we have examined. It is therefore all the more intriguing that there have been marked variations between one country and another in the social and political impact of condominium conversions. As a crude generalization, the advent of condo conversions in the USA was accompanied by a large volume of protest by tenants, and widespread media coverage, over the extent and consequences of tenant displacement (Drier, 1984; Shearer,1984). In the Netherlands, the opposition to conversions was more marked in the housing departments and city councils of the affected cities than it was among the tenants. In London, the protests were initially muted but have grown rapidly in intensity—particularly among the new long leaseholders. How can these variations be explained? Clearly, a variety of factors are likely to influence the extent of tenant protest over conversion and sales for owner occupation. These may include the prevailing state of the rental market, the existence of readily available alternative accommodation in the area at equivalent rent levels and the existence of compensation for disturbance. We would argue, however, that almost all tenants are likely to be unhappy about the prospect of enforced eviction from their home. The extent of tenant mobilization and protest is therefore likely to depend primarily on the extent to which large numbers of tenants in the same building, area or city are subject either to eviction or to the threat of eviction within a relatively short space of time—hence, on the existence of a known and shared external threat which may affect anybody and everybody. Only the existence of such a widespread mass threat or shared problem is likely to overcome the individualistic tendency to dismiss such a problem as the sort of thing which happen to other people.

In our view, variations in the three countries in the extent and incidence of protest and tenant mobilisation over the sale of rental property for owner occupation can be largely accounted for in terms of the interaction between variations in both the nature of real property law and the presence or absence of tenant protection legislation. Four possible combinations of circumstances can thus be identified, depending on the presence or absence of condominium legislation and the presence or absence of legislation protecting tenants from eviction.

In those countries where condominium legislation requires the registration of a condominium project and of a separate title to each individual unit in a project before a single unit can be sold, conversions affect all tenants simultaneously. But, in England and Wales, the existence of leasehold ownership means that units can be sold for owner occupation individually. When condominium legislation is combined with the absence of tenant protection legislation, as in the USA, the drive to sell as many units as quickly as possible usually results in a mass notice to buy or quit which mobilizes tenants and generates widespread opposition and protest. When condominium legislation is combined with legislation protecting sitting tenants from eviction, as in the Netherlands, conversions are unlikely to have much immediate impact on the tenants. Hence, tenant opposition and mobilization is likely to be much more limited.

In England and Wales leasehold ownership is combined with tenant protection legislation. This means that individual units can only be sold to sitting tenants with their agreement, or as and when the units become vacant. This is unlikely to generate the conditions for the mass mobilisation of tenants. One further potential combination of circumstances can be identified in theory if not in practice. Where leasehold title coexists with the absence of protection from eviction, tenant mobilization and opposition to sales could depend on whether the landlord decided to serve notices to quit to all tenants simultaneously.

The USA: tenants up in arms

The upsurge of renter unrest over conversion in the USA can be explained as a result of a combination of condominium legislation and the absence of security of tenure. Unlike tenants in Britain or the Netherlands where the Rent Acts provide most tenants with permanent security of tenure as long as they pay their rent and fulfil the terms of their lease, and where sales only take place gradually as tenants buy, move or die, tenants in the United States are subject to a 60 or 90 day notice to quit from their landlord. Not surprisingly, when a building is sold for conversion, one of the first steps is to issue a mass notice to quit to all the tenants. Although many tenants are offered the chance to purchase their apartments, often at a discount on the open market price, some are either unwilling or unable to purchase (US HUD, 1980). The issue of a mass notice to quit is therefore a remarkably effective radicalizing device which can immediately brings tenants together in a common cause.

As well as there being considerable pressure for action at the city and state level, a number of proposals and Bills to regulate condo conversion were introduced and debated in Congress, including the Condominium and Cooperative Conversion Moratorium Act of 1979 which proposed a 3 year moratorium on new conversions. The unrest reached a peak in 1979 when Congressman Benjamin Rosenthal of New York delivered a statement in the House of Representatives in which he stated (Condominium Conversion Crisis, 1979):

> Unless this Congress desires the forced displacement of millions of elderly and low—and moderate—income tenants from their homes, unless we wish to further restrict the mobility of Americans by allowing the rental housing supply to continue to dwindle, and unless we want to witness in our lifetimes the death of private rented housing in the United States and the onset of a costly government-owned and run rental housing industry, we must begin to ontrol and restrict the conversion of rental property to condominiums and cooperatives. We cannot afford not to act.

As a result of the continuing political outcry over condominium conversions, Congress directed the US Department of Housing and Urban Development in 1980 to prepare within 6 months a report on the scale, causes and impacts of condo conversions. The report's findings on the social impact of conversions are revealing. On the basis of a survey of households in 12 major metropolitan areas with high levels of conversion activity, it was found that whereas 42 per cent of all households occupying units that were converted after January 1977 remained in residence as either owners (22 per cent) or renters (20 per cent), some 58 per cent had moved out by January 1980. This reflects the degree of tenant displacement which has taken place. Of the 58 per cent of new residents, 17 per cent were renters and 41 per cent were owners.

The conversion process also resulted in considerable changes in the socio-economic and demographic characteristics of residents. Nearly two thirds of owner occupant household heads in converted buildings were professional and managerial, about a half were aged under 35, 57 per cent were single person households and 39 per cent had incomes of over $30,000 per annum. The new renters tended to have similar characteristics to those of owners, with the exception that their average income was rather lower. The former renters were much more mixed in terms of occupation, income and age, but, because the majority of converted buildings were at the middle to upper end of the rental market, and because rents were already high prior to conversion, the majority of former renters did not have low incomes. None the less, affordability was clearly a major factor in the purchase decision. Some 42 per cent of those who moved out of converted buildings had incomes which were too low to enable them to purchase their unit and 47 per cent of all former residents said that they could not afford to buy the unit despite discounts to tenants of between 10 and 20 per cent. Seventy per cent of former residents continued to rent after conversion and 28 per cent of them stated that they paid 25 per cent more in rent than previously. The parallels with our findings on the social consequences of the flat break-up process in London are striking (see Chapter 9). In both cases, older, lower income tenants were replaced by younger, higher-income buyers capable of supporting converter profit maximization by paying the price of living in converted buildings.

Britain: lessees up in arms

In Britain, where the existence of leaseholds permits a gradual process of individual flat sales and where most tenants have security of tenure, the radicalization of tenants has been a much more gradual process. Despite the aggressive sales tactics of some early flat breakers (see Chapter 6), the rapid growth of break-ups in London, instances of tenant harassment and offers of financial inducements to quit, there have been no mass notices to quit and the sales process has proceeded slowly and steadily. As a consequence, there has been neither the collective basis nor the necessity for mass tenant organization and protest as there has been in the United States. Instead, the pressure for action has built up relatively slowly, and more among the new leasehold owners than among the remaining rented tenants.

In order to understand why this has been so, we again need to look at the nature of English real property law. In the United States or continental Europe, once a building has been converted and the majority of units have been sold to buyers it is generally run and managed by a committee of unit owners. In England and Wales, by contrast, the management of buildings is conducted by either the head lessor or the freeholder who, under English real property law, is still the landlord of the building even when all the units have been sold. Where the new speculative owners of blocks have found that the rate of sales has proceeded more slowly than anticipated or hoped,they have sometimes sought to increase their cash flow by increasing the level of service charges, or reducing the level of service or maintenance, or both. Even where this has not occurred, residents often find it difficult to enforce basic maintenance and have little or no control over expenditure and the level of service provision (see Chapter 9).

Although most rental tenants have their service charges agreed by independent rent officers under the terms of the 1965 Rent Act,the great majority of leaseholders have clauses in their leases specifying that they have to pay whatever level of service charge the landlord deems necessary. Though both tenants and leaseholdershave been able to challenge the 'reasonableness' of such charges in the courts since 1980, unreasonableness is difficult to prove and, even if lessees win, they have often found that the landlord passes on the legal costs in the next year's service charge! In addition, as the years go by, a small but increasing number of long leaseholders have found that they own short leases which decrease rapidly in value and which, if they have less than 50 years to run, may be virtually unmortgagable. Not surprisingly, leaseholder militancy has increased sharply as an increasing proportion of units have been sold and as the remaining old-style investor landlords have been replaced by the new speculative landlords interested more in the maximization of short-term gains than in block maintenance or good landlord-tenant relations. Not only are the new leaseholders younger and more active, they also have a direct cash stake in the value of their homes. There is a large and growing ideological and political conflict between the desire of these new leaseholder owners for control over what they see as their property, and the determination of freehold ground landlords and head lessors to hang on to the overall ownership and control of the property and resist the threat to expropriate landlords' property rights. This conflict poses a threat to the ideology of ownership which has been so carefully fostered by the Building Societies Association among others. In 1983, the normally conservative BSA issued a report entitled *Leaseholds: Time for a Change* (Building Societies Association, 1983) in which it asserted that long leaseholders of flats were second class citizens and quoted Julia Eaton's comment: 'An Englishman's home, if held on a leasehold, is his landlord's castle.'

The Netherlands: municipal opposition

The relative absence of tenant protest over conversions in the Netherlands is a direct product of the strong tenant protection legislation which prohibits the tenants of conversions from being evicted in order that the converted unit can be sold. A large number of conversions have therefore been undertaken with a speculative eye on future vacancies. As in England, sales have been gradual, there have been no mass notices to quit and hence little direct pressure for tenant mobilization. Although there have been major outbursts of tenant protest in Holland (see Andriesen, 1981) these have tended to focus more on the shortage and expense of rental housing in general rather than on the long term problems for rental housing posed by conversions. As van Weesep and Mass (1984, p.1157) have pointed out, the existence of a large number of converted rented units means that: 'the main effects of conversion on the housing market are still to be felt'. It is this fact that has prompted municipal governments either to enact their own legislation or to press for national legislation in order to control conversions and protect the remaining rental housing market. We shall discuss these measures more fully in the following chapter, which examines the wide variety of government responses to the problems posed by conversions in each of the three countries.

Conclusions

In conclusion, we would stress two points. First, the economic and financial pressures for condominium conversion and break-ups have clearly been similar in the three countries we have examined. In every case, the principal motor of conversion has been the fact that it was more profitable for landlords to sell than to continue renting. The reasons for this are also similar in the three countries. The existence of mortgage interest tax relief has meant that potential buyers are able to pay more to own any given property than they are able to in rent. On the other hand, rising maintenance costs and changes in tax and subsidy legislation for landlords have meant that renting has declined in profitability. As the tenant investment value of the property has fallen relative to its vacant possession sale value, a growing 'value gap' has arisen which landlords and converters have been quick to exploit. But, for them to do so, it was first necessary for a market to be created in which apartments could be built for sale. Only when this had become accepted and mortgage finance became available, was it possible for rented apartments to be sold for owner occupation. In each case, the explanation of the process owes more to changes in financial conditions and taxation and relative profitability than it does to consumer preference. The second point we wish to make is that although the underlying economics of the process have been similar in each country, the extent of resident protest has not simply been related to the extent and rapidity of the break-up process. Instead, the social and political consequences have differed considerably depending on the interaction between the form of real property law and the strength of tenant protection legislation. In the next chapter we extend this analysis to look at variations in state intervention to control or ameliorate the effects of the process.

11 Resident protest and state intervention: a comparative analysis

Introduction

We showed in the previous chapter that, despite the underlying similarities in the economics of the conversion process, there were considerable variations in the incidence and extent of resident protest in the UK, the USA and Holland. It was argued that these variations could be largely explained in terms of the contingent national variations in the nature of real property law and the presence or absence of strong tenant protection legislation. In this chaper we want to extend this comparative analysis of the social consequences of condominium conversions by examining the considerable variations in political and legislative response to conversions in each of the three countries. To a large extent, the degree of state intervention to control or ameliorate the conversion process can be explained in terms of the level of tenant protest, the existence of tenant protection and condominium legislation, the extent to which legislative power is decentralized to the city or state level and the prevailing ideology regarding the desirability of state intervention in market processes.

State intervention to control or ameliorate the effects of conversions will partly depend upon the existence of a substantial level of resident protest. Where protest is absent or limited,the pressure for the state to intervene will generally be less. The existence of strong tenant protection legislation is also likely to militate against state intervention in that the effects of conversions are longer-term and unlikely to manifest themselves in terms of mass evictions. It can be speculated that the existence of leasehold legislation may be less conducive to intervention in that permission is not needed for a landlord to sell a long lease. Where condominium legislation exists, however, it is usually necessary for potential converters to apply for permission to convert and for approval of title. This offers greater scope for intervention, particularly at the local level, than does leasehold legislation where permissions are unnecessary. Similarly, where there is a federal system of government and/or a high degree of legislative autonomy at the city or state level, there is more likely to be some form of state intervention than where there is a centralized political system, because there resident protest and political pressure have to be sufficiently strong and widespread to force themselves onto the national political agenda. Put another way, the greater the degree of local legislative autonomy, the greater the possibility that local government will respond to problems and political pressures which manifest themselves at the local level. The limited power of local government power in Britain has severely restricted the scope for local government intervention in the process. Finally, where the prevailing political ideology is strongly opposed to state intervention in market processes, such intervention is likely to be either non existent or limited and extremely reluctant.

The policy response in Britain

We showed in Chapter 9 that the social consequences of flat break-ups in Britain have been considerable. But, despite growing pressure from the residents of the affected blocks and Members of Parliament, both Labour and Conservative Governments have been extremely reluctant to act until recently. There are a number of reasons for this, some of which we have already identified. First, because of the nature of English real property law and, in particular, the distinction between freehold and leasehold ownership, the sale of flats was a gradual process and eviction was inhibited by the security of tenure legislation. As a result, despite the outcry in the early 1970s when flat break-ups were at their peak, resident unrest and pressure for reform have been relatively slow to emerge, until recently when the proportion of long leaseholders began to increase substantially.

The second reason relates to the extremely marked geographical concentration of privately rented flats in London, and inner London in particular. Despite the close proximity of many of the affected blocks to the Houses of Parliament and the fact that a number of MPs actually lived in them, the problem was seen to be a highly localized one which affected relatively few people. Although local MPs were besieged with a growing volume of complaints and protests, it proved difficult for them to interest other MPs, let alone the Cabinet, in the issue. Indeed, given that at least one prominent Conservative MP and a Labour minister were actively involved in break-ups, and that a number of other Conservative MPs had residential property interests, it can be argued that there were strong counter pressures.

The third reason is essentially political. Given the Conservatives strong committment to the operation of market forces, their strong support for the sanctity of private property rights and their hostility to existing controls on rental property, most Conservative MPs were unwilling to see the government intervene in what was seen as an example of the market forces at work. It was felt that the predominantly middle class residents were quite capable of protecting their own interests in what was essentially a private matter between landlords and tenants. For their part, Labour were not particularly disposed to assist the well-heeled and well-to-do Conservative voters living in central London. The Labour attitude was that it was about time a few Conservative proponents of market forces had a taste of their own medicine. In the face of pressing national housing problems, the central London flat residents were left to stew in their own juice.

Finally, the chronology of the flat break-up process can be argued to have played an important part. Just as resident unrest was mounting in the early 1970s, the speculative property bubble burst and the Bank of England 'lifeboat' operation was mounted to limit the damage to the major financial institutions and prevent a major financial crisis. Then, with the spectacular collapse of the Stern property empire in 1974, it must have seemed that the worst was over. Certainly, the residential property market was depressed until 1978 but, as we have shown in earlier chapters, a new generation of speculators were buying blocks cheaply for a new round of breaking activity. And, although the central London Conservative MPs were becoming increasingly vocal by the late 1970s,the new 1979 Conservative Government was primarily concerned with the implementation of its controversial 'right to buy' provisions for council tenants in the 1980 Housing Act. The Act contained some concessions for tenants but these were very minor.

There were some early attempts to press for controls and greater tenants' rights—primarily from Conservative MPs representing central London constituencies with large concentrations of blocks. Sir Brandon Rees Williams, Conservative MP for Kensington, promoted a number of Private Members Bills from 1978 onwards which sought to give the residents of privately owned blocks of flats a right of collective purchase at an agreed market valuation.

Lacking Cabinet approval, none of these bills succeeded in becoming law. But, in 1980, the Conservative Government faced a small, but potentially embarrassing, challenge from five central London Conservative MPs who argued that it was inequitable to give council tenants a right to buy their homes without giving private tenants the same right. They put down several amendments to the 1980 Housing Bill which, had they been successful, would have given greater tenant control and a collective right to buy. Then, later in 1980, Peter Bottomly, another Conservative MP, promoted a Private Members Bill to ensure that tenants and leaseholders were informed when the owner of the freehold intended to sell and giving them a right of pre-emptive purchase at an agreed price.

All of these measures were unsuccessful. But collectively, they helped create a climate of opinion that government action had now become necessary to protect the interests of leaseholder and tenants alike. Little was done however until 1983 when a Working Party on the Management of Blocks of Flats established by the Royal Institution of Chartered Surveyors (RICS), the members of which play a major role in residential property management, published its report (RICS, 1983). Many of the recommedations were of a technical nature and related to the establishment of a 'code of good practice', but some required legislation. The government was impressed by the report but was unwilling to legislate without some hard evidence as to the scale and incidence of the problems. Thus, the then Minister of Housing, Ian Gow, announced the establishment of an independent committee of inquiry to be chaired by Edward Nugee, QC.

The Nugee Committee and its recommendations

The Nugee Committee's brief was:

> To collect and examine evidence of the nature, scale and incidence of problems for landlords and tenants arising from the management of privately owned blocks of flats; to assess the difficulties caused by these management problems and to make recommedations on how they might be resolved'. (Department of the Environment 1985)

The focus of the brief on problems arising *from management* rather than from the nature of ownership is significant, and it appears that the Department of the Environment wanted a Committee that would focus on the technical management issues rather than on the wider political issues surrounding the ownership and control of the blocks. In the event, although the nine person committee was said by the minister to be chosen on the basis of its expertise and experience of management problems, its membership was strongly orientated towards the property and legal world and included only one representative from residents' organizations and excluded the radical and militant Organisation of Private Tenants.

The composition of the committee influenced its conclusions on the key issue of ownership and control of blocks by residents. The committee received a large volume of evidence from both residents and landlords arguing that the divorce between resident leasehold ownership and landlord control lay at the root of most management problems, and that the key to good management lay in residents' ability to reunite the two. But the majority of the committee rejected any form of compulsory resident buyout of the landlords' interests on the prima facie grounds that management problems would not necessarily be resolved by a change of ownership and that the problems did not justify legislation which could lead to the acquisition of landlords property interests by residents against the wishes of the landlord. In other words, private property rights were to remain sacrosanct.

The only concession on this score was the unanimous agreement that tenants should have a right of first refusal where landlords wished to dispose of their property and that, if a landord sold without first offering the block to the tenants, they would have the right to buy the block from the new owner at the price paid. But, although this clearly represents an incursion into private property rights, it is limited solely to the rights of disposal and the British Property Federation had previously included such a recommendation in its own 'code of good practice' to members. The decision whether or not to sell or retain control was still to rest with the landlord.

Other, more radical proposals, to extend a right of collective purchase to residents where, for example, landlords were guilty of misconduct or in serious breach of their obligations, or where a block was entirely let on long leaseholds and where the residents owned the great majority of the equity, were rejected by a majority of the committee on the grounds that they involved the expropriation of private property and would not necessarily contribute to the solution of management problems. Nor did the majority of the committee support the proposal that residents should have the right to take over the management of their blocks without acquiring the ownership. The basic argument here was that freeholders had legal responsibility for the whole property and should therefore retain control over its management.

Apart from the recommendation of a right of first refusal, the committee's principal recommendation to strengthen the hand of tenants was that, in cases of persistent bad management or the failure of landlords to carry out their duties to uphold, maintain and repair their buildings, residents would be able to apply to the courts for the appointment of a 'reciever manager' to take over the control and management of the block from the landlord, to receive the rent and service charges and to carry out necessary maintenance and repairs. The committee unanimously rejected the extension of the 1967 Leasehold Reform Act (which was limited to house property) to enable individual leaseholders to purchase the freehold of their flats from their landlord. It was felt that the 'pepper potting'of individual freehold flats in mixed or otherwise wholly leasehold blocks would be likely to intensify rather than reduce management problems. The majority of the committee were unwilling to accept that the key to the reduction of residents' management problems lies in tenants' collective management and control of their blocks.

The Nugee Committee made a number of valuable, but more minor, recommendations regarding the disclosure of landlord identity, the control of service charge abuses, the variation of defective leases (retrospectively changing a lease which may, for example, allow landlords to levy a service charge, but does not compel them to provide any services in return), the establishment of residents' rights to check that the landlord had insured the block adequately and the like, but it is fair to say that many of the committee's recommendations were essentially marginal and conservative in nature. The pressures for greater control by residents over management and the extension of a collective right to buy were strongly resisted by the legal and property interests on the committee. The recommendations which emerged constituted the highest common factor of agreement between the various interests on the committee. While this largely guaranteed the acceptance of most of the recommendations by the Conservative government which established the Committee, it is significant that in accepting the report, the then Minister of Housing, John Patten, announced his intention to go further than the majority of the committee in two important areas. First, he proposed that residents should be given a right for landlords to consult them over the appointment of managing agents (a constant source of problems for residents), and second, he proposed that the residents of blocks which were wholly or substantially occupied by long leaseholders should have the right to purchase the landlord's interest at market price if they satisfied a court that the landlord had persistently failed to carry out his/her duties and responsibilities for maintenance and upkeep under the terms of the lease.

The government published the Landlord and Tenant (No. 2) Bill, based on the committee's recommendations, in March 1987. The Bill received all-party support in Parliament and at its second reading John Patten, stated (Hansard, 30th March 1987, p.770):

> This bill provides a framework for the orderly management of flats in private ownership. All residents, whether they are long leaseholders or renting tenants,have a right to expect that their homes will be properly managed....It is not an anti-landlord bill.There is nothing in the bill which the good and responsible landlord need fear. It is the bad, irresponsible and neglectful landlord at whom the bill is aimed.

John Frazer, MP, welcomed the Bill for Labour stating that: 'It carries with it much that we have campaigned for and much that is Labour party policy'. His major criticism was that the Bill did not go far enough along the road of leasehold enfranchisement. The Bill was nearly lost because of the announcement of a General Election, but, because it had all-party support, it was rushed through in the last week of Parliament and became law on 15 May. The major regret about the Bill is that it did not become law 10 or 15 years earlier. If it had, it would have halted many of the problems associated with break-up and saved resident's anguish.

All the discussion thus far has concerned the role of national government. Local government has been ignored. The reason for this is simply that local government has little or no power to intervene in the private housing market in Britain. Although local councils can build council houses (subject to Department of Environment approval and the availability of funds), and although they have a power to require private owners or landlords who allow their property to fall into disrepair, or who, in North American terms, are guilty of building 'code violations', to bring their property up to a certain minimum standard of 'fitness', they have few other powers. They can, in the case of persistent violations, apply for a Compulsory Purchase Order to take the property into council ownership but as CPOs can arguably be seen to represent a threat to private property rights and have to be approved by the Secretary of State, they are carefully scrutinized and often rejected. The Labour controlled central London borough of Camden did attempt in the mid 1970s to CPO several blocks of privately owned flats on behalf of the residents with the goal of then selling the blocks back to the residents, but these attempts were all rejected by the government. The recent success by the London borough of Lambeth in repairing and rehabilitating a block and then charging the landlord for the expenditure is an unususal and isolated occurrence.

The policy response in the United States

The policy response to condominium conversions in the United States has been more rapid and far reaching than in Britain, where leasehold and tenant protection legislation enabled the conversion process to proceed without mass evictions and without major tenant protest. Although the Department of Housing and Urban Development carried out a major study of the scale, extent and causes of the condominium conversion process in 1980, direct Federal intervention has been virtually nonexistent. The American Federal system of government, with substantial delegated powers of intervention and regulation, has ensured that the policy response has been almost entirely at the state and local levels. This is the complete reverse of the position in Britain. It also means that the policy responses have been more varied and complex.

Condominium statutes had been enacted by every state in the union by the early 1970s. For the most part, however, these statutes were designed to provide the legal basis for new condominium construction.They did not incorporate much in the way of consumer protection and they generally had no specific provisions for condominium conversions. The exception was New York where the conversion of rental apartment buildings into cooperatives had been taking place for 20 years or more and where a comprehensive system of rent control was already in place. As a result, it was established early on that the rent-controlled status of apartments occupied by renting tenants could not be terminated unless at least 35 per cent of all the tenants in occupancy agreed to purchase their units—an indication that the scheme was sound. In the great majority of states and local authorities, however, the sudden and unexpected boom in condo conversions led to the emergence of 'a broad-based demand on the municipal level for regulation or prohibition of residential apartment conversions to condominium status' (US HUD, 1980, Ch.XI, p.3)

The result was swift. The HUD conversion study comments that, by 1980; 'Almost half of the states have passed statutes that provide various types of protection for tenants and buyers in converted condominiums or co-operatives' (US HUD, 1980, ch.XI,p.1). The most significant form of protection requires that developers provide residents with prior notification of proposed conversions allied with some form of protection from eviction—usually 120 days in addition to any period of notice specified in the lease. Some states also provide extended notification periods for elderly or other categories of tenants, and some states have made provisions for a tenant's 'right to quiet enjoyment' of the property during the conversion process. In addition, some states have followed New York in specifiying that conversions cannot go ahead without a certain minimum level of tenant agreement, and many states require that tenants be given an unqualified right of first refusal to purchase their units. Finally, a few states require developers to pay tenants' moving expenses or establish a relocation assistance programme.

Almost half of the states have also revised their condominium statutes to include more protection for the buyers of new and converted condominiums. Most of the state statutes that provide for 'disclosure requirements' generally require a statement by the converter on the present condition of all structural and major mechanical components of the buildings, an estimate of repair and replacement costs, and a statement of the current and projected operating costs. A few states also require that when units are contracted for or conveyed, the developer must either 'post a bond' or place in 'escrow' some or all of the purchase price to ensure completion and to cover any uncompleted work on the unit or common areas. In addition, some states also provide a right for purchasers to cancel or rescind contracts of purchase. Finally, California has legislation which states that applications to convert or subdivide must take into account the preservation of the low and moderate income rental housing stock. Three states—New York, Minnesota and Connecticut—also provide special protection for tenants who are elderly, handicapped or have young children. In New York, tenants who are aged 62 or over may continue to rent their apartments even when the building is converted.

All the tenant and buyer protection provisions summarized above exist at the state level. In addition, there are numerous local municipal ordinances to regulate condo conversions, some of which have involved either a temporary moratorium on conversions or rent controls or both. Such emergency ordinances have often been hotly contested by developers and landlords, but the short duration of the notices—commonly between 30 days and 6 months—often makes it difficult for landlords to mount court challenges in time. The HUD report notes that such emergency ordinances have, not surprisingly, been most common in cities where conversion activity has been marked. In Washington DC, for example, there was a recurrent 180 day moratorium on conversions from 1976 onwards while the City Council considered permanent legislation. In San Francisco, any tenant can renew his or her lease for a year following conversion approval, and in Brookline, Massachusetts, the rent control by-laws state that no tenant can be evicted as a result of conversions. In addition, in Washington DC tenants have a collective right of first refusal to purchase their building if their landlord decides to sell, and in the city of Los Angeles, displaced tenants must be paid a rental subsidy for a year to meet any increase in rent. The city of Los Angeles also tried to control conversions by the introduction of a planning regulation which required that the number of car parking spaces required for condominiums had to be double that required for rental buildings. The alleged rationale for this was that the higher socio-economic status and income of owners would lead to a need for greater car parking. This was rapidly challenged by developers and struck down by the court as discriminatory.

The Federal Government has been unwilling to act itself for a variety or reasons. First, as van Weesep (1981a) has pointed out, there is a strong antipathy to direct Federal intervention in the housing market.

> The general opinion is that the government should not interfere in the market through direct participation; instead, its major responsibility is to guarantee the proper functioning of the market. The government's task is limited to formulating clear policies, mimimizing risk factors, safe-guarding the situation of healthy competition and stimulating construction for specific groups by means of various subsidy programs.

Second, as we have shown, the federal system allows considerable discretion to state and local governments and there is a large volume of state and local regulatory legislation. Third, the HUD study argued that, contrary to popular belief,the growth of condo conversions had only led to a marginal net decrease in the total number of available rental units. On the basis of a cross-sectional model of changes in supply and demand between 1977 and 1979 in 12 SMSAs with high levels of conversion activity, the study concluded that, because some converted units are bought by speculators and investors who continue to rent them in the short term and because some units are bought by renters themselves, the impact on the rental market is much less than was commonly supposed. The report concluded that for every 100 units of rental housing converted into condominiums, there was a net effect on the housing market of 5 extra vacant owner units and a loss of 5 vacant rental units. On the assumption that the conversion effect observed in the 12 SMSA's in 1977-9 is similar to what occurred nationally during the 1970s, the report concludes that between 1970 and 1979, 366,000 units were converted; the Nation's rental housing supply was reduced by 231,000 units, renter demand fell by 212,000 households; and a net total of 18,000 previously vacant rental units were occupied by former tenants of converted buildings' (US HUD, 1980, ch.VIII, p.10). Eillbot (1985) has also drawn rather similar conclusions, arguing that a high proportion of condominium units sold to investors continue to be rented.

This kind of analysis is open to challenge on a variety of grounds. First, it can be argued that the purchase of units by renters does not appreciably reduce renter demand in cities where rental accommodation is in short supply, where the vacancy rate is very low and where a large number of potential renters are effectively denied the opportunity to rent. Second, because most investor owned units are likely to be sold eventually,the figures for the long-term loss of rental units are likely to be considerably understated. Indeed, it can be argued that the very high interest rates in 1980/1 choked off sales and forced many investors to continue renting long after they had hoped to sell. The newly let condominiums are likely to have much higher rents than they had previously. It can also be argued that while the rental units lost are lost permanently and are irreplaceable, the decreased renter demand as renters have bought is a short-term phenomenon and the next generation of potential renters will face a permanently depleted stock. None the less, the HUD findings clearly weakened any incentive for direct Federal action. Finally, the Federal attitude to conversions has tended to be ambiguous at best. As Moon Landrieu, former HUD secretary, stated in his testimony to the Senate Subcommittee on Housing (US Senate, 1980):

> Conversions remove units from the rental market; yet ironically, by encouraging investment, conversion may be the best hope of preserving much of our existing housing stock. Conversions displace some lower income people, yet they also provide ownership opportunities for others priced out of the single-family housing market. As conversions contribute to the problem of urban displacement and the lack of rental housing, so do they contribute to neighbourhood revitalization and increase local tax revenues. Thus, conversions present a complex picture.

State intervention in the Netherlands: local and national

The level of state intervention in the Dutch housing market is far greater than that in the United States. A variety of measures such as rent control, security of tenure and housing allocation were introduced in 1940 in response to the wartime pressures, but they were not repealed at the end of the war. Instead, new policies were were added and successive governments have upheld, to a varying degree, the principle of intervention (van Weesep, 1984). Of the 3 million dwellings completed between 1950 and 1980, some 1.3 million were government financed public housing, 1.2 million were indirectly subsidized and only 600,000, or 20 percent, were entirely privately financed. Outside the 'expensive' decontrolled privately rented sector and the owner occupied sector, access is determined by the housing allocation system which aims to protect low and medium priced rental dwellings from encroachment by higher income groups. The housing allocation system is run and controlled by the municipal authorities and they play an active role in the Dutch housing market (Harloe and Martens, 1985).

Although there was not much tenant protest over conversions in the Netherlands, there has been considerable discontent over both speculation and the shortage of cheap housing (Andriesen, 1981),and the administrations of the large cities have been strongly opposed to conversions because of the threat they pose to the diminishing stock of affordable privately rented accommodation. The first attempt at control of conversions dates from 1975 when the National Housing Act was amended to allow cities to adopt a licence system for conversions. Under this law, owners have to register applications to convert. The building is then inspected to ensure that it is suitable for conversion and up to standard. If the building is satisfactory on both counts the conversion can proceed as long as the building is not within a designated urban renewal area. But van Weesep and Mass (1984) argue that the licence requirement has failed to stem the tide and that all that has happened in Amsterdam is that converters have shifted their activities from the dilapidated nineteenth-century neighbourhoods to areas which were developed between the wars and which are not yet subject to urban renewal. In Rotterdam, the 1975 law proved ineffective because the old inner city had been destroyed in 1940 and, as no conversion permit was required until 1979 for dwellings built since 1930, conversions were overwhelmingly concentrated in the interwar neighbourhoods which were not subject to control.

Another potentially effective municipal policy instrument was removed by national legislation. The freehold of most land in Amsterdam developed after 1900 is held by the city, and building leases always stipulated that any change or improvement to the property required the approval of the city. Subdivision could therefore be controlled by private contract, and until the early 1970s it was usual to refuse leaseholders permission to convert to condominiums, unless the dwellings were vacant or the renters themselves favoured conversion (van Weesep and Mass, 1984). But the laws governing leaseholds were amended in 1973 to protect leaseholders from interference from the landholder. Controls over changes to the property were abolished and all leases are now held to have been granted in perpetuity.

Tenants are protected from conversions by the security of tenure legislation. Eviction is very difficult to enforce and even if a property is sold for owner occupation, the principle applied is that 'sale does not break lease'. The new owner 'inherits' the tenants and there is no guarantee that the owner will be able to take up personal residence. Even if a new owner is successful in gaining an eviction order, tenants are usually granted a 3 year stay of execution. In the long term, however, conversions are likely to affect an increasing proportion of the privately rented stock as tenants move, buy or die. In order to try to halt this, Amsterdam introduced regulations in 1979 and Rotterdam in 1980. These stated that the owner of a converted rental dwelling would not generally be allowed to take up residence. As a result, the large number of already converted units became immediately unmarketable and the volume of new conversions fell sharply. But converters and property owners immediately took the cities to court where the regulations were struck down as arbitrary and malicious.

Rotterdam City Council introduced fresh housing regulations in early in 1981 in an attempt to circumvent this decision, but the court again ruled against it on the grounds that the city had not demonstrated the need for such regulations and could not quantify the negative distributional effects of conversions. Similar ordinances in Amsterdam and The Hague were also short-lived. The cities now look to the introduction of national legislation, but van Weesep and Mass (1984) conclude that,even if such legislation were forthcoming, it would come too late to nullify the effects of conversions. As they put it: 'Too many dwellings have already been converted, and there is little that can stop the converters from bringing these onto the market once the present tenants leave' (p.1159).

The Effective Regulation of Condominium Conversions

Van Weesep and Mass identify one of the fundamental problems with attempts to regulate conversions. Once sufficient conversion approvals have been granted, or once a substantial number of long leaseholds have been sold, the process is generally irreversible and legislation is likely to be restricted either to ameliorating the consequences ofconversions for residents or to attempting to lock the stable door once the speculative horse has bolted with the capital gains. The Nugee Committee's recommendation that residents be given first right of refusal where a landlord wishes to sell the block should eventually assist some residents to gain control over the ownership and management of their blocks but, given that the great majority of blocks have already been partly broken and sold, it will do very little to preserve the privately rented housing stock. All it will do is reduce some of the discontent among long leaseholders who have bought flats but find that the management and control of the blocks remains with their landlords. It is an important step forward for residents' rights but it is little more than a tidying up operation in the wake of market forces in search of greater profitability. And, if the landlords are unwilling to sell or ask too high a price for the freehold, there is little that the residents can do unless the landlords can be shown to be negligent in their duties and responsibilities under the terms of the lease.

In order to preserve the privately rented housing stock successfully, it is necessary either to intervene at an early stage in the process to prohibit further conversions or to impose restrictions on the subsequent transfer of housing units from one tenure to another as the Dutch attempted. Such attempts face strong opposition from landlords on the grounds of either discrimination or interference with private property rights. This is the nub of the problem. Although the introduction of security of tenure legislation in Britain and the Netherlands effectively limits landlords' freedom of action to evict their tenants at will, their rights to dispose of their property as they see fit have not been significantly constrained. Consequently, the tenure transformation from renting to owning has proceeded steadily in most Western capitalist countries. Condominium conversions and flat break-ups are merely the most recent expression of this transformation as landlords and converters have sought new routes to maximize the profitability of their housing investments. Any attempt to halt or slow this transformation and protect the long-term interests of residents and the community must therefore seek to control directly the right of landlords to dispose of their property at will. It is ironic that some cities in free enterprise California have been far more successful in doing this than in Britain.

12 Conclusions

Introduction

Our principal concern in this book has been to document and analyse the scale, causes and consequences of the break-up and sale for individual owner occupation of London's privately rented blocks of purpose built flats. As we have attempted to show, flat break-up has radically transformed the tenure structure of this sector of London's private housing market in little over 15 years. This transformation has been particularly marked in central London where purpose built flats comprise a large and important part of the private housing market. In the mid 1960s these flats were still almost all privately rented, but by 1981 the majority had either been sold or were being held vacant pending sale and the privately rented market had virtually ceased to exist as a functioning entity. Although perhaps a third of all flats were still privately rented, they would not be relet on vacancy. The process had advanced even further by 1987, aided by the rapid 60-100 per cent inflation in London residential property prices between 1984 and 1987. The private flat market in central London today is well on the way to becoming the exclusive preserve of high priced owner occupation or luxury letting and its social composition has changed accordingly. Although the central London flat market has always been dominated by the 'white collar' middle classes, it has now become increasingly drawn into the international luxury market with predictable consequences for costs, accessibility and social composition.

Flat break-up and the tenure transformation process

The flat break-up market in London is more than a one-off case study of limited interest and applicability. It is a particular expression of a more general and widespread process—that of the conversion of rented apartment buildings to owner occupation which has occurred in many Western capitalist societies over the last 10 to 20 years. Nor is this apartment conversion process unique. It, in turn, is a historically and geographically specific manifestation of the more general process of tenure transformation from private renting to owner occupation which has taken place with increasing intensity in many Western capitalist countries since the Second World War. Flat break-up, therefore, forms part of a much larger range of tenure transformations from private renting to owning.

But the process of tenure transformation has not proceeded in a geographically or historically even way across different sectors of the privately rented housing market. Although the underlying economics of private renting versus sale for owner occupation has increasingly tended to favour sales, the tenure transformation process has affected different sectors of the market at different times and in different places according to variations in a wide range of contingent factors such as the nature of the stock, the social composition of the tenants, ownership structure, interest rates, house price inflation, availability of mortgage finance and taxation changes. In Britain, the United States and Holland, the sale of privately rented property was first confined to house property and only subsequently, with the introduction of enabling legislation and suitable mortgage finance, did it spread to flats.

Because of the variability of the tenure transformation process, it is impossible to explain its development in any given area or at any given time solely in terms of the general economics of ownership versus renting. Instead, it is necessary to relate the analysis of underlying processes to the contingent factors which affect their specific manifestations. Conversely, the analysis of specific cases can throw valuable light on the nature of the general processes and the factors which influence them. By relating general underlying processes and their specific manifestations we gain a better understanding of both. Analysis of the break-up market therefore provides a useful insight into both the general decline of the privately rented sector and the way in which the general process of decline has manifested itself in specific circumstances. This is where the parallels with the rise of condo conversion in the USA and appartementen-splitsing in the Netherlands discussed in Chapter 10 are particularly valuable.

The key role of suppliers in transforming housing markets

The analysis of the flat break-up market in London also highlights the crucial role played by housing suppliers in the production and transformation of residential space. While earlier analyses of residential differentiation tended to stress the role of consumer choice and preference for different types of housing in different areas, it is clear from our analysis that household preferences are often severely circumscribed and take place in the context of a housing market whose structure is the result of decisions made by landlords and speculators regarding the relative profitability of different investments and types of supply. It must be strongly emphasized that the flat break-up market and the general process of tenure transformation from renting to owning *is not* the result of changes in consumer choice and preference for ownership over renting and the acquiescence of suppliers to changes in demand.

Although the flat break-up market and its counterparts elsewhere have been dependent upon a supply of potential buyers, consumer preferences have not been the principal causal mechanism underpinning break-ups. On the contrary, the flat break-up market has arisen as a direct result of changes in the relative profitability of renting versus sale for the owners of property. As a result, they have initiated policies which have had the direct result of rapidly contracting the privately rented sector. Not only have some households been directly displaced, but households seeking accommodation have been faced with a structure of supply which gives them a choice between buying or going elsewhere. There is no longer a real choice for most households of buying or renting. The economics of housing supply and the tenure structure are such that private renting has disappeared as a viable option. Nor is this process a product of the 1970s alone. Exactly the same thing was happening in the 1930s, and speculators in both periods derived their profits by persuading tenants to purchase and by appropriating a large part of the value gap between the tenanted investment and the vacant possession value of the properties. If this had not been profitable for landlords, sales would not have occurred, regardless of the level of demand. It has been the landlords, not the tenants, who have controlled the decision whether to sell or to rent. That this is the case is shown by the various attempts by flat breakers, and house traders before them, to create the market in which rented property could be sold to individual owner occupiers. Only then were sitting tenants given the choice to buy. This point is brought out very clearly in the United States where tenants generally have no security of tenure and where landlords wishing to convert have been able to issue a general notice to quit to tenants in a building they wish to clear for conversion. Here, tenants were offered no such choice.

Investment versus capital gains

The main reason why landlords have decided to sell rather than continue to rent is not the result of rent controls and security of tenure legislation although these undoubtedly played a role. It is that the emergence of owner occupation on a large scale in the interwar years created a new basis for the valuation of existing housing. Whereas rented housing had previously been valued on the basis of its rental income and the prevailing yields on capital—its tenanted investment value—the emergence of an owner occupied market based on vacant possession sale value created a dual value system. And, because of the growing tax advantages of ownership, the inflation of owner occupied house prices and the presence of rent controls which limited rent increases, the dual value system was reflected in the development of a 'value gap' between the two markets. The emergence of this value gap created the possibility for existing landlords and traders of transferring rented housing into the owner occupied market and realising a capital gain. As the dominance of the owner occupied housing market and the size of the value gap have increased, so vacant possession values have become increasingly important to the point where rent and profits of private renting are now measured against potential vacant possession values and the opportunity cost of not selling and reinvesting the proceeds elsewhere.

Changes in relative profitability

The next point we wish to stress is the crucial role played by profitability in the production and transformation of the private housing market and urban residential space by private capital. In market economies housing is a commodity, produced, exchanged and sold for profit. If production is not profitable, it will not be undertaken or it will take some other form. And if it is more profitable to invest in one sector of the market than another, then disinvestment and reinvestment is likely to take place as investors will move in search of greater profitability. If it ceased to be profitable to sell privately rented property for owner occupation then sales would stop, irrespective of the preferences of tenants and potential buyers.

Changes in the level of profitability also occur between the residential property market, other sectors of the property market and the non-property sector. This happened in Britain prior to the First World War when new investment moved out of housing and went abroad, and, as we have shown, it happened again during the 1960s as the commercial property boom led corporate landlords to disinvest from the residential property market and reinvest in commercial property. The tenure transformation of the private housing market is primarily a product of a change in the relative profitability of such housing for the producers and suppliers of housing, rather than a product of consumer choice. Although consumer preferences and supplier profitability may sometimes be congruent and reinforce one another, the break-up market provides a particularly clear illustration of the dominant influence of supplier profitability. Because of the dominance of the central London flat market by a relatively small number of large and usually profit-maximizing property companies which are responsive to changes in the relative profitability of different sectors of the property market and have the size and expertise to enable them to move between sectors, the break-up market offers particularly revealing insights into the way in which the private housing market can be transformed by private capital in the search for greater profitability.

Changes in the fiscal and financial environment

The shifts in the relative profitability of different sectors of the market do not occur of their own volition, of course. They are brought about by changes in external conditions, particularly by changes in the financial and fiscal environment. In Britain, as in many other Western countries, the shift to owner occupation has been underpinned by the favourable tax treatment of ownership relative to renting. Tax relief on mortgage interest for owner occupiers has meant that potential owners can usually afford to pay more for any given dwelling than a private landlord and that owning is a cheaper option than renting the same or an equivalent dwelling. Where, as in the United States, changes in the structure of tax allowances have reduced the attractiveness of investment in private renting, disinvestment has quickly followed. This can also occur as a result of changes in tax legislation not directly designed with housing in mind. We showed in Chapter 5 that the changes in British company taxation introduced in the 1965 Finance Act had unplanned effects on residential investment companies quoted on the Stock Market which suddenly found that they had to increase income rapidly in order to retain the after tax dividends to shareholders. This led to a shift into residential trading which was not as highly taxed as investment.

Similar changes have also been brought about by changes in interest rates and inflation. Investment in private renting is favoured by low interest rates which allow lower rents to be charged for the same return on capital. This tends to increase the competitiveness of private renting *vis-a-vis* owner occupation where the benefits of mortgage interest tax relief are reduced. The boom in new rental construction during the mid to late 1930s was partly a result of the rapid fall in interest rates in 1933. As we showed in Chapter 6, rapid increases in interest rates can also lead to a dramatic deterioration in the profitability of private renting, especially if property has been recently purchased on low yields and a high borrowing to asset ratio.

Changes in the structure of the residential mortgage market have played a central role in governing the development of owner occupation as a whole and the extent and rate of tenure transfers from renting to owning. Given that house purchase for the great majority of households is dependent on ability to obtain a mortgage, the decisions of mortgage lending institutions as to what types of property they are willing to lend on, and whom they are willing to lend to, are crucial determinants of whether the rental market is maintained or transferred into owner occupation. For example, there is considerable evidence that large scale housing abandonment in US cities is closely related to the switch in mortgage funding from inner city to suburban residential markets, coupled with a decline in landlord profitability in the inner city locations. In Britain, the development of a tenure transfer market for houses in the 1920s and 1930s was dependent on the availability of mortgage finance in a form suitable for individual owner purchasers. This was the radical break-through which occurred in the housing finance system at this time. As we saw in Chapter 5, the development of flat building for sale in the late 1950s and early 1960s and the flat break-up and flat conversion market in the late 1960s and early 1970s have been equally tied to changes in the availability of mortgage finance for individual flat owners. Similarly, the development of the condominium market in the United States in the 1960s depended on persuading mortgagors that condos were sound investments.

But the role of mortgage finance has not simply been limited to providing house and flat owners with the wherewithal to buy their own properties. As we showed in Chapter 6, the speculative activity of the flat breakers was itself fuelled by the ready availability of cash from the secondary banking system. Mortgage finance, for the suppliers as well as the consumers of flats, provided the crucial lubricant which greased the cogs of the break-up process. The flat break-up market illustrates just how intimately the housing finance system is linked to the wider financial investment market which controls the form and quantity of capital flowing into both the housing consumption and the housing production processes.

But the flat breakers did not passively sit and wait for financial institutions to decide to lend on purpose built flats being sold for owner occupation. They were active in arranging mortgage finance for individual mortgagees from the insurance companies and fringe banks. As in the 1930s, the new breed of property traders had to create their market. Clearly, tenure transformations do not simply happen. They are made to happen by those who stand to profit.

The variability of response

The variety of influences affecting the profitability of the residential investment market also highlights the role played by the variety of landlord responses in the break-up process. Although general conditions of profitability may change in response to changes in the wider fiscal and financial environment, these changes are not automatically reflected in a predictable set of landlord responses. First it is necessary for landlords to perceive these changes in the market, and second, for them to decided how to react to them. Not only can perceptions of market changes vary considerably from one landlord to another, but the way in which landlords react to them are shaped by their own market position, orientation and conditions of profitability. While some landlords react in an aggressive, profit-maximising way, other, more conservative landlords are likely to place more trust in the tried and tested traditions of long-term residential investment. And while some of these conservative landlords eventually changed strategies, the realization of the need to change comes too late to prevent some being snapped up by predators quick to perceive the profitable opportunities inherent in undervalued or under-utilized assets. In attempting to explain the variety of landlord behaviour it is therefore necessary to relate the changes in underlying market conditions, the landlords' perception of those changes and their own internal structure and position in the market. There is no one automatic response to changes in market conditions.

Exactly the same point applies to attempts to explain resident protest over break-ups and government intervention to control or ameliorate the process. As we argued in Chapters 10 and 11, there is no single explanation which can be put forward to account for the presence or absence, form, extent or timing of either of these responses. In both cases, the specific outcomes are the result of the interaction of a number of contingent factors, and the comparative analysis of a variety of different manifestations of, or responses to, the same underlying general phenomenon is useful in enabling the effects of different combinations of contingent factors to be examined.

One thing is quite clear, however. Government intervention to attempt to control or mitigate the worst effects of flat break-up and similar processes elsewhere has generally been little more than a clearing up operation to sort out the mess left by private capital in its search for greater profitability. As a result of the withdrawal of traditional investor landlords from the market, and the arrival of a new breed of property speculators interested solely in short-term capital gains, the residents of many blocks in Britain have been left facing a legacy of poor or non-existent maintenance, rising repair costs and service charges, declining services, absentee landlords and indifferent managing agents.

In Britain, the opportunity for central government to intervene and control the flat break-up process presented itself in 1972 when concern over the tactics of flat breakers was first raised in Parliament. But with the collapse of the property boom in 1974, the pressure to intervene died down and nothing was done, despite the subsequent spectacular collapse of the Stern Empire. It was not until the Royal Institute of Chartered Surveyors became concerned about the effects of the growing management problems of blocks of flats and published its report in 1983 (Royal Institute of Chartered Surveyors, 1983) that government was prompted to establish a Committee of Inquiry, headed by Edward Nugee, QC. It is to their credit that the Conservative Government acted quickly and positively in response to the findings of the committee after it reported in 1985 (Department of the Environment, 1985).The most positive feature of the 1987 Landlord and Tenant Act, which incorporated the main recommendations of the Nugee Committee, is that by giving residents the right of first refusal on a landlord's decision to sell, together with some limited entitlement to buy out the landlord's interest or have an independent manager appointed in the case of gross neglect or bad management, tenants have established a foot in the door of the traditional rights of landlords to manage and dispose of their property as they see fit without consulting residents. This constitutes an important breach in the hitherto almost unfettered rights of private property ownership.

However, we are forced to conclude that if action had been taken in 1972 instead of 1987, many of the problems subsequently exposed by the Nugee Committee could have been avoided. Residents are now paying the price of a 15 year delay. In the meantime, the bulk of the profits have already been made and the flat breakers have either retired on the proceeds or gone on to new and more profitable ventures which are not, as yet, subject to such control. As in many other policy arenas, attempts to control the excesses of speculation in the central London flat market, the sort of speculation which Edward Heath once termed 'the unacceptable face of capitalism', have lagged well behind the speculative activity itself. By the time politicians have discovered the issues and the relevant protests have been made, research called for and action contemplated, the speculators have banked the proceeds and simply moved on.

A future for the private landlord?

Finally, what does our analysis of the decline of the private rented sector imply for the future of privately rented housing? If our understanding of the reasons behind the fall of the investor landlord is correct, then the current political interest in the revival of the private landlord is likely to fail. Unless there is a commitment to a subsidy and taxation system at least as generous to potential landlords and tenants as that currently provided for owner occupiers, it is likely that few of the tenants for whom renting is deemed to be of most benefit (i.e. those excluded from home ownership) will be able to afford the level of rents needed to tempt private investors back into the residential lettings market. For those who are able to afford home ownership, there will be little incentive to change tenure given the current tax system.

So long as the fiscal and financial incentives which are so attractive to investors in the home ownership market remain, proposals by the new Conservative administration to stimulate the privately rented market will remain little more than pious dreams. The political party which has so assiduously and at huge public expense nurtured its image as the champion of the individual home owner and the property owning democracy cannot have its cake and eat it. Owner occupation and private landlordism are incompatible over the long term as they are currently funded. We suspect that given the number of votes to be garnered by the Conservatives from home owners who continue to benefit from the present subsidy system, it is unlikely that this government will do much to alter the prevailing direction of investment. With the exception of the pension funds and larger building societies, which may be persuaded to assist in the transfer of the public rented stock out of the control of local authorities and into a form of state-assisted institutional private landlordism, and those landlords providing high-rent, short-let accommodation for the young and mobile, the private landlord is most unlikely to be revived. There can be no other conclusion while the principle of tax-assisted individual home ownership remains the hub of housing policy.

References

Allen, J. (1983) 'Property relations and landlordism: a realist approach', *Society and Space*, 1, 191–203

Allsop and Co. (1967) *Allsop Flat Rental Index.*

Allsop and Co. (1983) *Property Rental Index.*

Badcock, B (1984) *Unfairly Structured Cities*,

Blackwells, Oxford

Balchin, P. (1981) *Housing Policy and Housng Needs*, London, Macmillan.

Ball, M. (1978) 'British housing policy and the housebuilding industry', *Capital and Class*, 4, pp 78-99.

Ball, M. (1981) 'The development of capitalism in housing provision', *International Journal of Urban and Regional Research*, 5, pp 145-77.

Ball, M. (1983) *Housing Policy and Economic Power*, London, Methuen.

Barnes, H. (1923) *Housing: The facts and the Future*, London, Ernest Benn.

Barras, R. (1978) The new property boom, *Estates Gazette*, Oct 6th vol 252, pp 41-43

Bassett, K. and Short, J. (1980) *Housing and Residential Structure:Alternative Approaches*, Routledge

Boddy, M. (1976) 'The structure of mortgage finance: british building societies in the British social formation', *Transactions, Institute of British Geographers*, N.S. vol 1, no. 1. pp 58-71

Boddy, M. (1980) *The Building Societies*, London, Macmillan.

Boddy, M. (1981) 'The property sector in late capitalism: the case of Britain', in Dear, M. and Scott, A. (eds) *Urbanization and Urban Planning in Capitalist Society'*, Methuen

Bonnar, D. (1979) Migration in the South East of England: an analysis of the interrelationship of housing, socio-economic status and labour demand, *Regional Studies*, 13, pp 345-359

Bourne, L. (1976) 'Housing Supply and Housing Market Behaviour in Residential Development', in D.Herbert and R. Johnston, eds *Social Areas in Cities*, vol 1, John Wiley, pp 111-158

Bourne, L. (1981) *The Geography of Housing*, Edward Arnold

Bowley,M.(1945) *Housing and the State 1919-1944*, Allen and Unwin.

Brennan, J. (1978) *History of the Bradford Property Trust: 1928–1978,* London, B.P.T.

Brett, M. (1972) *'Could the break-up men break down' Investors Chronicle,* 14 April, 137–7.

British Property Federation (1977) *Review of the Rent Acts,* London, B.P.F.

Broackes, N. (1966) 'Reflections on the new tax structure', *Investors Chronicle,* March 26th, pp xivii-l.

Burgess, E.W (1925) 'The growth of a city' in Park, R.E et al *The City* University of Chicago Press

Burnett, J. (1978) *A Social History of Housing 1815—1970*, London, David and Charles.

Byrne, D. and Damer, S. (1980) 'The State, the Balance of Class Forces and Early Working Class Housing Legislation' in *Housing Construction and the State*, Conference of Socialist Economists.

Campaign for Homeless in Central London (1986) *Central London House Price Survey, 1986*

Cannadine, D (1980) *Lords and Landlords: the aristocracy and the towns, 1774-1967*, Leicester University Press

Chalklin, C.W. (1968) Urban Housing Estates in the eighteenth century, *Urban Studies*, 5, 1 pp 67-85

Chown, J. (1967) 'Facing up to taxation' *Investors Chronicle*, March 17, pp xxvii—xxx.

Clark, S. and Ginsberg, N. (1975) 'The political economy of housing', in *Political Economy and the Housing Question*, Conference of Socialist Economists Housing Workshop.

Coakely, J. and Harris, L. (1983) *The City of Capital*, Blackwells

Community Development Project (1976) *Whatever Happened to Council Housing?*.

Dashwood, R. G. (1969) 'Selling flats on long lease', *Investors Chronicle*, March 14th, pp. 22-23.

Daunton, M. (1983) *House and Home in the Victorian City*, London, Arnold.

Dennis, R. (1985) *English Industrial Cities of the Nineteenth Century*, Cambridge University Press

Department of the Environment (1971) *A Fair Deal For Housing,* London, HMSO.

Department of the Environment (1977) *Housing Policy: A Consultative Document and Three Technical Volumes*, London, HMSO.

Department of the Environment (1985) *Report of the Committee of Inquiry into the Management Problems of Privately Owned Blocks of Flats,* (Nugee Committee), Vols I and II, London, HMSO

Dickens, P. (1977) 'Social change, housing and the State: some aspects of class fragmentation and incorporation', in Harloe, M. (ed) *Urban Change and Conflict*, London, Centre for Environmental Studies.

Drier, P. (1984) 'The tenants movement in the United States', *International Journal of Urban and Regional Research,* 8 (2), 255–79.

Dyos, H. J. (1961) *Victorian Suburb*, Leicester University Press.

Dyos, H.J. (1967) 'The slums of Victorian London', *Victorian Studies, Studies,* 10, 5–40.

Dyos, H. J. (1968) 'The speculative builders and developers of Victorian London', *Victorian Studies*, 11, 641-690.

Economist, The (1977) 'The Trouble with Freshwater', *The Economist,* 29 October, 111-19.

Ellibot, P. (1985) 'Condominium rentals and the supply of rental housing', *Urban Affairs Quarterly*, 20 (3), 389–99.

Elliot, B., and McCrone, D. (1975) 'Landlords in Edinburgh: some preliminary findings', *Sociological Review*, 23 (3), 539-62.

Engels, F. (1969) *The Condition of the Working Classes in England*, St Albans, Panther Books.

Escott, T.H.S. (1879) *England: Its People, Policy and Pursuits*, London.

Fielding, N. (1984) 'Who is subsidising whom?' *Roof*, March/April, 11–14.

Firey, W. (1945) 'Sentiment and symbolism as ecological variables', *American Sociological Review*, 23 (3) pp 539–62.

Forrest, R., and Kemeny, J. (1982) 'Middle class housing careers: the relationship between furnished renting and owner occupation', *Sociological Review*, 30 (2), 208-22.

Form, W.H. (1954) 'The place of social structure in the determination of land use', *Social Forces*, 32, pp 317-23

Galvin, P. (1966) 'The damaging policy of 'Priorities not Profits'', *Investors Chronicle*, March 25, pp xvii-xxii.

Gauldie, E. (1974) *'Cruel Habitations: a History of Working Class Housing 1780-1918'*, London, Allen and Unwin.

Gough, I. (1979) *The Political Economy of the Welfare State*, Macmillan

Gray, F. (1975) 'Non-explanation in urban geography',*Area*,7,228-35

Gray, P.G. (1947) *The British Household*, (Social Survey, 1947) London, HMSO.

Grebler, L. and Mittelbach, F.G. (1979) *The inflation of housing prices: its extent, causes and consequences*, Lexington, Mass., Lexington Books.

Greve, J. (1965) 'Private Landlords in England', *Occasional Papers on Social Administration*, No. 16,.

Hamnett, C. (1983) 'Regional variations in house prices and house price inflation', *Area*, 15 (2), 97–109.

Hamnett, C. (1984) 'Housing the two nations: socio-tenurial polarisation in England and Wales', *Urban Studies*, 43, 389–405.

Hamnet, C., and Randolph, W.I (1981) 'How far will London's population fall?' *London Journal*, 8 (1), 95–100.

Hamnett, C., and Randolph, W. (1983) 'The changing tenure structure of the Greater London housing market', *London Journal*, 9, 153–64.

Harloe, M. (1985) *Private rented housing in the United States and Europe*, Beckenham, Kent, Croom Helm

Harloe, M., and Martens, M. (1985) 'The Housing Crisis in Britain and the Netherlands', *Environment and Planning*, A, 17.

Harvey, D. and Chatterjee, L. (1974) 'Absolute rent and the structuring of space by governmental and financial institutions', *Antipode*, 6, 1, pp 22-36.

Harvey, D. (1973) *Social Justice and the City*, London, Edward Arnold.

Harvey, D.(1975) Class structure in a capitalist society and the theory of residential differentiation, in Peel, R., Chisholm, M. and Haggett, P (eds)

Harvey, J. (1981) *The Economics of Real Property*, London, Macmillan.

Heath-Saunders, P. (1972) 'Property share performance', *Investors Chronicle*, April 7, pp 129-132.

Hennock, E.P. (1973) *Fit and Proper Persons*

Hillmore, P. and Raw, C. (1972) 'The housing finance of William Stern', *The Guardian*, 16 June

House of Commons (1982) 'First report from the Environment Committee, Session 1981-82', *The Private Rented Sector*, HMSO.

Ishino, S.A., (1979) 'Condominium conversions in the Bay Area,' *Unpublished Master's Thesis*, Berkeley, CA, Dept. of City and Regional Planning.

Jackson, A.(1974) *Semi-detached London*, Allen and Unwin

Jenkins, S. (1975) *Landlords to London*, London, Constable.

Kellett, J.R. (1961) Property Speculators and the Building of Glasgow 1980–1830' *Scottish Journal of Political Economy*, 8, 211–32.

Kemeny, J. (1981) *The Myth of Home Ownership*, London, Routledge & Kegan Paul.

Kemp, P. (1980) 'Housing Production and the Decline of the Privately Rented Sector: Some Preliminary Remarks', *Urban and Regional Working Paper*, No. 20, University of Sussex.

Kemp, P. (1982) 'Housing landlordism in late nineteenth century Britain', *Environment and Planning* A, (14), pp 1437-47.

Kreiger, C. (1972) 'Trends in Flat break-up', *Investors Chronicle Property Supplement*, 7 April, pp 31-2.

Lamarche,F.(1976) 'Property development and the economic foundationof the urban question', in Pickvance, C.G. (ed) *Urban Sociology: Critical Essays*, Tavistock, London

Langton, J. (1976) 'Big profits from flat break-up market', *Evening Standard*, October 15.

Margo, A. (1973) 'Flat break-ups', in *The Property Development Process*, Property Study No. 7, College of Estate Management Reading.

Marriot, O. (1968) *The Property Boom*, London, Pan.

Marshall, J.L. (1968) 'The pattern of housebuilding in the inter-war period in England and Wales', *Scottish Journal of Political Economy*, pp 184-205.

Massey, D. and Catalano, A. (1978) *Capital and Land*, London, Edward Arnold.

Massey, D. and Meegan, R. (1982) *The Anatomy of Job Loss*, London, Methuen.

Merrett, S. (1979) *State Housing in Britain*, London, Routledge

Merrett, S. with Gray, F. (1982) *Owner Occupation in Britain*, London, Routledge & Kegan Paul.

Methesius, S. (1982) *The English Terraced House*, New Haven, Connecticut Yale UP

Milner, R. (1969) 'First National turns the £10m Flat Key,' *Sunday Times*, 3 August, p 12.

Milner Holland (1965) *Report of the Committee on Housing in Greater London*, Cmnd 2605,London HMSO

Morton, J. (1970) 'The Marks and Spencer of London Housing', *New Society*, October 15th.

Murie, A. (1974) *Housing Movement and Housing Choice*, Occasional Paper no 28, Birmingham, Centre for Urban and Regional Studies.

Murie, A., Niner, P. and Watson, C. (1974) *Housing Policy and the Housing System*, London, Allen and Unwin.

Nationwide Building Society (1986) Local Area Housing Statistics 1986, No. 15 London Boroughs.

Nevitt, A. A. (1966) *Housing, Taxation and Subsidies*, London, Nelson.

Offer, A (1981) *Property and Politics, 1870-1914: Landownership, Law, Ideology and Urban Development in England*, Cambridge UP.

Olsen, D. (1976) *The Growth of Victorian London*, London, Batsford
Paley, B. *Attitudes to Letting in 1976*, London, OPCS Social Survey Division, HMSO
Paris, C. 'Private rental housing in Australia,' paper given at conference on *The Housing Question in Australia and Britain,* Australia Studies Centre, Institute of Commonwealth Studies.
Parry Lewis, J. (1965) *Building Cycles and Britain's Growth*, London, Macmillan.
Pawley, M. (1978) *Home Ownership*, London, Architectural Press.
Plender, J. (1982) 'Regalian Properties: anything goes in a paperchase market'. *Investors Chronicle,* 31 March,
Plender J. *That's the Way the Money Goes*, London, Andre Deutsch.
Preston, W.J. (1968) 'Taxation and the Property Market', *Investors Chronicle,* 25 March pp 25–8.
Prince, H. (1964) 'North-West London 1814–1914'; in Coppock, J.T. and Prince, H.C. *Greater London,* London, Faber.
Prior, P (1980) 'Dis-investment in privately rented housing: the concept of total returns', Unpublished, Manuscript, Open University.
Rassmussen, S.E. (1982) *London: The Unique City*, Cambridge, Mass. MIT Press.
Read Hurst Brown & Co. (1972) *Property Share Review,* London.
Reeder, D.A. (1965) 'Capital Investment in the western suburbs of Victorian London' Unpublished Ph.D. thesis, University of Leicester Press.
Reeder, D.A. (1965) *Capital Investment in the western suburbs of Victorian London*, Unpublished Ph.D thesis, University of Leicester.
Rex J., and Moore, R. (1967) *Race, Community and Conflict,* Oxford University Press.
Robinson, R. (1979) *Housing Economics and Public Policy*, London, Macmillan.
Robson, B. (1969) *Urban analysis: a study of city structure,* CUP
Robson, B. (1975) *Urban Social Areas*, OUP
Saunders, P. (1981) *Social Theory and the Urban Question*, Hutchinson
Saunders, P. (1984) 'Beyond housing classes: The sociological significance of private property rights and means of consumption' *International Journal of Urban and Regional Research*, 8 (2), 202-27
Shearer, D. (1984) Citizen Participation in local government: the case of Santa Monica, California, *International Journal of Urban and Regional Research,* 8, 573–86.
Short, J. (1978) Residential mobility in the private housing market of Bristol, *Transactions of the Institute of British Geographers*, NS, 3 (4), 533-47
Stacey, J. P. (1959) 'Sale of Flats', *Chartered Auctioneer and Estate Agent*, January.
Stafford, B. and Doling, J. (1981) 'Rent Control and Rent Regulation in England and Wales', *Occasional Paper No. 2 (New Series)*, Centre for Urban and Regional Studies, University of Birmingham.
Steadman-Jones, G. (1971) *Outcast London*, Harmondsworth, Middx., Penguin.
Stern, W. G. (1966) 'A Magna Carta for tenants—and landlords' *Investors Chronicle*, 25 March,pp. lxii-lxiv.
Summerson, Sir John. (1978) *Georgian London*, Harmondsworth, Middx., Peregrine Books
Svensson, J. (1965) 'A fate worse than death', *Investors Chronicle*, 26 March, pp. l-lv.
Swennarton, M. (1981) *Homes Fit for Heroes*, London, Heinemann

Tarn, J. N. (1969) *Five Per Cent Philanthropy*, CUP
Tarn, J. N. (1974) 'French flats for the English in nineteenth century London'; in Sutcliffe, A. (ed.), *Multi-Story Living: The British Working Class Experience*, Beckenham, Kent, Croom Helm.
Thompson, F.L.M. (1974) *Hampstead: Building a Borough, 1650–1964*, London.
Tyler, R. (1971) 'Flats: the break-up operation', *Estates Gazette*, 30 October, pp 663–6.
US HUD (1980) *Condominium—Cooperative Study*, Washington DC, US Department of Housing and Urban Development.
van Weesep, J. (1981a) Condomania: the proliferation and impact of condominiums in the U.S.A., *Geografische en Planogisch Notities, no. 6*, Geography and Planning Institute, Free University of Amsterdam.
van Weesep, J. (1981b) *The Sponsors of Condominiums in Large US Cities, occasional paper, Center for Metropolitan Planning and Research, Johns Hopkins University, Baltimore, Md.*
van Weesep, J. *(1984) Condominium Conversion in Amsterdam: boon or burden, Urban Geography*, 5, 165–77.
van Weesep, J. (1987) 'The creation of a new housing sector: condominiums in the United States' *Housing Studies*, 2, (2), 122–33.
van Weesep, J., and Mass, M. (1984) 'Housing policy and conversion to condominiums in the Netherlands', *Environment and Planning*, A (16), 1149–61.
Walker, R.A. (1978) 'The transformation of urban structure in the nineteenth century and the beginnings of suburbanisation', in Cox, K.A. (ed.), *Urbanisation and Conflict in Market Societies*, London, Methuen.
Walker, R.A. (1981) 'A theory of suburbanisation: capitalism and construction of urban space in the United States'; in Dear, M., and Scott, A.J. (eds), *Urbanisation and Urban Planning in Capitalist Society, London, Methuen.*
Walton, J. (1968) 'Will house prices stablise?' *Investors Chronicle*, 29 March.
Wheatcroft, P. (1979) 'Black Jack Dellal is back', *Sunday Times*, 2 October.
Whinihan, M. (1984) 'Condominium conversion and the Tax Reform Acts of 1969 and 1976', *Journal of the American Real Estate and Urban Economics Association*, 12, 461–71.
White, P. (1984) *The West European City*, Harlow, Longman.
Wohl, A. (1971) 'The housing of the working classes in London, 1815–1914; in Chapman, S.D. (ed.), *A History of Working Class Housing*, Newton Abbot, David & Charles.
Wolman, C. (1982) 'Life in Bergerland, *Roof*, November/December, 11–13.

INDEX

For Product Safety Concerns and Information please contact our EU
representative GPSR@taylorandfrancis.com
Taylor & Francis Verlag GmbH, Kaufingerstraße 24, 80331 München, Germany

www.ingramcontent.com/pod-product-compliance
Ingram Content Group UK Ltd.
Pitfield, Milton Keynes, MK11 3LW, UK
UKHW021505240926
475702UK00035B/431
* 9 7 8 0 3 6 7 6 8 2 1 1 8 *